Communication Control in Computer Networks

WILEY SERIES IN COMPUTING

Consulting Editor

Professor D. W. Barron

Department of Mathematics, Southampton University, Southampton, England

BEZIER • Numerical Control — Mathematics and Applications
DAVIES and BARBER • Communication Networks for Computers
BROWN • Macro Processors and Techniques for Portable Software
PAGAN • A Practical Guide to Algol 68
BIRD • Programs and Machines
OLLE • The Codasyl Approach to Data Base Management
DAVIES, BARBER, PRICE, and SOLOMONIDES • Computer Networks and their Protocols
KRÖNSJO • Algorithms: Their Complexity and Efficiency
RUS • Data Structures and Operating Systems
BROWN • Writing Interactive Compilers and Interpreters
HUTT • The Design of a Relational Data Base Management System
O'DONOVAN • GPSS — Simulation Made Simple
LONGBOTTOM • Computer System Reliability
AUMIAUX • The Use of Microprocessors
ATKINSON • Pascal Programming
KUPKA and WILSING • Conversational Languages
SCHMIDT • GPSS Fortran
PUŽMAN and POŘÍZEK • Communication Control in Computer Networks

Communication Control in Computer Networks

Josef Pužman
Federal Ministry of Technology and Investments
Prague, Czechoslovakia

Radoslav Pořízek
Institute of Applied Cybernetics
Bratislava, Czechoslovakia

A Wiley — Interscience Publication

JOHN WILEY & SONS

Chichester · New York · Brisbane · Toronto

Published in co-edition with ALFA, Publishers of Technical and Economical Literature, Bratislava

British Library Cataloguing in Publication Data:

Puzman, Josef
Communication control in computer networks.
(Wiley series in computing).
1. Computer networks
I. Title II. Porizek, Radoslav
001.64'404 TK5105.5 80-41259

ISBN 0 471 27894 7

Printed in Czechoslovakia at ZT, n. p., závod Svornosť, Bratislava

To Eva and Rita
and
to Danka and Katka

Contents

Preface

Notions such as communication protocol, network architecture, communication function, communication control, and the like are generally connected with computer networks. Communication control is necessary in any data communication system or in any communication network, regardless of its scope, design, and application. This book is entitled "Communication Control in Computer Networks", since computer networks may be regarded as the most comprehensive of the distributed data processing and communication networks. As such, they embrace nearly all the principles and forms of communication control used in various networks. Moreover, many new communication control principles have been developed for computer networks, or for the communication subnetworks of various computer networks. The principles and results explained in this book apply also to simpler sorts of networks.

Several years ago, when we wrote a book on protocols[1]) we wished to describe several existing communication protocols by using a unified notation. This was intended for those readers who wanted to become acquainted with a new and rapidly developing discipline, namely communication control in data transmission systems and in computer networks. It was an arduous task since most publications describing protocols are widely dispersed in periodicals, in proceedings of various international and national conferences and seminars, in internal publications of firms, or in research reports often accessible to a very limited group of readers.

But it has become evident that a unified notation is not sufficient or adequate to express all the interdependences concerned with communication control and aimed at the required values of performance measures used. However, the deficiencies can be overcome by the introduction of communication functions as parts of the entire communication control in a network.

When in a given network we want to obtain (and maintain) the required values of performance measures, adequate communication functions and methods of their

---

[1]) POŘÍZEK, R.—PUŽMAN, J.: Data Transmission Control Procedures and Protocols (In Slovak), VVS OSN — Alfa, Bratislava, 1976, (254 p.)

realization in the course of the communication control design must be selected and implemented by appropriate communication protocols. In the sense of the above interpretation, communication protocols are formal tools intended for the implementation of selected communication functions methods. The differentiation between communication functions and communication protocols is essential. As the description, or notation, of a communication protocol need not necessarily show the functions implemented by the protocol, it is better to specify these functions separately.

Therefore this book on communication control deals with communication functions and communication protocols, not with protocols alone. Nowadays, the formal properties of protocols represent quite an extensive discipline and, therefore, protocols take up a substantial part of the present book. Some actual protocols are briefly characterized in appendices, in order to illustrate the implementation of some communication functions. However, these appendices can in no way replace the appropriate full text of standards, recommendations, and other original documents.

We have tried to keep within reasonable limits the difficulties arising from the "Babel like" character of the protocol terminology, by coining a unified terminology which is, of course, valid only within the scope of this book. This terminology, being rather unusual in places (for which we apologize), does not claim, of course, the right to general validity. It is intended only to ensure a unified and clear presentation of the material in this book.

As for communication control literature references, we had to give up the initial scheme of presenting an extensive bibliography in the book, because the number of communication protocols publications alone amounts to roughly one thousand. Therefore we have focused on publications containing surveys of individual problems and on publication containing significant new principles and approaches. We apologize if some publications (as well as the names of their authors) have been omitted and we shall be grateful to readers for bringing our attention to such cases. We have omitted various working materials and documents, especially those of various institutions dealing with standards. Very good surveys of references may be found, especially in monothematic issues of some periodicals[1]) and, of course, in bibliographies[2]).

It is customary with books written by more than one author to indicate the contribution of the individual authors. In our case this is not possible, because the extent of discussions, criticisms, and supplements supplied by either author is very great. Therefore the chapters are the joint products of both authors.

Moreover, the origin of the book was either directly or indirectly influenced by many communication control and computer and data network specialists who contributed to the writing of the book by giving advice, providing publications and

---

[1]) Proc. IEEE, No. 11, 1972 and No. 11, 1978, IEEE Trans. on Communications, No. 3, 1972, No. 1, 1977, and No. 4, 1980

[2]) Computer Networks (Bibliography), SZENTIVÁNYI, T., and TALLÓCZY, I. (Eds.), SZÁMKI, Budapest, 1980

documents not commonly accessible, organizing conferences, seminars, or workshops, etc. From among all those above we shall name N. Abramson, D. Barber, M. Bazewicz, A. Butrimenko, A. Danthine, D. Davies, M. Gien, J. L. Kulikowski, H. Meier, S. Noguchi, H. Petersen, L. Pouzin, W. Price, J. Seidler, T. Szentiványi, B. S. Tsybakov, and E. A. Yakubaytis. It is our very pleasant duty to acknowledge their contribution here.

Praha, Bratislava 1980

J. Pužman, R. Pořízek

Part 1
Distributed Processing Networks

1.1 Kinds of Distributed Processing Networks

Distributed processing networks is the proposed name for various networks containing both programmable (primarily) and nonprogrammable elements connected in various ways both locally and remotely. The following are examples of networks covered by the term: multiaccess terminal networks, computer networks, data collection and/or distribution networks, transaction type networks, etc. Use of some form of data transmission is typical for all these networks, and both simpler and more complex forms of communication can also be found in all of them.

In the distributed processing networks, various network elements can communicate, including computers, terminals, node computers or communication processors, concentrators, various kinds of controllers, etc. There are also programs or processes communicating in distributed processing networks, and not only the network elements as a whole, but also the individual parts which can communicate. One generic term will be used for all these communicating elements: stations.

Communication basically encompases both exchange of data messages between two or more stations and the control of the exchange. The tasks of such control will be explained in Chapter 2.1. Communication control must be implemented in the corresponding stations. The exchange of control information comprising commands, responses, status information, addressing information, etc., must be performed between communicating stations in order to make the communication control possible.

The aim of communication is to exchange data messages between the source station and the destination station. This transfer can be one-way or two-way. In the latter case, both source and destination stations are at both ends. For example, a terminal sends data messages to a computer and the computer sends data messages back to the terminal. The transfer of data messages is one-way or two-way. The transfer of control data should be two-way in any case. Controlling any communication in networks requires negotiation to take place between the stations. A station must know the state of the other station and of the communication medium as well. The activities of the stations must be synchronized in the sense that they wait for one another from time to time.

Communication can be local or remote. When remote, the common communication medium for both data messages and control information is generally used.

The pair of communicating stations seems to be a useful and adequate basic element in the analysis of complex communication control structures. There are many various communicating pairs in distributed processing networks. Such pairs of communicating stations can be permanent, or temporary i.e. dynamic, and they can operate alone or in close relation with other communicating pairs. These relations will be treated in Chapter 2.3, in connection with network architectures. But even without explaining these relations one can expect local and global communication control to take place in the networks. Local communication control manages individual pairs of communicating stations; the global communication control manages the cooperation of such pairs.

The development of communication control, and in particular that of communication protocols, has been mostly influenced and stimulated by computer networks and by packet switching networks. It was the rise and development of these networks that have brought a range of new problems related to various aspects of communication control. Dealing with these problems enriches substantially the principles, methods, and forms of communication control and adds to the profiling of communication functions, communication protocols and network architectures.

However, there was communication control long before packet switching networks arrived. Any line used to transmit data had to be controlled in some way. Common telephone and telegraph lines in switched networks are controlled. It does not matter that signalling is used to denote this control and that the set of control functions is limited, mostly because man participates actively in this control.

Communication control in distributed processing networks is much more complex and extensive; the fact that it is fully automatic adds to the complexity. Computer networks represent the most complete example of new communication control principles and methods, which is why communication control in computer networks was chosen as one of the subjects of this book. However, the description of principles, methods, and aims will be given rather generally, so that they can be applied in simple computer communication systems as well.

There exist many distributed processing networks in the world. By way of some examples let us mention the multiaccess terminal systems, reservation systems, message switching networks (e.g. SITA), packet switching networks (e.g. DATAPAC, TRANSPAC, EPSS, DX-1, CIGALE), and finally computer networks (e.g. ARPA, TYMNET, CYCLADES, EIN, ALOHA). The structure of these networks influences strongly the ways in which communication control is dealt with in them.

Besides networks, comceptions of how to build distributed processing networks from existing vendors' hardware and software products are known and are mostly categorised by the term "architecture". Thus we have the SNA of IBM, DNA of Digital Equipment Corp., DCA of Sperry UNIVAC, etc. In all of these architectures a certain structure of communication control in networks is defined. This structure is, of course, necessary when various networks have to be created by connecting together individual pieces of hardware and software, and cooperate properly. Well organized and adequately implemented communication between network elements is needed in all such networks.

New networks have brought with them new principles and methods of communication control. This is a natural development in other fields too, and is very useful and desirable for advancement of networks and of relevant theoretical disciplines, but it is unsuitable from the point of view of compatibility of present day and future networks.

Already, therefore, efforts in the form of international standards and recommendations have been made in order to try to achieve mutual agreement on the structure of communication control in different networks. These will be treated elsewhere in this book, e.g. in Chapter 2.6.

Various principles, methods, and forms of communication control in networks are primarily determined by the configurational structure of networks. The configurational structure defines various network elements used in the network and various means of their interconnection. The following are examples of possible network elements: host computers (HOST), node computers (NC), concentrators (C), multiplexors (MUX), front-end processors (FEP), terminal controllers (TC), communication controllers (CC), data entry system controllers (DES), terminals (T), etc. The following sorts of terminals can be distinguished: teletype terminals (TT), display terminals (DT), intelligent terminals (IT), graphic terminals (GT), batch, or remote job entry terminals (RJE), data entry terminals (DET), etc. As far as the communication control aspect is concerned, we can recognize scroll-mode, page-mode and packet-mode terminals, as well as start-stop terminals.

As we have already mentioned, all such network elements are considered to be stations from the aspect of communication control. But there are other activities (operations) being performed by network elements besides communication control. Therefore, stations refer only to the communication parts of network elements.

For the sake of completeness we give here a short description of most of the network elements. There is no doubt about what host computers do in networks: they represent the processing and storage resources of networks and they communicate primarily in order to provide access to these resources for large communities of users. Node computers act primarily as packet switchers, but they can serve other purposes too. For example, they can connect terminals to networks (e.g. TIP in the ARPA network). Communication controllers, multiplexors and front-end processors all have one common main task: to support terminals in accessing a host computer. The multiplexors (do not confuse with communication multiplexors) perform this task exclusively by use of hardware. The communication controllers and front-end processors use software for that purpose and free the host computer from the burden of communication line and terminal management. Concentrators concentrate parts of data messages coming from remote terminals (remote with respect to the concentrator), merge them into other data messages, and send these messages over a few lines that have much larger transmission capacity than the lines connecting the terminals to the concentrator. Terminal controllers perform the concentration function too, but the terminals controlled are local (i.e. connected by means of cables). Controlling of terminals is performed to various extents by these controllers. Data entry system controllers can be regarded as terminal controllers for data entry terminals. However, depending on the data entry system concerned, various amounts of preprocessing are performed by them as well.

Network elements can be connected by means of various communication media that will be treated in some detail in the following chapter. In the configurational model, it is enough to distinguish a local connection (mostly parallel transmission) and remote connection (mostly serial transmission). The simplification of the model is considerable, but it allows for all basic considerations concerning the network. Also it is much more general, because superfluous and misleading details are excluded.

Figure 1.1 shows the graphical symbols used for individual network elements and for the above mentioned two basic types of connection. The symbols will be used in several configurational schemes that follow and also elsewhere in the book.

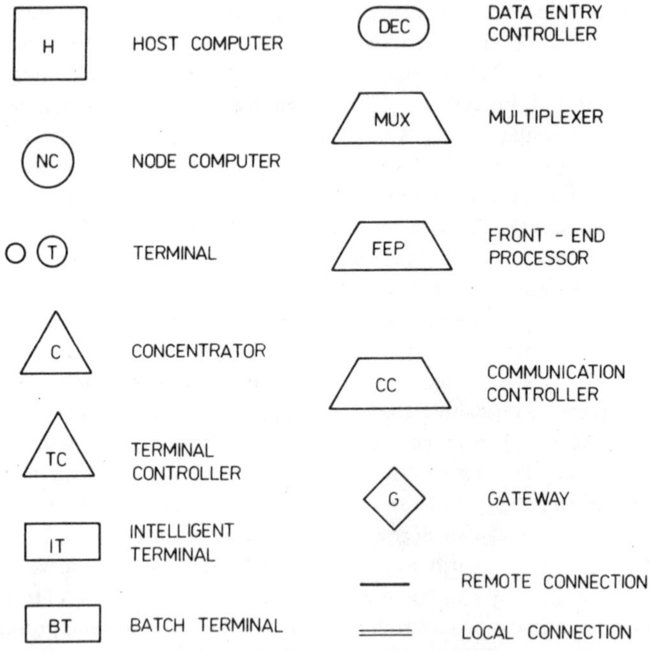

Figure 1.1 Overview of network elements and of their graphical symbols and acronyms

Various distributed processing networks, or their configurational models, are shown in the following figures.

A simple, one-level, multiaccess terminal system is shown in Figure 1.2. The data transmission subnetwork, consisting of telephone lines, modems, and modem adapters, is indicated by a dashed line.

The three-level multiaccess terminal network, comprising concentrators and a terminal controller, is shown in Figure 1.3. The front-end computer is used instead of a hardware multiplexor. Specialized communication controllers can be used to replace the front-end processor, the latter being often a general purpose minicomputer equipped with additional hardware and software.

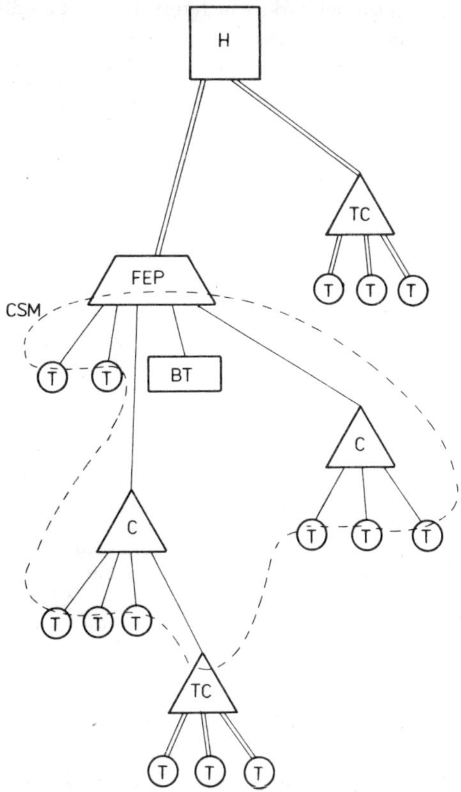

Figure 1.2 One-level multiaccess terminal network.
(Key: see Figure 1.1, CSM = communication subsystem)

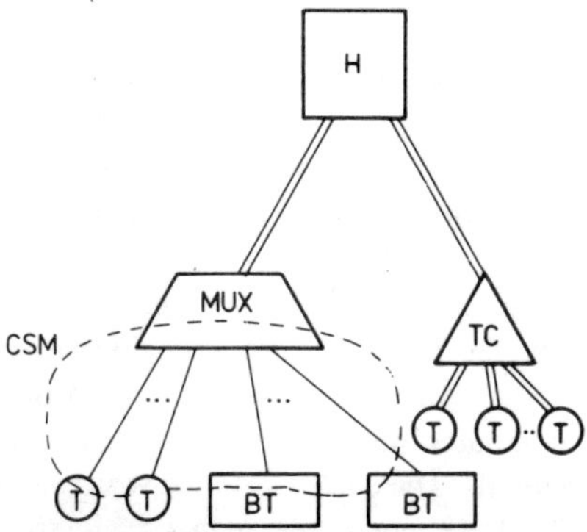

Figure 1.3 Three-level multiaccess terminal network.
(Key: see Figure 1.1, CSM = communication subsystem)

The data transmission subnetwork, which mostly is not a self-contained part of the terminal network, is indicated by the dashed line.

Similarly, the first computer networks did not use an independent data transmission subnetwork, as can be seen from Figure 1.4. This situation soon changed, however, especially with the development of packet switching networks.

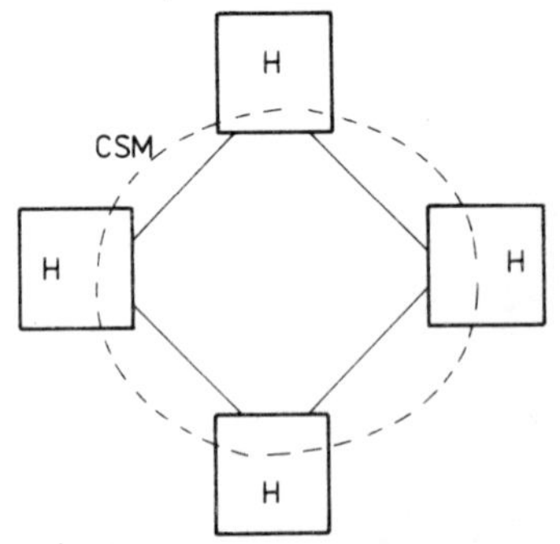

Figure 1.4 Computer network without explicitly separated communication subsystem. (Key: see Figure 1.1, CSM = communication subsystem)

To give an example, the basic configurational structure of the ARPA computer network is shown in Figure 1.5. TIP and IMP are two kinds of node computers. TIPs and IMPs, together with the inter-node links, constitute the self-contained data communication subnetwork that makes use of the packet switching principle. Only IMP node computers were used in the initial ARPA. They switched packets and provided for local connection of up to four host computers (not necessarily of the same make). Terminals were connected to host computers. Later the function of concentration and servicing of start-stop terminals were added changing the IMP into the TIP.

As can be seen from Figure 1.5, several (up to four) host computers can be connected to one node computer, but no host computer is connected to more than one node computer. There is only one path between any host computer and the corresponding node computer. The alternative, or redundant, paths are not necessary in this case, because the connection is local and the probability of transmission breakdown is very low.

When host computers are connected to node computers remotely, failure rates may be much higher than in the previous case and alternative paths can improve the reliability substantially. Of course, to have more than one path between the host computer and node computer means more complex communication control and different addressing methods. The configurational structure of such a network, similar to that of the CYCLADES computer network, is shown in Figure 1.6. Host computers are mostly connected to two node computers. Interconnected node computers create a packet switching subnetwork. The function of concentration is

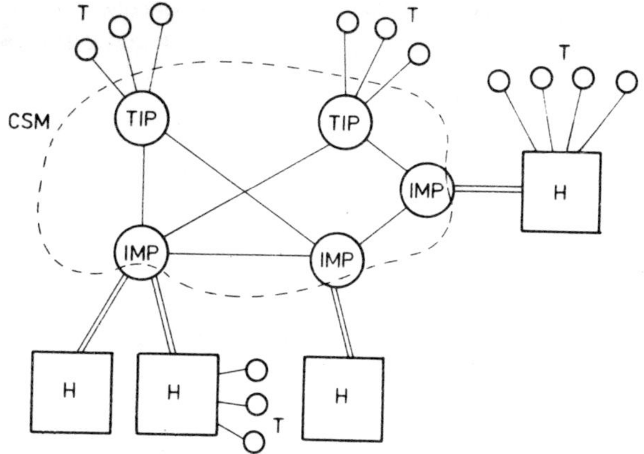

Figure 1.5 Configurational structure of the computer network with locally connected host computers, e.g. of the ARPANET. (Key: see Figure 1.1, CSM = communication subsystem)

taken out of the packet switching subnetwork and is implemented in special concentrators. A gateway processor is also shown in Figure 1.6: this performs the conversion functions required when interconnecting two computer networks or packet switching networks.

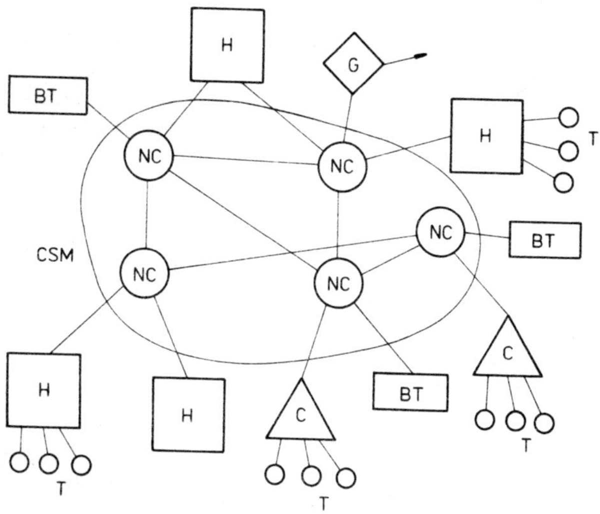

Figure 1.6 Configurational structure of the computer network with remotely connected host computers and concentrators. (Key: see Figure 1.1, CSM = communication subsystem)

A packet switching subnetwork can replace the set of concentrators in a multi-level terminal network (see Figure 1.7). It is clear that addressing will be changed accordingly.

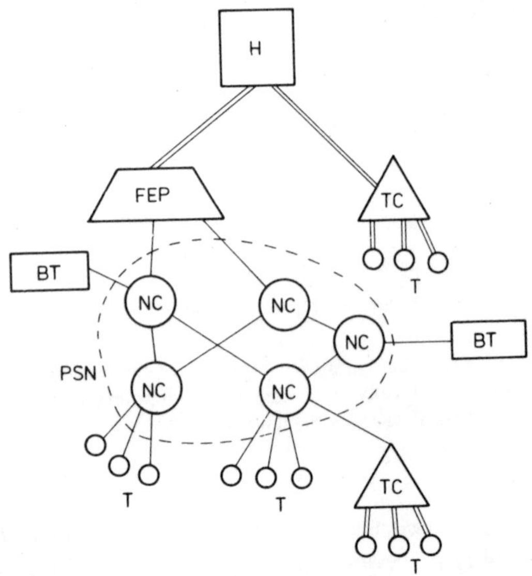

Figure 1.7 Terminal network using a packet switched network. (Key: see Figure 1.1, PSN = packet switched network)

Figure 1.8 shows an example of data entry and a data distribution system. In this network, concentrators perform other functions besides the concentration of messages from terminals and the distribution of messages to terminals. We nevertheless do not regard them as node computers, because they do not switch packets (leased lines are utilized in the network).

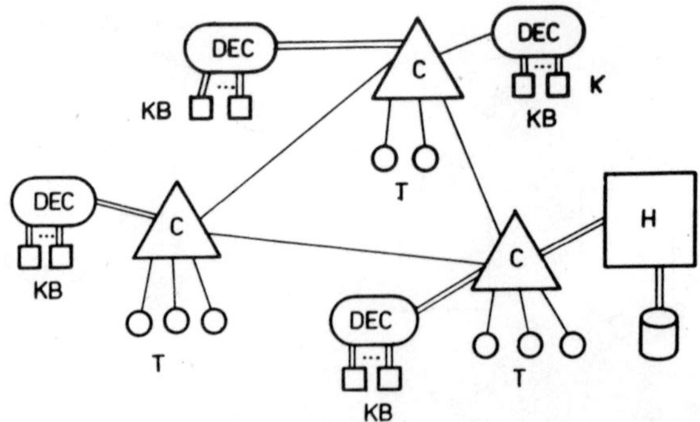

Figure 1.8 Data collection, transmission, and distribution network. (Key: see Figure 1.1)

In all examples of network structures shown so far leased or switched telephone (or telegraph, or wideband) lines are utilized as an ultimate service obtained from the common carriers or post offices. But now, when public packet switching networks are provided, a new situation arises. The subnetwork is characterized, besides other things, by the fact that it is a sort of black box for users. This is not entirely so, because marginal subnetwork nodes are "visible" and the interface between them and various subscriber equipment is well defined. In the terminology of CCITT, the public data network nodes are called Data Communication Terminating Equipment — DCE, and subscribers' equipment is called Data Terminating Equipment — DTE (see Figure 1.9).

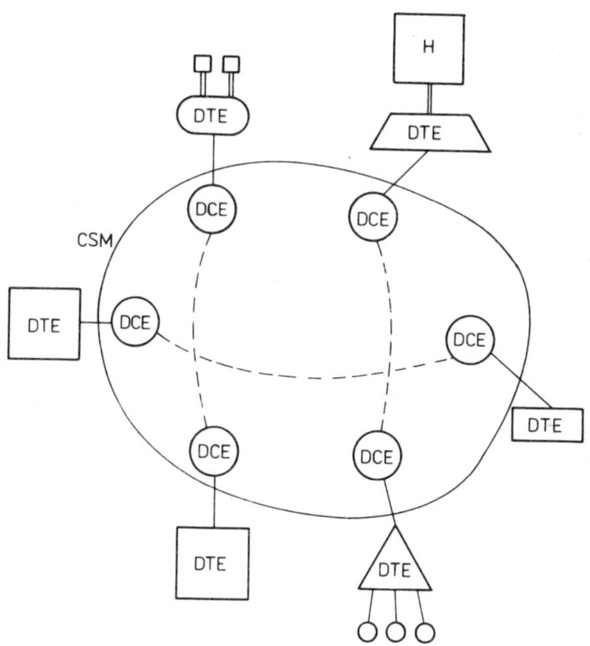

Figure 1.9 Public data network according to CCITT

Configurational structures represent only one of the factors that determine the requirements for communication control in a given network. Various kinds of connection between network elements constitute another factor. The influence of these connections will be analysed in the next chapter.

Because the basis of any configurational structure is represented by a simpler and less informative topological structure, we shall summarize the structures observed as follows.

From the point of view of communication control three basic network topologies can be distinguished (see Figure 1.10):

a) tree topology,
b) ring topology,
c) polygonal topology.

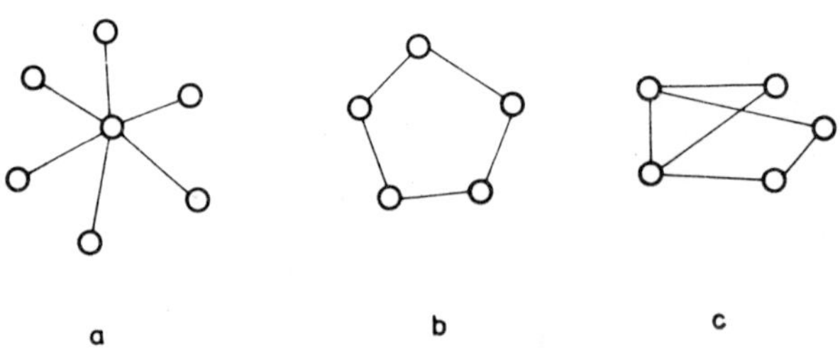

Figure 1.10 Basic one-level network topologies:
a) tree (star) topology, b) ring topology, c) polygonal topology

Of course, when applying graph theory measures to these topologies, the ring structure (a cycle) is only one special case of the polygonal structure. But here we are not interested in such an abstract approach.

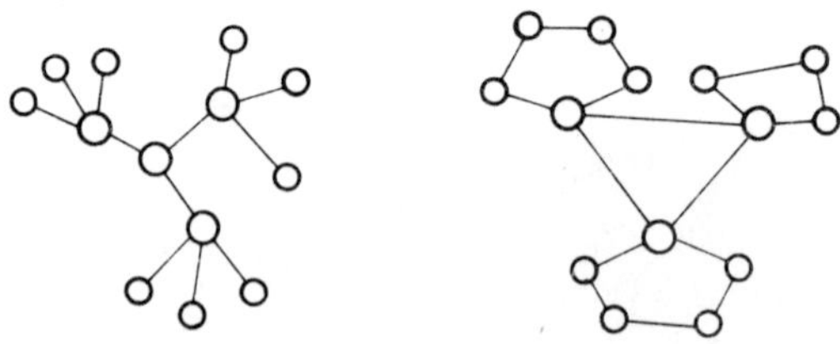

Figure 1.11 Two-level network topologies

The basic topologies can be one-level or multi-level. Examples of two-level topologies are shown in Figure 1.11. They are used with hierarchical networks.

1.2 Communication in Distributed Processing Networks

In distributed processing networks communication between various stations is realized by means of transmission devices and transmission media. Any configuration of transmission facilities existing between any two communicating stations may be called a communication medium. Although basically communication control proper may be treated abstractly, at the algorithmic level, without unnecessary details inherent to hardware or software implementation, nevertheless it may simplify further explanation if we recall some basic concepts of data transmission and data communication. Therefore, in this chapter we shall present a concise survey of data transmission techniques and networks. Those readers who are well acquainted with data transmission may take this chapter as a recapitulation, or they can simply leave it out.

In the same way as we have telephone lines for telephone signals transmission, and telegraph lines for transmission of telex messages, so, naturally, we may have data links for data transmission. The notion of a data link is not quite common and in various publications its meaning differs. Therefore it deserves more attention.

Data signals belong to discrete signals and therefore they cannot be transferred directly over analogue lines, e.g. over telephone lines. Even when using discrete lines (e.g. telegraph lines), it is not always possible to connect a data station to such lines directly, because the data station may not be adjusted to the type of line. Therefore some transmission device is needed which can modify or change discrete signals into analogue ones, or into discrete signals of an other type, and vice versa. Such a device, generally called a data set, is introduced as an interface between the line and the data station. Several kinds of data sets are known. For telegraph lines we use telegraph signal converters, in the case of telephone lines modems perform the signal conversion, and for other links (e.g. PCM links) special converters are utilized. Figure 1.12 shows a general scheme of the data link where the link can transfer any kind of signals and the data set represents, according to the lines used, a modem or a telegraph signal converter.

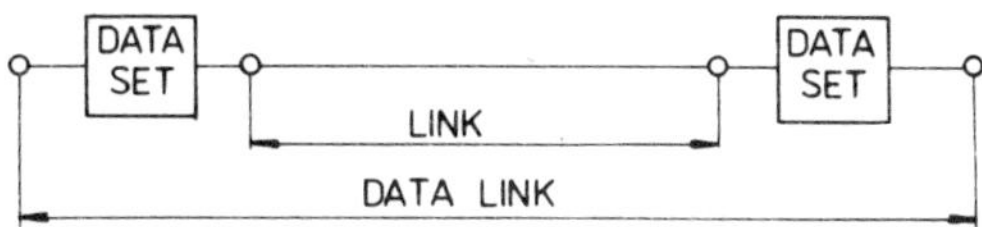

Figure 1.12 Scheme of a data link

Until now only telephone and telegraph lines have been considered. However, there are further possibilities. After all, in public telegraph or telephone networks various technical means are used for the required links. The same is true for data links. Therefore we shall say more about transmission links, because they have their specific features and communication control must reflect these features.

Links are generally divided into cable links and radio links. Cable links may utilize wires (as when interconnecting exchanges or when connecting subscribers to local exchanges), or twisted pairs, or symmetrical and coaxial cables (for trunks and long-haul lines). Waveguides and optical fibres have been utilized recently, because of their large bandwidth yielding higher data rates. Figure 1.13 gives some idea about the bandwidth of individual sorts of transmission media. If, according to the modulation method used, we know the number of carrier frequency cycles per one bit, we can also estimate the data transmission rates.

A feature of cable links is their negligible propagation delay, even for long distances. Of course, they may be used only for immobile stations.

The bandwidth ranging from very long radio waves up to laser generated light waves (see Fig. 1.13) is utilized by radio links. Wavelengths under 10 m, e.g.

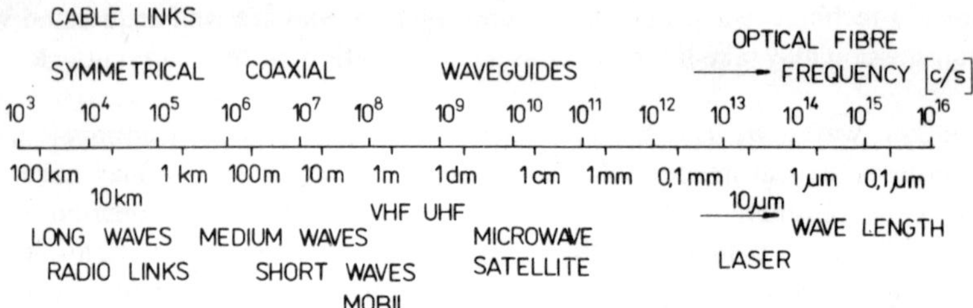

Figure 1.13 Use of frequency spectrum

wavebands for mobile radio services, for radio relay communication, and for satellite communication systems, are mostly used for data transmission. Radio links are suitable for mobile stations as well, but their quality is not stable (it depends on ionospheric and/or atmospheric conditions, for example). Shorter wavelengths require direct visibility between communicating stations which may not always exist. When the visibility is poor or even non-existent, difficulties (known, for example, from television) arise and transmission is hardly feasible. Therefore it can happen that some stations are "hidden". They require the intermediary services of control stations used to retransmit messages (signals) exchanged between pairs of such hidden stations. When a geostationary satellite is used to perform this intermediary function, the delay of 240—270 ms must be considered. This delay depends on the distance between the stations, which is variable. Moreover, even with fixed distance the delay is not constant, but fluctuates. These disadvantages prevent the use of some communication control methods. But, on the other hand, some new methods are feasible (e.g. the sending station may be able to "hear" itself).

A link of any nature can serve for signal transmission as a whole, or several transmission paths may be created by means of various multiplexing devices. The transmission path may be one-way (simplex) in which case it is termed channel, or it may be two-way (duplex) in which case it is termed a circuit. A similar situation arises

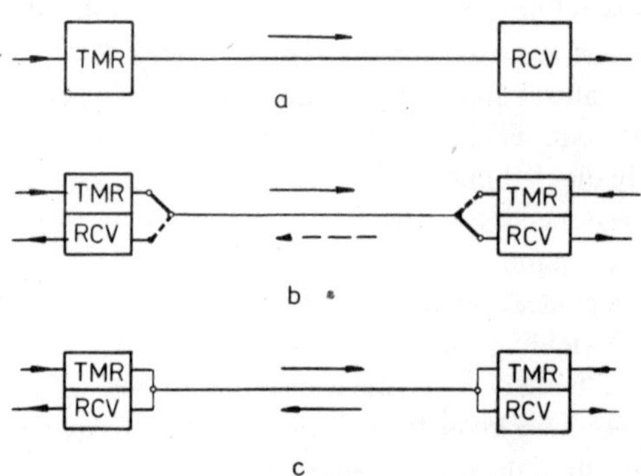

Figure 1.14 Types of data links
a) simplex (SX) TMR — transmitter
b) half-duplex (HDX) RCV — receiver
c) full-duplex (FDX)

with the data link, which can be simplex, half-duplex, or full-duplex not only according to the transmission path, but also according to the data sets. Fig. 1.14 illustrates this situation. Case a) corresponds to a simplex data link in which a sending data set (TMR — transmitter) is connected with a receiving data set (RCV — receiver) by means of a channel. Case b) relates to half-duplex operation which is characterized by both kinds of data set at both ends of a circuit (but with only one of them working at any one time). Finally, case c) illustrates the full-duplex operation over a circuit.

In the given example a common circuit is used for both data and control. Sometimes, especially with error control, forward and backward channels are used between the stations. In order to obtain these two channels, either a physical circuit is established between the stations or the two channels are allocated for the purpose within the scope of more multiplexed channels created by means of one physical link. In the latter case full-duplex operation is determined by transferring either data or control information in both directions simultaneously (e.g. data in one direction and control information in the opposite direction).

The transmission path can also be created by cascaded connection of several transmission circuits or channels. This is the way the transmission path is created in the circuit switched network. In such network cascading may be combined with multiplexing (voice frequency telegraphy — VFT, carrier telephony). All these techniques are well known in data transmission engineering, and therefore they need no further explanation. Let us recall only that circuit switching is generally utilized in telegraph and telephone networks and that subscriber extensions, by means of which the subscribers are connected to the nearest exchange, are two-wire and operate in half duplex. When required, namely in the case of data transmission, the four-wire extension is used extending the circuit up to the subscriber.

Data transmission rate can be utilized as another criterion for data link classification. According to data transmission rate we can distinguish low-speed links (up to 1200 bit/s, namely 50, 100, 150, 200, 300, 600, and 1200 bit/s), medium-speed links (up to 10 800 bit/s, namely 2000, 2400, 3600, 4800, 5600, 7200, 9600, 10 800 bit/s) and high-speed links (e.g. 19,2, 40,8, 48, 56, 64, 72 kbit/s). This classification reflects the purpose of the links, and is identical with classes of data links provided by common carriers or, especially, by post offices. And with post offices on the scene a further criterion emerges, based on subscriber — owner relation.

Data links (or corresponding transmission facilities) may be owned by users (private lines) or by PTTs. In many countries the PTT is the only common carrier allowed, i.e. the PTT has a monopoly in telecommunications. Subscribers can use dedicated lines or links (leased from the PTT) or shared lines or links within the scope of public telephone, or telegraph, or data transmission networks.

Sharing of links is achieved by switching. Three methods of switching are utilized: circuit switching, message switching and packet switching. Subscribers may get the link needed for a relatively short communication in the form of a switched link, which is the opposite to the leased link mentioned above. Leased lines are used especially for high-speed links. PCM links, wideband links and television links are examples of such high-speed links.

From the point of view of communication control, the difference between switched links and leased links is twofold.

First, switched links must be selected from the set of all links available in the public network and assigned to subscribers for one call or for one session. When the subscribers finish their data exchange and have nothing more to say to each other, the link used is returned to the network, i.e. the link is released. Of course, if the above operations are to be performed automatically, they must be controlled.

Second, switched links have a substantially larger bit error rate (from ten to thousand times larger than leased lines) which means more demand on error control.

In order to give the reader a real picture of bit error rates existing in public networks, Table 1.1. presents some values related to several networks and data transmission services. The values given in the table are not the result of measurement, but rather are typical values for comparison. There are differences not only between public networks in various countries, or between different public networks in one country, but also between values measured at different time intervals (days, months, etc.). In this sense, the numbers in the table are estimates. As far as the error rate in packet switched networks is concerned, it should be emphasized that good error control is provided by these networks resulting in low residual error rates.

Table 1.1 Comparison of error rates in typical links and paths

Type of link	Bit error rate
switched telephone lines	5.10^{-4}
telex	10^{-4}
leased telegraph	10^{-5}
leased telephone	5.10^{-6}
message switched network (e. g. AUTODIN)	10^{-8}
public line switched data netwrok (e. g. EDS)	10^{-9}
packet switched data network (e. g. ARPANET)	10^{-12}
possible public packet switched data network	10^{-15}

The last criterion which will be used in this chapter for classification of data links is their topology, or configuration. Stations will be considered further. The simplest and most often used link connecting two stations (or two points) is the so-called point-to-point link shown in Figure 1.12. When more stations (points) have to be interconnected by means of a single link, a multipoint link or a ring configuration is a suitable approach. Both these arrangements are presented in Figure 1.15. They differ in the way stations and data sets are connected to the link, and in transmission. The former can be regarded as a means for connecting stations in parallel to a common transmission medium. The latter enables communication between any two stations, and also among more than two stations (group calling service or broadcasting). It is immaterial that some stations may be switched off or have failed to cooperate.

The ring (or loop) is characterized by serial connection of communicating stations (or, more precisely, of data sets). The ring may be simplex or duplex, i.e. signals pass stations in one direction, or in both directions. At least one of the ring stations acts as a signal regenerator in order to reform the shape of circulating signals and to perform synchronization. From the point of data transfer, frames are circulating in a loop link. Each frame can transfer a certain amount of data, and each station can insert its data into the passing frame if the frame is free, i.e. if it is not already carrying some data. And each station can empty the frame if the data are addressed to it. The station can empty the frame and at the same time load it with data to be sent. In this sense, even the simplex loop can operate in full duplex. The serial connection of stations yields lower reliability of loops because the failure of a single station can put down the whole ring.

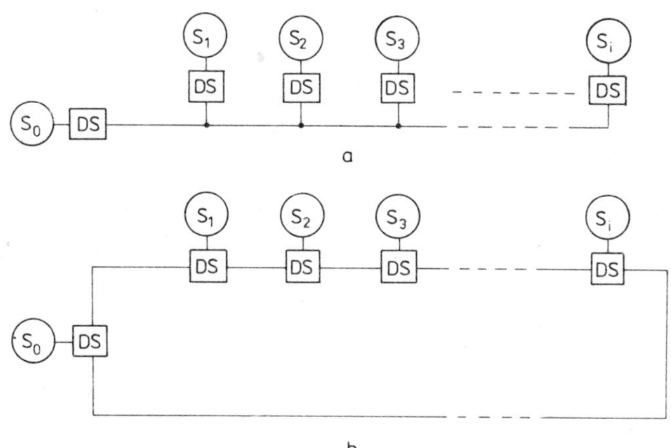

Figure 1.15 Structures of data links
a) multipoint structure, b) ring (loop) structure
S — station, DS — data set

Several times in this chapter PTTs have been mentioned as the owners and operators of transmission facilities. PTTs provide services of great variety, and because services are closely related to communication control it is necessary to deal with them briefly.

The simplest service consists in offering asynchronous or synchronous data links. Asynchronous data links utilize data sets that are not controlled by a common clock. Users (subscribers) have to take care of establishing and maintaining adequate synchronization (see Chapter 3.2). In synchronous data links a subnetwork provides synchronization and there is no need for users to bother with it.

Other services relate to the switching methods used in public data networks. A switching method, i.e. circuit switching (or line switching), message switching, and packet switching, determines to a considerable extent the distribution of responsibilities or activities between the network and users (subscribers).

Circuit switching is used in all telephone networks, in most telegraph networks, and in some data networks (e.g. in the West German EDS network). The principle of circuit switching lies in creating one link (physical or virtual) between subscribers or end stations. Blocks are sent over this link without intermediate storing. The link is temporary only (because the network is switched). PTTs specify rules for the operation of such switched links.

Direct connection of subscribers by means of a tie data link is the advantage of circuit switching. But there are many disadvantages that show themselves especially in data transmission. Because the resulting data link is created (built) from serially connected sections, the quality of the whole data link depends considerably on the quality of the worst section. This limits the speed and worsens the error rate. Although link establishment is normally automatic (though in many cases it is still manual, i.e. it is performed by operators), the supervising is predominantly manual. When an unsuccessful attempt has been made to establish connection, then the user (operator) decides if the attempt is to be repeated. An unsuccessfull attempt may be done not only to all lines being engaged, but also that the addressed station may not be available (busy, not prepared, in failure, etc.). Therefore the message switching and/or packet switching is being used more and more.

Message switching means that a network takes up the whole data message from a user (subscriber) and the network is fully responsible for delivery of the data message to the addressed station. A user need not trouble any more about the message. The network controls the hops of the message from one store-and-forward switching node to another. The message is temporarily stored in each intermediate node. By practising hops related to sections created by neighbouring nodes better utilization of network resources is achieved. Message switching is used in some telex or telegraph networks (e.g. the Swiss system ATECO).

Message switching systems either limit the message lengths and guarantee (to some extent only) the delivery times (delays), or, if the message lengths are not limited, the network operation is inefficient and slow, because many sections are blocked by long messages. This deteriorates the throughput substantially and makes the cost of such data transmission much higher. Therefore packet switching systems were elaborated and put into operation, both experimental and routine.

Packet switching utilizes the same basic principle as does message switching, i.e. the store-and-forward principle. Packets are data blocks of reasonably limited length (say, one or several thousands of bits only) and of well structured and agreeed formats. Both small length and unified formats make implementation much simpler and operation much more efficient.

There is another principle, not always utilized in packet switching networks, namely that of sending packets of one message over different paths or routes through the network, aiming at even better utilization of partial data links and improvement of other performance measures. But allowing packets to travel via different routes brings some new problems, e.g. sequencing and reordering.

In this connection two broadly discussed data transmission services have to be mentioned here. They are the datagram service and the virtual call (virtual circuit) service.

The datagram service represents the system in which the principle of using different routes for packets called datagrams is utilized. However, sequencing, or reordering, is not included in the subnetwork (i.e. in the packet switching network): users (subscribers) are supposed to take care of the proper order of packets and some others matters. In this sense the datagram network transfers individual and independent packets — datagrams.

Virtual circuits represent the case when the principle of using different routes for individual packets is not used, or, at least, is not made visible to users (subscribers). Therefore there is no need to reorder the delivered packets as they travel over the same virtual circuit and so cannot become out of order (except, of course, when error recovery is provided).

There can be permanent virtual circuits created in the virtual circuit network. These are analogous to leased lines in telephone or telegraph networks.

Figure 1.16 shows a survey of switching services that are used in public data networks operated by various PTTs.

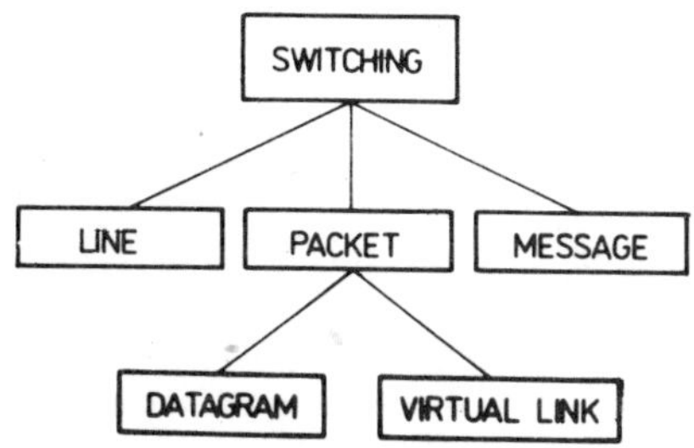

Figure 1.16 Services in public networks provided by PTTs

The physical principles of data links and data networks determine the selection of appropriate communication control methods and their realization by communication protocols. This is the main reason why these physical principles have been treated in this chapter.

Part 2
Communication Control

2.1 Communication Control Principles

2.1.1 Fundamental notions

Communication control in computer networks may be connected either with notions of communication protocols and network architecture or with the control of a communication subnetwork aimed at maintaining and/or optimizing the performance of the communication subnetwork.

It is the control theory viewpoint that represents the advanced approach to communication control problems and which is receiving growing attention nowadays.

In general, each communication in a network consists of the data exchange proper and of a set of auxiliary operations which in themselves are not data exchanges but which are indispensable for the data exchanges to be performed and, moreover, must be of required quality under all predictable and even under some unpredictable conditions. The set of these auxiliary operations can roughly be regarded as communication control. Later, namely in Chapter 2.2 and in Part 3, we shall show in detail the nature of these operations, what purpose they serve, and how they are realized. We shall identify suitably selected groups of these operations as communication functions.

Here, and throughout the book, we shall distinguish between two quite different aims and the corresponding nature of the individual communication functions. In other words, two main approaches to communication control in computer networks may be recognized. They can be characterized as the performance approach and the implementation approach.

These two approaches originate in two different meanings of the term control. In a computer, various control units or controllers are utilized to perform operations that are not themselves processing, but that are indispensable if processing is to take place at all. These control operations constitute a subset of all operations performed in computers.

Similarly, in a network, communication control covers those operations that enable data exchanges to take place. This aspect of communication control represents the implementation approach. It primarily concerns structure and elements, not the subnetwork as a whole.

On the other hand, in computer systems and in networks changes of both external and internal conditions occur during the operation. For example, load (either processing load or communication load) can fluctuate considerably, because it is generated by users (or subscribers) that certainly do not provide a uniform source of traffic. Moreover, the environment in which computers and networks operate can exert a disturbing influence on individual computer units or network elements, especially on transmission lines or channels used. As for internal changes, various failures can occur. All these changes must be treated adequately if the performance of a computer or network is not to deteriorate. Such treatment, in general, is the task of control.

Let us recall some basic ideas concerning control. The general model of a control system shown in Figure 2.1 can be used to clarify the explanation. The controlled system is expected to yield required values of the relevant objective function, which it normally does. But when external influence is exerted, in the form of extended changes of environment, it is no longer capable of coping with such conditions. Similarly, failures inside the controlled system have generally the same effect. In these cases controlling intervention may help, being provided by the control device or controller and based on proper observations of the controlled system and/or of its outputs and inputs. There exists a great variety of control system models: the one shown in Figure 2.1 is only a simple example of such models.

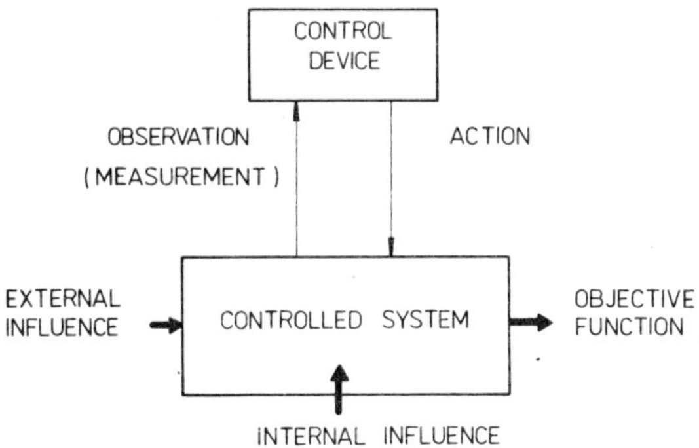

Figure 2.1 General model of a control system

When applying the control system model to communication control, we must first identify the controlled system. This identification can be hardly unique because the model is general and as such it can be applied to several actual systems or configurations.

Communication control essentially concerns either pairs of communication stations or the communication subnetwork as a whole. So these two may be regarded as controlled systems.

Figure 2.2 reminds us of the various network elements that can communicate in a distributed processing network. Several pairs of communicating stations are clearly distinguished in Figure 2.2. The individual pairs are marked by geometrical symbols (squares, triangles, etc.) and also the individual communication paths are distinguished graphically.

These pairs of stations illustrate the obvious fact that at least two stations are needed for communication to take place. On the other hand, however, neither should there be more than two stations. So we can generalize the situation shown in Figure 2.2 and define the basic communication element as is shown in Figure 2.3. When applying this basic communication element to any pair of stations in Figure 2.2, we can identify the communication medium with the corresponding communication paths or with the whole communication subnetwork (which is not shown in Figure 2.2). The individual communication paths influence each other inside the subnetwork.

The basic communication element may be considered to be a controlled system (in the sense of Figure 2.1). But the basic communication element is more often used to express what the stations have to do (or will do). The main reasons for control come

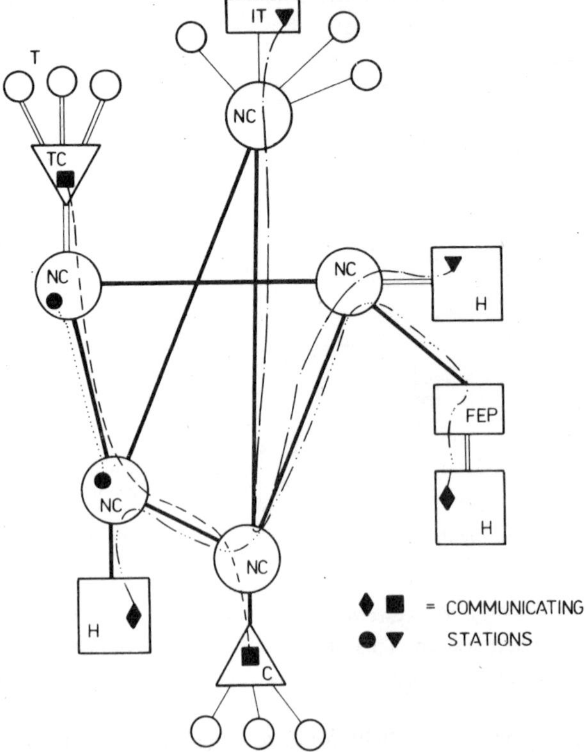

Figure 2.2 Examples of communicating pairs of stations in a network. (H = host computer, NC = node computer, C = = concentrator, TC = terminal controller, FEP = front-end processor, T = terminal, IT = intelligent terminal)

from the communication medium which is the main source of disturbances and changes anyway. Therefore we shall first deal with the subnetwork that may be regarded as a case of a communication medium.

The configuration shown in Figure 2.2 can be generalized as shown in Figure 2.4. The network comprises the communication subnetwork and subscriber stations only.

Offered traffic entering the subnetwork represents the external influence. Failures of subnetwork nodes and/or data links are internal influences. Both the influences are stochastic or definitely nondeterministic. The subnetwork should provide for simultaneous communication of many individual pairs of subscriber stations. Subnetwork performance serves as an objective function. The control device, in this case, is included inside the subnetwork.

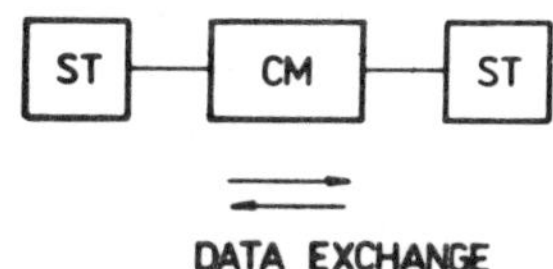

Figure 2.3 General communication element

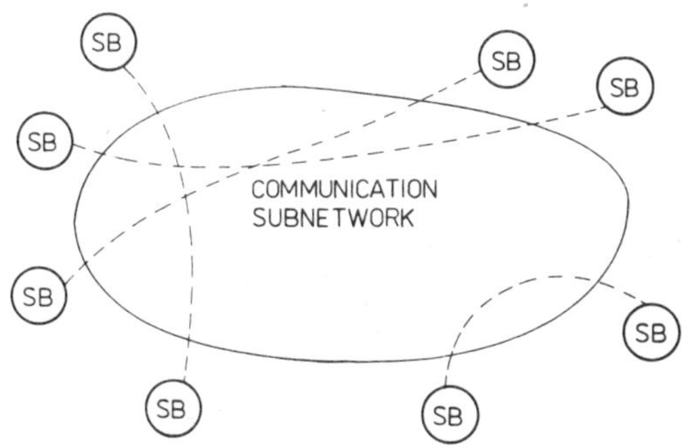

Figure 2.4 General network model.
(SB = subscriber station)

Here one must differentiate between identifying the control algorithms used (i.e. identifying the control device) and implementing these control algorithms somewhere. One common control centre (a special subnetwork node) can provide for implementing such algorithms, or they can be implemented in all subnetwork nodes and even in subscriber stations (partly only).

The subnetwork performance is not a single variable, but is rather complex, being composed of several performance measures, such as throughput, transit time, delivery time, round-trip delay, utilization of nodes and/or lines (generally: of subnetwork resources), residual error rate (concerning either bits, or characters, or blocks, or messages), recoverability, reliability, etc. Most of the performance measures may be defined for any pair of subscriber stations, or for some subset of subscriber stations i.e. for stations belonging to some class of service, or for one particular pair of stations only.

Besides the performance measures user requirements may be introduced, such as accuracy, readiness, reliability, and costs. Accuracy relates to error-free transfer of blocks or messages. Readiness covers all delays, transit times, response times, etc. Reliability comprises recoverability and all other means of decreasing vulnerability. Costs need no comment. Such user requirements are useful in the early stages of network (or subnetwork) design when overall requirements on network properties (characteristics) are to be transformed step-by-step into some more technical and more detailed variables (i.e. into the values of individual performance measures).

Resulting values of performance measures are determined by values of so called design variables (or components) that can be also global or detailed. As examples of global design components we can mention network topology, capacity assignment (i.e. selecting the processing and buffering capacities of network elements and/or of subnetwork nodes, and transmission capacities of lines or links used), and communication control. The values of design variables are selected (after estimation, or calculation, or modelling) so that the required values of performance measures are achieved if possible. However, even this static design (i.e. the design neglecting dynamic changes and stochastic influences) may not be feasible, because of conflicting dependencies of various performance measures on design variables or because of constraints that generally exist and which must be taken account of in the design.

Communication control plays a double role in communication subnetwork design. This double role enables us to differentiate between static design and dynamic design, or between the design of control units and the selection of dynamic control algorithms, respectively.

During the static design stage the rules for communication of all possible pairs of communicating stations and of their possible cooperation should be specified. Such rules are most often called communication protocols, and essentially they relate to individual pairs of communicating stations rather than to all such pairs together, i.e. to the system as a whole.

The dynamic design takes care of both external and internal influences, and can be identified with the design of communication control proper. It means that some new group of operations, or corresponding communication functions, aimed at suppressing the effect of the individual influences is to be chosen, specified, and implemented during the dynamic design stage. So the second role of communication control leads to the implementation of additional groups of operations in the appropriate controllers. These operations, generally requiring the cooperation of two or even more stations, must be supported by relevant communication protocols.

From what has been written above it is clear now that from the two roles of communication control the basic one is that which corresponds to the static design. This is so because without some basic rules for communication specified (and implemented, of course) no communication can take place. So the implementation approach represents the step in the design of a subnetwork that must be made first.

Only after designing the static part of communication control can we proceed with the dynamical change, i.e. with communication control proper.

An example may illustrate this. The basic communication element shown in Figure 2.3 may be detailed by distinguishing the static communication control part first, as shown in Figure 2.5. The control parts of stations, which will be called protocol stations in this book, implement the rules for the exchange of control information between the stations. These rules must be specified and realized within the scope of a relevant communication protocol. Both in Figure 2.3 and in Figure 2.5 it is assumed that data source and data destination are parts of stations (communicating stations). This assumption may not be true when the stations are identified with the whole network elements, e.g. with host computers, and it certainly is not true when communication is structured into layers, as will be explained later. Therefore it is better to differentiate between the basic communication element comprising both data source and data destination, and the communication control element which contains protocol stations only. The communication control element is shown in Figure 2.6, and fully represents the static communication control model.

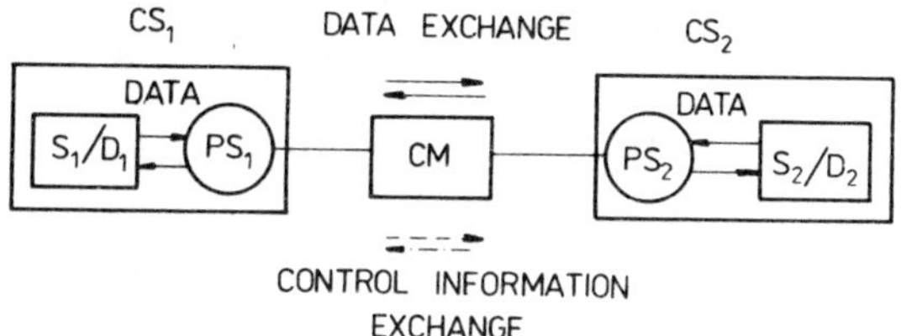

Figure 2.5 Communication element.
(CM = communication medium, CS = communication station, PS = protocol station, S/D = source/destination)

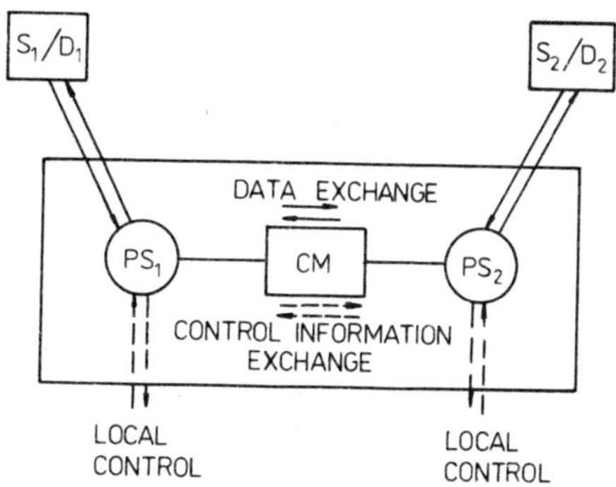

Figure 2.6 Communication control element.
(CM = communication medium, PS = protocol station, S/D = source/destination)

Now let us assume that in some part of a subnetwork an alternative communication path is to be used as a means of dealing either with high traffic, or with the failure of a line. The switching on and off automatically of this path is an example of dynamic control. The alternative path expressed by means of communication control element in Figure 2.7 is switched on and off by actions of an adequate control device when exceptional conditions occur (or when they are recognized by the control device). The control device may be placed either externally (see Figure 2.7) or internally (see Figure 2.8). Of course, the control algorithm used is essentially the same in both cases: only the network elements in which the algorithm is performed are different, with the communication paths for transfer of both measured values and action values being correspondingly different. Note that the same communication medium (e.g. the same communication lines) is used for both data exchange and for control information exchange (and, moreover, for both static and dynamic control information exchange). Both static and dynamic control functions are performed by protocol stations.

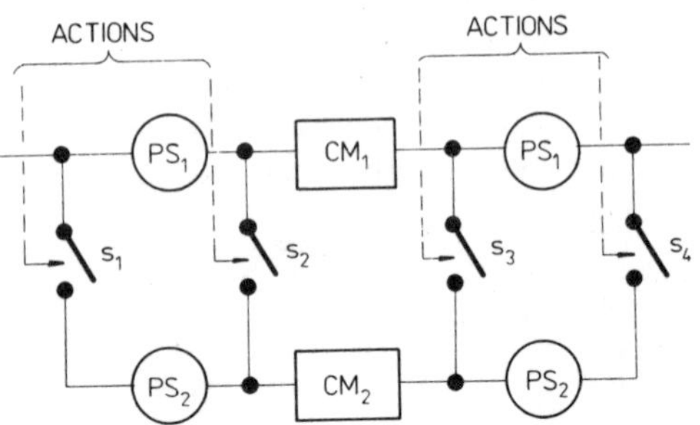

Figure 2.7 Communication system with alternate path and with external control device. (CM = communication medium, PS = protocol station)

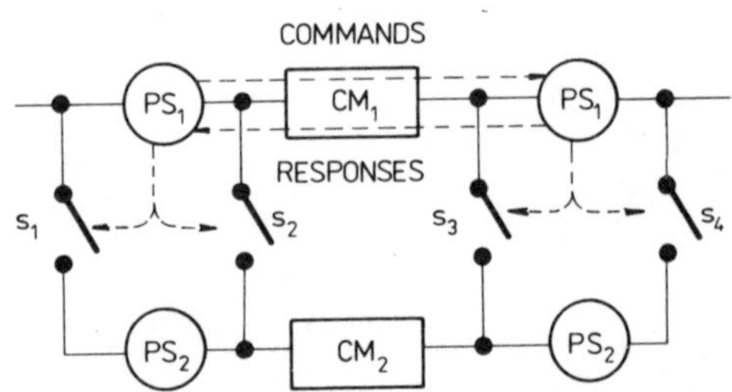

Figure 2.8 Communication system with alternate path and with internal control device. (CM = communication medium, PS = protocol station)

The communication control part of any network element may be represented by one station (or by one protocol station when the communication control element representation is used). For several reasons, it is not very suitable to use one station only. For example, when the network element is complex, its communication part is complex too and thus it is advantageous to decompose it into several simpler parts, usually into a hierarchy of horizontal layers. The resulting layered structure is commonly called network architecture (see Chapter 2.3). In most layers (but not necessarily in all) both communication control elements and corresponding communication protocols are specified, because there may be several layers implemented in one network element. When the network element is complex, its communication control part is also represented by several relatively simple stations.

We have already described communication control as consisting of communication functions. This also can be regarded as decomposition, namely as the decomposition of a set of all control operations into several subsets corresponding to the individual communication functions. Because some communication functions can be implemented in several layers, or even in all layers of the network architecture, this decomposition may be considered to be vertical.

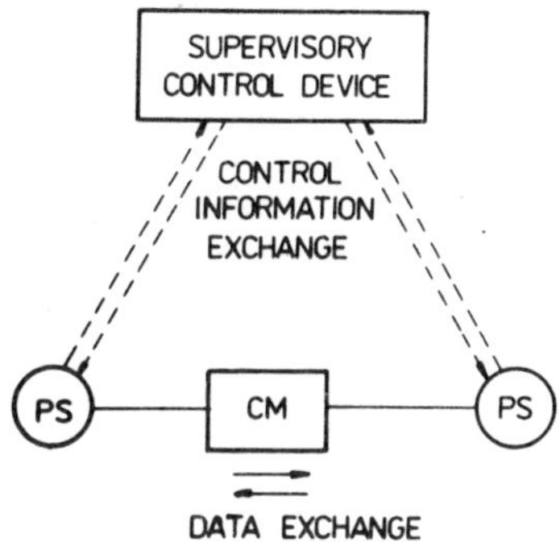

Figure 2.9 Communication control element with supervisory control. (CM = communication medium, PS = protocol station)

Both decompositions of communication control illustrate a basic principle, namely the simplification of a complex system by dividing it into several simpler and therefore much more comprehensible parts.

The communication control element shown in Figure 2.6 corresponds to direct control that is characterized by a control device being implemented directly in the two protocol stations. This means that the protocol stations, in this case, comprise both static control and dynamic control.

We can recognize indirect control also (see Figure 2.9) which rather resembles the control system model shown in Figure 2.1.

The general schemes of Figure 2.6 and Figure 2.9 can be applied to various systems. The systems may be distinguished when some of the following criteria are applied to them. The two stations and the supervisory control device can be either local or remote. When local, they can reside in one network element (e.g. in different layers of the network architecture) or in independent network elements, these being connected by means of cables. Also, serial or parallel transmission can be utilized. Of course, in all the above cases, the corresponding communication medium must be used. All the alternatives mentioned can be combined, yielding a variety of systems or communication control elements.

Basic communication elements and communication control elements are building blocks for communication control of the whole subnetwork. The existing communication control in a network can be decomposed into such basic elements when the analysis of the network is performed. Alternatively, the synthesis of the communication control system can be performed by combining individual communication control elements into the required overall structure, generally according to some network architecture selected. Both in the analysis and in the synthesis, various chains of communication control elements (or basic communication elements) may be recognized and created respectively. More details concerning this subject will be presented in Chapter 2.3 and 2.4.

First, however, communication functions will be examined from various points of view and explained in the next chapter.

2.1.2. Bibliographical notes

Some control aspects of communication control problems are, in varying depth and scope, dealt with for example in [85, 176, 177, 188, 230].

Adequate principles of general system theory and control theory may be found in excellent books of Mesarovic et al. [161, 162].

Issues of communication systems design approaches and of relations between internal (or secondary) system variables (which comprise the selected methods of communication functions) and external (or primary) system variables (which represent the system performance) are treated for example in [196, 224, 225].

2.2 Communication Functions

2.2.1 Communication phases

Let us refer to Figure 2.6 which depicts the communication control element, i.e. the model of a controlled communication system. Let us assume that the system has such a property as to start operating from outside, for example by entering data to be transferred, and then to operate autonomously by virtue of its control until all the data are transferred. The start of the autonomous operation may be called the start of the communication and the end of the operation may be called the end of the communication. The course of the communication, i.e. all operations between its start and its end, may be called the communication process.

Let us introduce a simple example. We can assume that the communication system consists of the leased line, the terminal, and the communication control unit of the computer. When the computer has got the message to be sent to the terminal, it must start the communication system, i.e. it must send a request to the communication control unit which, in accordance with the appropriate protocol, will further find out if the terminal (the other station) is connected, prepared, not busy, and willing to communicate. If any of the above conditions is not fulfilled, the attempt is unsuccesful. When the conditions are fulfilled, the positive acknowledgment comes from the terminal and the data exchange may start. The data exchange goes on until all data are transferred, or until one of the stations expresses its request to stop the transmission. Both such events are well recognizable. Finally, one of the stations will terminate the operation of the communication system, for example by sending the appropriate request to the other station and by receiving the corresponding response (if required).

In the above example we have recognized several events between the start and the end of the communication. Thus we divide the communication process into smaller parts which will be called the communication phases. So the communication phases are parts of the communication process delimited by well defined events. By the term "well defined" we mean that the occurrence of such an event is clearly recognizable under all possible conditions. Examples of well defined events are the occurrence of control characters, or of certain bit sequences, or changes of communication system states (e.g. states of the protocol stations).

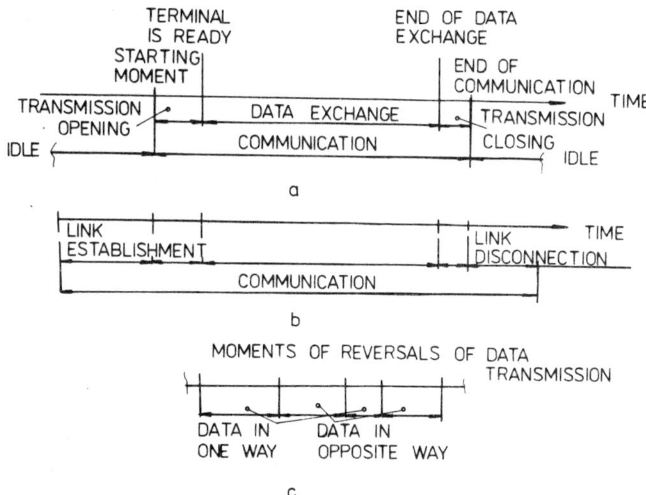

Figure 2.10 An example of communication phases
a) phases of leased data link
b) phases of switched data link
c) subphases of data exchange phase

Figure 2.10a illustrates the communication phases assigned to the above example. The first phase may be called the transmission opening phase, the second phase may be called the transmission maintaining phase or the data exchange phase, and the third phase may be called the transmission closing phase. The transmission opening phase is delimited by the starting event of the communication and by the situation of both stations being prepared to exchange data. The other phases may be defined similarly.

The phase between the ending event and the next starting event is an idle phase.

The phases may be not only merged, but also decomposed. For example the data exchange phase may be divided into subphases according to the direction of the data transfer (Figure 2.10c). To give another example, the operations assigned to the error detection and correction of a transmission error may be distinguished and regarded as subphases too. We could continue to divide the communication phases into subphases until the elementary events, i.e. the individual commands and responses are reached.

The number of communication phases can also be increased by other operations being added to the control of the communication system considered. For example, when using the switched line instead of the leased one in the system shown in Figure 2.10a, we must build into the communication control the operations or functions of the establishment and releasing of the line and we can assign two more phases to these operations (see Figure 2.10b). So instead of three phases we have five phases. Of course, the start of the communication will be shifted to the beginning of the line establishment phase and the end of the communication will be shifted to the termination of the line releasing phase.

In order to show the significance of the communication phases for the communication control explanation let us come back to Figure 2.10b depicting the five communication phases. What is the role of the communication control in the individual phases? In the first phase the establishment of the data link, according to the rules given for the switched network used, is the main task of the communication control. However, not only must the line be established, but also this must be accomplished within the required time limits. The line establishment time may be considered to be the performance criterion used with the first phase.

The operations used for establishing the line are generally not repeated in other phases; or they may be repeated, in the case of the link releasing phase, but in reverse order. On the other hand, it is clear that the data exchange operations are of no use during the line establishment phase. There are other performance criteria used during the data exchange phase, namely residual error rate, transfer time, availability, etc. Other communication control operations are necessary in order to reach and keep up the required values of the criteria.

Similarly, we could continue to assign the performance criteria to the other phases and to analyse the corresponding communication control operations. But now we shall go on with the analysis of Figure 2.10c, presenting the division of the data exchange phase into subphases assigned to the individual directions of the data transfer. The communication control operations need not be the same for both directions, although the differences will not be great. For example, other values of the performance criteria may be required for one of the directions. Nevertheless, the above differences can require slightly different control methods, although both groups of control methods i.e. for both directions will belong to one common class, namely to the classs of data exchange control methods.

From the point of view of the communication control the decomposition of the data exchange phase into further subphases yields no advantages.

The decomposition of the communication process into phases provides for differentiating various groups of operations performed within the scope of the communication control. Such a group of operations was called a communication function in Chapter 2.1, and this means that corresponding communication functions may be assigned to the individual phases of the above example. So we can recognize the line establishment function, the transmission opening function, the data exchange function, the transmission closing function and the line releasing function.

However, it is also possible to distinguish several communication functions in one communication phase. Because of the deep significance of the communication function notion for the decomposition of the communication control, the communication functions will be dealt with elsewhere in this book, namely in the next section and in Part 3.

2.2.2 Communication functions and services

As we have already mentioned, there can be several communication functions distinguished in one communication phase. We shall consider the performance of certain defined groups of operations, which are part of the communication control, to be the communication function. There are many other functions in the data processing systems, namely various processing functions, processing control functions etc., but these will not be dealt with.

Generally, each communication function has some purpose assigned to it. This purpose is achieved by means of operations belonging to the communication function. Everything that was stated about the communication control in the preceding chapter fully holds for individual communication functions. For example, for each communication function one or several performance criteria must be selected and the required values of this performance criteria must be maintained within the prescribed limits. But it should be noted that one communication function cannot influence all performance criteria used in the system, that it is not possible to optimize more than one performance criterion, and that it is not possible to prescribe values of several performance criteria, because of existing interrelations.

In order to know more about the achievement of the required purpose, the communication function methods must be described. Generally there is more than one method for the communication function. The most suitable method must be selected, according to the purpose required and the conditions present, in the course of the communication system design.

When the communication function and its method have been selected the next step is communication function method implementation. First, the place of the implementation must be determined. Communication functions can be implemented in only one node of the communication subnetwork, in two nodes, in several nodes, or even in all nodes. Some communication functions demand a knowledge of the states of the communication system. This means that the variables to be measured must be specified, and the places of measurement, processing and utilization must be determined. When the above places are not the same, the transfer of the measured and processed data must be specified as well.

For each communication function we should know the corresponding conditions for starting the function.

Now let us come back to the example shown in Figure 2.10b and to the line establishment communication function. The purpose of this function is clear: to create the physical line between the two stations in the required time. The method is determined by the switched network used, and it can concern the way of addressing or identifying the called station, the signalling between the calling station and the exchange node, the signalling between the calling station and the called station, etc.

Even in one switched network there can be several methods of line establishment. The method is selected according to the purpose. The line establishment communication function must be implemented primarily in the calling station, but the called station must also be active in the last steps of the line establishment procedure. The data about the network are obtained in the exchange nodes during the line establishment phase. These data must be transferred to the calling station. The line establishment function is started either by a request from the users(i.e. from outside), or by a signal from the network stating that the previous attempt was not successful.

Now let us try to find other communication functions in our example. During the transmission opening phase the calling station must not only find out if the called station is able and willing to communicate, but it must also make sure that the called station is really the one which was originally called. It can happen in the switched communication network that failures occur and, as a result of such an occurrence, nonaddressed stations are connected. Therefore two communication functions may be differentiated in the transmission opening phase, namely the transmission opening function proper and the identification of the connected station. Because these two functions are not performed simultaneously, but sequentially, the corresponding communication phase may also be decomposed into the two subphases.

When analyzing the transmission techniques more deeply, we find that data transmission cannot be accomplished without synchronization of the transmitter with the receiver. The synchronization requires additional control operations, and hence a synchronization control communication function is needed.

Now let us have a look at the most important communication phase, namely the data exchange phase. The performance criteria of accuracy and readiness are assigned to this phase. What situations can occur during this phase? One is that a transmission error can occur which decreases the accuracy of the transferred data. In order to prevent this the error control communication function must cope with this situation. This function must be able to detect the error and provide for recovery from it. It also can happen that the receiving station will not be able to receive the transferred data, for example because of occupied buffers. Overload or congestion can occur which may cause the increase of delay and even the loss of data blocks. In order to prevent this, another communication function must be introduced, namely the flow control function.

Let us compare the error control and the flow control functions. Each of them copes with a different unwanted situation and exerts its influence on the communication process under different conditions. The two communication functions can be applied sequentially. Independent subphases can be assigned to them, but it can happen that they will both use the same mechanism. For example, the negative acknowledgement mechanism (see Chapter 3.4) may be used both in the case of transmission error detection and in the case of buffer overflow. The receiving station does not know, after receiving the negative acknowledgment, what was the reason for sending it, but nevertheless reacts in the same way, i.e. it retransmits the corresponding data block. Of course, this is possible only because the same reaction of the receiving station is required for both the starting situations. When we look only at the data blocks (or at the commands and responses) exchanged by both stations and when we do not consider the states of the communication system, we are not able to differentiate between the subphases assigned to the two functions.

Communication functions provide for distinguishing additional subphases assigned by corresponding control operations, which is one of the roles they play in the decomposition of the communication control. From the point of view of the communication system the communication functions are internal means for achieving and maintaining the prescribed performance.

Some communication functions may be accessible to the communication system users. In such a case the user does not have to know the communication functions methods used, because he wants to use the communication system for communication per se. This is the case of the public telephone or telegraph network users. These users want to communicate, and as long as the network fulfils their requirements, they are not interested in the internal structure of the network.

But the situation is different when the user wants to use the whole communication subnetwork in some higher system which also must perform some communication functions. Then it is not enough for the user to know only the values of the performance criteria. He must also know the communication functions methods used, in order to be able to design the adequate interfaces. The communication functions, as seen from outside the communication systems, are usually called services, because the results of the corresponding control operations have the form of services offered by the communication system to its users. So the services (we should say communication services, but we do not deal with other types of services here) can be regarded as the results of the communication functions operations observable and usable outside the communication system. The details of communication functions implementation are not necessary when the services are to be specified. For example, it is enough to know that the communication system offers the service of improving the residual error rate by the factor of 10^3 (i.e. decreasing the, say, 10^{-3} error rate to the 10^{-6} error rate) and that the rules for the use of this service are such and such. If the above improvement is

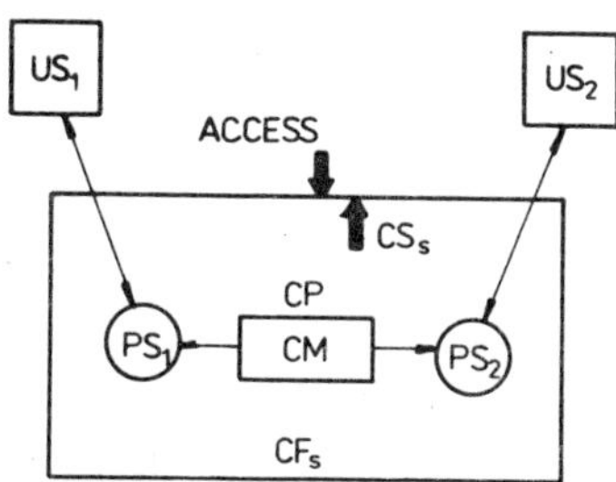

Figure 2.11 Basic element of a network architecture. (CP = communication protocol, CM = communication medium, CFs = communication functions, CSs = communication services, US = user station, PS = protocol station)

not sufficient, the user must add a supplementary error control function to the higher system (or to the higher adjacent layer).

The services sometimes have the same name as the corresponding communication functions, and sometimes not. But the background remains the same.

We can now extend our model given in Figure 2.6 by adding communication functions, services, and users (Figure 2.11). When interpreting blocks marked "users" generally, not only as human operators, we obtain the model which is able to express the basic pattern in the network architectures (see Chapter 2.3), namely the pair of adjacent network layers.

2.2.3 Types of communication functions

Before presenting at least the basic communication functions and services we shall show examples of their classification. One approach to the classification of the communication functions is to identify them with the communication phases and to arrange them according to their occurrence in the communication process. An example of such linear ordering of five communication functions is given in Figure 2.12.

Figure 2.12 An example of linear ordering of communication functions

The other classification scheme utilizes classes and subclasses of communication functions. The class of all communication functions may be decomposed into the subclass of the transport connection establishment functions which contain resource scheduling, security procedures, call progress signals, accounting, execution of connection, etc., and the subclass of data phase functions which contains blocking, segmenting, sharing, link multiplexing, multiple links, flow control, exceptional conditions recovery, data security, data blocks priority, sequenced delivery, message delimiting, etc., and, finally, the subclass of ancillary functions which contains end-to-end error control and error reporting, routing, "escape" to nonstandard heading, etc. Some of these functions may be further decomposed, e.g. the data security function may be divided into the control of closed user groups, into remote authentication, and into encoding[1]).

Figure 2.13 gives another example of the hierarchical ordering of communication functions determined by their implementation. The relations between the three levels are shown in Figure 2.13, because one communication function may belong to more than one class (e.g. the link control, according to Figure 2.13, belongs to all three classes).

---

[1]) This classification scheme is taken from [275]

Some communication functions may contain, either fully or partially, other communication functions. For example, the data exchange function can contain both error control and flow control functions. Most of the methods used by the two functions require the division of the transferred data messages into shorter data blocks — fragments — and the reassembly of the fragments into the original messages. A positive or negative acknowledgment is also required. These functions will be described in Chapter 3.4.

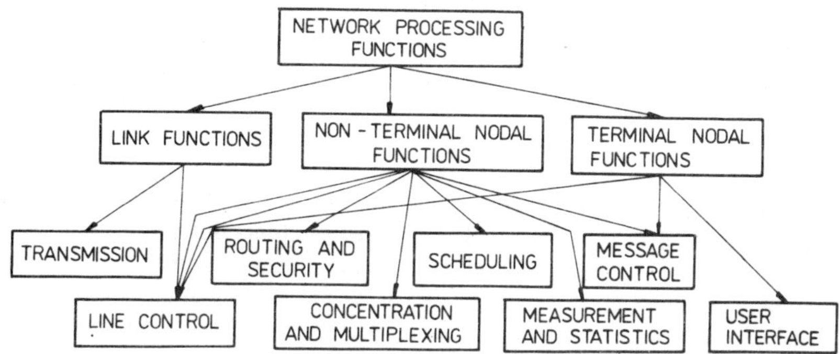

Figure 2.13 An example of the communication functions hierarchy according to their implementation

The latter situation is shown in Figure 2.14, which also contains an instance of a pair of communication functions, namely the assembly/disassembly pair. In fact, these two functions can be quite different. There are such pairs e.g. establishment/ /releasing of a line, opening/closing of a transmission, etc. In all these cases the two communication functions are two complementary transformations. The first transfers the communication system to a new state and the second shifts it back to the original state. These functions occur in phases which generally are not adjacent: there are other communication phases between them. Of course, the mechanisms of these complementary communication functions are generally different.

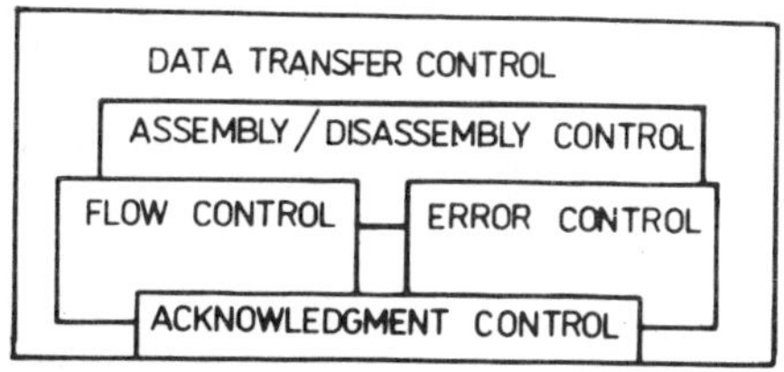

Figure 2.14 An example of inclusion of communication functions

At the end of this section some examples of classification of communication functions will be given. Readers interested in details of these classifications are advised to use the literature referenced in Section 2.2.4.

When using purpose as the classification criterion we can divide the communication functions into basic or necessary ones, functions providing the required performance, and functions devoted predominantly to the overall control operations. Examples in the first group are synchronization (see Chapter 3.2), opening/closing of a transmission, and establishment/releasing of the link. The second group can contain the following functions: error control, fragmentation/reassembly, flow control, routing, transmission capacity assignment, exceptional states recovery, etc. The functions of the third group are congestion control, network and communication monitoring, etc.

Communication functions can also be divided into transport functions, such as synchronization control, transmission opening, error control, flow control, etc. and supporting functions, such as buffer management, addressing, etc.

The place of implementation of the communication function can be used as the other classification criterion, according to which the protocol functions and the internal or nonprotocol functions may be distinguished. The following are examples of the protocol functions: transmission opening/closing, error control, flow control, routing, exceptional states recovery. The nonprotocol functions may be represented by fragmentation/reassembly, multiplexing/demultiplexing, address transformation, buffer management, etc. The protocol functions are implemented in two stations, whereas the nonprotocol functions are implemented either in only one station, or in more than two stations (e.g. measurement, routing, congestion control, etc.).

Further examples of the classification of communication functions will not be presented here. Realization methods of some selected communication functions are dealt with in the whole of Part 3.

2.2.4 Bibliographical notes

Although the notion of the communication function has existed for a long time (functions, communication functions, and services are used commonly in the descriptions of nearly all communication systems) a more exact interpretation, namely that of the transformation, was introduced by Elie [78] only in 1972. Since that time many classifications of communication functions have been described in the literature, although without any exact definitions. Because we do not know of any compiling publication general and comprehensive enough and because many descriptions of the communication functions classification, analysis, or implementation have their unique and specific approach, the following selection of literature references is suggested to provide a wider and deeper understanding of the communication functions: [51, 56, 65, 66, 79, 83, 84, 89, 118, 192, 195, 247, 257] (in [83] the communication functions are called mechanisms). This selection is far from being a complete list of references.

For example, in [209] the communication functions are described within the scope of the communication protocols, in [227] the communication functions for the data link control are dealt with, in [108] nine transport layer communication functions (see Appendix E) are specified (being called the communication primitives). Lists of communication functions and services with respect to the open systems architecture are, of course, in [231, 263, 275].

The communication phases generally are not described independently. The one exception is the description of the BSC line control procedures and the corresponding ISO standard (see Appendix A). These phases are illustrated in Figure 2.10b.

2.3 Network Architectures

2.3.1 Introduction to network architectures

In this book the term network architecture will be used for the structure of communication control in networks, although the term may have several other meanings elsewhere. Communication functions represent the decomposition of the contents of communication control. Network architecture also represents a decomposition, namely the decomposition of the form and of the implementation of communication control. Often a set of communication protocols used in a network is regarded as network architecture. It will be shown later that such an interpretation of a network architecture is not precise enough.

The notion of network architecture is naturally connected with the configurational structure of a network described in Chapter 1.1. But in the field of communication control and communication protocols the assignment of network architecture to communication control structure is already deep-rooted.

Architecture, generally, resembles structure. In networks we have topological structure, network operation control structure, and communication control structure. And we also have configurational structure. All these structures may be covered by the term network architecture, but only communication control structure will be dealt with in this book.

Such a selection is in agreement with many existing network architectures, e.g. with the network architectures of computer networks like ARPANET and CYCLADES, with the architectures of packet switching networks as described in various documents of ISO, CCITT, and IFIP-INWG, and also with some network architectures of firms (e.g. with SNA of IBM, DCA of Sperry UNIVAC, DNA of DEC, etc.).

Communication control structure is also used in Open Systems Architecture — OSA (see Appendix F) — which is described in the working document of ISO.

The existing network architectures are quite different, because they were designed for different purposes. Four main purposes may be distinguished:

a) Easing the implementation of communication control in various networks and network elements and supporting the operation of a network by well arranged documentation.

b) Defining the uniform philosophy of designing various networks from various hardware and software products of the same make (network architectures of main producers of computers).

c) Creating a common background for a consistent system of standards and recommendations which are necessary in order to achieve a high level of compatibility of both networks and network elements (as the basis of international standards).

d) Creating a uniform methodological tool for the analysis, comparison, and evaluation of various network architectures and for facilitating their investigation (reference architectures, or reference models of architectures).

Though these purposes have some common points, they differ enough to yield different network architectures.

It is not possible here to go into details of the several existing network architectures. Therefore, in this chapter, elements and principles common to the network architectures will be dealt with and then an outline of a single reference network architecture will be presented.

2.3.2 Layering

Layering is one of the basic principles used in network architectures. It represents the manner of decomposition employed.

It has already been said that communication control in a computer network (or in a distributed processing network) may be decomposed by the identification of individual communication elements. For example, in the ARPANET the following communication elements were recognized: IMP-IMP, HOST-IMP. But when one communication station is assigned to the whole network element, the station may be too complex. Therefore such a station is divided into several substations, or the communication control part of the network element is decomposed into several layers. In this way, for example, instead of having one communication protocol for the host computer-node computer communication element several communication protocols corresponding to layer communication elements may be used.

Another approach utilizes the decomposition of the set of all possible communication functions into nondisjoint subsets and hierarchical arrangement of these subsets. In the network architecture each layer has its subset of communication functions assigned. There may be a layer containing one communication function only, and there may be a communication function assigned to one layer only. On the other hand, some communication functions may be assigned to several layers, or even to all the layers. Of course, there remains to be explained how to select the communication functions for individual subsets. We shall comment on this problem later, but essentially it is a complex task that needs to be solved individually in the course of design of the relevant network.

Layering is one way of decomposing a complex system into several simpler and, therefore, more comprehensible parts. It is used because of the well known fact that man cannot cope with too extensive systems without dividing them into manageable parts. Of course, there are other kinds of decomposition, but layering expresses in the best way the step-by-step, or onion-like, adding of equipment, services, protocols, modules, etc. which is typical of distributed processing networks.

Two basic kinds of layering will be differentiated in this chapter: logical and configurational layering. First logical layering will be described as the background of the reference network architecture.

Though there is no simple answer to the question of how to determine the number of layers and how to specify their contents, some general points may be presented here that can influence the choice. They are: the relative independence and close relations of some communication functions, relations to topological structure and to the addressing used, specific features of existing hardware and/or software, existing communication protocols (especially standardised protocols), existence of formally or functionally independent parts, the required modularity of the overall system, specific requirements based on assumed implementation, locations of fragmentation of data messages into data blocks, locations of multiplexing, etc.

One simple example of layering is presented in Figure 2.15. For a more complex example of layering we refer the reader to the Open Systems Architecture (see Appendix F) or to some descriptions of existing network architectures.

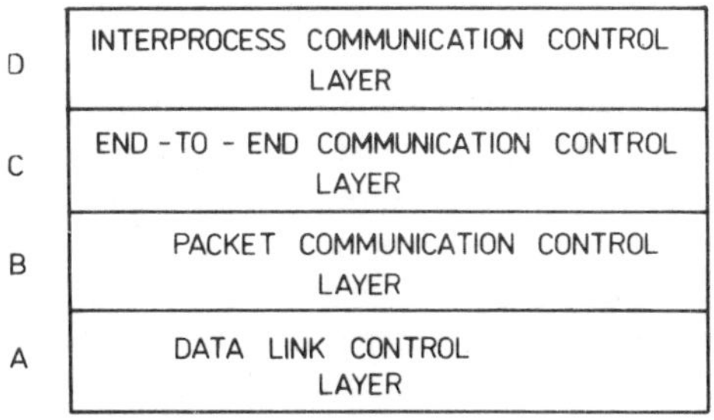

D	INTERPROCESS COMMUNICATION CONTROL LAYER
C	END-TO-END COMMUNICATION CONTROL LAYER
B	PACKET COMMUNICATION CONTROL LAYER
A	DATA LINK CONTROL LAYER

Figure 2.15 Example of structuring of communication control into layers

Referring to Figure 2.15, the first, lowest, layer comprises data link control, which is a selfcontained area of communication control concerned primarily with point-to--point data transmission. It has been developed over a period of many years. In computer networks, it controls the communication between adjacent nodes at the lowest level. Many data link communication protocols (or control procedures, as they are sometimes called) have been developed and utilized. Some of them are standardized internationally (see Appendices A, B and C).

In the second layer, the control is accomplished by means of the transfer of packets through the packet switching network comprising node computers as packet switchers. This requires some groups of operations to be added to the operations already being performed in the data link control layer. It seems natural to assign these operations to this second layer, which can be called, say, the packet control layer.

The third layer, marked C, relates to a kind of end-to-end communication control. We can see in Figure 2.2 that communication paths generally cross several nodes, so we can differentiate end nodes and intermediate nodes. Because of the special position of end nodes, additional communication functions are needed to provide for all the tasks of the communication control governing the communication between end nodes. These additional functions and the corresponding communication protocol create the basis of the third layer.

The fourth, highest, layer contains the control of exchanges of data messages between system programs and application programs in distributed processing networks, or generally between processes. Of course, processes are to be found not only in host computers, but in all programmable devices which belong to the network. Control of communication of all these various programs or processes can be concentrated in one layer which may be called, say, the interprocess communication control layer.

The simple structure depicted in Figure 2.15 and containing only the names of the four layers can hardly be regarded as a network architecture. Therefore it should be complemented by other elements and information.

2.3.3 Step-by-step communication

In the example given one communication control element has actually been assigned to each layer. Such an element comprises two protocol stations and provides for two-way communication. A communication protocol is assigned to each such element. When mapping the four layers and corresponding protocol stations into two fictional network elements, we can express the communication control structure relating to the two network elements as shown in Figure 2.16. Dashed lines correspond to communication protocols while solid lines indicate a physical communication path for transferred data blocks passing through the individual layers. The layers, stations, and protocols are labelled with capital letters A, B, C and D.

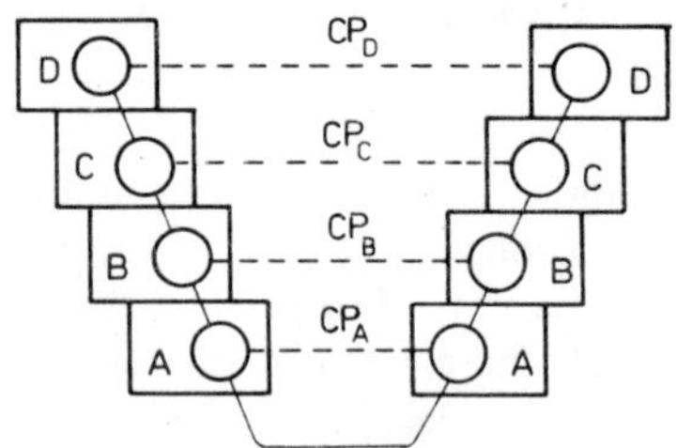

Figure 2.16 Scheme of the V-communication

The scheme we have introduced in Figure 2.16 resembles the chain of interlocutors as defined in the theory of colloquies (see Chapter 4.2).

Because of the stepwise form of communication control depicted in Figure 2.16, which means layer-by-layer transferring and processing of control information, such a communication control may be called V-communication. Figure 2.16 shows the scheme of V-communication.

The layers of a network architecture can be mapped into real network elements as well as fictional ones. In the real case we can distinguish groups of network elements according to subsets of layers mapped into them. In order to show all the representations of network elements in one picture, a graphical form different from that of Figure 2.16 will be used, namely the form of concentric circles and sectors. The circles show the boundaries of the layers and the sectors (or parts of them) represent the individual network elements (see Figure 2.17). So the resulting scheme shows a relation between the network elements used and the defined layers of the communication control.

The structure of V-communication illustrated in Figure 2.16 can be found also in the upper part of Figure 2.17. Of course, the scheme of V-communication holds for any pair of network elements shown in Figure 2.17.

Any two equally labelled stations (layers) may communicate under the control of a similarly labelled communication protocol. This means that in this case we have only one protocol for all possible pairs of communicating stations of the same sort. It follows from the above that Figure 2.16 shows the kinds of communication control elements (or protocol stations) and the kinds of communication protocols used in a given network architecture, whereas Figure 2.17 informs about the kinds of network elements differentiated by the mapping of various subsets of layers into them.

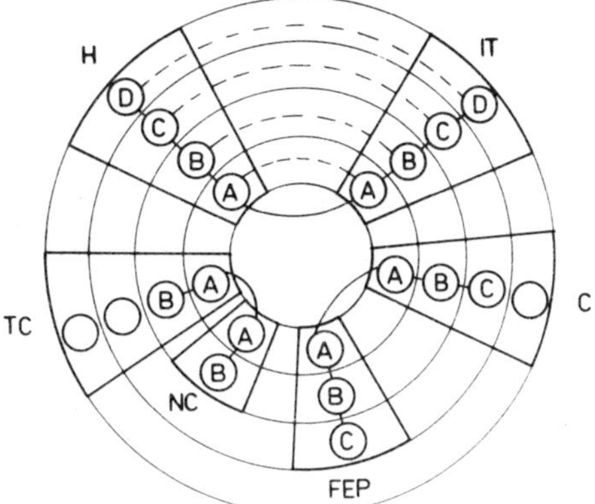

Figure 2.17 Assignment of the layers to individual network elements. (H = host computer, NC = node computer, C = concentrator, TC = = terminal controller, FEP = front-end processor)

Again we can see that communication protocols for some pair of network elements are decomposed into several basic communication protocols selected form those defined in Figure 2.16. For example, the protocol for the communication of a concentrator C with a front-end processor FEP may be interpreted as a set of three partial protocols, namely that of CP_A, CP_B, and CP_C.

V-communication is an example of the step-by-step communication with steps being identified with the layers of a network architecture. The other possibility is to identify steps with nodes, i.e. to recognize a node-by-node communication. Such communication is inherently connected with the store-and-forward principle typical for computer networks and basic for packet switching networks.

The node-by-node communication, or the communication utilizing intermediate nodes, is depicted in Figure 2.18. This figure expresses the situation when two stations (or protocol stations) communicate not directly but via several mediating stations. In other words, a chain of communication control elements mediate such a communication. Of course, when treating the communication of stations in layer C we could consider the node computers as a communication medium, i.e. a kind of black box. But if we want to know all the steps of the communication control and all parts of the communication path, then such a simplification is not appropriate.

Figure 2.18 depicts the communication of an intelligent terminal with a host computer over a packet switching network and over the FEP computer. It is assumed that host and FEP computers are connected locally.

There are some differences between Figure 2.17 and Figure 2.18. The first, formal, difference consists in the use of a linear graphical representation instead of a circular one. The linear representation allows us to express clearly more network elements within the frame of network architecture, i.e. with layers mapped into the elements and with representative protocol stations assigned to the network elements. The lowest strip (layer) in Figure 2.18, corresponding to the inner circle in Figure 2.17, represents the basic transmission facilities that are no longer included in the network architecture.

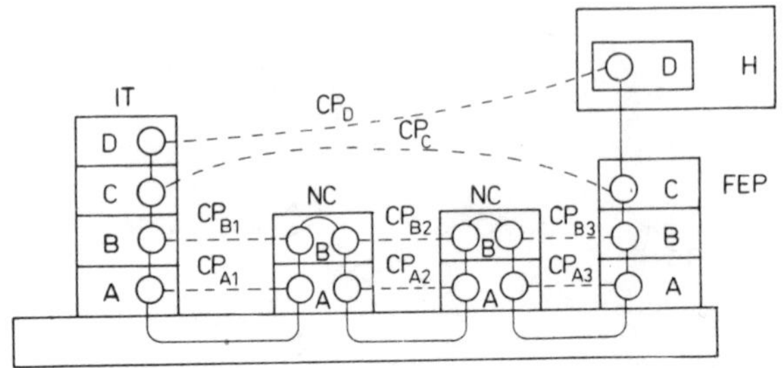

Figure 2.18 Illustration of communication control acting through intermediate nodes. (IT = intelligent terminal, NC = = node computer, FEP = front-end processor, H = host computer, CP = communication protocol)

The second difference lies in the fact that Figure 2.18 illustrates a chain of communication elements. The scheme given in Figure 2.18 can be considered to be a pattern or a representative expression of such a chain or cascade. Of course, the whole network with all network elements connected in various ways cannot be suitably expressed in this way.

The third difference relates to the communication protocols CP_A and CP_B. There is only one layer protocol shown in Figure 2.17, but there are three possible layer protocols in layers A and B in Figure 2.18.

The fourth difference concerns the interlayer protocol CP_{CD} assigned to the host-FEP communication element. This protocol is distinguished here because the two protocol stations are located in two different network elements, though the elements are placed near each other.

It should be noted that no quantitative aspects resulting from higher numbers of network elements connected in the network have been considered here. We have only dealt with the qualitative aspects, i.e. with the kinds of network elements, with the kinds of communication control elements and corresponding communication protocols and protocol stations, and with the kinds of relations among them.

In reality in each network element, and even in each layer being mapped into such element, there are several protocol stations. For example, the number of protocol stations in layer A in some network element is equal to the number of data links connected to the network element. However, we shall not consider here the quantitative aspect.

2.3.4 Data messages and data blocks

Layers of a network architecture are often differentiated by different data blocks which are assigned to individual layers. Therefore we shall come back to the scheme of V-communication in order to augment it with data messages and data blocks transferred. To each layer, or more precisely to each communication control element, a data block is assigned. Such a data block is characterized by its header (or by its envelope) and by its length (more precisely: maximum length). As a matter of fact it is not one block only that is assigned to the layer, but a group of blocks of similar characteristics. The data blocks in the group generally have equal maximum lengths, but have different envelopes and serve different purposes. Each communication control element generates and recognizes only such headers as are assigned to it. It does not understand any other headers and it does not even separate them from the text part of a message or of a block.

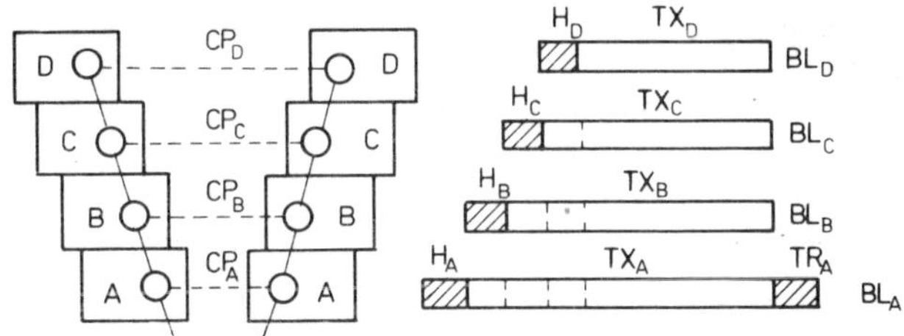

Figure 2.19 Assignment of data blocks and headers to layers. (BL = data block, H = header, TX = text, TR = trailer, CP = = communication protocol)

The data message sent by the S_D protocol station in one network element to the S_D protocol station in another network element passes through all layers, and each layer generally adds (in one direction) and takes away its header (see Figure 2.19). Sometimes both header and trailer are used, resulting in an envelope. So passing of the message through the layers is accompanied, besides other things, with packing it into envelopes and then unpacking it from them step-by-step.

In this book, when dealing with two adjacent layers the data blocks assigned to the higher layer will be called data messages and the data blocks assigned to the lower layer will be called simply data blocks.

Data messages can generally be longer than data blocks. For example, when files are to be transferred they are surely longer than, say, packets of some packet switching network. In such cases data messages must be disassembled into fragments of adequate length. But data messages may also be shorter than data blocks. For example, transactional terminals generate (and receive) short data messages. In this case, several data messages have to be packed into one data block. Details will be given in Chapter 2.5. We have mentioned it here because such disassembling/ /assembling and packing/unpacking often motivates the introduction of a new layer in a network architecture.

Data blocks, in general, serve as one of the criteria for distinguishing the layers.

2.3.5 Protocols in network architecture

The V-communication scheme is primarily the form of communication in the highest level (level D in our case). The communication of any two protocol stations S_D is controlled according to the communication protocol CP_D. We have already said that stations S_D cannot exchange their data blocks directly, but only through the mediating services of other layers, because such is the principle of V-communication. This means that data messages from the layer D must in some way enter the layer C. Basically two ways are possible for the exchange of data blocks between adjacent layers (or between protocol stations in adjacent layers). Either the whole data block is transferred from one layer into another one, or control information is only exchanged. In either case there exists some kind of communication between the layers. The contents, extent, and form of this communication depend on the location of the corresponding protocol stations (or modules) in network elements and on the location of these elements.

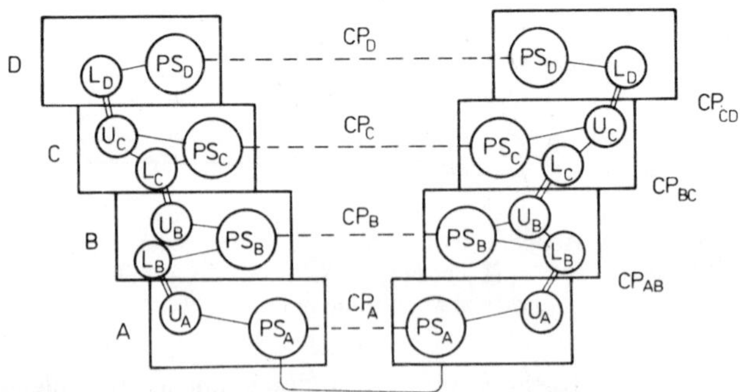

Figure 2.20 Scheme of the logical network architecture with protocols. (PS = protocol station, U, L = protocol stations of inter-layer communication protocols)

Although interlayer communication mostly takes place in one network element, i.e. in the form of interprocess communication performed in the software environment of one computer or other programmable device, it need not be so in all cases. For example, it is not so in the case of connecting a host computer to the FEP, as is shown in Figure 2.18. Therefore, if a universal scheme of reference network architecture is to be designed and if this scheme is to be so complete that it allows for expressing the individual network architectures by simply deleating some of its elements, not by adding additional elements, then interlayer communication must be explicitly included. This can be done by means of interlayer communication protocols.

This means that a universal scheme of network architecture will contain two kinds of communication protocols: layer protocols and interlayer protocols. Because each communication protocol is assigned to some communication control element, the corresponding communication control elements should be incorporated into the scheme designed. Figure 2.20 shows the result.

We note again that interlayer communication may be very simple, and not require a communication protocol. And it also can be invisible from outside the network element, being implemented within the network element software. After all, from the point of view of the compatibility of network elements the interlayer communication control is of secondary importance. But because it exists, it is important to include it into the universal scheme of reference network architecture.

The two new kinds of protocol stations that are present in the layers, namely the stations labelled U and L, are basically the same. The reason for labelling them differently lies in the need to differentiate the interlayer communication from the upper layer (station U) and from the lower layer (station L).

2.3.6 Supervisory control and common parts

The layers of a network architecture may be implemented in one, two, or even more network elements (see, for example, Figure 2.18). In most cases there is more than one layer implemented in one network element, and in such cases some operations common to all implemented layers are often concentrated into some common parts. Such operations can be buffer management, queue management, scheduling, statistical data recording, network element status monitoring, etc. These common operations may be concentrated in one functional block that will be called a supervisory control block in this book. The supervisory control block can act as an independent operational system, or it may be a part of some other operational system, or it may serve as an interface to some larger and independent operational system (especially in the case of medium or large host computers).

Common parts are implemented in the supervisory control block (SC), not in layers. Therefore there must be some communication between the layers and the supervisory control, as shown in Figure 2.21. Sometimes local control in layers can be distinguished too, and therefore it is also included in the general scheme of Figure 2.21. So we have modules of local control C_i in individual layers, one supervisory control block SC, and modules SC_i in this block assigned to the individual layers. Again, from the point of view of compatibility of network elements, the supervisory control may be invisible and therefore is not directly involved in ensuring compatibility.

It should be noted that the scheme presented in Figure 2.21 primarily satisfies these implementation requirements.

When the layers of a network architecture are implemented in two network elements, two supervisory control blocks are necessary, as shown in Figure 2.22.

Several classifications of communication functions were presented in Chapter 2.2, including the differentiation between protocol and nonprotocol communication function. We assume the protocol communication functions to be implemented in protocol stations. The nonprotocol communication functions are not covered by

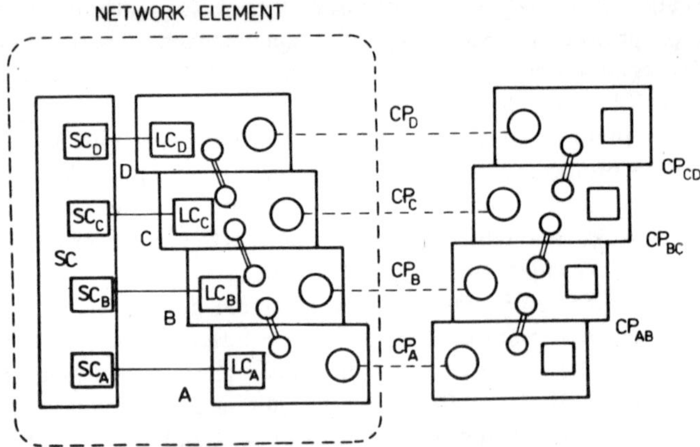

Figure 2.21 Supervisory control block and layers of a network architecture. (SC = supervisory control, LC = layer control, CP = = communication protocol)

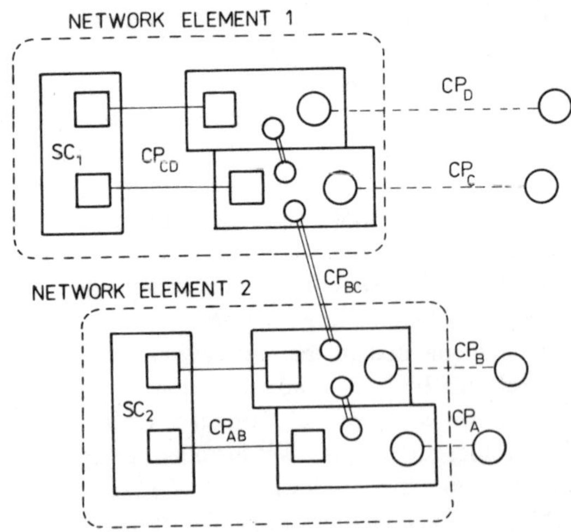

Figure 2.22 Implementation of layers in two network elements

communication protocols and therefore they have not been included in layers so far. Therefore the modules NCF_i (Nonprotocol Communication Functions subset of the layer i) are inserted into the layers. The resulting graphical representation of a layer is given in Figure 2.23.

Two of the nonprotocol communication functions will be dealt with separately now, because sometimes they cause the introduction of a new layer. Graphically both are represented by branching. Upward branching expresses the effect of multiplexing, while downward branching corresponds to multiple links.

Multiplexing generally means utilizing one communication element (i.e. one virtual or physical link) by several user or subscriber stations residing in the adjacent higher layer (see Figure 2.24). The principle of multiple links is that several communication elements in the layer being investigated serve for one user or subscriber station in the adjacent higher layer (see Figure 2.25).

Although we have so far excluded the quantitative aspect from our network architecture considerations, in this case we are making an exception for the reason that a new layer can be distinguished by one or both of the two functions.

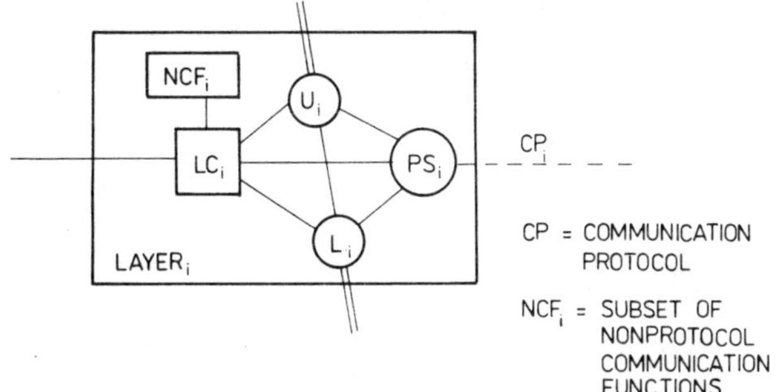

Figure 2.23 Scheme of a universal layer *i*. (LC = layer control, PS, U, L = protocol stations)

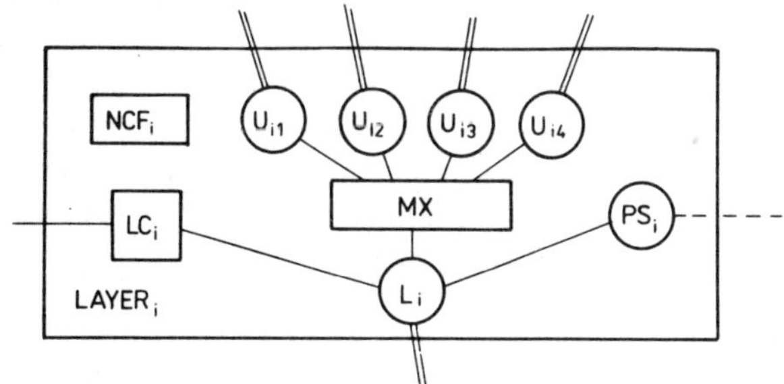

Figure 2.24 Representation of multiplexing in a network architecture layer

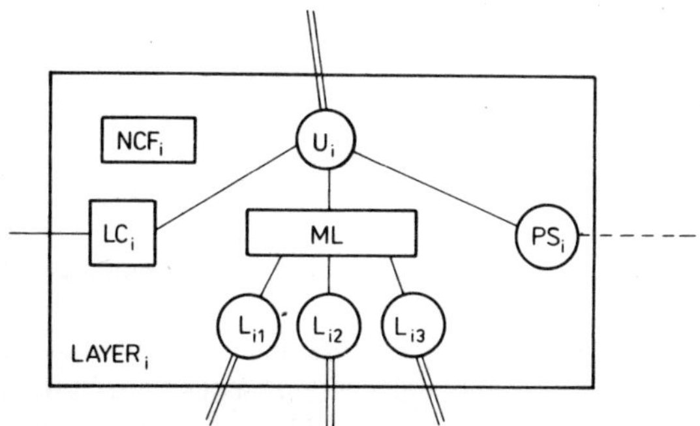

Figure 2.25 Representation of multiple links in a network architecture layer

2.3.7 Two basic kinds of network architecture

Based on the results of the analysis of existing network architectures, the following two basic kinds may be distinguished:

— the logical network architecture,

— the configurational network architecture.

These reflect two fundamental approaches to communication control in networks: the implementation approach and the performance approach (see Chapter 2.1).

The logical network architecture primarily defines elements and kinds of communication control, and their relations. It represents the decomposition of communication control, i.e. of the set of all communication functions used in the network, into layers. It identifies the kinds of communication protocols and communication control elements used and it specifies various relationships between them. It does not cover larger numbers of elements of the same kind and is not concerned with subnetworks. Therefore it is not suitable for investigating the subnetwork (or the communication system) performance. On the other hand, it is indispensable for designing the implementation of communication control in individual network elements, and also it is adequate for specifying the compatibility requirements. Because they so strongly focus on implementation, it is not surprising that some network architectures of computer producers can be used as typical examples of logical network architecture.

All schemes of network architecture presented until now in this chapter relate to logical network architecture. Because all such schemes can be expressed by means of two fictional network elements, the notion of V-communication is both sufficient and suitable for representing graphically the logical network architecture.

Configurational network architecture is primarily the decomposition of the set of network elements, or of the set of certain parts of network elements. The layers are identified by network elements (or types of network elements), or by parts of network elements, assigned to them. The layers determine the boundaries of individual subnetworks. Subnetworks contain all the network elements of a certain kind, i.e. any number of them; these elements are not isolated, but interconnected. In this sense, configurational architecture may be regarded as the decomposition of the whole network into several onion-like structured subnetworks.

It is therefore quite natural to emphasize the access of the subscriber stations, i.e. of the communication stations in the adjacent higher layer, to the services provided by the subnetwork as a whole. Focusing on subnetworks is the usual approach for the purpose of performance investigation. The significance of configurational network architecture for public data networks is quite obvious, too.

Now some differences between the two basic kinds of network architecture will be shown.

In both kinds there are layers and in both kinds communication functions are assigned to individual layers. These communication functions implemented in layers are the sources of services that may be utilized by the stations in the adjacent higher layer by means of access specified in the definition of architecture. But it is clear that the services offered are different for the different kinds of network architecture, because the logical network architecture comprises qualitative aspects only, i.e. it expresses what two network elements can produce and offer, whereas the configurational network architecture represents all the subnetworks (or better: subnetwork elements), i.e. it comprises the quantitative aspects as well. Further, the coordinated action of several interconnected network elements using several lines yields other kind of service than the action of two elements only.

However, when designing the network architectures, this substantial difference is not necessarily visible. For example, Figure 2.26 shows the logical network architecture with five layers. In the case of a logical network architecture layers define subsystems (not subnetworks, as in the case of configurational network architecture). The access to the subsystem SS_C may be defined by means of the interlayer protocol CP_{CD}. The services offered by the subsystem SS_C are determined by communication functions implemented in the subsystem SS_C, i.e. in layers A, B, and C. The access to

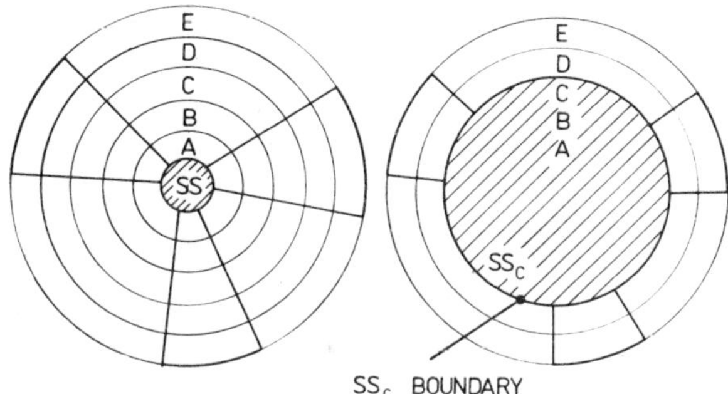

Figure 2.26 Subsystems in a logical network architecture. (SS_C = the subsystem bounded by the layer C)

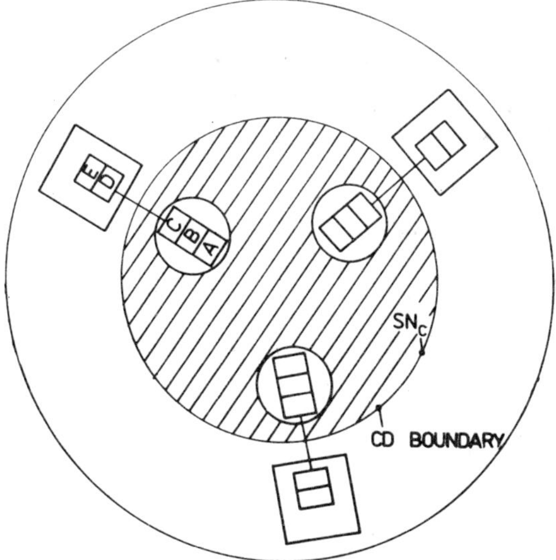

Figure 2.27 Configurational network architecture — network elements connected to the subnetwork SN_C (to subnetwork nodes) locally

the services can be defined precisely, without knowing the detailed contents and structure of the subsystem SS_C.

Figure 2.27 depicts a configurational network architecture, also containing five layers. The same boundary, namely the layer C, is used. Subscriber stations are connected to the subnetwork SN_C locally.

There is a variation of the configurational network architecture in Figure 2.28 that corresponds to remote connection of subscriber stations to the same subnetwork SN_C.

Comparing schemes depicted in the last three figures we can see that while there is no difference visible between Figures 2.26 and 2.27, i.e. the graphical interpretation of the logical network architecture and the configurational network architecture is the same, Figure 2.28 shows a quite remarkable difference. It should be noted especially that the boundary CD which relates to the layers of logical network architecture is separated from the boundary of the subnetwork SN_C.

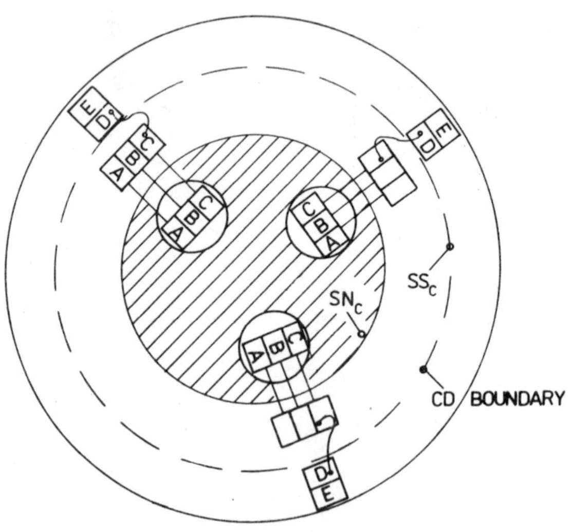

Figure 2.28 Configurational network architecture — network elements are connected to the subnetwork SN_C remotely (SS_C = subsystem C)

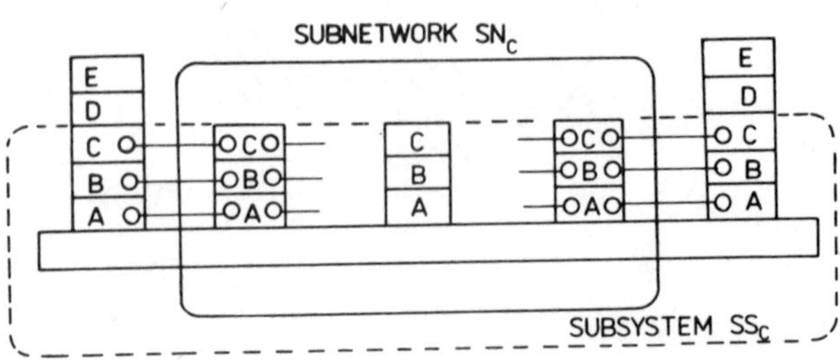

Figure 2.29 Illustration of the difference between the subnetwork SN_C and the subsystem SS_C

Figure 2.29 illustrates expressively the difference between the subsystem (logical network architecture) and subnetwork (configurational network architecture).

It is also clear from a comparison of Figures 2.26 and 2.28 that the interface is quite different. In the case of the subsystem the interface may be defined by means of only one interlayer communication protocol, whereas in the case of the subnetwork (Figure 2.28) three layer communication protocols create the interface. An example of such a situation is the structure of protocols defined in CCITT X.25 Recommendation concerning the interface between the DTE and DCE (see Appendix D).

As one can see in Figures 2.26 to 2.28, the layers defined for a logical network architecture are mapped into network elements assigned to the subnetworks of configurational network architecture. Therefore we can consider the logical network architecture to be the primary of the two architectures.

2.3.8 Reference network architecture

When summing up all considerations, principles, and elements described so far, the resulting reference network architecture as depicted in Figure 2.30 may be drawn.

The reference network architecture contains both layer and interlayer communication protocols (generally in each layer), and also contains the corresponding communication control elements and protocol stations. It further contains subsets of communication functions assigned to the individual layers and modules of local control.

The module MX/ML_i corresponding to multiplexing and/or to multiple links is drawn independently, because of its special role.

Of course, when this general scheme is applied to some real network architecture, some of the elements may be deleted. For example, in some layers there may be no layer communication protocol specified. Such is the case when multiplexing is assigned to a whole layer. On the other hand, there can be more than one layer protocol in one layer (e.g. several link control protocols as BSC, SDLC, HDLC).

The supervisory control block is not included in the reference network architecture. However, it is drawn in Figure 2.30 in order to facilitate communication control structure description for implementation purposes. Local control modules C_i ensure the cooperation of individual layers with the supervisory control block.

When specifying some network architecture by means of the reference network architecture, we determine the elements that are not included in the architecture investigated and then we try to identify the detailed specification of remaining elements of network architecture.

As we have already mentioned, interlayer protocols may be largely simplified, or they may be replaced by the indirect communication control performed by the supervisory control block and by the local control modules C_i.

This reference network architecture, being basically a logical one, does not contain the specification of the addressing scheme used, because addressing depends on the topological and configurational structure of a network. The principles of addressing are described in Chapter 3.3. The implementation of addressing is included in module NCF_i, because addressing belongs to nonprotocol communication functions.

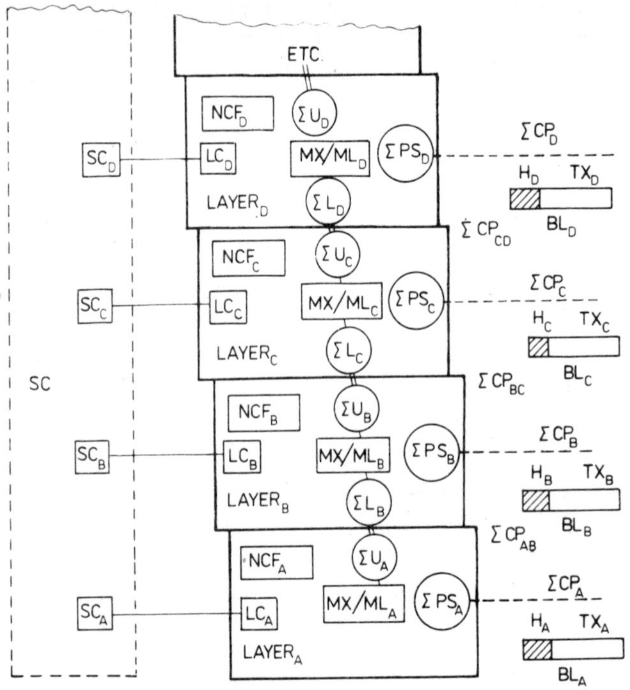

Figure 2.30 General scheme of the reference network architecture. (ΣPS_i = the set of protocol stations of layer communication protocols, ΣCP_i = the set of layer protocols, ΣCP_{ij} = the set of interlayer protocols. ΣU_i, ΣL_i = the sets of protocol stations of interlayer protocols, LC_i = layer control module, SC_i = supervisory control module, NCF_i = the subset of nonprotocol communication functions, MX/ML_i = the module of multiplexing and/or of multiple links, BL_i = data blocks, i = A, B, C, D, etc.)

For the specification of compatible network elements three architecture elements must be specified for each layer: layer communication protocols, modules (or subsets) of nonprotocol communication functions, and data blocks.

2.3.9 Bibliographical notes

Although various structural characteristics of distributed processing networks can be described as network architectures [12, 39, 51, 90, 91, 144, 202, 287], a growing number of publications use the more narrow meaning, namely that of communication control structure [50, 191, 193, 209, 230, 231, 294]. This is also the meaning used in network architectures such as SNA of IBM [50, 151, 256], DCA of UNIVAC [152], or DNA of DEC [70]. It can also be found in network architectures of various networks [77, 79, 158, 258, 279], and it creates the background for standardization activities [34, 84, 113, 217, 231, 247].

The backbone of network architectures is the layered structure [294] which reflects the basic theoretical principles [76, 142, 143, 164, 204].

The relation of the network architecture and communication protocols is presented in many publications, from which we have selected [57, 77, 96, 170, 192, 205, 209, 288, 289].

The network architecture cannot be avoided in the treatment of interconnections between various networks [36, 203, 231].

As far as we know, there is only one book devoted entirely to the network architecture, namely the book of Cypser [50] treating comprehensively the SNA architecture.

Well written tutorials partially concerning the subject are [144, 209].

2.4 Communication Protocols

2.4.1 The notion of the communication protocol

We already know that a communication protocol is one of the basic components of communication control in networks, that it expresses communication control rules, and that these rules mostly concern a pair of communicating stations, or a communication element, or a communication control element (see Figures 2.5 and 2.6).

This basic notion was sufficient for the explanation of the role of communication protocols in network architectures. In the preceding chapter we also learned that several layer communication protocols are needed when communication control is structured into layers and that several communication protocols may even be assigned to one layer. Thus it follows from the network architecture principle that different communication protocols are used for the communication control in networks.

The reality confirms this assumption. Each computer network has its own set of communication protocols. For example, the following protocols may be found in the ARPANET computer network: the Network Communication Protocol (NCP) and the Transmission Control Protocol (TCP) for host-host communication, the File Transfer Protocol (FTP) for transferring files through the network, the IMP-HOST protocol, and several others. In the CYCLADES computer network, mainly transport protocols or end-to-end protocols were designed and investigated. They are based on so called transport stations and form the basis for host-host communication, or for interprocess communication. As examples of the European Informatics Network (EIN) protocols we may choose the Bulk Transfer Function (BTF), which is a file transfer protocol and the Scroll Mode Virtual Terminal (SMVT), which is a virtual terminal protocol.

In each network a data link control protocol must be used. Examples of such protocols are the ISO and CCITT control procedures (see Appendices A, B and C) and protocols of computer manufacturers such as BSC and SDLC (IBM), BDLC (Burroughs), DDCMP (DEC), UDLC (Univac), etc.

Standardisation also concerns the communication protocols of higher layers of network architectures. As examples the protocol from the CCITT X.25 Recommendation (see Appendix D) and the end-to-end protocol specified in documents INWG 96 and INWG 96.1 (see Appendix E) may be mentioned here.

Until recently the number of different communication protocols was growing proportionally to the number of various computer communication networks, because an appropriate set of communication protocols had to be designed for every network. However, only some of them have met with broader acceptance and have become the basis of the existing standardized communication protocols or of those being developed at present.

The increase in the number of publications treating communication protocols has been even more marked. But though there are tens of communication protocols and hundreds of publications describing, analysing, and evaluating them, the notion of the communication protocol has not been unified until now.

It does not matter too much that communication protocols are also referred to as network protocols, computer network protocols, computer communication protocols, control procedures (especially in connection with data links), or simply protocols, although in the latter case some caution is advisable due to the fact that sometimes algorithms of noncommunication operations (e.g. conversion operations) are also referred to as protocols.

The cause of confusion is the fact that all the above terms, including the basic term communication protocol, may describe the overall communication control in a network, one communication function, or communication control rules only. In the first case, the term "ways of communication control in a network" is actually replaced by the term "a network protocol". The routing protocol, the error control protocol, the flow control protocol, or the connection establishment protocol are examples relating to the second case.

We prefer the third case in this book, i.e. we consider the communication protocol to be only a formal tool for the implementation of selected communication functions. So we shall differentiate between communication functions, or methods of communication functions, and the ways of their implementation by means of communication

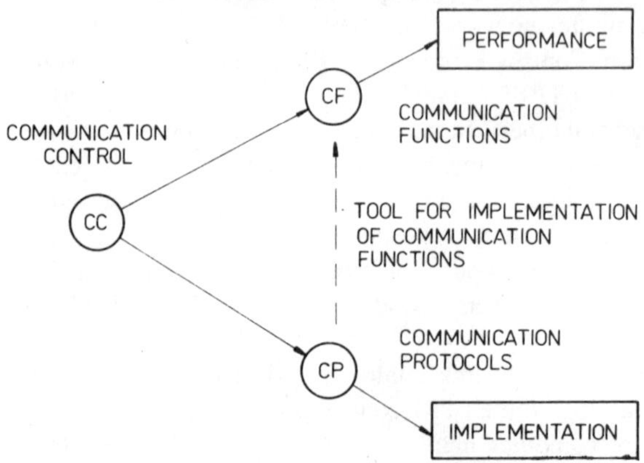

Figure 2.31 Performance and implementation approaches to communication control — the place of communication protocols

protocols. Such an interpretation of a communication protocol, which is illustrated in Figure 2.31, is closely connected with two basic approaches to communication control in networks that have been explained in Chapter 2.1.

A communication protocol is often defined as a set of rules and formats facilitating the control of communication between two stations. Such a definition is not sufficiently precise, complete and detailed. We should like to know what these rules are, and what must be known about the subject of communication control, i.e. about the communication element, or about the communication control element. More detailed information may be useful for both the protocol implementation and for the investigation of compatibility of two different protocols.

Communication protocols represent the implementation approach to communication control (see Figure 2.31). They primarily serve as a formal tool for implementing selected methods of communication functions and mechanisms. In this sense they are also formal tools for implementing the communication control as a whole, because communication control is composed of individual selected communication functions.

However, not all communication functions are implemented by communication protocols. The protocols only implement protocol communication functions and cooperate on the implementation of network communication functions. Communication protocols do not implement nonprotocol communication functions. It means that corresponding protocol stations do not comprise functional modules for nonprotocol communication functions. Such modules are included in layers of network architecture as the NCF modules (see Figure 2.29).

Protocol stations contain buffers for both data blocks and state variables, the latter being internal states of protocol stations.

The communication control element and the corresponding communication protocol may be applied to various pairs of communicating stations, for example to a host-node pair, or to a node-node pair, etc. In any case, the interpretation of protocol stations and of the communication medium is a crucial point in such an application. In order to illustrate the point, it may be enough to note that the communication medium may represent both a telephone line and a whole packet switching network (e.g. in the case of an end-to-end protocol).

It follows from the unique assignment of a communication protocol to the communication control element that the corresponding protocol stations must be present at all places of a network where the communication protocols are used.

The protocol stations of the communication control element may, but need not, be equal. Such an asymmetry is necessary if the communication control element has to model all possible situations. For example, there are primary and secondary stations used in unbalanced modes ARM and NRM of the HDLC control procedures (see Appendix C).

2.4.2 Principles of communication protocols

A communication protocol essentially defines the necessary negotiation between protocol stations. This negotation is performed in the form of the control and status information exchange. The negotiation is indispensable, because each protocol station controls the communication according to its momentary image of the other protocol station's state and that of the communication medium state. Naturally, within the framework of the above negotiation both status information and various commands are exchanged. However, these commands also carry information about the state of the sending station, because the command sent depends on the instantaneous state of the sending station.

Because the negotiation takes the form of a kind of conversation, the control and status information exchanged may be regarded as words. This means that protocol stations exchange words which will therefore be called protocol words. Communication stations (of communication elements) exchange primarily data blocks containing both the texts and protocol words mentioned. Although data blocks are exchanged between protocol stations too, when treating communication control we shall focus on the control and other auxiliary parts of data blocks only and therefore we shall mostly use protocol words. The control and status information exchanged is structured in various ways in communication protocols, or in their formats. Various names are used for individual parts of the structuring mentioned, examples can be found in the Appendices. Most often use is made of the name commands, or commands and responses, or control codes. But here, because of its uniformity and general validity, the term "protocol words" will be used.

A protocol station reacts to each protocol word in a way which has been agreed upon and which forms an integral part of the communication protocol definition. Of course, the reaction depends on the state of the protocol station, i.e. different reactions correspond to different states of the protocol station.

At least two stations are required for the negotiation referred to, this being typical for communication protocols. We have already mentioned protocols denominating such algorithms as do not require the cooperation of two or more stations because they define the operation of one module or network element. Such algorithms, of course, will not be considered to be communication protocols.

Although generally one common channel is used for both data and protocol words, these both being contained in the data blocks transferred, sometimes separate channels are used. But in both cases the channels used are such that the occurrence of various distortions, errors and failures is rather high. Under such conditions, more often than not, a data block transferred is lost or impaired. Of course, protocol words may be lost or impaired too, which results in an improper functioning of the protocol stations, because they will not get the right image of the other station's state. This possibility must be taken into consideration and adequate means must be built into the relevant communication protocol in order to provide for reliable negotiation between protocol stations even under the above conditions.

Protocol stations of one communication control element may be implemented either in one network element, or each of them in a different network element. In the latter case the network elements may be situated close to, or far from, each other. Accordingly, the exchange of protocol words is either internal, or external local, or external remote.

In the case of internal protocol words exchange the data blocks are generally transferred in parallel. With the local exchange either the parallel or serial transfer of data blocks is used, whereas the remote exchange mostly necessitates the serial transfer of data blocks. In all three cases a communication protocol can be used. Of course, this is only possible when a communication control element can be identified, i.e. when parts of the network elements can be interpreted as protocol stations.

It has already been stated in Chapter 2.1 that indirect communication control cannot be expressed by means of a communication control element. Therefore the communication protocol is not concerned with indirect control. This means that when no direct communication control is applied to adjacent layers of a network architecture, but, instead, the indirect control is used, then no interlayer communication protocol may be defined.

2.4.3 Principles of communication protocol definitions

Basically there are two approaches to the communication protocol definition, one concerning sequences of data blocks (or protocol words) exchanged between protocol stations, the other focusing on the internal structure of the communication control element and on reactions of protocol stations to the entering protocol words.

Specifications of communication protocols presented in various publications contain primarily definitions of formats, namely those of protocol words. So protocol words used are defined as well. Sometimes conditions for the generation of protocol words and reactions of protocol stations to individual protocol words are specified, too. Finally, various sequences of protocol words are defined. These sequences, which express the course of communication, correspond to various typical situations and are assigned to typical parts of protocol stations activities. In connection with communication functions they result from the activities of individual functional modules or mechanism modules. Sometimes various state diagrams are also presented. Samples of such specifications are given in the Appendices.

When generalizing the above facts the following simplified formal definition of the communication protocol may be written:

$$CP = \{V, F(V), L(V)\}$$

where CP stands for the communication protocol, V is the set of the protocol words used, $F(V)$ is the set of formats, and $L(V)$ is the set of sequences of the protocol words used. Set V may contain as special words results of error and failure occurrences, and results of internal timers' activities. $L(V)$ may be considered to be a formal language defined on the set V. The definition presented is an example of the first approach.

The number of theoretically possible sequences of protocol words is generally infinite. Even the number of practically observable sequences of protocol words is so high that it is not feasible to list them all when defining the protocol. In order to by—pass this difficulty, either formal grammars or finite state machines may be utilized. Under certain conditions, namely when the formal grammar used is regular, both formal tools are dual.

The outline of the communication protocol definition utilizing a formal grammar looks like this:

$$CP = \{V, F(V), G(L)\}$$

where $G(L)$ is the relevant regular grammar capable of generating language $L(V)$. The above expression is not formally exact because the grammar alone can define the whole communication protocol. This, in turn, is due to the fact that the grammar contains set V and that set $F(V)$ may be expressed formally by some other grammar. So the communication protocol can be defined by the hierarchical set of formal grammars only. This will be explained in Chapter 4.2. But here we only want to point out that language $L(V)$ may be replaced by grammar $G(L)$, and for this purpose the expression is satisfactory.

The communication protocol definition utilizing finite automata may be expressed as follows:

$$CP = \{V, F(V), FA(PS_1), FA(PS_2)\}$$

$FA(PS_1)$ and $FA(PS_2)$ being finite automata corresponding to protocol stations PS_1 and PS_2. Needless to say, when the protocol stations are the same, only one automaton is used. There are other possibilities of interpreting the communication control element by means of state models. But these will be treated in Chapter 4.2 which deals with communication protocol models. The utilization of state models represents the other approach to communication protocol definition.

2.4.4 Procedures, phases and communication functions

Communication functions and communication protocols were clearly differentiated (see Figure 2.31) according to the two basic approaches to communication control. In this sense, any communication protocol implementing selected communication functions serves as a formal tool for such an implementation, but is not identical with communication functions. On the other hand, for each communication protocol it should be known which communication functions, or which methods of communication functions, it is capable of implementing.

The methods, or sometimes the mechanisms, of communication functions are implemented by means of functional modules which are contained in protocol stations. By activities of such modules specific sequences of protocol words are produced. Each specific sequence may be called a procedure, and corresponds to one method of one communication function, or to one mechanism. By concatenating such procedures the phases of communication may be derived, resulting eventually in a whole course of communication containing several phases and many procedures.

Procedures are subsets of the language $L(V)$. These subsets need not be disjoint, because some mechanisms (e.g. the window mechanism described in Chapter 3.4 and elsewhere) may be used for several communication functions methods.

It should be pointed out that the procedure may acquire different meanings, too. That is, it can be regarded as a subprotocol in the following sense: if we add an appropriate subset of $F(V)$ and an appropriate subset of V to the subset of language $L(V)$, then the resulting triple defines a communication protocol which is partial with respect to the original protocol. In this sense we may use the terms "a connection establishment protocol" or "a data transfer protocol", or "a procedure".

Moreover, there is the connection establishment communication function, the connection establishment phase, and connection establishment methods. Clearly there is a lot of redundancy in utilizing these terms. For the purposes of this book we suggest not using the term "protocol" for what can be expressed by terms "procedure" or "phase".

2.4.5 Communication protocols parameters

Although communication protocols primarily represent fixed agreements on communication control rules, nevertheless certain protocol parts can be modified or adjusted even in the course of operation of the relevant communication control element or communication system.

The following variables may be regarded as communication protocol parameters:

a) various lengths (e.g. the data block length, the header length, header fields lengths, etc.),

b) numbering module M,

c) window size K,

d) the maximal allowed number of retransmissions E,

e) lengths of individual time-out intervals T_0,

f) generation polynomials of the code used, etc.

Details concerning the parameters listed under points b) to f) may be found in Chapter 3.4 whereas the first parameter is discussed in Chapter 2.5.

When the communication protocol design (or selection) has been completed, the modification of values of protocol parameters is the only means of influencing the performance of the communication subnetwork.

Though the parameters listed above are more concerned with communication functions (the window size, the number of retransmissions, time-outs) or with the entire communication system (the data block length), almost all of them are implemented in protocol stations and therefore they may be called protocol parameters (not communication functions parameters). But in the sense of differentiating between communication protocols and functions, the parameters are essentially connected to communication functions.

2.4.6 Reference specification of communication protocols

The exact, complete, and unique specification of communication protocols, which is the subject of Chapter 4.2, and which utilizes various protocol models, is generally too extensive to be of great practical value.

When comparing and/or selecting protocols, or when performing the basic design of protocols, we must characterize protocols in more detail, though not so much as to lose the overall picture. We therefore suggest the following frame of reference for the specification of communication protocols:

A: What configuration is the protocol assigned to and what kind of communication is to be controlled?

B: What data blocks are to be transferred (what length)?
C: What communication functions are to be implemented?
D: What are the protocol words and formats?
E: What are the values of the protocol parameters used?
F: What are the sequences of protocol words and what are the phases of communication?
G: What should be the reaction to protocol words (and what are the state diagrams)?

A communication protocol mostly relates to the communication control element. It means that we should know more about the communication medium used (A1), about communication stations (A2) and also about the environment in which the communication control element must operate (A3). So the location of the element in either the network architecture or communication subnetwork must be characterized and basic communication properties must be specified as well (A4). For example, it should be known whether the communication is to be two-way alternate or two-way simultaneous, whether the transfer is to be serial or parallel, etc. If communication modes are required (A5), as for example balanced or unbalanced modes, or "lettergram" or "liaison" modes (see Appendix E), they must be specified, too. When the configuration differs from that of a communication control element, it must be specified in details (A6).

Point B covers all information on data blocks with the exception of formats.

Point C comprises the specification of communication functions (C1) broken down to communication functions methods (C2) and mechanisms (C3).

The definition of the protocol words used (D1) and of the corresponding formats (D2) creates the contents of point D. Protocol parameters are specified under point E.

Points A to E should be specified for any protocol, points F and G being alternatives: it is enough to specify one of them.

Point F contains the definition of protocol words sequences (F1), i.e. the definition of procedures. The assignment of procedures to communication phases (F2), or the definition of communication phases by means of procedures, is of secondary importance only.

Point G focuses on the specification of protocol stations. It contains the specification of reactions to individual protocol words (G1), or it may contain state diagrams (G2).

The above reference specification frame represents a methodological tool which is considered useful by the authors of this book. It is by no means an agreed upon, or generally accepted, way of structuring the description of communication protocols.

2.4.7 Couplings and transformations of protocols

A communication protocol has been assigned to a communication control element. This element serves as the basic element for the analysis of communication control in networks, but its usage is rather limited. It can primarily serve for point-to-point links. In configurations which are more complex, either topologically (more nodes) or architectonically (more layers), communication control must be expressed by means of chains of communication control elements. The general scheme of such a chain is depicted in Figure 2.32.

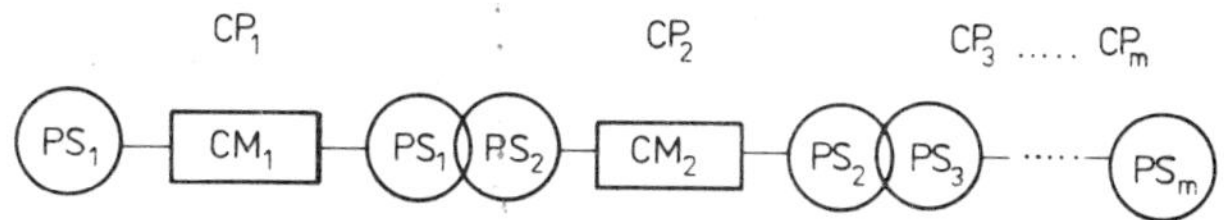

Figure 2.32 Chain of communication control elements

The contact between two communication control elements may have the character of a coupling or that of a transformation.

The contact will be regarded as a coupling when both communication control elements use the same communication protocol. This means that the two protocol stations merely exchange appropriate control information and that no conversions are required.

When different communication protocols are assigned to the contacted communication control elements, the contact is considered to be a protocol transformation. This situation occurs when various networks are interconnected, or when several layer communication protocols are utilized in one layer (see Figure 2.18).

In networks more than two protocol stations may be contacted (see Figure 2.23).

This very brief description of the topic was intended to give an outline of the problems; more details will be given in Chapter 4.4.

Communication protocols are basic components of computer networks, both in theory and in practice. As such, they can hardly be described adequately within the limit of a few pages. Therefore they will also be treated in Part 4 of this book, where protocol design, modelling, verification, and evaluation will be explained.

2.4.8 Bibliographical notes

Comprehensive treatment of communication protocols (with many references) can be found in [21, 197, 205, 209, 264]. Very valuable is the proceeding of the Computer Network Protocols Symposium (see, for example, [56]).

Communication protocols may be classified according to network architecture layers, for example into line protocols [44, 59, 75, 95, 186, 223, 276], packet transfer protocols [34, 37], transport protocols, or end-to-end protocols [37, 216, 217, 258, 293, 295] and higher-level (or function-oriented, or host-to-host) protocols [33, 48, 283]. Among the latter the virtual terminal protocols are the best known example [248, 249].

From among the protocols used in existing networks the following have been selected [8, 190, 198, 279, 290, 293]. Sets of protocols are described in [77, 170] and, of course, in [8]. In general form, such a set is characterized also in [231].

Interprocess communication protocols are dealt with in [4, 178, 282]. Examples of comparison of protocols are in [58, 200].

General and analytical treatment of communication protocols may be found, for example, in [21, 35, 55, 143, 146].

2.5 Formats

2.5.1 The role of format in protocol

In the previous chapter we have defined the protocol and we have claimed that the description of protocol contains also formats of commands, responses, data, etc., that are transferred between stations. In this chapter we will describe the formats in greater detail because we can take them as one of the basic terms in the field of communication control.

The fact that the stations are not able to understand the semantics of the transmitted data in the same way, for example, as a man who works on the teletype, is the reason for the necessity to implement perfect syntax, that, from the standpoint of communication control, will partly supply these semantics. The strict ordered sequence of bits, characters, or words creating the message makes it possible for the receiving station to recognize which parts of the data are control data and which part are user's data (note that the control commands and user's data are transmitted together in the same way). Suppose we agree that in simple point-to-point communication the user's data will always be preceded by the control command consisting, say, of 8 bits. Hence the receiving station can distinguish user's data from the control commands, because the first eight bits (octet) from the received bit sequence, or the first eight bit characters after decoding, are sufficient information saying what kind of command has been sent and how the receiver should react to the message. This convention (between two stations, or in a communication network or in a data processing system) describing the order of characters or bits in data, commands, and responses is usually called the format. As this definition is not quite sufficient, we will study it in greater detail.

Let us presume the following simple format. The station has at its disposal just the five control commands C_1, C_2, C_3, C_4, and C_5 and a transmission data block size of D bits without code restriction. When we have a block, consisting of the control command and a sequence of D data bits, then the format of this block can be described by means of the rule that the first part of a block must contain one of the control commands C_1 through C_5, immediately followed by the D data bits. Another description can be based on the results of the format realizations, i.e. from the description of all possible blocks, that is 5.2^D (if we admit data expressed in a binary code). They are the following formats:

$$
\begin{array}{l}
C_1\,TXT(1),\ C_1\,TXT(2),\ C_1\,TXT(3),\ \ldots,\ C_1\,TXT(2^D),\\
C_2\,TXT(1),\ C_2\,TXT(2),\ C_3\,TXT(3),\ \ldots,\ C_2\,TXT(2^D),\\
\cdots\cdots\cdots\cdots\cdots\cdots\cdots\cdots\cdots\cdots\cdots\cdots\\
C_5\,TXT(1),\ C_5\,TXT(2),\ C_5\,TXT(3),\ \ldots,\ C_5\,TXT(2^D).
\end{array}
$$

Till now we have been interested in format macrostructure, that is its composition of commands and data. Now it is necessary to describe the structure of the format parts. For any code, the rules or the description of all possibilities of command and data construction from characters must be defined. In the case of a sequence of bits the same must be done within the scope of the bit structure. In this way we arrive at the basic building stones which comprise the blocks and which have assigned their format. Therefore we will still stay at the format microstructure.

Data are classified according to the type of their processing and the type of computer, constructed of bytes (byte-oriented processing), or of words. A byte is usually formed from an octet of bits, representing one alphanumeric character, or perhaps two numeric figures (code BCD). A word is a longer sequence of bits that represent a number, item, etc. The important thing is that in computer processing a byte and a word are processed simultaneously. Higher data formations are record, segment, file, etc., but we will not use these terms because they are not quite stabilized and the term message will be sufficient (it means data message). By a message we will understand a comprehensive set of bytes or words, usable as input or output data in any task, program, etc.

In the field of data transmission, however, the situation is different. While computer processing is parallel, data transmission, in most cases, is serial, bit after bit. If we pass over the technical design of the sender or receiver, which can handle smaller parts of signals carrying bits (e.g. samples), the smallest element of every data message is a bit. An antipole of the byte (in the case of byte oriented data) is the character that belongs to some code (ISO/CCITT, EBCDIC). The fact is made use of that byte oriented data may have certain features which can also be utilized for data transmission, as, for example, the parity bit. But it is necessary to realize that besides the codes that have characters which are 7—8 bits long there exist other codes that have characters with fewer bits (five bits code ITA 2, six bits code SBT). So the character need not agree, in every case, with the byte. To avoid misunderstanding we shall hereafter write about characters in the case of characters belonging to some code, regardless of the fact that they are or are not bytes. In particular, we shall call the eight-bit characters octets.

Another data transmission formation mentioned already is a block, which is processed as a whole during data transmission. Synonyms for the packet switched network are packet, datagram, letter, etc. In this book other term than block will not be used; the Appendices are the only exceptions because they use the same terms as appear in original documents. The block has no relation to any data formation in the processing. Its size is determined by other than processing demands: it is selected on the basis of transmission features of the system and must be capable of fulfilling the needs of protocol.

In the previous example we introduced a block consisting of the command and D data bits. When the data message can be transmitted from one station to another, it must, at first, be divided into long portions, e.g. D bits. These portions, which we shall call fragments, are usually independent of the structure of the processed data, as are blocks.

Let us return to the definition of format. The format of a block must be defined in terms of a structure which is constructed of the smallest possible, further indivisible, elements, i.e. bits or characters. Therefore we will differentiate between bit oriented format, defined by the structure of bit sequences, and character-oriented format associated with a particular code or codes (e.g. character-oriented format of link protocol BSC working with the ASCII, EBCDIC, and SBT code), where the data as well as other commands in a block are expressed by the characters. In the latter case it makes no difference if the transmission is mostly realized serially and if the stations send and receive bits and not characters; the advantage of character oriented format is that it includes the possibility of parallel transmission by characters.

Besides bit or character oriented formats there may exist cases where the commands and the data are formed by bit sequences of different lengths, especially when the data part of a block is actually the original data message. Although not entirely accurate, since this format is actually bit-oriented, the term message-oriented format is also used (e.g. format in the DDCMP link protocol). Since it is not necessary to deal with message orientation, we will only use the term bit or character orientation.

We have seen that format can be defined in two ways in the same way that a protocol was defined in the previous chapter. The definitions are brought about either through rules for creating blocks or through specifications of all blocks created in this way. In the first case, the format will be the system of rules for the arrangement of bits in a block (in bit-oriented format), or for the arrangement of characters (octets) in a block (in character-oriented format). This kind of format description is shorter but more complicated than the other method: the format is a set of all permitted blocks.

The complexity of the description based on the specification of all blocks can be seen in the previous example, where we dealt with a finite data sequence. When the number of data bits in a block is not constrained (*D* has no limit), then there can theoretically also be an unlimited number of blocks in the concrete format while the number of rules is always limited. The description by means of rules is more complicated, because their exact specification is not a simple affair (the verbal description we have used in the example is not always exact). Formally it is possible to define the format by the rules of regular grammar, by transitions of the states of finite automaton, etc.

For practical applications priority is given to a mixed definition: all macrostructures are specified (in our example it is only one macrostructure C TXT) and then the rules for the construction of particular block portions are defined (C could be chosen from the five commands and each command is, for example a five-tuple of bits, in which there are always only 1 one and 4 zeros; TXT are all the binary combinations *D* bits long). Looking at the standardized protocols, we can practically always find this kind of description: e.g. in X.25 all of the block structures are specified (in this case they are packets) in octets assigned with rules for the creation of 8-tuples of zeros and ones.

The syntax of the format itself is sufficient for the formal realisation of the protocol, but for its activity it is necessary to add the conditions for which cases this or that rule and this or that block can be used. We can talk about a certain semantic feature of the format definition: a certain block will be used by the sending station to open the transmission, the other one is for the response of the receiving station confirming the received data. The syntax only tells us that after using one block as the response of the opposite station, only one of the blocks that have been defined in advance can be sent, though which of them will be the reaction to the state of this station must be specified separately.

Finally, we must not forget that a format, like the protocol, is defined by variables — the parameters of format. The parameters of format include block length, length of the portions of a block, especially the length of data embedded in the block, etc. Although the majority of format parameters are determined by procedures or protocols it is necessary to specify the extent of parameter values in the format description. But to this we will return later.

Though the macrostructure of the format will be the topic of the next section, we shall mention here the basic portions of format. In block and in format we shall always separate the portion which carries the user's data; we will call this portion the data portion. Anything that precedes the data portion is called header, and anything that follows after the data portion is called trailer. There also exist formats in which characters or bits are inserted into the user's data portion. Header, trailer, and inserted bits (characters) included in the data portion form the envelope (notice that the terminology resembles the terminology used for telegraph, postal, and mail services: every telegram is equipped by a heading and sometimes is terminated by a trailer, every letter in an envelope is furnished with the name of the sender and the addressee). The basic macrostructure of a block is shown in Figure 2.33.

HDR	DTA TXT	TAIL
HEADER	DATA MESSAGE OR FRAGMENT	TRAILER

Figure 2.33 Basic block format

At the end of this section we will mention some terms important from the point of view of the format. We can divide formats in terms of dependence on block length, because some formats create blocks of the same length and others create blocks with different lengths. In the latter case the block length can vary in the user's data part only, or in the envelope, or in all parts.

We often encounter the term transparent or nontransparent format. The term transparency is connected with the code of the transmitted data. The transparent (code independent) format of a block is given when it is possible to transmit all the 2^D binary sequences in the data portion of a block D bits long. When the number of transmitted data sequences that are admissible is less than 2^D (some sequences are not allowed) the format is nontransparent (code dependent). It follows from this that, chiefly in the character-oriented format, which uses a certain code, not all the characters represent data: some of them designate control, (for instance the control characters of ISO/CCITT code), and as such are not allowed to form an element of the data portion. We will return to this problem in the section about format operations (Section 2.5.3).

Finally, we can mention the role of the formats in network architecture (Figure 2.34). The block format on a certain layer of the architecture, from the viewpoint of the nearest underlaying layers, is taken as a data fragment that creates the data portion in the format of this layer, to which the header, trailer, and if

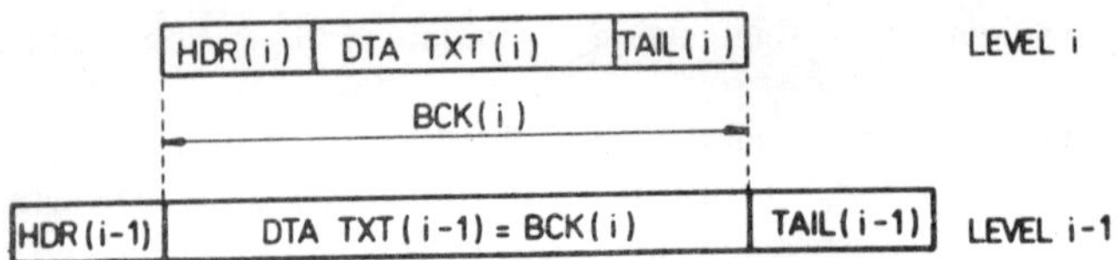

Figure 2.34 Block formats in neighbouring levels of architecture

necessary other internal bits or characters, are added. This kind of wasting of overhead could be reduced to some extent by a special arrangement of the header and the trailer, but we will write about that in greater detail in Section 2.5.3.

2.5.2 Macrostructure of format

Let us again look at Figure 2.33 which contains the basic macrostructure of block format. It consists of the header (HDR), the data fragment (DTA TXT), and the trailer (TAIL). The header and the trailer are too large, while the character or bit structure is, for the purpose of our explanation of communication control, in too great detail. Therefore we shall introduce another level of structuring: partition into fields. By a field we will understand that portion of the block which has complex control or complex data meaning, regardless of whether it is a part of the envelope or a part of the data. The result is that the whole data fragment, for our purpose, will be a (data) field, the header which consists of only one command will be a single (control) field, while the header with command and address will consist of two fields. An example of the block format structure is shown in Figure 2.35.

There is an advantage in recognizing the fields according to symptoms. Hence we can speak of a data field that contains the user data and may be completed with inserted characters (bits) of envelope, and of a non data field. The non data fields are, for instance, the check field and the control field, and are further divided into command field, address field, identification field, numbering field, synchronization field, phasing field, etc. Before we describe some fields in greater detail, let us look at the way of dividing fields in a block.

Theoretically the differentiation of parts, given in advance of bit sequences (fields), can be solved generally. Note that the fields have the same length, and the main task is

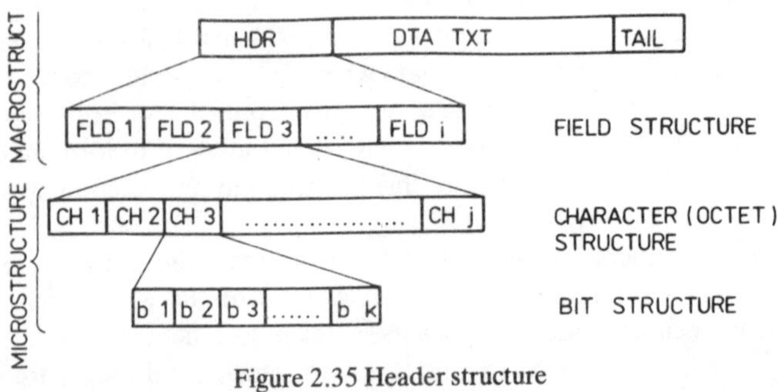

Figure 2.35 Header structure

to find a structure on them that provides the possibility of finding the initial point of any sequence that forms the format. It is evident that in this case it is impossible for the field to consist of any combination of zeros and ones, because otherwise the division could be realized on an arbitrary point, regardless of the format macrostructure. The limitation of field structure could be solved either by special coding or by a separator.

The special coding (known in the literature as comma-free) relates to the decoding of genetic information in the DNK string, where it is necessary to divide a bit sequence correctly into fields beginning from the position of any bit. As an example, in Table 2.1 there are all possible field structures 4 bits long having this feature. Let us try to make out any sequence of four bits from Table 2.1. Starting from any position, we will find the beginning of some field after testing 3 bits at the most. For instance in the sequence 10010101101110111001100, where the first bit is omitted, by a sequential comparison of the groups of four bits 1001, 0010, 0101, 1010 with the words from the table we will immediately find out the first right field, 1010.

Table 2.1 Example of the comma-free code and of the code with a separator

Comma-free code				Code with a separator			
1	1	0	1	0	1	1	1
1	0	1	0	0	1	1	0
1	1	0	0	0	1	0	0

Because differentiating fields by means of a comma-free code is pretentious on the receiver decoding, there is another possible way: the comma code. Let us again presume a field 4 bits long, but now the first two bits will be of fixed structure and will represent the comma. In Table 2.1 the combination 01 is chosen as the comma; the number of all structures of the fields has not been altered. The reader can try himself to take any sequence of groups of four bits from Table 2.1 and he can recognize the right fields, independently of where the separating search begins. The advantage is that now it is not necessary to use the decoding table as in the preceding case, but it is sufficient to find the commas that determine the beginnings of the fields.

In formats normally used this method is unnecessarily extravagant, because the receiving station is not supposed to have to work with incomplete blocks. Block phasing solves the problem of how to find the beginning of the block (note the details in Chapter 3.2) and so it is sufficient either to keep a constant field length in all the formats or to use separators, which is much more simple than in the case with commas.

When we use a constant field length the problem is quite evident: the receiving station counts the proper number of bits or characters (octets) from the beginning of the block and thus the format is divided. When even the block end is known, then the length of one field can be altered because the receiving station can count from the beginning or from the end of the block or from both. It naturally has sense only in the case when the variable field is a data field (the format of the data block in the HDLC link protocol is designed in this way).

As soon as a bit pattern (character from some code) has been chosen representing the separator, this pattern must not appear in the header, the data field, or the trailer fields, otherwise it will lead to an incorrect separation of the fields. Thus the separator has the same function as a comma, but there is a difference in that in a bit sequence of the comma code the appearance of a separator is never allowed. On the other hand in a bit sequence with separator the appearance of the chosen separator in the place of another character (in character-oriented format) or in the place of an octet (in bit-oriented format) is not allowed. If we presume the field length to be equal to an eight-bit character or octet, then the total number of the characters (octets) usable in the field is $2^8 - 1 = 255$; one character (octet) is reserved for separation, while in the code with a separation character the reduction is much greater (note Table 2.1 where from the 16 possibilities only three are usable).

Now we shall pass to a description of the individual fields, beginning with the data field.

The data field can be transparent or code dependent; we will write about this in the following section. In either case the content of the data field is a fragment of the data message plus, if need be, the envelope bits (characters) necessary for keeping transparency. When we want to keep the same length of data field, the last fragment, usually shorter, must be completed, e.g. by zeros, but that increases the overhead (Figure 2.36b). When we allow a variable data field length in order to reduce the overhead, a special character (special bit sequence) is to be used either at the end of a shorter fragment or at the end of a block including a fixed length trailer (in the latter case the receiving station side can recognize the end of the data field by means of counting from the end of a block). This way of indication is shown in Figure 2.36a and is used, for example, in the INWG end-to-end protocol, where the end of a fragment (INWG notation of a letter) is indicated by the character EOL (end of letter).

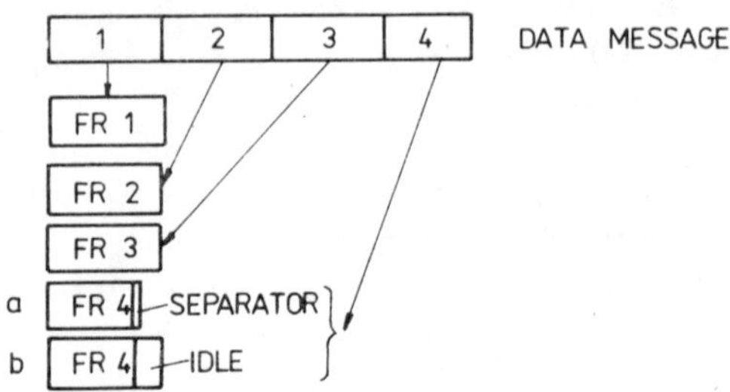

Figure 2.36 Methods of data message decomposition
a) using a special separator
b) using fixed-length fragments and an idle

The data field length can be arbitrary, except that in character-oriented format it must be an integer multiple of the number of bits in the character. From the transmission viewpoint the entire block length and also the data field length are chosen with regard to error control, flow control, and other procedures (in the header and in the trailer there are no greater reserves for altering the length). Besides, the data field length can be adjusted to data processing and the length should correspond to the length of words in the HOST computer. That is why in universal protocols (especially of international standards) the data length is chosen with regard to the most often used word length, or the length is an integer multiple of their least common multiple. For instance, when we presume using 16, 18, 24, 32, or 36 bit length words, the length of the fragment (and without interleaving the data field, too), must be an integer multiple of 288 (this is the case of the INWG end-to-end protocol in datagram service, where the fragment length is 6.288 = 1728 bits, that is 216 octets). When the word length is 8, 12, 18, 24, and 36 bits it is an integer multiple of 216 bits, when the word length is 6, 8, 12, 16, 18, 24, 32, 36, and 64 (this is the really universal format) then the data field length must be an integer multiple of 576 bits. We are talking about data field lengths, but we really mean fragment lengths; when other bits (characters) of the envelope are inserted between data bits or characters for transparency, then the data field length is larger, and moreover, variable.

The control field is necessary for the control of data transmission between stations and usually contains commands, responses and other data necessary for control. The control field length depends on the way of coding the commands and on their number. When binary coding uses all the code combinations, the control field of length C can contain 2^C commands, addresses, etc. For the commands, responses, identification symptoms, synchronizing and phasing combinations a code is chosen which attaches C long binary combinations to commands. For addresses and numbers of blocks direct binary coding is used. This is all valid when the control fields are under error control; otherwise it is better to use some error detecting and/or correcting code. Commands in which an incorrect receipt can be expected because of errors during transmission, it is better, in binary representation, to remove as far from each other as possible (in terms of Hamming distance).

The error checking field is usually a part of the trailer, or even forms the whole trailer. It serves for the transmission of the check bits of a block, so that errors can be corrected or detected. The bit length of this field depends on the correction or detection code used (note Chapter 3.4), but usually the length is an integer multiple of character length (in character-oriented format), octets, or word length (in the bit-oriented format). This rule is also used for other fields, because the advantage during processing exceeds the contingent loss of throughput.

The fields that have been enumerated are not the only fields used in the envelope of a block. For instance in the message switching systems (in the public telegraph service) the header or the trailer are usually much more complicated than in line switching or packet switching systems. In the header the date and time of passing the message to the communication system is written, together with the urgency of delivery (this indication may be used in packet switching, too), the tariff values, and many others, some of which may be repeated again in the trailer for error protection.

There now remains the question of how the data field should be ordered in the block, which field can be introduced first, and the order in which the fields should follow each other.

In the first place it depends on whether or not the block is error protected. When it is error protected and the protection also covers the envelope, then it does not depend on the field ordering because the whole block must first be received, acknowledged, and perhaps asked for a repetition. When the receiving station is assured of the correctness of the block, it can read the header and maybe the trailer and in this case it does not matter which field is read first. Only in the cases when some items of the header can be changed in the course of block transmission, and we wish to transmit its value "up-to-date", is it placed at the end of the block (an example is in Chapter 3.4, where "piggybacked" commands in a transmitted data field are discussed).

The reading algorithm, of course, takes care of the order of importance of fields.

In the case when the block is not under error protection (e.g. in formats on higher layers of architecture) or the error protection does not cover the envelope (the link protocol BSC), a rule of ordering the fields according to their importance is natural, so that the receiving station must be informed first of a field containing data or commands. For instance in the link protocol of multipoint or loop lines the data of the addressee is most important, and that is why the address field should be on one of the first positions before the control field. On the packet layer the type of the block should be first, followed by the field containing the priority degree and routing information. When the envelope holds information of security, it should precede the address field, or should be placed in the very beginning of the header, otherwise it could happen that the block will be placed in the unprotected part of the memory.

The order of fields in the envelope is becoming the subject of intensive study and the first proposals of standards are occurring.

2.5.3 Operations with formats

During transmission and processing in nodes of the network, during transfer from one network to another and finally when blocks are formed based on user demands, we cannot avoid the transformation and the modification of format. In principle the modification (change) of the whole format of the block (transformation of the block) or the modification (change) of some block part only (header, data portion, trailer) is concerned.

The simplest modification of the whole block consists in taking the whole block as a fragment and adding a new envelope. This modification is necessary when passing from a higher layer of architecture to a lower one (note Figure 2.34). We have mentioned that this modification usually increases overhead, because some data in the envelope of the block in the i-group layer can contain the data for the $(i-1)$ layer, hence it is unnecessary to repeat them. If the same data can be used for both layers of the architecture, it is sufficient to order the fields in the format in such a way that in the lower layer only part of the header or maybe of the trailer is put in. The fields that are shared with both adjacent layers must be placed at the beginning of the header and at the end of the trailer in the format of the higher layer, in the format of the lower layer they will be at the end of the header and at the beginning of the trailer (Figure 2.37). In this way a system of formats in end-to-end protocol is formed according to INWG (see Appendix E).

When blocks are passed from one network to another through the gateway the protocol that controls the transmission is also altered, hence a modification of the format may be necessary. If a change of the structure of the format takes place and the block length does not change, there is no other way than to perform the whole transformation, that is unpack the fragment from one envelope and substitute the envelope with another one. But often the block length is changed and then the problem arises of dividing one block into several smaller sub-blocks, or alternatively to compose one larger multiblock from several original blocks. In such cases it is possible to proceed in two ways. Either the whole block is divided and every part is

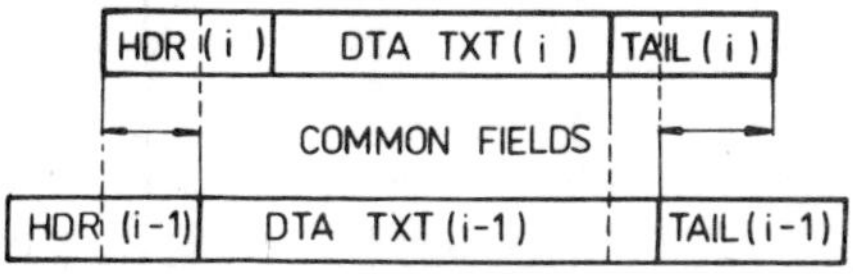

HDR (i) | DTA TXT (i) | TAIL (i) LEVEL i
COMMON FIELDS
HDR (i-1) | DTA TXT (i-1) | TAIL (i-1) LEVEL i-1

Figure 2.37 Block formats in neighbouring levels of architecture using common fields

handled as a fragment (there is an example of division into two sub-blocks in Figure 2.38a) or only the data field is divided without the envelope (without inserted bits or characters) and thus formed subfragments are completed with a new envelope (Figure 2.38b). As far as numbering is concerned, either the new blocks are renumbered, or the original numbering is kept and the sub-blocks are recognized by an additional digit. In the case of a return transformation during which blocks or fragments are composed into a multiblock or multifragment, the numbering can remain, too, with the condition that multiblocks are always numbered by the number of the first fragment in the multifragment (e.g. a multifragment contains 4 smaller numbered fragments: the first multifragment contains the fragments 1, 2, 3, 4 and is numbered 1, the second multifragment with fragments 5, 6, 7, 8 has number 5, etc.).

For security purposes data are coded and this can also be done with whole blocks. In this case there is no transformation of format, but only its code, which in order to keep the meaning of all control data of the envelope must be repeated in each node of the network. When only data (fragments) are encoded there is no change in the composition of the format, but it is necessary to take care on a code dependent format that the rules for forming a data field are not broken.

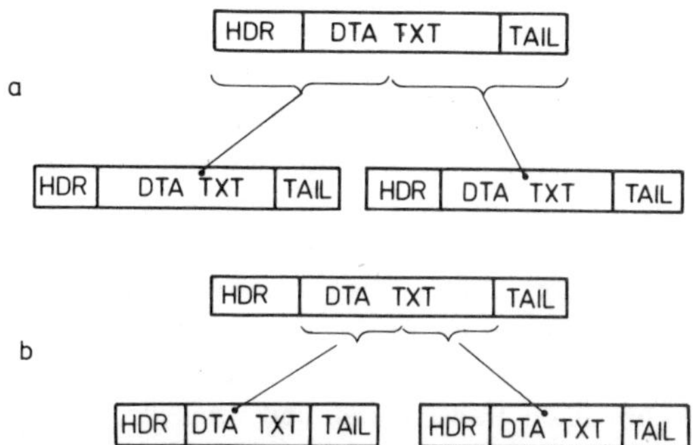

Figure 2.38 Methods of decomposition of blocks into subblocks
a) Decomposition of the whole block
b) Decomposition of the data field

Now we come to the operations on block fields. We shall treat the data field since it is most important. When we want to achieve code independency, and the data field length is variable, we must ensure such a transformation of fragments as will provide a possibility of recognizing all the fields in the format. Let us look at a few solutions of this problem.

The least economic way, suffering from great overhead and from small throughput, is the global encoding of data. Let us consider character-oriented data in the a-unit code. When we encode these data into the $(a+1)$-unit code, e.g. to each a-tuple group a zero is added, we get 2^a free combinations which can be used for control. The same is true also for bit-oriented data; there all octets are transformed into nonets (9-unit combinations with zero at the beginning, for instance). It is quite understandable that this method has some disadvantages and will not be used in practice, because much more economic methods exist.

The method of encoding commands and all other control combinations belongs to them. The data can be in any form and can also hold the control combination of bits or characters. If we want to differentiate between actual commands in a format, we must encode them, e.g. we complete it with a prefix (a bit or character combination preceding a command) or a suffix (a bit or character combination following a command) having a constant structure. Since the prefix (suffix) can also appear in the data, and the possibility is not excluded that they are followed (preceded) by a certain chosen control combination which would be regarded as a command by the receiver, the prefix (suffix) must be extracted from the data, e.g. by duplication. That then means that if a combination of the prefix (suffix) appears in the data it is duplicated for all cases and at the receiving site it is again excluded. The receiving station reads the block and wherever it finds a prefix (suffix) it checks the following (preceding) combination. When this combination is again a prefix (suffix), data are indicated and one combination is cancelled. When a control combination follows (precedes), it is evident that a header or trailer or separation combination is concerned. Of course, this kind of transformation also changes the length of nondata and data fields. This method is used in the format of the BSC link protocol, where the prefix is the character DLE from USASCII.

When we can keep the length of the all nondata fields fixed and only the length of the data fields is changed, while the blocks are transmitted asynchronously (with idles), it is sufficient to find out the beginning or, if necessary, the end of the block and take care about the nonappearance of separating block combinations in the data (the result is that the receiving station would regard this combination as the beginning of a new block and would count off the relevant number of bits or characters of the trailer). Thus the content of the nondata fields will stay unchanged but the content of the data field will change, more exactly, it is necessary to encode them. As an example we can recall the HDLC link protocol: the block separator is the octet 01111110, thus it is sufficient if 6 adjacent ones followed by a zero do not appear in the data. The data are checked before their transmission, and whenever 5 ones are detected an overhead zero is inserted so that, regardless of the value of the following bit, the octet 01111110 will not occur. The receiving station must, of course, extract these zeros and handles only the remainder of the content of the data field.

The last way is the most efficient because the overhead increases least. However, by inserting bits (zeros), not only is the length of the data field changed, but the length does not comprise an integer number of octets; thus it is not possible to transmit this format in parallel, one octet after another. The method of encoding commands keeps the character orientation if the prefix (suffix) has the same length as the used characters (in the case of the BSC protocol, for instance).

In all cases overhead bits or characters that can be included in the envelope are added to the data, because their function is only concerned with transmission and they have nothing in common with the transmitted user data (fragments).

The transformation of other data fields is not so interesting. The heart of the matter is in the encoding, changing the numbers, addresses, priority degrees, error detecting code, etc. However it is not possible, for understandable reasons, to change the security designation if it is part of the envelope. The actual mechanism of transformations is very simple and the reasons for the transformation of the non-data fields are related to the corresponding procedures. We shall talk about them in Part 3.

2.5.4 Bibliographical notes

The reader can only become acquainted with the structure of formats from all the descriptions of protocols (see the Appendices). They are discussed summarily in various books about data transmission and its control (e.g. [165, 197], where other references are mentioned). No special study on this topic is well known to the authors, though maybe [285] is near while in [65] the principle of the format structure choice is dealt with. A review of standard formats in link protocol si in [197] and [253], the format of messages used in message-switching systems is summarily discussed in [15] which is very valuable, because it is therefore not necessary to search in the CCITT recommendations and in the descriptions of the commercial systems. At the time that this book was being written the first proposal of the ISO standard [215] was issued, dedicated so far to the structure of the header from the viewpoint of communication function in the end-to-end protocol. As for the refragmentation of blocks with respect to networks interconnections, a summary may be found in [259] while in [35, 268] some special problems are dealt with.

2.6 Role of Standards

2.6.1 Organizations for standardization

Before discussing the evolution of standards in communication control we shall recapitulate, for the benefit of those who have had few dealings with standardization, the basic organizations for standardization which play the chief role in forming protocol standards. It is not by chance that, in the main, organizations connected with the standardization of data processing equipment, telecommunication equipment and data transmission equipment, work on protocols for communication control.

The first step towards standardization in the data transmission field was made by CCITT, i.e. by the international telecommunication organization of PTTs belonging to the International Telecommunication Union — ITU, the resident specialized organization for telecommunication and radiocommunication of UNO. The abbreviation CCITT denotes the first letters of this organization's French name (Commité Consultatif International Télégraphique et Téléphonique). This literally means the international consulting committee for telegraphs and telephones. After the first Plenary Assembly in December 1956 in Geneva at which study question 43: "What general characteristics should be standardized to permit international transmission of accounting data?" had been set up, Working Party 43 was appointed for the solution of this problem. From it Special Study Group A, abbreviation SG SpA, developed in December 1960 at the second Plenary Assembly. This group treated data transmission from all viewpoints up to December 1972, when a new study group VII "Public Data Networks" was formed which took over a part of the work concerning standardization of the interface between subscribers and public data networks and the cooperation of these networks. SG VII originated in the joint SG X/SpA working party, known under the denotation GM/NRD at the IVth Plenary Assembly in 1968. For the sake of completeness let us note that, at the VIth Plenary Assembly of CCITT in October 1976 SG SpA was renamed SG XVII.

Besides study groups VII and XVII, other SGs also deal partly with data transmission, e.g. SG VIII (Telegraphic devices), SG X (Telegraph switching), SG XIV (Telegraphy, facsimile), and others.

CCITT publishes recommendations (rather than standards) which are approved at plenary assemblies and published in books of diverse colour, one colour for each four-year period. The Plenary Assembly VI in 1976 approved the recommendations published in orange books.

It has, however, become obvious lately that development in data transmission is so rapid that a four-year interval between plenary assemblies is too long and therefore provisional recommendations have been published at intermediate times since 1977.

Within the framework of ITU, CCIR has been working on radiocommunication performance, separately from CCITT. CCITT or UIT cooperates with a number of further standardization bodies such as IEC (International Electrotechnical Commission) and with ISO and ECMA (see later), with ICAO, IATA, UIC, CEPT (Conference of European Post and Telecommunications Administrations), and others, through the intermediary of mutual representatives or in the form of exchange of documents.

The second main international organization for standardization, as far as data transfer and data processing and thus also protocols are concerned, is the International Organization for Standardization (ISO). It was founded in 1946 for questions of the exchange of goods and data, for technological, economic and scientific cooperation. Quite a number of technical committees (TC) are working within the framework of ISO, including TC 97 (Computers and Data Processing). Within TC 97 a number of subcommittees (SC) have been formed, e.g. the well-known SC 6 (Data communications) which has prepared many standards from the field of procedures and codes and the new SC 16 (Open System Interconnection), established in February 1978 in which four working groups (Reference Model, Application and System Management, Application and Presentation Layers, and Session and Transport Layers) are engaged in the standardization of architectures and protocols for heterogeneous computer networks. In particular a reference model of open system architecture has been proposed.

For those who deal with ISO standards let us note that ISO has been publishing standards, particularly for remote data processing, since 1972 (series IS — International Standards); until then these standards had been denoted as recommendations (R). In view of the fact that in the majority of cases a rather long time passes between the draft of a standard and its approval by all the member states, it is useful to follow even the DIS (Draft International Standards), which are forwarded for critical examination.

Other international organizations for standardization have more of an application character and are oriented only to certain fields. Besides receiving and applying ISO standards and CCITT recommendations they sometimes also develop new standards which are either valid only for their members or are sent to ISO and CCITT as contributions. One of these organizations is ECMA (European Computer Manufacturers' Association) which was established in 1961 and which prepares, in its technical committee TC 9, standards from the field of computer networks, specially regarding interfaces and protocols (problem oriented Tasking Group TG A), and from the field of public data networks (TG B).

Standards for socialist countries are published by CMEA (Council for Mutual Economic Assistance), and in the field of computer techniques standards are dealt with by the CMEA Intergovernmental Committee for Computer Technology.

International standards are usually so flexible and are conceived so generally that it is necessary for individual countries to adapt them to their specific conditions. That is why all the member states of ISO, CCITT, and CMEA have their own national standard organizations, and some of them show their activity by elaborating standards and submitting them to international organizations for standards before they are accepted internationally. Of the most important ones let us mention the American organizations ANSI (American National Standards Institute), NBS (National Bureau of Standards), and EIA (Electronic Industries Association), the English BSI (British Standards Institution), the French AFNOR (Association Francaise de Normalisation), and the German DNA (Deutscher Normenausschuss).

Even though international and national organizations for standardization draft standards and recommendations they are not the only institutions which can come forward with a draft of a new standard or with an amendment or improvement to an old one. Anyone can cooperate in the creation of standards through his national organization. Besides these there exist independent groups of specialists who work in this field within the framework of some organization and submit suggestions for application in the process of standardization. An example of such a group for communication control is Working Group 6.1 (originally called the Group for International Networks) which works within the framework of Technical Committee 6 Data Communication of IFIP (International Federation of Information Processing) although it is not an organization for standardization but rather an organization for science and technology. The group is the most active source of protocol designs for international cooperation of data networks.

The three fundamental international organizations for standardization (ISO, ITU,

ECMA) are shown in Figure 2.39 with their organizations (solid lines) and mutual cooperation (dashed lines).

2.6.2 Evolution of protocol standardization

As already mentioned, the development of the standardization of protocols for communications control in computer networks is closely linked to the standardization of computer systems and their peripherals and data transmission devices. Should it be required to go through the history of protocol standardization then one would first encounter the standardization of codes and alphabets. Although these were meant for data recording they have since been used also for data exchange and remote transmission. Besides the International telegraph alphabet (ITA), which was proposed by D. Murray (although it is sometimes, less precisely, called Baudot code) and is used the world over in teletype operation, a seven-bit code alphabet has also been standardized. This was first introduced as an American national standard USASCII, but later was taken over both by ISO (IS 646) and CCITT (V.3 and X.4). In view of the fact that the international alphabet standard affords space for national peculiarities (for this purpose it leaves 10 combinations vacant) it is accepted as a national standard in almost all countries which use the free combinations for their special printed characters.

A matter which received attention in the next stage is the interface between data processing machines and peripheral units (the parallel interface for which the British BS 4421 standard was used most often), between DTE and the data set (series V and X of CCITT standards, e.g. V.24/X.24, V.10, V.11, X.26, X.27, ISO standards for mechanical interface characteristics IS 2110, DIS 4902, and 4903), and between DTE and DCE which must be included already among protocols (CCITT X.25, X.20, and X.21).

On the link level data link control protocols were first compiled with bit-oriented format (CCITT V.41), then later the conversational mode was solved in character-oriented format (ISO IS 1745 and complements 2111, 2628, and 2629), and finally the bit-oriented format was returned to, though for a wider use (HDLC protocols which, from the American ADCCP proposal, were eventually standardized by ISO as IS 3309 and 4335, DIS 6159 and 6256, and were used by CCITT as LAP B in the X.25 recommendation). The basic standardized link protocols are presented in brief in the Appendices (see Appendix A through C), where the history of their origin is also given.

The standards and recommendations given so far (especially the CCITT V series) were mainly used for forming so-called closed systems within the scope of the architecture of individual companies (SNA, DNA and others). Earlier, against the background of SG VII CCITT, the public data network was beginning to be considered and interfaces were specified between subscribers (DTE) and DCE terminating the public circuit-switched data network (X.21 for synchronous DTE, X.20 for asynchronous DTE) and a packet switching network — PSN (X.25 and X.29 for packet DTE, X.28 for start-stop DTE). Even though some protocols on the data network interface (X.60, X.70, X.71, X.75) had been specified, the architecture of public PSN had not yet been defined at the time the book was being written. What is now normally called open systems architecture, in which control layers are specified and functions (services) are defined, was missing.

The first step towards removing this disadvantage was made by a group of experts gathered in WG 6.1 TC6 IFIP, namely by the design of an end-to-end protocol, or by a protocol in the transport layer. But the actual specification of the open system architecture was conceived within the framework of TC/97 SC/16 WG1 in cooperation with WG2 and WG3 of ISO in March 1980 by the preparation of the document "Provisional Model of Open System Architecture" and later of the document "Reference Model for Open Systems Architecture". That seems to have set the basis for the development of further standardization activity in the communication control field and to have created the space required for a unified concept of control and protocol layers.

2.6.3 Bibliographical notes

More detailed information on organizations for standardization on an international scale and on some more important national bodies can be gained from [9, 27, 112, 113, 119, 124, 145, 168, 175, 228, 251]; in [251] the relations and cooperation between such organizations are depicted in more detail than in Figure 2.39. A series of papers analyses the importance of standardization of data transmission and protocols together with the reasons for individual standardization steps from codes (alphabets [82] through interfaces [84, 101] up to protocols and the of open architecture systems [23, 80, 119, 244]). A matter which was important at its time was that of considerations about what should be standardized, and when and how [27, 206, 280].

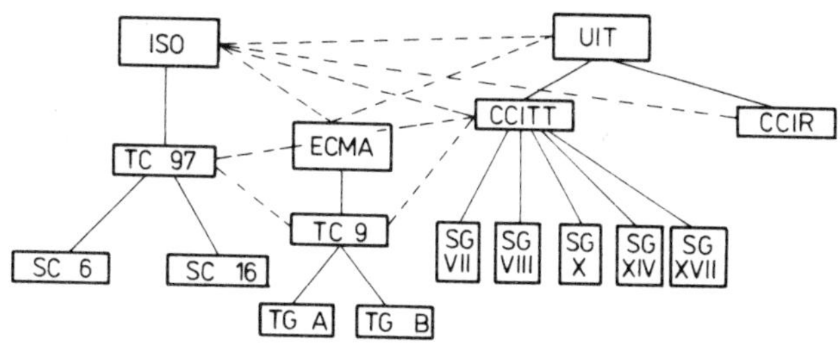

Figure 2.39 Diagram of organization (solid lines) and cooperation (dashed lines) of main international organizations for standardization

The actual standards and recommendations must be studied from the original documents [34, 59], but there exists a number of more or less complete summaries [47, 66, 84, 145, 147, 168, 222, 244, 251] which serve not only as guides and aids in orientation but also present complete wordings of standards, sometimes with comments, as e.g. [60] which contains 89 CCITT recommendations and ISO, ANSI, EIA, and FTSC (Federal Telecommunications Standard Committee) standards.

It is sometimes useful to remember the development of some standards even after some years. Thus, for instance, in [237] the origin of link protocol standards in the

ANSI framework is treated as is the standardization of interfaces by EIA, CCITT, and ISO in [47], where a whole series of further references can be found which we do not mention here because of lack of space.

While this book was being written a few contributions appeared concerning the standardization of public data networks [97, 113, 114]. Finally, considerations of the further development of standardization of protocols were very instructive at their time, especially when they can, after a period, be confronted with reality. In lieu of all others let us mention [174, 206, 209].

Part 3
Communication Functions

3.1 Establishment and Releasing of Links and Connections

3.1.1 Examples

In any communication subnetwork several operations must be performed before the transfer of data blocks starts and after it terminates, in order to set the prescribed states of the communicating stations and of the communication medium. These operations are performed within the scope of the link establishment/release phases and transmission opening/closing phases which were described in Chapter 2.2. The types and the number of these operations depend on the properties of the communicating stations and of the communication medium used. The set of these operations may be divided into four parts, namely into the communication functions of link establishment, transmission opening (or connection establishment), transmission closing or termination (or connection releasing), and link releasing (remember connections are regarded as virtual links). Synchronization control operations are not included in the above four communication functions, because they represent an independent communication function of the synchronization control and phasing (see Chapter 3.2).

First let us get acquainted with several examples taken from actual protocols and/or networks. There are five phases, or communication functions, specified in the ISO character-oriented data link control procedures (see Appendix A): link establishment in a switched network, transmission opening, data exchange, transmission terminating, and link releasing (in the original document a different terminology is used). The transmission opening function comprises, for example, the setting of master and slave states in the protocol stations according to the polling or selecting operation mode.

The transmission opening (or connection establishment) function in HDLC data link control procedures contains operations such as operational mode setting (e.g. NRM, or ARM, or ABM — see Appendix C) and state variables initialization.

Generally, the link establishment/releasing function is used only in switched networks. The operations or procedures used depend, of course, on the type of switching.

In packet-switched networks, two basic types of service are used, namely the datagram service and the virtual circuit service. The virtual circuits are store-

and-forward analogies of physical circuits. Hence, they can also be fixed or switched. A special kind of link establishment function must be provided for switched virtual circuits, but no such function is required in the datagram service network. Data are just inserted into packets and sent to the destination station. When the latter is not prepared, or is busy, the packets either may be dropped, or they may wait for a while (being stored in a subnetwork node) and be dropped later. The higher level control must provide for the retransmissions of such packets.

In the ARPANET computer network the connection is established between two communicating stations called sockets. These are protocol stations with assigned network addresses. First the connection (a half-duplex communication path) must be established and only then may the processes communicate.

In all the above cases the establishment and opening functions are counterbalanced by corresponding termination and releasing functions which provide for reaching the required final states.

Based on the analysis (not presented here) of the above and other examples, the following criteria concerning link establishment/releasing and transmission opening/terminating functions may be stated:

a) What is to be established? — physical links, virtual links, various connections, various sessions, etc.

b) Between what stations? — node computers, transport stations, ports, sockets, processes, host computers, terminals, etc.

c) Through what medium? — physical lines, switched network (line switching or packet switching), datagram network, virtual circuits network, multipoint links, etc.

d) What is to be transferred? — data blocks, data messages, packets, letters, files, telegrams, single-packet messages, multi-packet messages, etc.

Referring to c) and d) we should note that the connection is established (or the transmission is opened) for one data block, for one data message (i.e. for several data blocks), for several data messages, (i.e. for a session).

3.1.2 Connection establishment/releasing within the network architecture

The more complex the communication stations, the more complicated are the procedures of transmission opening/terminating, because the higher number of state variables and a multitask environment make the processing more difficult and more time-consuming.

We know from Chapter 2.3 that virtual links may be established in each layer of the network architecture, between corresponding protocol stations. The basic condition for the establishment of such a virtual link is given, for example, in the Open Systems Architecture document (see Appendix F). In order to establish (or to release) the connection in layer X one must have the connection in layer (X-1) established. But the connection in layer X remains established even when the connection in layer (X-1) is released. Of course, one must be careful with the interpretation of the connection here. The connection primarily concerns protocol stations, not the communication medium, whereas the link primarily concerns the communication medium, not the protocol stations.

Within the scope of the connection establishment function the protocol stations must agree on the operational modes, must initialize all state variables, must allocate the corresponding buffers, must load the required programs (if any), and must activate the required processes. Moreover, several auxiliary operations, such as measurement, statistics gathering, diagnostics, etc., may be started by the connection establishment function.

The connection releasing function, besides setting the required final or idle states of both protocol stations and of the communication medium, must also perform several auxiliary operations, e.g. the processing and evaluation of measurement results, the reporting or recording of these results, etc.

3.1.3 The influence of public networks and services

The couple of link establishment and releasing functions is influenced by the communication means used (see point c) from Section 3.1.1). In this section we shall notice an influence of public networks and services afforded by them, on these functions.

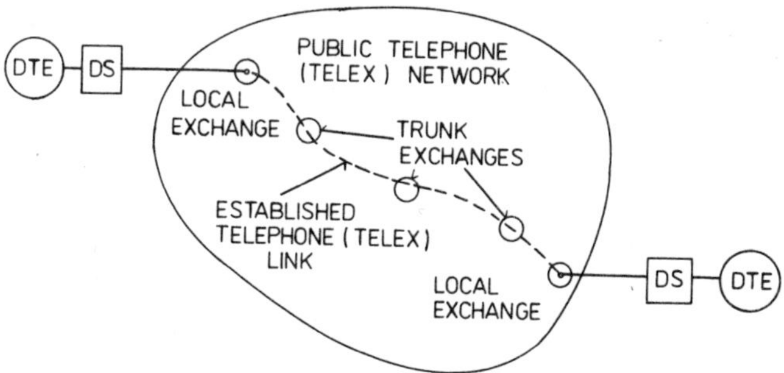

Figure 3.1 The interconnection between two DTEs over a public telephone (telex) network
DTE-data terminal equipment, DS-data set

In general, two cases can be considered. The first and original one concerns public telecommunication nondata networks, such as telephone and telex networks. These networks were not originally designed for data transmission so that the data terminal equipment (DTE) cannot be directly connected in the same way as telephone and telegraph sets. Between the DTE and a network, a data set (e.g. a modem) must be inserted in order to adapt the DTE signals to normal network conditions (see Figure 3.1). For the establishment/releasing purposes the DTE must generate all necessary signalling sequences for which the network is designed. Moreover, such signalling must be able to govern and control all active switching and transmission elements in the same way as in the case of normal use by telephone or telegraph sets.

As an example consider a long distance data transmission over a circuit switched telephone network equipped with echo suppressors. Recall that the telephone traffic needs to put down continent echoes while the data transmission traffic necessitates the FDX operation. The link establishment procedure must take this into account and generate an appropriate signal (e.g. 2100 Hz c/s in international connections) as an answering tone to disable echo suppressors. Such a requirement is, of course, not necessary if the data transfer takes place in nationwide or regionwide conditions.

The above example described the case of how to influence the network from the viewpoint of the special data transmission features. On the other hand, the DTE must adapt its actions to the network requirements. In telex operation only the ITA 2 code is permitted during the link establishment phase and no other characters are to be used. Because of the lack of some necessary control characters in the ITA 2 code the signalling to switch the remote station from telegraph operation to data operation (e.g. to synchronous transmission and the IA 5 code) can be provided by a combination of five-unit characters (e.g. by SSSS). The telex clearing signal which leads to the link releasing consists of more than seven continuous space (start) conditions (seven continuous zeros) so that the occurrence of such a signal must be avoided. This concerns all phases except the link releasing one in which the clearing zero signal is in turn indispensable.

It must be taken into consideration that the time required for the link establishment phase in public telegraph and telephone networks can vary from several seconds up to hours (provided switching is manual). Even lower call set-up time values would be inconsistent with data users requirements. There are two ways of improving this situation. Either from the user site, i.e. to shorten the call set-up time by means of special link establishment methods (e.g. without waiting for an acknowledgment from the remote exchange), or from the network vendor site, which leads to building new public networks designed with respect to stringent demands.

Before dealing with public data networks services we shall at least enumerate the duties and titles of DTEs which influence methods implemented in the link establishment/releasing function. In public telephone and telex circuit switched networks the DTE is responsible for almost all actions connected with the link establishment and link releasing. It must connect itself to the network (to the nearest local exchange), put a dial tone on line, answer with an appropriate signal (e.g. 2100 c/s in the international telephone call), ask for and reply by an identification code (if necessary), take care of all faults and exceptional states (the remote DTE is busy or out of order, an exchange in the path is overloaded and refuses further interconnections, a circuit is disconnected, etc.) and recover them. It follows from the fact that public nondata networks are modified for intelligent manual control from the subscriber site that these networks offer only a limited range of services.

As has been already mentioned, public data networks are planned, designed and built in order to improve services provided to data subscribers. These networks can be circuit-switched or packet-switched and in the latter case the datagram or the virtual circuit (call) are provided.

Relating to link establishment/releasing functions the call set-up time is much shorter (tens, maximally hundreds, of milliseconds), the network inspects the behaviour of all calling and called stations including data switching exchanges and quickly recovers prospective faults and failures. From the data subscriber viewpoint the public data network is a "black box" in contradistinction to nondata networks, the structure and actions of which are usually well known. In order to disburden a subscriber of most of the duties necessary for the link establishment and the link releasing, an appropriate sophisticated control element must be built in as an opposite to the DTE. Such an element is called the data circuit-termination equipment, abbreviated DCE, and takes care, inter alia, for creating data paths (physical or virtual, depending on the type of service). The DTE then only handshakes with its own DCE according to the rules specified for the interface between the DTE and the DCE (Figure 3.2). The main role of the DTE begins after the link or the call has been established, i.e. during the data transfer phase.

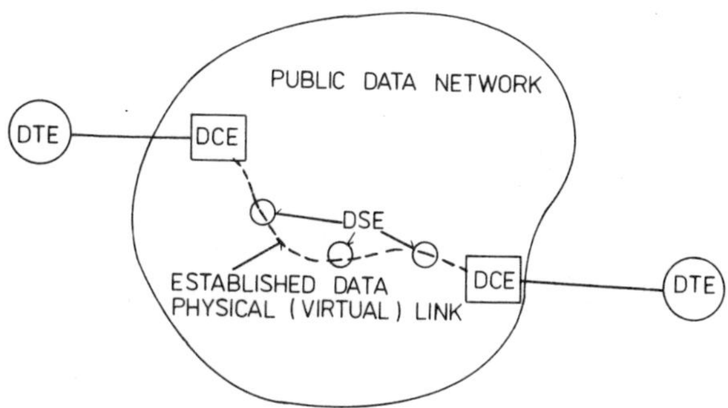

Figure 3.2 The interconnection between two DTEs over a public data network
DTE-data terminal equipment, DCE-data circuit-termination equipment, DSE-data switching exchange

Let us look at Figure 3.3. It follows from it that the DCE is responsible for the whole link establishment (and, indeed, the link releasing) operation. The calling DTE only requests the link (the called DTE either accepts a call or clears it), transmits the selection signals containing the address of the called DTE, and may also confirm the clearing signals from the DCE. In all cases it must permanently inform the DCE about its own state (e.g. ready, not ready, temporarily not ready). The DCE being an intercessor between the DTE and the network must accept the call request, form a link or a path with the called DTE via the corresponding remote DCE, and release it. Moreover, it is responsible, e.g. for call collision recovery (when the DTE receives the incoming call from the DCE in response to the call request, or when the DCE receives the call request from the DTE in response to the incoming call).

If the network provides for additional facilities such as called line identification, connection in progress, calling line identification (the last is not pictured in Figure 3.3), the DCE answers for their correct and successful courses.

Methods of link establishment/releasing function implemented in DTEs are influenced not only by public network services but also by time courses of network behaviour. All time-outs defined in the network with respect to the DTE (on the interface between the DTE and the DCE) must be considered when the establishment and releasing methods are designed or choosen. That is why the descriptions of interface handshaking procedures are mostly based on time diagrams.

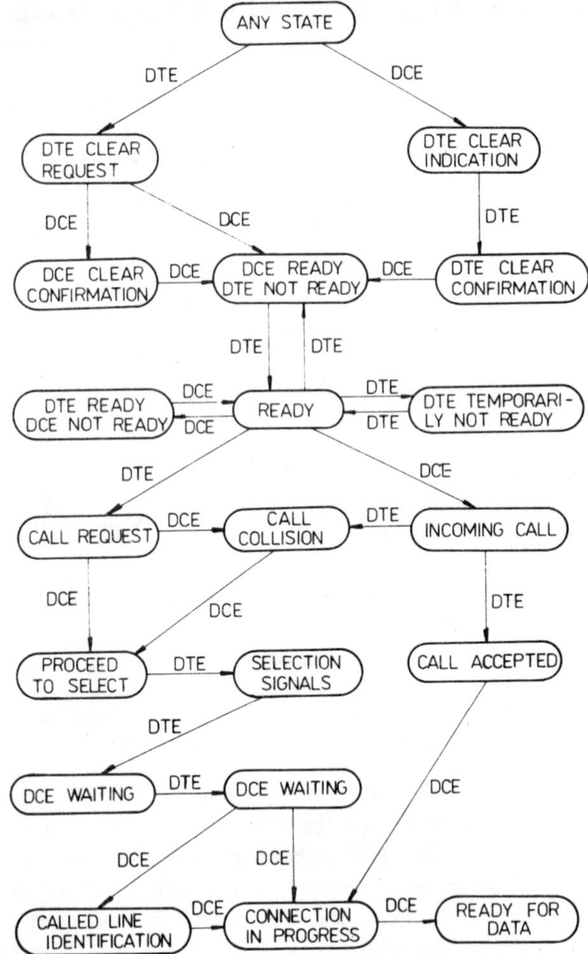

Figure 3.3 State diagram of link establishment/releasing procedures

3.1.4 Bibliographical notes

The transmission opening/terminating functions are implemented in almost all communication protocols (the transport protocol on datagram service is an exception, see e.g. the lettergram mode in [37]) while the link establishment/releasing functions are mostly left to the communication subnetwork (in higher level protocols) or to public networks (in particular in link level protocols). The latter case is due to PTTs or public network vendors and the corresponding procedures are ruled according to CCITT recommendations V.26, X.20/X.20 bis, X.21/X.21 bis [34], X.3, X.28 and X.29 [216], X.75 [217]. (The reader acquainted with the CCITT recommendations will realize that Figure 3.3 is taken from X.21 in modified form.) Those who want to study the procedures of call progress signalling in public telecommunication (non-data) networks more deeply are referred to the CCITT documents and also to national PTT standards and rules.

The analysis of link establishment/releasing and transmission opening/termination functions, most often concerning the verification of their procedures based on some formal models, is dealt with e.g. in [24, 56, 141, 159, 271]. Link establishment/releasing within the network architecture is explained in more details in [231].

3.2 Synchronization and Phasing

3.2.1 The synchronization problem

So far we have studied communication and its control by protocol without considering time. For example, we have assumed that the stations function quite naturally one after another. We have not dealt with the problem of how to achieve the state in which both stations (expressed for example by automata) work with the same speed. In this chapter we shall introduce a new variable, time, which we have so far not needed, although using time-out has been useful.

As soon as we begin pursuing the time course of activities controlled by some algorithm (procedure, protocol) we are up against processes. The general meaning of a process is a precisely defined time course of an activity, and if the process is controlled by an algorithm it is possible to describe it by the moments corresponding to each step (event). We ought to note that the processes which we use while programming multiprocessor systems are included in our definition of a process, although they have many more specific properties. However, since we shall not need them we shall stay at processes in general and shall consider their contents in relation to communication control.

Let us consider a procedure. It is defined by a set of commands and responses, rules for their use and exchange between stations, and, if need be, values of parameters (if they form part of the procedure). By means of this procedure we can recover certain situations in communication, i.e. certain communication functions. We shall describe the use of the procedure for two stations for instance by a table of functions of both stations (see, for example, Table 3.5 on page 125). Everything seems to be in order because we know how the stations react to commands and replies, but a "dispatcher" is necessary to follow both stations and give them instructions when to listen and when to work (transmit and execute). It is not possible, however, to apply the procedure to stations which can work self-containedly and cooperate without supervision. That is why also a time diagram must be plotted, according to which the procedure shall take its course. A procedure with a time table shall then become a process.

Let us now consider two processes without regard to their contents. The first process (say A) shall consist of steps A_1, A_2, A_3, etc., the second (B) is a sequence of steps B_1, B_2, B_3, ... We shall regard the steps as activities defined beforehand (remember the protocol phases, program instructions). It is not necessary for the step

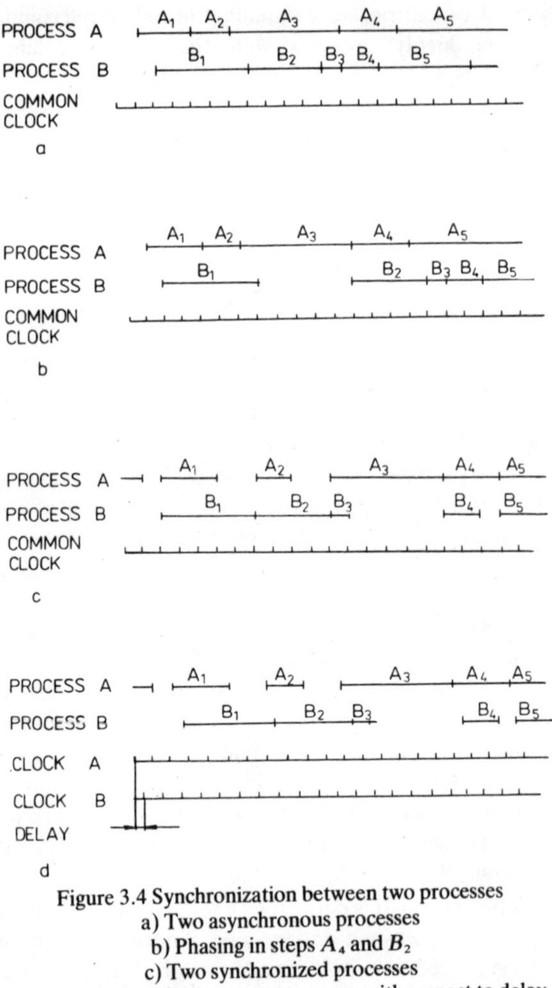

Figure 3.4 Synchronization between two processes
a) Two asynchronous processes
b) Phasing in steps A_4 and B_2
c) Two synchronized processes
d) Two synchronized remote processes with respect to delay

length of the process to be the same. The time course of both processes is shown in Figure 3.4a.

When both processes are performed self-containedly and are not coordinated in any way, i.e. neither the beginnings nor the ends of the steps of the processes are the same at the same instants, we call them asynchronous. Asynchronous processes can be performed not only in different stations, as in the case when two computers or processors communicate, but also in one multiprocessor computer, even when the operations of all the processors are controlled from a common clock, for the length of the steps need not be the same. We are, however, chiefly interested in fully asynchronous processes, taking place on different devices.

Now let us assume that one process (for instance B) needs the cooperation of another process (A), i.e. it needs to communicate with A. In particular, in step B_2 it needs to utilize the results of step A_4. From Figure 3.4a we can see that without certain measures being taken this is not possible because, at the time when step B_2 takes place, process A is still at step A_3 and cannot afford the necessary results to process B.

It is possible to achieve the cooperation of two asynchronous processes in two ways. Either the slower process is quickened or the quicker process is slowed down. Usually the quickening is not possible without interference with the structure of the process (we assume that the speed of the processes, which is controlled by internal clocks of the devices on which the processes are performed, cannot be influenced) and it is therefore only possible to slow down the quicker process, which is not difficult to accomplish. Slowing down can be realized only by interruption because of the speed of the clock being constant and that is, of course, very ineffective because overhead time is caused during which it is necessary to wait. An example of an interruption of process B and of phasing of step B_2 to the beginning of step A_4 is shown in Figure 3.4b.

We have used a new concept: phasing. By the phasing of two processes we shall understand making the beginnings (ends) of certain steps, determined beforehand, coincide, so that they will take place at the same instants. Between these moments the processes will remain asynchronous.

It is possible to apply the process of phasing to each step, and both processes can be phased with each other. If the beginnings (ends) of all the steps are phased, the asynchronous course of the processes shall become synchronous, more precisely synchronous in steps and both processes take their course at the same speed (Figure 3.4c).

As far as data processing processes are concerned, although in the literature only the synchronization of processes is discussed, for our purposes it is more advantageous to differentiate between synchronization and phasing in the sense of what has been mentioned above. We shall need it for controlling the operation of the communicating stations.

Let us return to the operation of two communicating stations. Contrary to the processes, the examples of which were given in Figures 3.4a to 3.4c, it is not possible to compare the processes which take place in remote stations according to a single time scale. The communication medium between stations is characterized, inter alia, by its delay due to propagation time, so that from the time when one station needs the cooperation of another station to the time when this cooperation takes place, a certain time interval passes. If we represented the course of both processes on a single time scale, the coincidence of the beginning of the steps would not be reached even with synchronous processes, but one process would be shifted in time in relation to the other by a constant value (Figure 3.4d). That makes the problem of synchronization and phasing in the case of processes communicating at a distance more complicated, and it is necessary to reckon with it henceforth.

In order to consider the delay originating in the course of the processes it is better to regard the synchronization as an activity which guarantees the performance of the steps of the processes in a certain time, decided on beforehand. In the case of two communicating stations the process executed by one station shall be synchronized with the process of the other station if it takes its course according to a time schedule set beforehand which is given by the course of the other process. It is not necessary, and not even possible, for both processes to take place at the same moments. From the technical viewpoint synchronization has a more narrow meaning, but that will be discussed in the next section.

One thing is quite clear: communication as the cooperation of processes taking place in remote stations needs the synchronization of both processes. From the protocol (procedure) viewpoint this means synchronizing the steps by the realization of the protocol (procedure); from the station viewpoint the state of their actions is synchronized. The same is true when two people communicate: they must also "synchronize" themselves while the actual synchronization is derived from the contents (semantics) of the exchanged news. In data communication controlled by protocol the semantics must be replaced by syntax, and that is the subject of the communication function of synchronization control.

3.2.2 Synchronization of processes

We can generalize the above idea of synchronization to phases, commands/ /responses, instructions, characters, and even bits. It is very important to determine the level of synchronization because solving the synchronization at one level does not necessarily lead to synchronization at another level. For example, processes which are synchronous in steps need not be synchronous in terms of instructions if the speed of the processors on which the processes take place are not the same. On the other hand two processes working at the same speed will, of course, be synchronous up to the level of instructions; but if they are built up of steps of different lengths, they will not be synchronous at the step level.

We shall speak of synchronization when, at the lowest level we are interested in, the speeds are the same. From the viewpoint of the macrostructure of communication control the level of commands and responses, i.e. the actions of the stations, will play an important role, so that both stations shall be synchronized when they work at the same speed and shall alternately exchange messages. Because of link control we shall want to know what speed is used at bit level (in a protocol which is bit-oriented) or at character level (in a character-oriented protocol), i.e. we shall be interested in bit or character synchronization.

Synchronization can be applied not only to completely asynchronous processes, as we have shown in the previous section, but also to processes which are mutually dependent and in which the subordinate process cannot work self-containedly. The first case is much more complicated because it must take care of independent functions, whereas in the second case one process is controlled by the other.

Processes which function self-containedly can be controlled either by a third process (centrally by the "dispatcher" we have spoken of) or by each other (in a decentralized manner). The decentralized control of synchronization can, however, lead to deadlocks: one process waits for the other and the other does the same, and if this situation is not resolved in a higher layer of the architecture neither process can continue in its activity. There exists a number of ways of preventing deadloks, we shall speak of one of them — a semaphore — in connection with the control of the synchronization of the sending and receiving communication processes.

Let us assume we have two stations: the sending station (S_1) can among other things send data blocks to the receiving station (S_2), which is also engaged by some activity of its own. Overhead time necessarily arises from interruption. Something must be done so that both stations can cooperate and overhead time is distributed as best as possible and burdens neither one nor the other station unduly. This means they must inform each other of their activity and control each other according to their own state and the state of their partner.

Let us, therefore, introduce a two-value variable B connected with sending and receiving data blocks and two operations on B: $P(B)$ subtracts one from a positive value of B (does not change a zero value), $V(B)$ on the other hand adds one to a zero value of B (not changing value one). If B reaches a zero value after applying $P(B)$, then the process which fulfils this operation must stop and wait. When the process applies operation $V(B)$ and B reaches value one, it can restart or continue in its activity.

At the beginning let $B = 1$. The sending station S_1 is preparing a data block for station S_2 and receiving station S_2 is occupied by other work (another process). After ending the process S_2 applies operation $P(B)$ to B which leads to a zero value of B, so that, according to the rules given above, S_2 must stop while the station S_1 can start the sending process and send the block. When transmission ends, value B is changed by operation $V(B)$ to one which means that it has to give over further activity to station S_2, but can be engaged by other activity if this does not require a common transmission medium. Hence station S_2 takes over a block, processes it, and again changes value B by the operation $P(B)$, which for station S_1 means that it can send a data block if it has been prepared. If not, it gives over activity to station S_2 by operation $V(B)$ on B.

Table 3.1 An example of process synchronization by means of semaphore

Sender (S_1)	Receiver (S_2)	Semaphore (B)
block preparing	process (S_2)	1
	$P(B)$	0
block sending		
$V(B)$	block receiving	1
	$P(B)$	0
$V(B)$	process (S_2)	1
⋮	⋮	

In Table 3.1 there is an example of the synchronization of processes in two stations utilizing a common transmission medium. Variable B acts as some form of semaphore: it shows when the communication medium is free to be utilized by one or the other process. Let us note that in this case we are mainly concerned with the division of activities between both stations which on one hand work on their own tasks and on the other cooperate.

The semaphore method is, of course, not as simple as we have shown in the example. Generally the semaphore is a multivalue variable and in many cases one semaphore is not sufficient. The number of a block is an example of a semaphore; others are the window size and other parameters of a protocol which we shall discuss in further chapters, not calling them so.

The synchronization (centralized or decentralized) of asynchronous processes shall be of use in protocols of higher layers of the architecture (e.g. on the level of process control). In lower layers, especially on the level of link protocol, one process is subordinate to another and the problem of synchronization of one station is solved by the other station.

3.2.3 Bit synchronization control

Let us consider bit synchronization, which is very important in order that the receiver can function well and that errors do not occur, as Figure 3.5 convinces us. The influence of transmitting properties evokes not only noise, but also distortion of the original digital signal. One such distorted signal at the input of the receiver is represented in the illustration. Using sampling pulses the receiver scrutinizes the received signal and decides if it is zero or one. The positions of the sampling pulses must, however, be in the centre of the characteristic intervals (Figure 3.5a), otherwise an incorrect decision is taken and error occurs (Figure 3.5b). This so-called technical synchronization consists in the keeping up of the same speed (frequency) and the same phase. Figure 3.6 shows the difference between periodic signals of different frequencies a) and of the same frequency and different phase b). In both cases the signals are not generally synchronized; only in the case when the signal coincides with the original one (except for possible channel propagation time), do we speak of full synchronism.

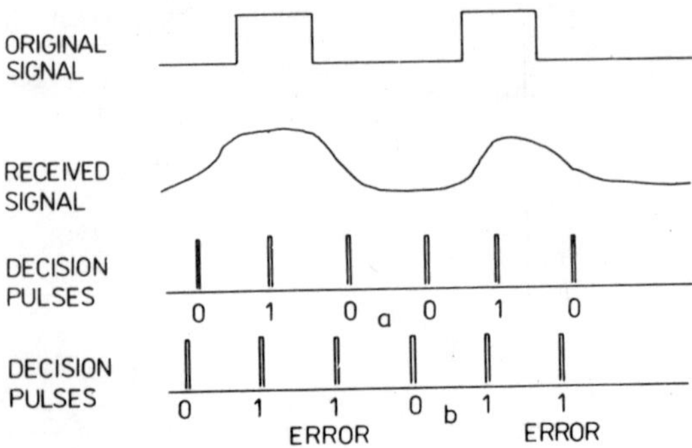

Figure 3.5 The error occurrence due to false synchrónization
a) Decision pulses at the centres of characteristic intervals
b) Decision pulses shifted

Although the protocols usually do not deal with the technical solution on the signal level, synchronization control is an exception as long as data are not transmitted over synchronous links (channels), as is now the usual case. Up-to-date data communication equipment (modems) has, on going from the speed of 1200 bit/s, its own synchronization circuits which establish and maintain data link synchronization without regard to data transmission and protocol control. That is why the problem of bit synchronization is not solved in some link protocols, e.g. in the DDCMP protocol. Should the protocol be universal it must be able to tackle even this communication function, as in the case of HDLC protocol which is able to control bit synchronization (although it assumes synchronous links).

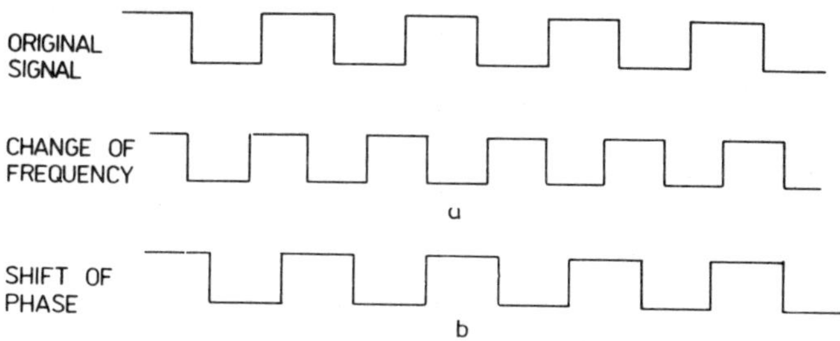

Figure 3.6 An example of the change of frequency (a) and of the shift of phase with the same frequency (b) in comparison with the original signal

It will not do any harm to state briefly a few fundamental principles of bit synchronization control as it is treated in protocols, especially link protocols, even though we shall not be concerned with circuity (readers can gain information on this subject from the literature mentioned in Section 3.2.5).

We should note that, of the two stations studied, one is a control station, at least as far as synchronization control is concerned. In principle it is necessary to differentiate between two cases: that of two stations which both have clock (in other words, both can work self-containedly but the task of the controlling station is to keep up the frequency and phase of the tributary station), and the case of stations of which only one has its own clock and the other utilizes the same clock. The first case is called a synchronous transmission and the second an asynchronous one.

In the case of a synchronous transmission the control station must take care of special synchronization information, according to which the tributary station corrects the rate of its clock. In the second case every bit is accompanied by a special synchronizing signal followed by the actual data or control bit. Hence the tributary receiving station using the synchronizing signal finds out the position of the bit or, more precisely, the centre of the characteristic interval and so enlarges the probability of a correct reception.

There also exists a third method, where both stations have their own clock, but the clock of the tributary station only function for a certain short time of a few bits. Therefore the clock of the tributary station need not be as precise as is necessary for a synchronous transmission because they are needed to keep up the frequency and phase for a short time only. This form of transmission is called start-stop: the clock in the tributary receiving station are started up by a start signal and after a synchronous transmission of a few bits a stop signal is transmitted to stop it and prepare the receiver for the next start signal.

Without regard to the manner of transmission for bit control synchronization it is necessary to decide about suitable synchronizing commands and also to take care of their transfer from the controlling station to the tributary one. It is necessary for the synchronizing commands to differ, in the case of an asynchronous transmission, from the bit that follows them (this can be an impulse of greater amplitude). In the case of a start-stop transmission the start and stop signals must differ (e.g. by opposite polarities). In the case of a synchronous transmission it should have a sufficient number of transitions (0 to 1 and 1 to 0), onto which the receiver can synchronize itself. In the last case (in a character-oriented protocol) special characters are chosen as, for example, the character SYN = 0110100 from ISO/CCITT code or sequences of bits (in the case of bit-oriented protocols) as, for example, the sequence 0101 followed by an arbitrary sequence of zeros and ones with at least 28 transitions (CCITT V.41).

A synchronizing command can be transferred by a special channel (if the stations are not at a great distance from each other and if such a channel is available), before data exchange and at intervals between data and command transmission, or piggybacked directly in commands and data. The last case can concern us only with regard to synchronous transmissions, and then it is necessary to ensure transitions often enough (in particular, data sequences of zeros or ones are not permitted). It suffices either to use a nonlinear code (see Section 3.4.4 where the odd parity is mentioned) or to put zeros into longer sequences of ones as the HDLC link protocol does, even though this is done primarily for code transparency (the zero sequence can be avoided by the NRZI coding).

To end this section let us mention the efficiency of different methods of synchronization control. Work on synchronous links without a solution of synchronization problems even in link protocol is most advantageous. Throughput is lessened least by synchronization through a special channel and then by deriving from transferred data, i.e. by a synchronous transmission. Asynchronous and start-stop transmission greatly increases overhead.

3.2.4 Phasing

Whereas bit synchronization is only the concern of link protocol and is not dealt with on higher layers of architecture, phasing (i.e. character, octet, word, block, letter, etc.) synchronization must be established and maintained in practice on all layers of architecture including the link layer.

Phasing methods can be derived or used straight from the separation of characters, octets, blocks, etc. in formats (see Chapter 2.5). If separating has been guaranteed in any way, it is sufficient to attend to the decoding and adjustment of the phase. That is why we shall not speak of the method of autophasing by use of comma-free code in this part, but shall pass straight to special phasing patterns, which are used most often.

As we have stated in the preceding section and in Chapter 2.5, a phasing pattern can appear only at the beginning of a character, block, etc. so that a wrong interpretation and thus an error should not occur. Further demands are made on the phasing pattern.

If a short phasing pattern is chosen (by which losses of throughput are reduced), it can happen that in some cases it must be used more than once, especially when the same pattern is also used for bit synchronization. In this case it is necessary to ensure that in the sequence of phasing patterns immediately following each other, there should be no other phasing patterns which could contain the original one. It is very easy to check this property. If a phasing pattern is given (as an example let us take the above mentioned synchronization character 0110100 from ISO/CCITT code), then let us form a sequence of two identical phasing patterns and let us leave out the first and last bit (in our example we get 110100011010). A sequence thus formed must not contain the original phasing pattern. If this happens then the receiving station could make a mistake because of transmission errors and may phase at a sequence shifted in phase and the whole block which follows would be received incorrectly.

Let us again show an example. The phasing pattern 011011 does not have the above stated property, as can easily be seen. If we repeat it a few times, e.g. twice (011011011011), and in the first three bits there occurs at least one error during transmission (e.g. 001011011011) the receiver takes for phasing the first six bits which have the same structure as the original phasing pattern (in our case they are the six bits beginning with the fourth bit, which means they are shifted three bits to the left). When this is not the precise position of the original phasing pattern, the whole following transmission is incorrect.

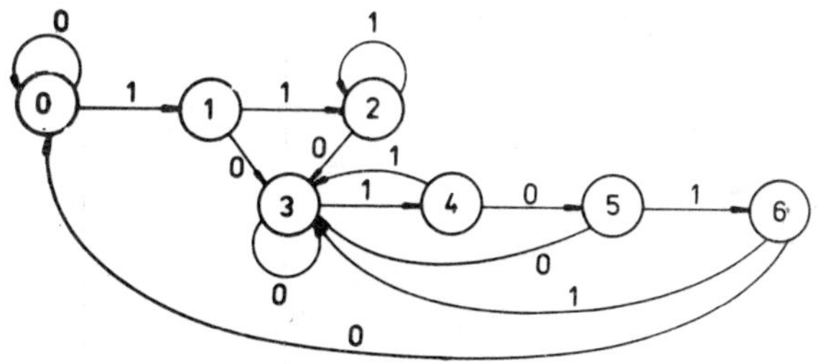

Figure 3.7 The state diagram of a phasing automaton

The next property of the phasing pattern is connected with its decoding and the establishment of the initial state of the receiving station. Let us imagine that the receiving station works as an automaton. An example of a state diagram of such an automaton with seven states is shown in Figure 3.7. The phasing pattern must be able to transfer the phasing automaton from any state to the initial state in a precise number of steps. Such a phasing pattern for the automaton in Figure 3.7 is 0010010100, which can be verified by applying this pattern gradually to different states of the automaton (Table 3.2). In all cases in the ninth bit of the phasing pattern the automaton will pass to the initial state regardless of which state it was in when the first bit of the phasing pattern was applied. The last, tenth, bit is a safeguard in case of any failure.

Finally the phasing pattern length must also be chosen appropriately. The greater the length, the smaller the probability that improper phasing may take place even

Table 3.2 State sequences of phasing automaton by different initial states

Initial state	Input (phasing word)									
	0	0	1	0	0	1	0	1	0	0
0	0	0	1	3	3	4	5	6	0	0
1	3	3	4	5	3	4	5	6	0	0
2	3	3	4	5	3	4	5	6	0	0
3	3	3	4	5	3	4	5	6	0	0
4	5	3	4	5	3	4	5	6	0	0
5	3	3	4	5	3	4	5	6	0	0
6	0	0	1	3	3	4	5	6	0	0

when errors occur. On the other hand throughput decreases and delay increases. The influence on protocol performance is also dependent on the communication mode: in a batch transmission when long blocks of a constant length are exchanged, it is not necessary for every block to be phased. Phasing is required for the first block or else after failure or stopping. Then even long phasing patterns do not burden the throughput unduly. That is the case of the link protocol according to CCITT V.41, which uses a 16-bit pattern for phasing (see Appendix B). On the other hand the HDLC link protocol chooses a short phasing pattern of 8 bits (flag in Appendix C), because of the possibility of exchanging small blocks of different lengths, where every block must be phased. It is even possible to use more phasing patterns according to the kind of transmission, i.e. DDCMP link protocol phases by 8 units for a serial start-strop transmission while for a serial synchronous transmission it phases by the octet 10010110 (for bit synchronization several transitions are necessary) and by an octet of all zeros for a parallel transmission. In protocols using codes with a small number of control characters phasing patterns must be helped by combinations of characters. A recommendation of CCITT (S.4) exists for expressing phasing and other commands by a combination of characters of the ITA 2 code.

3.2.5 Bibliographical notes

From the technical (transmission) viewpoint the problems of synchronization and phasing have been treated rather long ago in connection with other than data transmissions. We have not dealt with a detailed technical solution, but refer to relevant literature [26, 61, 65, 229, 281, 286]. Pouzin and Zimmermann [209] deal more widely and in an unconventional way with synchronization for computer networks. Synchronization and phasing is expounded in more detail in paper [95], from which we have also taken the example of a phasing automaton in Figure 3.7. In [61] synchronization in modems is solved, whereas a summary of the solution of synchronization and phasing in most link protocols is published in [227], and to a certain extent also in [281]. The first to deal with the problems of synchronizing general processes was Dijkstra [73], who also introduced the semaphore. Further methods of process synchronization are also presented in other special articles on programming; for communication control we shall only mention a more detailed application in [65] and a short comment in [91]. The reader is also referred to the interesting approach in [139].

We have supposed tacitly in the whole chapter that transmission delay is constant although positive, which in practice holds for cable links. On satellite links, however, delays fluctuate to a large degree and when the transmission rate is very high this fluctuation presents many problems. [172] tells about them and solves them in detail theoretically and practically.

Finally we cannot forget the synchronization of whole networks, not only data but digital networks in general. We have not mentioned these problems, for it is not the subject of this chapter or indeed of the book. For readers who are interested in a more detailed interpretation, let us call attention at least to two papers: [106] examines many synchronization techniques in circuit-and packet-switched data networks, whereas [46] deals with the synchronization in general digital networks.

3.3 Addressing

3.3.1 Addressing principles

In the literature concerning computer networks we can find terms such as addressing, naming, or identification, all of them reflecting the fact that several parts of computer networks are shared by many users and that some distinction must be made between these users. If every communicating pair of stations had a dedicated link within the network, then there would be no need for addressing (or there would be the need to distinguish only one station of the pair from the other). But the variety of computer networks and distributed data processing networks are designed to make use of the possibility of sharing various network resources, including communication resources. This is due to the fact that sharing allows a substantial rise in efficiency. But, as we have just mentioned, sharing requires addressing, especially in the case of communication.

Right at the outset we wish to point out that both the methods of addressing and the implementation of addressing are referred to as addressing. We find it suitable to differentiate clearly between the methods of addressing, and the implementation of addressing as one of the communication functions. The selection of the most appropriate method of addressing for the given network is one of the steps. The operations determined by the selected method are then to be implemented in the relevant network elements.

These operations vary from very simple ones (reading of the address) to very complicated ones. Of course, this depends on the addressing method, which also determines the type and the scope of services offered by the subnetwork (see Figure 3.8). Or vice versa: if we know what kind of addressing services are required, we can (when designing the network or the subnetwork) choose the most appropriate addressing method.

Thus addressing is closely related to the services offered by the subnetwork. It is also closely related to network topology, to network architecture, and to geographical distribution of network elements. Adressing reflects primarily the characteristics of

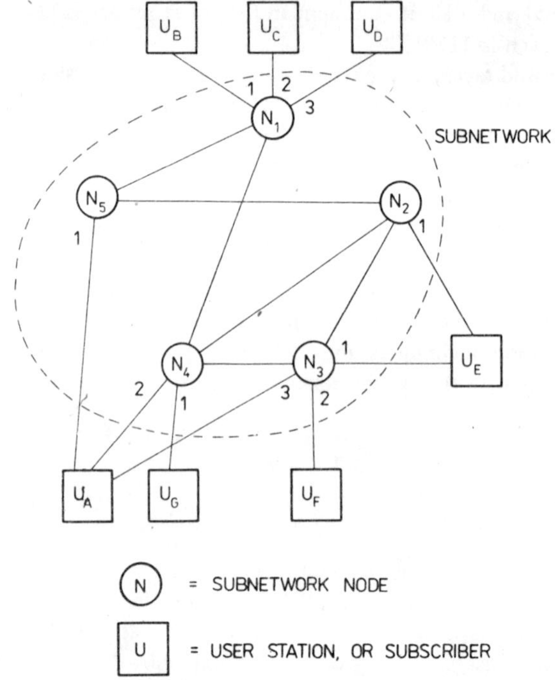

Figure 3.8 Scheme of a two-level network

various hierarchical structures which are present in networks and which contain various branch forms and occurrences of branching.

The address form can be structured according to the location of communicating stations within the network hierarchy. Figure 3.9 shows one example of such a structuring related to the packet switching network with host computers connected to it. The structure corresponds to the hierarchy: process — host computer (subscriber station) — node computer (the subnetwork node). The advantages of address structuring become evident in the course of implementation. To give an example, let us mention address transformation tables, which are used in conjunction with some addressing methods. Structuring allows for a substantial reduction of table sizes. Address structuring bears also upon branching and sharing of physical lines or logical links.

In the given example, two processes have communicated, each of them being situated in a different host computer. The communication was made possible by a packet switching network providing the necessary communication medium. In this

NODE COMPUTER ADDRESS	HOST COMPUTER ADDRESS	PROCESS ADDRESS

Figure 3.9 Example of address structuring

case, host computers belong to the generic class of subscribers, which contains all actual or prospective users of the subnetwork — the packet switching network. But there are other subnetworks, e.g. various VANs, which can support communication, and communication can also take place inside subnetworks. The communication control elements were defined and used in Part 2 of this book, which contained an explanation of the principles of communication control. When considering these principles in relation to addressing, they mean that each protocol station must be addressed, regardless of whether the protocol station is used in a user-oriented communication (through the subnetwork or in contacting the subnetwork) or in a system-oriented communication (inside the subnetwork). The system-oriented communication can serve the purpose of network operation management, or of networkwide communication control.

The communicating station can be labelled by numbers, by letters, or by both. The terms to be used are addressing and naming respectively. We do not use "numbering", because this term acquires quite a different meaning in communication control (see Chapter 3.4). Users and computers (sometimes) give preference to letters, while networks and systems prefer numbers.

The addressing methods can be classified according to the following criteria:

a) the number of hierarchical structure levels,
b) the kind of addressing services offered by a subnetwork,
c) the number of addressed stations,
d) the address allocation mode.

As mentioned before, the hierarchical structure can be found in the network topology (e.g. several subscribers connected to one node), or in the network architecture (e.g. several processes in one host computer connected to one transport station — see Appendix E). Examples of a two-level network and a three-level network will be presented in Section 3.3.2.

Physical and logical addressing can be distinguished according to the kind of addressing services offered by the subnetwork. In the case of physical addressing, the detailed location of the destination station must be known to the subscriber, because he is supposed to insert into the header not the name of the destination station (of the other subscriber), but the detailed structured address, such as in Figure 3.9.

In the case of logical addressing, only the name of the destination station (subscriber) is announced to the subnetwork, which searches the tables and, having found the physical address assigned to the name (to the logical address), transfers the relevant data block to the destination station determined by this address. This situation may be compared with the telephone network. The first case is equivalent to the common telephone network where each user or subscriber has a telephone directory at his disposal. In the second case, subscribers have lists of subscriber names, not directories. The subnetwork stores directories in its nodes and performs the transformations of names supplied by subscribers into numbers recognized by the subnetwork.

Sometimes hybrid addressing is used, i.e. the address contain both the name part and the physical address part.

The number of addressed stations can be as follows:

a) one — single addressing,

b) several } multiple addressing
c) all }

Single addressing prevails in existing computer networks; the potential advantages of multiple addressing methods have not been exploited yet. Multiple addressing methods will be described in Section 3.3.2.

The address allocation mode can be either static, or dynamic.

Addressing criteria and the corresponding addressing methods will all be explained in the following section.

3.3.2 Addressing methods

A survey of addressing methods is given in Figure 3.10. The methods were classified by means of criteria a) to d) from page 109.

The universal two-level network, depicted in Figure 3.8, will be used for the clarification of methods of logical and physical addressing.

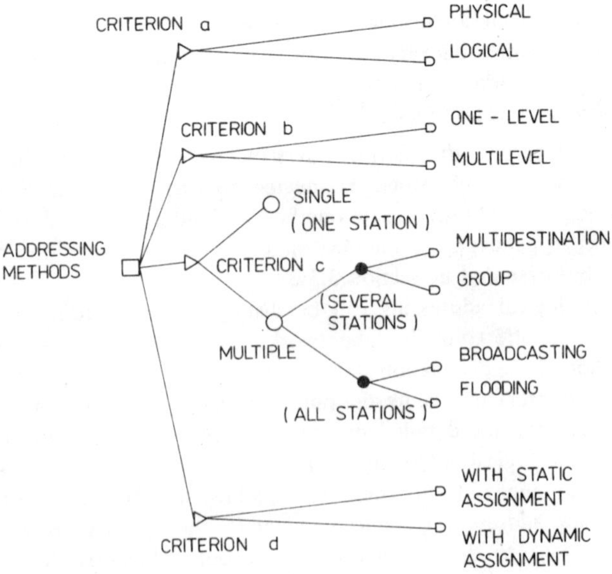

Figure 3.10 Overview of addressing methods

Physical addressing

The principle of physical addressing lies in an explicit specification of the destination station address. In the case of the two-level network it means that both the node number and the subscriber number have to be specified. The subscriber number may be replaced by the number of line connections. Taking the example from

Figure 3.8, the physical address of the subscriber station U_B has the form $\langle N_1 \rangle \langle 1 \rangle$. To be able to specify such an address, subscribers must have detailed knowledge of the internal structure of the subnetwork.

Physical addressing cannot be used in the case of multiple homing (i.e. when one subscriber is connected with more subnetwork nodes), which is a drawback, because multiple homing adds substantially to network reliability.

Multidestination addressing

We have already described single physical addressing. We wish to point out here that physical addressing is used also in the case of multidestination addressing, when physical addresses of several destination stations are announced explicitly to the subnetwork. The subscriber sends one block containing addresses mentioned to the subnetwork. The subnetwork will deliver the block to the destination stations indicated by physical addresses. This can be considered to be an extended addressing service. Of course, the price for this better service is a higher complexity of the subnetwork nodes. But, on the other hand, the higher complexity is offset by the reduction in the transmission overhead, i.e. by a higher throughput.

Logical addressing

In the network depicted in Figure 3.8, logical addresses are identical with labels of subscriber stations: U_A, U_B, U_C, etc. It is enough for subscribers to know the names (labels) of destination stations. Having searched through the tables which must be implemented somewhere in the subnetwork, the subnetwork will supply the physical addresses. The tables can be complete or partial, and may be implemented either in all nodes of the subnetwork or in several of them only. When the number of addresses is large and consequently the searching complicated, a data bank (either centralized or distributed) can be used for this purpose. One or several physical addresses can be assigned to one logical address.

Logical addressing enables destination subscribers to change their locations without changing their addresses, i.e. logical addresses. The physical addresses must be modified, of course, but this modification is invisible to subscribers. In computer networks, such features are very useful and are required by users.

Logical addressing permits the implementation of multiple homing. Subscriber stations U_A and U_E are examples of such a redundant way of connection to the subnetwork. Multiple homing represents the case when several physical addresses are assigned to one logical address. Of course, the assignment must be defined in the tables. For example, the table entries corresponding to the logical address U_A are: $\langle N_3 \rangle \langle 3 \rangle$, $\langle N_4 \rangle \langle 2 \rangle$, $\langle N_5 \rangle \langle 1 \rangle$. The selection of one of the three possibilities is made by the subnetwork, and is based on criteria like reliability (alternate route), optimization (routing), etc.

Group addressing

Group addressing can be considered to be multiple logical addressing. Several physical addresses are assigned to one logical address which becomes a group address in this case, hence the term group addressing. The sender must notify the subnetwork of the group address only. Taking an example from Figure 3.8, it can be, say, $KONF = U_C, U_E, U_G$. The subnetwork assigns the three logical addresses to *KONF*, and the corresponding physical addresses to U_C, U_E, and U_G, respectively. And, of course, it delivers the block to all the three destination stations. So the subnetwork must perform some additional operations which are not needed when simpler addressing methods are employed. Therefore the subnetwork nodes will be more complex.

Again this disadvantage is offset by better services offered to subscribers and by the ability to optimize performance by managing the traffic distribution.

Broadcast addressing

Both the principle and the method of sending one data block to all destination stations are referred to as broadcast addressing.

The principle will be dealt with first. Broadcast addressing, as well as multiple addressing, is useful for both the subscribers and the subnetwork itself. Internal needs of the subnetwork probably prevail, because they require the control or management messages to be sent by the subnetwork control centre to subscriber stations or to subnetwork nodes and, conversely, from subnetwork nodes to the control, or measuring, or routing centres. More about the network routing centre can be found in Chapter 3.6.

Of course, a block may be sent to all destination stations by sending it to one individual destination after the other, with each block containing one address only. But broadcast addressing is more efficient and involves lower overhead and a higher throughput. The block enters the subnetwork only once, carrying the logical address, say, *TO ALL*, which tells the subnetwork what to do. The two methods of broadcast addressing which we are going to describe determine the action taken by the network.

First of all we shall introduce one common element used in both methods. This is the so-called broadcast address, which has the form of an r-bit vector (r is the number of subnetwork nodes). All the bits corresponding to addressed destination stations are set to one in this vector. The broadcast address is generated by the node through which the block enters the subnetwork. This input node sends the copies of the block in all directions, providing each copy with the corresponding broadcast address. The contents of these addresses differ in the two methods. When a block copy is received by a subnetwork node, the bit corresponding to the node is reset. The block copy is then either transferred to a subscriber or passed on to another node. The block copy can be received by the node only on condition that the corresponding bit is set. In this way, multiple passing of blocks through nodes is precluded.

Now let us look at the method of broadcast addressing. A characteristic feature of this method is that any node and any (but not each) line connecting two nodes is entered by a block copy at most once. In order that this may take place, the input node must make some routing calculations and decisions resulting in the generation of broadcast addresses for outgoing copies such that each copy is assigned to a distinct subset of destination stations. The close co-operation with routing has already been mentioned. The corresponding method of routing is also called broadcast routing. A certain optimization can be achieved in this way.

Flooding addressing

This is the second method of broadcast addressing. Its algorithm is simpler, and consequently it is less exacting on subnetwork facilities. On the other hand it yields higher overhead.

According to the principle of flooding addressing, each node sends one copy of the received block in all directions (this was performed by the input node only in the previous method). Of course, the direction from which the block has arrived is excluded. In order to limit the number of blocks passing through the subnetwork, the block copy is allowed to enter any node only once. It is the broadcast address again that serves this purpose. The input node sets all bits in r-vectors for all outgoing copies in this method (except for the bit which corresponds to the input node, of course).

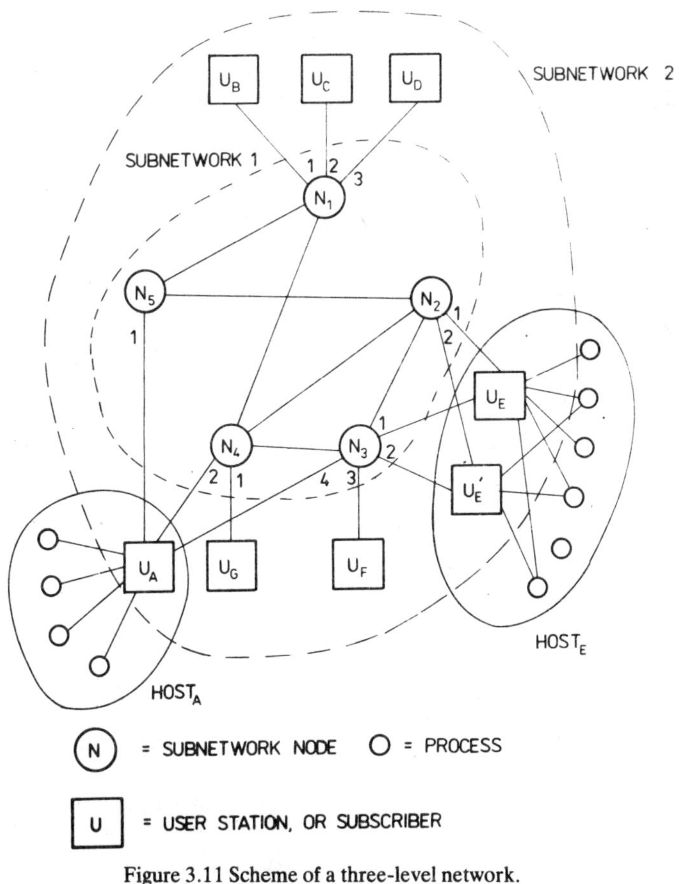

Figure 3.11 Scheme of a three-level network.
(HOST = HP)

There is also flooding routing (see Chapter 3.6) which is closely related to flooding addressing.

Though flooding addressing may at the first sight look very impractical and inefficient, that is not in fact the case. When analyzing its requirements of the network performance at the network design stage it may happen that flooding addressing is the best choice, and in several cases it proves to be better than the method of broadcast addressing.

Figure 3.11 shows an example of a three-level network. This network can be regarded as an extension of the two-level network, characterized by adding processes (in the third level of addressing) pertinent to host computer subscribers of subnetwork № one. This is the case of the previous U_A and U_E subscriber stations. Subnetwork № two can be seen in Figure 3.11. Multiplexing (HP_A and HP_E) and multiple homing (HP_E), both related processes, i.e. to the third level, are also shown in Figure 3.11.

Of course, there are other interpretations of the three-level network, and there are higher than three-level networks. But we could hardly derive further addressing principles from them and therefore they will not be treated here.

The processes taking place in computers are not of the same type. There are system processes which are assumed to communicate more often than user processes do, to give just one example. Therefore it is convenient to distinguish between processes in addressing, too.

The reason for this differentiation lies in an effort to make better use of the virtual communication channel used for the communication of remote processes. In principle, such a channel is created by one basic communication element. This means that it contains the protocol stations which must have buffers reserved for state variables. If such a channel (or the corresponding protocol station) is assigned permanently to a process with occasional communication requirements (e.g. once per hour), the resources of such a channel are not exploited efficiently. Though this problem is to be solved by buffer management primarily, nevertheless it is reflected in addressing too.

The situation mentioned above may be handled by dynamic allocation of buffers to protocol stations. The corresponding scheme related to addressing is shown in Figure 3.12, where we can find the so-called ports representing the permanent protocol stations (end of virtual channels). R ports are to be assigned dynamically to M processes, $M > R$. The processes are temporary, i.e. they do not communicate (are not called) often. There is one special process, labelled ALC and called the allocation process, which is responsible for the dynamic allocation. All requests for communication with any of the M temporary processes go to the ALC process that allocates a free port (if available) to the addressed M process, or refuses to do so (if there is no free port at the time). The ALC process can inform the sender that there is already a free port (after some of the ports have been released).

What we are interested in now is the structure of addresses reflecting the above situation. There will be a modification in the process address subfield which involves dividing this subfield into two parts: into a process number and into a port number (see Appendix E).

Another demand for address transformation arises in connection with processes. This transformation is based on differences between the subnetwork and the subscribers. Numbers and very short address codes are preferred in the communication subnetwork, this being dictated primarily by efficiency. Users, and for historical reasons also computers, prefer names, not necessarily the shortest ones. Because users and computers are used to the local naming, which differs from that required by the subnetwork, address transformation is a feasible answer to this discrepancy. Such a transformation is also included in the addressing communication function, which can be implemented elsewhere (for an example, see Appendix E).

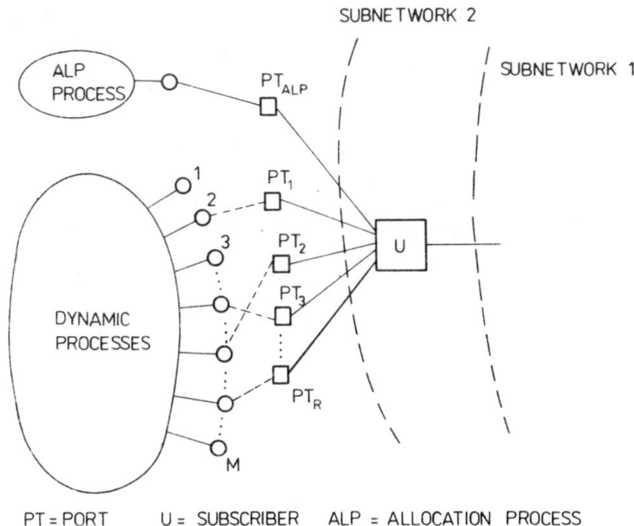

Figure 3.12 To dynamic allocation of ports to processes

As far as the relation of addressing and other communication functions is concerned, addressing is very closely related to routing, and also to multiplexing and sharing. We have also shown its relation to buffer allocation and management (if this is to be considered a communication function).

As we can see, in some cases it is very difficult to distinguish between addressing and routing. Therefore it might be useful to draw attention to the root of the difference. Operations connected with address generation and identification are assigned mostly to the addressing communication function, whereas activities resulting in finding another block route (and the corresponding address of the neighboring node, of course) form the basis of routing.

3.3.3 Bibliographical notes

Although there are many papers and documents (most of them describing either some networks or network design) dealing with addressing as an independent topic, the authors of this book know only of two papers devoted entirely or prevailingly to addressing, namely those of McQuillan and Pouzin [154, 209].

Among the others the following can be recommended: [6, 51, 65, 86, 91, 157, 208].

3.4 Error Control

3.4.1 Errors and their influence

In protocol performance error-free transmission is provided by the accuracy component which is expressed by error rate, or more precisely residual error rate, RER, measured by the ratio of the number of bits (characters) transmitted and delivered with error to the total number of transmitted bits (characters). Hence the requirement of introducing error control is given by the necessity of a certain accuracy of delivered data even over noisy links and is expressed quantitatively by the residual error rate.

By accuracy we understand above all the data being delivered to sink in the form in which the source has sent them. An error then occurs if, when we compare the sent and received data, differences come to light. It is not important whether the differences are in one or several bits in the same position, or even if all the bits of the message are different. (In the last case such an error would not matter because it would suffice to invert the received bit sequence and an error-free data message would be gained, but the receiver usually does not know about this.) Accuracy understood in this way means, however, that both sequences (sent and received) have the same length. In practice it may, however, happen that, due to the influence of noise in the transmission medium, some bits creep into the transmitted message, or on the other hand, some bits disappear. Then it is impossible to compare the sent and

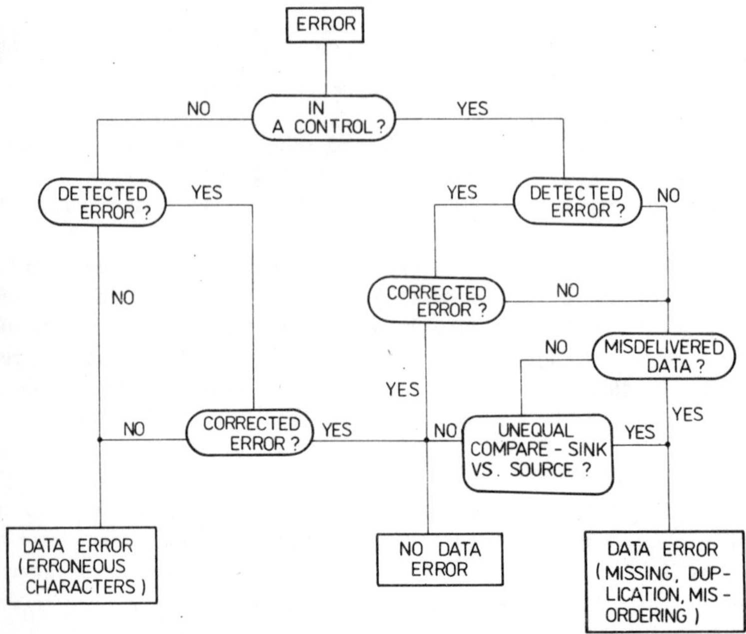

Figure 3.13 Types of error occurrence

received messages because their lengths are not the same, and usually the whole message is regarded as erroneous.

If the message is divided into blocks (which, as we shall see later on, is essential for control purposes) the residual error rate can also be expressed by the ratio of the number of blocks delivered with errors to the total number of transmitted blocks (block error rate). The block shall be regarded as transferred error-free if it is identical with the sent block and the message shall be transferred error-free if all the blocks it contains are received error-free. As a loss or embedding of bits can take place, so a loss or duplication of blocks can take place, which is again the result of noise or failures in the transmitting media, but can also be influenced by certain error control methods. We shall return to this later.

It is possible on a control level higher than the link protocol level that data message blocks, although they have been transmitted in the order in which the message is formed, do not arrive in this order (they have been shuffled). If a datagram service is concerned, which does not guarantee that the blocks are received in the correct order, then this phenomenon does not mean an error. If, however, the protocol guarantee a virtual link service then block shuffling is regarded as an erroneously transferred message even if the blocks have been correctly received.

Finally, we cannot disregard the case in which the transmitted data do not reach their addressee in the time given beforehand, e.g. because of an address error or an overload or some other failure of the transmission system. That is then quite naturally characterized as a loss of block or message and is hence regarded as an error.

All studied cases of error occurrence are shown in Figure 3.13.

3.4.2 Error control function

If we use communication functions to describe communication control we can also consider error control from this point of view. As has been stated in Part 2 error control is a communication function which keeps the values of residual error rate within given limits (below a given limit), even against noise, failure, interruption, distortion and other influences which are indivisible parts of a real transmission process.

In contradistinction to communication functions being active outside an actual data transfer phase, error control accompanies data transfer and data exchange. In the transfer phase, however, error control function does not act on its own: other functions take part, e.g. flow control. It is necessary to consider this fact when choosing the error control mechanism and designing the protocol.

We have called the part of the protocol which controls communication in some phase a procedure. Hence error control together with flow control is realized by the error control and flow control procedures, and these comprise part of a chain of procedures, which forms the protocol. In this chapter we are only going to deal with error control and the appropriate procedures for its realization; flow control is the subject of the next chapter.

The error control procedure (like the protocol) is specified by a set of commands and responses, their formats and data formats, the rules for their exchange, and the parameter values. In what follows we shall not deal with command, response, and data formats in detail because it is possible with all these to use the same mechanism for error control and flow control. For formats in general, see more in Chapter 2.5. Individual methods or error control will be characterized by the rules for exchanging commands and responses and perhaps by parameter values.

Here it is necessary to note, in connection with procedures and phases, the possibility of a further decomposition of the transfer phase from the viewpoint of error control. Some methods of error control operate with the acknowledgement of transferred blocks, i.e. after blocks are accepted and evaluated the acknowledgment process takes place. For simplicity the phase of exchanging data proper and of exchanging acknowledgement commands are differentiated between and the error control function is sometimes decomposed into the data exchange function and the acknowledgment function. From the method viewpoint this approach is justified because the acknowledging scheme is not always directly dependent on the data exchange method. We shall deal with the acknowledging system separately, if only for the reason that it can also be used for flow control. We regard acknowledgment as an integral part of error control, and so it is included in the error control function in this book.

In some protocol descriptions the occurrence of data errors is regarded as an exceptional state and the system's subsequent function is called exceptional states solution or recovery control after such a state. Since, however, we consider error occurrence a quite normal situation which is registered and solved by error control, we shall not refer to the correction of errors as recovery but as a part of the error control procedure.

3.4.3 Fundamental error control methods

The basis of data transmission error control is as follows. An n-bit long block is formed which is processed at the receiving side intact. The block consists of two parts: the information or data part (k bits which carry data) and the error control part $m = n - k$ check bits long. In terms of format description the information part is a data field and the error control part mostly a trailer; a header is not needed for the time being.

The error control part of the block is formed on the basis of the information part according to a coding algorithm determined beforehand. At the receiving side the same algorithm is used to find out if the bits of the error control part agree with the bits of the information part. According to the kind of code in use disagreement either shows that an error exists or enables the position of the erroneous bit to be found; if binary bit symbols are concerned, it is sufficient to invert the bit transmitted with error at the determined place. Thus the codes in use are divided into error-detecting codes (intended only for the detection of the presence of errors) and error-correcting codes (besides detecting errors, their position can also be found); both codes together are called error detecting-correcting codes.

According to the fundamental result of information theory (coding theorem) in certain circumstances encoding is possible for which the resulting error probability (residual error rate) is arbitrarily small for a non-zero block coding rate BCR $= k/n$.

The smaller the residual error rate we require, the longer the blocks which must be encoded. This makes decoding more complicated so a large receiving buffer capacity is needed. That is why methods have been and still are being looked for, which, although not as effective as demanded by theory, will be applicable in practice.

The error control procedure using correction codes — abbreviated FEC (Forward Error Control) — has been developed, thanks to the discovery of many suitable codes for correcting not only independent errors but even error bursts occurring in real channels. Thus besides traditional Hamming and cyclic (e.g. Bose—Chaudhury—Hocquenghem or BCH) codes, Fire, burst-trapping, Reed—Muller, and Reed—Solomon codes have been used recently for correcting individual errors as well as bursts of errors. Of course, the FEC method still has a disadvantage, i.e. the impossibility of achieving an acceptable block coding rate for the limited block length because decoding is difficult and a large storage capacity is necessary. No doubt the FEC method keeps up the information rate k/n without regard to the channel error rate, but with an increasing channel error rate RER also increases so that the use of this method is limited to a narrow class of channels. The method is nevertheless not only used on radio channels but has lately also started asserting itself on satellite links where a large transmission delay precludes the use of other methods.

Even such simple error control methods as fixed block repetition and majority decoding (e.g. for triple transmission of the same block a bit is supposed to be transmitted correctly if, after passing through a noise channel, it appears at least twice) belong to the FEC method. The method concerned is, in fact, a very uneconomical one, affording a low information rate, but it is very simple and easy to apply.

A much more effective and simple method is the use of error-detecting codes. Table 3.3 convinces us of how the number of check bits grows and the information rate decreases with the number of corrigible and detectable errors. Even for such a short information field (in Table 3.3 it is formed of 7 bits) using the correction code is uneconomical from triple errors onwards, whereas the same number of check bits is necessary for the detection of as many as 6 errors.

Table 3.3 Check bits needet to correct and detect t and less errors for data field lenght $k = 7$

t	Error correction		Error detection	
	number of check bits	BCR	number of check bits	BCR
1	4	0,64	1	0,88
2	8	0,47	4	0,64
3	11	0,39	5	0,58
4	18	0,28	8	0,47
5	20	0,26	9	0,44
6	25	0,22	11	0,39

Error-detecting codes can be used for error control only to a limited extent, because the aim is not only to find the presence of an error but also to correct it. It is nevertheless sometimes sufficient to detect the error and ensure its correction in some other way (e.g. later during data processing). We shall revert to this subject later in connection with feedback error control procedures.

3.4.4 Error-detecting codes

Error-correcting and detecting codes can be considered from different standpoints. Systematic linear codes are used most. These are codes for which the information part can always be separated from the control part (the format of block mentioned earlier is an example of a systematic code) and, moreover, check bits are linearly dependent on information bits. Hamming codes and cyclic codes are systematic linear codes. The simplest example is the simple parity code with an arbitrary number of information bits and one check bit, the value of which is chosen so that the number of ones in the whole block is even. This code is very favourable for error detection: it detects all odd numbers of errors. It cannot be used on its own for error control for transmission over noise channels, because it does not yield an acceptable residual error rate.

The opposite of linear codes are nonlinear codes, which are not used so often because they have no better properties than corresponding linear codes. The only application of nonlinear codes is their use in synchronization control. During synchronous transmission when the information for receiver control is gained from the transmitted signal, no signal which does not contain any transition 0—1 or 1—0 may occur. A signal carrying only zero bits is a signal of this kind. It can occur in a linear code, whereas a nonlinear code ensures the occurrence of at least one transit and thus also the possibility of deriving the synchronization information. As an example we mention the simple nonlinear parity code, where the number of ones as information bits is completed by the check bit to an odd number.

Codes of the type "a-out-of-n" belong to the category of nonsystematic codes. In them all n-long blocks have precisely a ones. For error detection the codes "2-out-of-5", "3-out-of-7", "4-out-of-8", twice "1-out-of-4", etc. are used. As far as detection capability is concerned, nonsystematic codes usually give larger error detecting capability than systematic codes with the same block length n, though at the cost of a lower information rate which, for nonsystematic codes, is equal to the binary logarithm of all different blocks divided by the block length n. Thus, for instance, for the "2-out-of-5" code the total number of different blocks is $\binom{5}{2} = 10$, so that BCR is $\log_2 10/5 = 0{,}664$. On the other hand for the simple parity code of block length 5, BCR = 0.8, while the ratio of undetectable errors to the number of all possible error combinations is 0.29 for the first and 0.48 for the second code.

We have mentioned the detecting capability of a code which is a further characteristic of error-detecting and correcting codes such as RER. Detecting capability can be defined by the probability that an error shall occur during transmission of a block over a certain noisy channel and shall not be detected at the receiver side (probability measure), or by the ratio of the undetectable error combinations to the number of all possible error combinations (combinatoric measure). Thus, for instance, for systematic codes with m check bits the probability of undetected errors during transmission over a binary symmetric channel is smaller than 2^{-m}, for cyclic codes the proportion of the number of undetected m-long error bursts to all error bursts of the same length is equal to $2^{-(m-1)}$, and for longer bursts this ratio decreases to one half.

For error control by error-detecting codes, we have on the one hand codes with longer blocks, and on the other hand codes that allow easy encoding and decoding. Cyclic and iterative codes belong to the latter group.

Cyclic codes form a wide class characterized by the property that every cyclic transition of an encoded block is also part of the code. This property permits cyclic codes to be studied with the use of polynomial algebra and every cyclic code to be defined by a generating polynomial of order m, where m is the number of check bits. Encoding the data field is done by dividing this data block, expressed as a polynomial, by just the generating polynomial. The check field is given by the remainder after division converted back into a sequence of zero and one bits. Decoding is also simple: the received block is again divided by the generating polynomial and the occurrence of a detected error is determined by the fact that the remainder is not zero (if it is zero then either an error has not occurred or there is an undetected error). Encoding and decoding of cyclic codes is done to great advantage by hardware (shift register with feedbacks). A software solution is more difficult and therefore further methods of encoding and decoding and new codes are sought.

Let us show encoding and decoding on cyclic codes on a simple example. The data field is e.g. the character 0001011 of the ISO/CCITT code. The character polynomial X^3+X+1 corresponding to the binary character chosen will be coded by means of the generating polynomial $X+1$.

First of all the character polynomial is multiplied by X^m (in our example $m=1$) in order to shift all character binary digits m places to the left (to add the zero sequence of length m on the right side):

$$(X^3+X+1)\cdot X = X^4+X^2+X$$

The result is then divided in modulo 2 algebra where addition and substraction is the same and $X^r+X^r=0$ for all r, by the generating polynomial:

$$\begin{array}{l}
X^4 \quad + \quad X^2+X : X+1 = X^3+X^2+1 \\
\underline{X^4+X^3} \\
0 \ +X^3+X^2 \\
\quad\ \ \underline{X^3+X^2} \\
\quad\ \ 0 \ +0 \ +X \\
\qquad\qquad\quad \underline{X+ \quad 1} \\
\qquad\qquad\quad 0+ \quad 1 \text{ remainder}
\end{array}$$

The remainder is directly the check polynomial (1 in our case) and after adding it to the character polynomial multiplied by X^m wè get the encoded character polynomial $X^4 + X^2 + X + 1$ which corresponds in binary to 00010111.

Note that in our example the check bit is an even parity so that the linear parity code is also cyclic and can be generated by the polynomial $X+1$.

Now suppose three errors (in the 1st, 3rs and 4th places) occurred in the encoded character during a transmission. The decoder thus receives 10100111 corresponding to $X^7 + X^5 + X^2 + X + 1$ and divides it again by $X+1$:

$$
\begin{array}{l}
X^7 \quad + \quad X^5+X^2+X+1 : X+1=X^6+X^5+X \\
\underline{X^7+X^6} \\
0 \ +X^6+X^5 \\
\quad \underline{X^6+X^5} \\
\quad 0 \ +0 \ +X^2 \\
\qquad \underline{X^2+X} \\
\qquad 0 \ +0 \ +1 \quad \text{remainder}
\end{array}
$$

The nonzero remainder indicates the error occurrence.

The zero remainder can be achieved even if a detected error occurs but it must be unique, known in advanced and different from the remainder in the case of no or undetected error. This may be useful for synchronization, phasing and other control purposes. Such a modification is the result of an inversion of some block fields (control, check, phasing, etc.) before or during encoding and/or decoding. We lay accent on it because sometimes the same generating polynomial need not yet guarantee the same error control procedure (see e.g. the link protocols CCITT V.41 and HDLC or LAP of X.25 in the Appendices A and C or D, respectively, which are not fully compatible with respect to the error control).

Cyclic code parameters are the number of error control bits m (degree of generating polynomial) and the maximum block length n at which the code does not lose its detection properties. If we do not know the block length beforehand, then there is an advantage in choosing a cyclic code with a very large n. Surpassing n means a considerable deterioration of error detecting capability.

In Table 3.4 some cyclic codes used for error control in different protocols (most often link protocols) are shown. Every cyclic code is given by its generating polynomial and hence also by the number of check bits (m), maximum block length n, and block coding rate BCR. The table is supplemented by the names of codes, the detection capabilities, and the firm or standards organization which has used it.

The second class of detection codes is iterative codes. Their name follows from the fact that two or more codes (same or different) are in turn applied to a single data field. Most often it is a case of double iteration and a simple parity code (linear or nonlinear). Data bits are arranged in a matrix with a rows and b columns so that

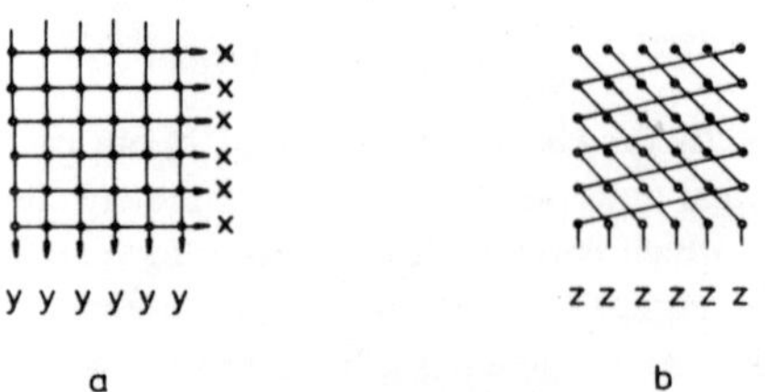

Figure 3.14 An example of forming an iterative code
a) Double iteration (character-x and block-y parity checks)
b) Spiral parity (z)

Table 3.4 Most commonly used cyclic error-detecting codes

Generating polynomial	Block length bits	BCR	Code type	Detecting capability	Application
X^6+X^5+1	2^6-1	0,9	BCH Hamming	single and double errors; bursts up to 6 bits; 96,9 % bursts of 7 bits; 98,44 % longer bursts	IBM
$X^{12}+X^7+$ $+X+1$	2^6-1	0,8	Fire	odd number of errors; double errors; bursts up to 12 bits; 2 bursts of total length up to 7 bits; 99,95 % bursts of 13 bits; 99,98 % longer bursts	TESLA
$X^{12}+X^{10}+$ $+X^8+X^5+$ $+X^3+1$	2^9-1	0,98	Fire Abramson	odd number of errors; double errors; 2 pairs of adjacent errors; bursts up 12 bits; 99,95 % bursts of 13 bits; 99,98 % longer bursts	RFT
$X^{12}+X^{11}+$ $+X^3+X^2+$ $+X+1$	$2^{11}-1$	0,994	Hamming Abramson	odd number of errors; double errors; 2 pairs of adjacent errors; bursts up to 12 bits; 99,95 % bursts of 13 bits; 99,98 % longer bursts	IBM
$X^{16}+X^{12}+$ $+X^5+1$	$2^{15}-1$	0,9995	Hamming Abramson	odd number of errors; double errors; 2 pairs of adjacent errors; bursts up to 16 bits; 99,997 % bursts of 17 bits; 99,998 % longer bursts	CCITT
$X^{16}+X^{15}+$ $+X^2+1$	$2^{15}-1$	0,9995	Hamming Abramson	odd number of errors; double errors; 2 pairs of adjacent errors; bursts up to 16 bits; 99,998 % longer bursts	IBM
$X^{20}+X^{17}+$ $+X^6+1$	$2^{17}-1$	0,9998	Fire Abramson	odd number of errors; double errors; 2 pairs of adjacent errors; bursts up to 20 bits; 99,9998 % bursts of 21 bits; 99,9999 % longer bursts	ROBOTRON

$k=ab$, and to each row and column a check bit is added to make the number of ones even or odd so that $n=(a+1)(b+1)$ (Figure 3.14a). The maximum BCR is achieved for $a=b$; nevertheless, in practice, a character length (in bits), e.g. $b=7$, is chosen for b, so that the encoding is as simple as possible.

The information rate of an iterative code does not reach the information rate of a cyclic code, but its error detecting capabilities are high, e.g. the iterative code detects, apart from all odd numbers of errors and double errors, also all bursts up to the length $b+1$ and a large percentage of longer bursts.

It is possible to increase the error detecting capability of an iterative code by increasing the number of iterations (data bits are arranged in a three-dimensional, four-dimentional, etc., formation and errors are checked in all dimensions), by using a more complex code than a simple parity code, or by creating another error detecting character of length b by means of so-called spiral parity (Figure 3.14b).

In conclusion of this section it may be said that error-detecting codes used at present (cyclic, iterative and others which cannot be discussed in detail due to lack of space) are, from the viewpoint of error detecting capability, nearly equivalent and can be used for transmission even over very noisy channels. A more conclusive criterion for the choice of a code today is the complexity of encoding and decoding and the compatibility of protocols. That is why only very few types of error-correcting and detecting codes are encountered in practice. The importance of error-detecting codes grows, however, in the case when feedback is used for error control, which will be the subject of the following section.

3.4.5 Utilization of feedback

If a backward channel is available, besides the forward channel between the sending and receiving stations, its existence affords the same if not a greater error control efficiency that can, moreover, be achieved by more simple and cheaper means than with the FEC method. All error detection methods utilizing a backward channel in some way are called feedback methods. In contradistinction to the FEC method, their common property is that, with the increasing error rate of a forward channel, the block coding rate BCR and thus also the throughput decreases, but the residual error rate does not change. That means that feedback methods are suitable wherever it is not possible to define the channel error rate in use well beforehand while demands are made for an error-free transmission.

Feedback error control methods belong to the oldest adaptive methods. They are adaptable to changing link properties and can keep the specified error rate within given limits. They are therefore given preference over FEC methods wherever possible (see the restriction recalled in Section 3.4.3).

Feedback methods can best be classified according to the decision position (note that with an FEC method the decision is always on the receiving station side) as follows:

a) decision feedback (decision at receiving side end — Figure 3.15a),
b) information feedback (decision at sending side end — Figure 3.15b),
c) combined feedback (decision at both sides — Figure 3.15c).

Let us study the individual feedback methods in more detail. Decision feedback is based on a decision at the receiver (e.g. on a detection code, link state, signal distortion basis) whether an error has occurred or not. In the first case the receiving station demands block repetition, in the second it asks for the next block to be sent (if the sending side is prepared). Data blocks are transmitted over a forward channel, whereas commands from the receiving station are transmitted on a backward channel. This method is also called the automatic request for repetition method, ARQ for short.

Hence the ARQ method needs a decision criterion, according to which the receiving station requests repetition or continuation of transmission (most often the detection code is the one concerned) and, furthermore, at least two commands, one for block rejection and a request for repetition (REJ), the second for a continuation of transmission (ACC). In Table 3.5 there is an example of part of an error control procedure using ARQ, where data blocks (trailer included) are denoted by the abbreviation BCK and for better understanding individual rows are accompanied by a commentary with function description.

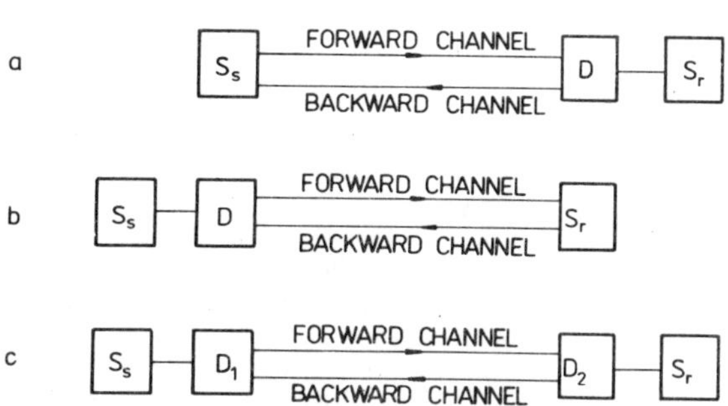

Figure 3.15 Types of feedback methods (S_s — sending station, S_r — receiving station, D — decision)
a) decision feedback (ARQ)
b) information feedback (echo-check, loop-check)
c) compound (hybrid) feedback

Table 3.5 Example of an ARQ procedure

Station S_1 (sending)	Station S_2 (receiving)	Notes
BCK		block 1 has been sent
	ACC	block 1 has been received and S_2 asks for a new block
BCK		block 2 has been sent
	REJ	after an error detection S_2 requests a repetition
BCK		repetition of block 2
	ACC	reception of block 2
BCK		block 3 has been sent
	ACC	reception of block 3

Information feedback requires activity on the part of the sending station which decides whether the transmitted block shall be repeated or the subsequent block shall be transmitted. The sending station can again utilize a few decision criteria: either the block received over the backward channel from the receiving station is compared with the earlier transferred block still in its buffer (echo-check), or both stations have an agreed error-detecting code but the corresponding check field BCC is transmitted over the backward channel and the sending station then compares it with its check field BCC (loop-check). Since in both cases the receiving station does not know whether the received block is error free or not, it must always keep it in the buffer and wait for a command from the sending station over the forward channel, saying if the block has been repeated or if it is the next transmitted block.

We can again demonstrate an example of information feedback in a table (Table 3.6). This table shows both decision alternatives (the case of transmitting only the check field BCC is shown in brackets), a repeated block declaration is denoted by the prefix RPT.

Table 3.6 Example of an echo-check procedure

Station S_1 (sending)	Station S_2 (receiving)	Notes
BCK		block 1 has been sent
	BCK (BCC)	block 1 (or its BCC) is sent back to S_1 for a comparison
BCK		block 2 has been sent
	BCK (BCC)	block 2 (BCC) is sent back to S_1
RPT BCK		after an error has been detected,block 2 is retransmitted
	BCK (BCC)	block 2 (BCC) is sent back to S_1
BCK		no error has been detected, so block 3 is transmitted
	BCK (BCC)	block 3 (BCC) is sent back to S_1

We shall not analyze both feedback methods here in order to reach a comparison of them. A rough analysis is insufficient and for a more detailed one the exact conditions must be determined, particularly the kind of channels and their transmission properties. The chief difference, as we have already said, is in the position of the decision term: in the case of decision feedback greater demands are made on the receiving station, while information feedback requires a more complex sending station. Information feedback usually also requires a wider band backward channel yeilding greater transmission rate (either the whole block or the check field are transmitted over it), data are, however, transmitted over the forward channel with a greater throughput (it is not necessary to transmit the check field). Decision feedback (ARQ) can use a narrow band backward channel which has also a lower noise level and hence a lower error rate. This leads to a greater transmission accuracy of commands and so to a smaller RER and a higher throughput.

In the summary of feedback methods we have also mentioned a combined method which is characterized by the existence of a decision device in both stations (Figure 3.15c). There is more than one such method, so it is worth mentioning them in this short summary, although we shall not classify them.

The method of ensuring minimum residual error rate is a combination of a decision and information feedback (compound feedback). The price which has to be paid is, of course, a lower throughput and an increased complexity. Blocks transmitted over the forward channel are provided with decision criteria (most often using the error-detecting code) and the receiving station either detects an error and then the system works as with decision feedback or the error-detecting error checking result is negative (because either an error has not occurred or it is not a detectable error) and then the system behaves as with information feedback (the whole block is returned to the sending station for comparing).

Another combined method, called hybrid, is a combination of decision feedback and FEC when, at the request of the receiving station, the whole block is not sent again but only further check bits are sent which, together with the original check bits, enable the detected error to be corrected by the receiving station. This method, however, requires completely new codes, where part of the error detection bits would serve for error detection and together with other check bits would form a sufficient criterion for determining the position of an error. Both methods also require a larger receiving buffer capacity (up to $2n$ if a block is repeated); hence memory ARQ or simply MRQ.

Error-correcting codes and decision feedback can be simply combined in the following way. Blocks are provided with check field for error correction in a way similar to that of the FEC method. When a number of errors occurs in excess of the correction capability of the chosen code the receiving station at least detects the erroneous block, and its correction by repetition is requested by a backward channel command.

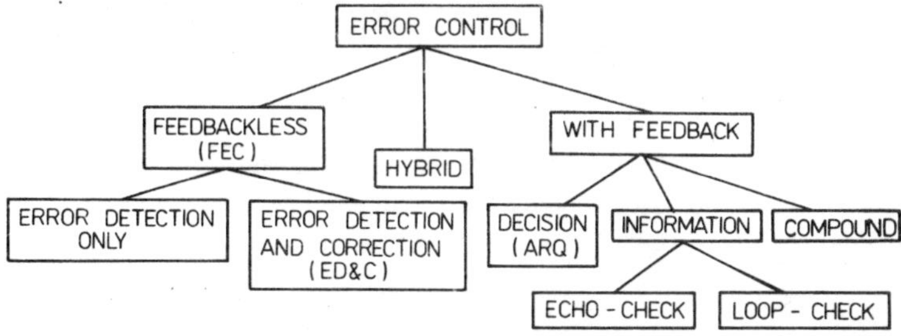

Figure 3.16 Classification of error control methods

In conclusion of this section let us present a short classification diagram of the error-control methods we have just described (Figure 3.16). Since the ARQ method is used most often and has been developed into a series of modifications, we shall devote the next section to decision feedback.

3.4.6 Modified ARQ method

The basis of the ARQ method is the scheme in Figure 3.15a with error-detecting code and receiving end decision, where the receiving station requests a repeat of the transmission or the transmission of further blocks by a command over the backward channel. Nevertheless, technical facilities as well as user demands necessitate a modification of this basic method.

First we shall suppose data are transmitted in one direction (in simplex mode), i.e. one station is a sending station, the other a receiving one. The backward channel then only serves for transmitting commands from the receiving station to the sending station. The example in Table 3.5 is the most simple of such methods when the sending station transmits one block and awaits a command from the receiving station. This method is, therefore, also called "stop-and-wait". A one-block buffer is required of the receiving and sending stations but the throughput is evidently very low, especially when channels with a long propagation time are used.

The low throughput of the "stop-and-wait" method is caused, on the one hand, by the transmission delay of a repeated block, and on the other hand by the time during which the receiving station waits for a response. The former time can be partly cut down by repeating only the incorrectly received part of the block. It is therefore necessary to use an appropriate error-detecting code and to transmit, over the backward channel, information about the position of the error, gained by decoding the received block, instead of the REJ command. The sending end then determines which part of the block should be repeated so that, on average, $k/2$ bits are repeated instead of $k+m=n$ bits. It is, however, evident that the price of an increased throughput is the necessity of a wide band and error — free backward channel.

The waiting time can be eliminated by FDX between the forward and backward channels with the sending station transmitting block by block and the receiving station reacting to the received blocks by commands over the backward channel. It goes without saying that in this case commands concerning individual blocks shall not arrive immediately after these blocks. There must be a certain delay between the command and the corresponding block. This delay shall be dependent on the propagation time and the times required for a decision about the reception on the part of the receiving station (reception and block control) as well as of the sending station (reception of commands over the backward channel). The time behaviour can best be seen in Figure 3.17.

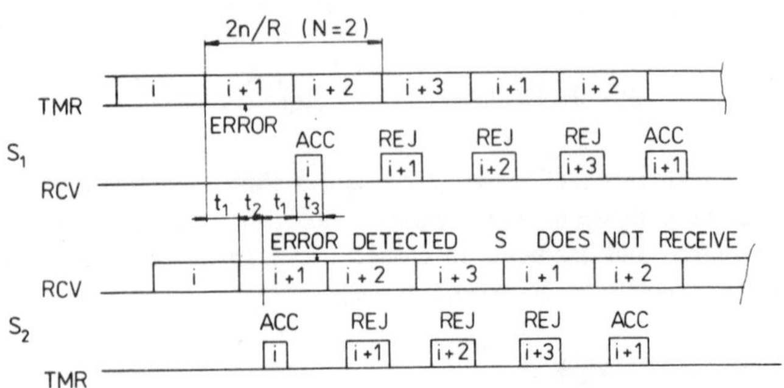

Figure 3.17 Time diagram of continuous ARQ method

In this figure the time schedule of all active parts of both stations is shown: the sending part TMR and receiving part RCV of the transmitting station S_1 and the same parts of the receiving station S_2. The sending station sends one block after another (in Figure 3.17 the blocks are denoted, for the sake of greater clarity, by serial numbers, which are not considered for the time being). These blocks arrive at the receiving part S_2 with a delay t_1 determined by the propagation time. From the checking part S_2 finds out if there is an error and after the time t_2, necessary for a final decision, sends the appropriate command (REJ or ACC) to station S_1 over the backward channel. After some delay the command returns to station S_1 (for simplicity, suppose both channels have the same propagation time, so that the command will also have a delay of t_1). Only after receiving and recognizing the command (which takes up the time t_3) is station S_1 informed about the state of the block received by station S_2.

This method is at first sight more efficient then the "stop-and-wait" method, because between the transmission of individual blocks idle or overhead times do not arise. We must, however, ask how the sending station recognizes, according to the accepted command, which block it concerns and how to dimension the buffers in both stations.

It is evident from Fig. 3.17 that the station S_1 comes to know about the reception status of the i-th block after the time $T = 2t_1 + t_2 + t_3$ from the moment when transmission ceases, when it receives command ACC or REJ. Within this time it sends TR bits, where R is the transmission rate in bits/s. If the block length is n, then, at the moment when the command about the i-th bit is being received, the $\left(i + \left\lceil \frac{TR}{n} \right\rceil\right)$-th block shall be transmitted, where the symbol $\lceil x \rceil$ denotes the smallest integer greater than or equal to x. When REJ is received, the sending station S_1 must return $\left\lceil \frac{TR}{n} \right\rceil$ blocks and open retransmission. Let us denote this value by N; so the method of returning N blocks (go-back-N) or the continuous ARQ method offers the possibility of raising the throughput while the residual error rate is not affected due to the repetition of each block which has been erroneously received by the station S_2.

When a block is rejected, S_1 must return N blocks and hence must repeat $N+1$ blocks. Therefore a buffer capacity $N+1$ blocks long is necessary. Station S_2, however, after finding an error, receives neither the erroneus block nor the N blocks following it, so that for it a buffer capacity of one block (Figure 3.18) is sufficient.

It now remains to determine the number N which is the parameter of this error control method. Either it is defined beforehand and then the procedure is suitable only for of data links (with very small deviations) or it is always determined separately before transmission (e.g. by means of measuring propagation delay T). It is, however,

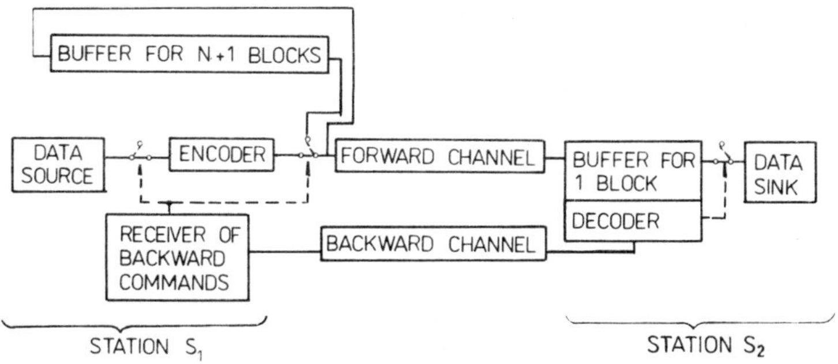

Figure 3.18 Block scheme of stations operating in the go-back-N ARQ

preferable to number blocks as well as backward commands, in which case it is not necessary to know the value of N during transmission, though it must be reckoned with in the dimensioning of the sending buffer.

So far we have only considered the situation in which, in the case of a block being rejected by S_2, all blocks which were transmitted after the erroneous block are repeated by S_1. Again, a modification of this method is possible leading to a higher throughput: instead of repeating all blocks after an error has been found, only the erroneous block is retransmitted. If we use Figure 3.17 for our explanation, then, when an error is detected in the $(i+1)$st block, S_2 receives the next blocks $(i+2)$, $(i+3)$ and only requests a repetition of block $(i+1)$. The station S_1 evaluates the requests from S_2 at the time that the $(i+3)$rd block is being transmitted, so that the next transmitted block shall have number $(i+1)$ and shall be followed by the $(i+4)$th block, etc. The price paid for this way of increasing the throughput is determined by buffer dimensioning. Although on the sending end there remains a buffer capacity of $N+1$ blocks, the receiving end must enlarge it from 1 block to $N+1$ blocks.

Even though, at first sight, the ARQ "stop-and-wait" method seems to give the lowest throughput in comparison with the continuous ARQ method, which is further exceeded by the method described last (which may be called a selective repeat method), this is not true for all values of the channel error rate. If the channel is of a rather poor quality, i.e. its error rate is high, then even a mean number of repetitions is much larger than 1 and the total throughput decreases rapidly. A method which raises the throughput was therefore designed for channels with a high error rate. Its description follows. As soon as an erroneous block is detected and station S_2 requests retransmission of it by its command REJ, the sending station S_1 does not repeat it only once but, for example, s-times ($s > 1$ is a parameter of the procedure). S_2 receives all s repeated blocks and requests new retransmission only in a case when, in the s transmitted repetitions, neither block has been received without a detected error.

All ARQ methods can be modified in this manner. In the "stop-and-wait" method the parameter s is dependent on transmission speed and block length (e.g. for 2400 bits/s, $n = 980$ bits and at a block error rate of 0.6 the result is $s = 2$), while with both other methods (continuous and selective) an outstanding optimum of throughput

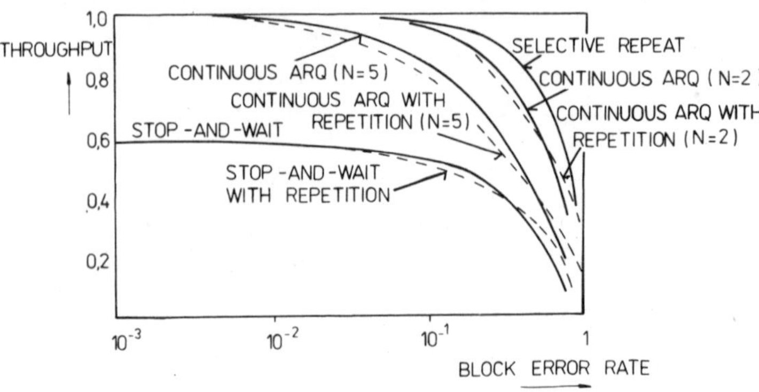

Figure 3.19 A comparison of several ARQ methods

can be found for a definite range of channel error rates at different values of s. For example, with the continuous ARQ method, repeating s times (regardless of the value of $s > 1$) gives a higher throughput with a block error rate higher than 0,5 assuming an independent error occurrence.

Figure 3.19 shows the dependence of the throughput on the block error rate for all the ARQ methods studied above. They are examples of dependence courses and therefore the remaining parameters, like block length, data field length, transfer rate and, perhaps, delay T are not given. However, in Figure 3.19 the advantages and drawbacks of the individual methods are shown: for low error rate values there is practically no difference between continuous and selective methods, whereas the "stop-and-wait" method is always markedly worse. The throughput decreases, of course, with an increasing N. On the other hand, with a growing error rate the selective ARQ begins to predominate, and with continuous ARQ the advantage of repeating s times begins to manifest itself. That is why it is always necessary to choose an ARQ method (and that holds true for all error control methods) according to the desired transfer system if we want to reach optimum values of performance.

All feedback methods are accompanied by one more parameter. So far we have assumed that the number of retransmissions of one and the same block is arbitrary. On links with a low error rate this assumption does not lead to performance degradation, but even in as exceptional a state as link interruption, sudden deterioration of link transfer properties, synchronization loss, etc. cannot be ruled out. In such a case of failure the unlimited number of repetitions would lead to a deadlock or cycles in the error control procedure and in the whole protocol. That is why the number of repetitions of the same block is limited by the value E and the method of exceptional state recovery must be determined after this value is reached. Although this is more a problem of recovery control, here we shall only say that, in this case, one may proceed in either of two ways. Either the E-times repeated block is received although an error has been detected in it (this error is knowingly allowed at the end S_2), or control is passed to a higher level protocol. The latter is better and does not lead to a decrease of RER. Or, if need be, the operator is summoned. The reason for it is that the communication system state concerned can be often recovered only by a higher level protocol or human intervention (see Chapter 3.8).

So far we have been interested in the ARQ methods used in the case of simplex data transmission. As soon as data are transferred over the forward as well as the backward channel we get other modifications of the decision feedback. We shall mention some of them briefly.

The "stop-and-wait" ARQ method does not change anything on the actual both way data exchange. One station sends a block and awaits a command together with a block from the station on the other end. It is only possible to transfer commands for either retransmission or for continuation of transmission (ACC and REJ) separately, e. g. as independent blocks, or to insert them into blocks, e.g. into their header (piggybacking).

With the continuous ARQ method the situation is different. First let us assume that the transmission over the forward and backward channels is synchronous, i.e. in both directions blocks of the same length are transmitted and all their beginnings are kept in synchronism. It is not unduly important whether the control commands are part of the data blocks or are independent. In view of the continuous transfer blocks are transmitted immediately after one another, so that independent control blocks can either be regarded as a header of the following data block or as a trailer of the preceding data block. An example of the time course of both stations is given in Figure 3.20, where blocks are numbered for greater clarity and the number in brackets is always the number of the block, transmitted from the station at the other end, to which the inserted command applies. The duration t_3 of the backward command is equal to the duration of the whole block in the case of a command inserted into the data block (in such a case the backward command is only evaluated on the basis of the reception of the whole block), and that duration is n/R, where n is, as usual, the length of the block in bits and R is the transmission rate in bits/s. Hence the number of blocks N which the sending station must return in the case of retransmission is equal to $1+\left\lceil\frac{T'\cdot R}{n}\right\rceil$, where $T'=2t_1+t_2$. Consequently FDX data transmission increases the value of the parameter N during the continuous ARQ method, thus making greater claims on the buffer capacity of the sending parts of both stations.

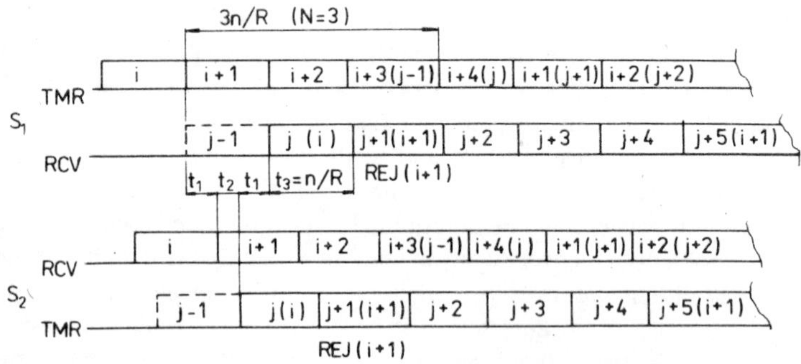

Figure 3.20 Time diagram of the FDX continuous ARQ

The mechanism of evaluating backward commands shows, however, a way of decreasing the value of N by at least 1. If the receiving part of the station is able to evaluate the received block during the time that the sending part sends another data block back, then the backward command ACC/REJ can, to advantage, be embedded into the trailer of this block and thus reach the station at the other end one block earlier. Shown in Figure 3.20 by dashed lines is the $(j-1)$st block which has precisely this property in the sending part of station S_2. If the receiving part of station S_2 can process data block i and form a backward command during less time than t_2, then it is possible to insert this command into block $j-1$ and thus N decreases from 3 to 2.

We must also return to the problem of disregarding the N blocks following the block in which the receiving part of the station has detected an error (Figure 3.17; in Figure 3.20 these blocks are not denoted). Whenever data blocks also contain backward commands, then no received block can be omitted because the commands it carries would also get lost. So the receiving stations must receive all blocks regardless of whether ARQ is continuous or selective. In the former case, however, it need not take care of the recording of data parts in a buffer; it is sufficient to recognize the command in the header or the trailer. When the blocks are numbered, which we shall deal with in Section 3.4.8, a "pure" synchronization is not achieved, because the numbers of transmitted blocks do not have the same counterpart in the numbers of acknowledged blocks (independent numbering). That can, in fact, be seen in Figure 3.20.

If we should want to maintain synchronisation, with throughput not being important, the following method could be used. As soon as the receiving part of some station (e.g. S_2) detects an error in a received block, it steps N blocks back and its sending part begins retransmitting $N+1$ blocks which had been transmitted before, even if the other station S_1 has not requested them to be repeated. The receiving part of the station at the other side receives the command REJ and its sending part also steps N blocks back and begin repeating $N+1$ blocks, so that the mutual numbering shall be adhered to, of course, at the cost of unnecessary repetition. However, this method is important chiefly when backward commands are replaced by numbering and that is why we shall discuss this further in the section on numbering mechanisms.

If we want to maintain block synchronization in both channels (forward and backward) between stations S_1 and S_2, and both stations are not controlled from the same clocks (e.g. one will transmit at a higher data transfer rate than the other), it is sufficient to insert a stuffing block at the moments when the transfer in one direction begins to lead by more than one block. Although the stuffing block contains a data field it carries no backward command. In this way the different data transfer rates are temporarily equalized as far as the ACC/REJ commands belonging to the received blocks are concerned.

3.4.7 Acknowledgment mechanisms

A further modification of the ARQ method is achieved by the choice of backward commands from the receiving station to the sending station. There exist several points of view according to which the ways of acknowledging (ACC) or rejecting (REJ) can be divided up. We shall mention all of them, at least briefly.

So far we have considered two backward commands: ACC requires sending the next block and REJ requires the block to be retransmitted. In practice, however, we should not omit the case when, because of failure (noise, drop-out), no response comes over the backward channel (or more precisely it is so distorted that the receiving part cannot evaluate it). That is why a reaction to such a state must also be introduced. Here time-out T_0 or a retransmission interval is useful, which serves the purpose of enabling the station to react in some way after the expiry of it in case it gets no response from the other end.

Commands thus introduced (a time-out may also be included among commands, even though it is not transmitted by the station but the whole communication system reacts by it) enable us to differentiate between three kinds of acknowledgements: using 2 commands (ACC and T_0 or REJ and T_0) or using 3 commands (ACC and REJ and T_0). The first mechanism (let us abbreviate to P-scheme) only uses the positive command ACC (hence P) in the case that transmission continuation of the next block is requested and for all the other cases (request for retransmission or loss of ACC) time-out T_0 is utilized. Similarly the second mechanism (N-scheme) utilizes the negative command REJ for repetition and otherwise the sending station activity is controlled by T_0. Finally the third mechanism (A-scheme — meaning all-acknowledgment scheme) is the method described above with both commands ACC and REJ to which time-out has been added for the event of a loss of some command.

If the time-out T_0 were the same as the time $T = 2t_1 + t_2 + t_3$ (Fig. 3.17) then, from the viewpoint of throughput, all three schemes would be equivalent. However, then would be lost the significance of T_0 as a criterion that the command from the opposite station has not been delivered, whether because it has not been sent or because it has

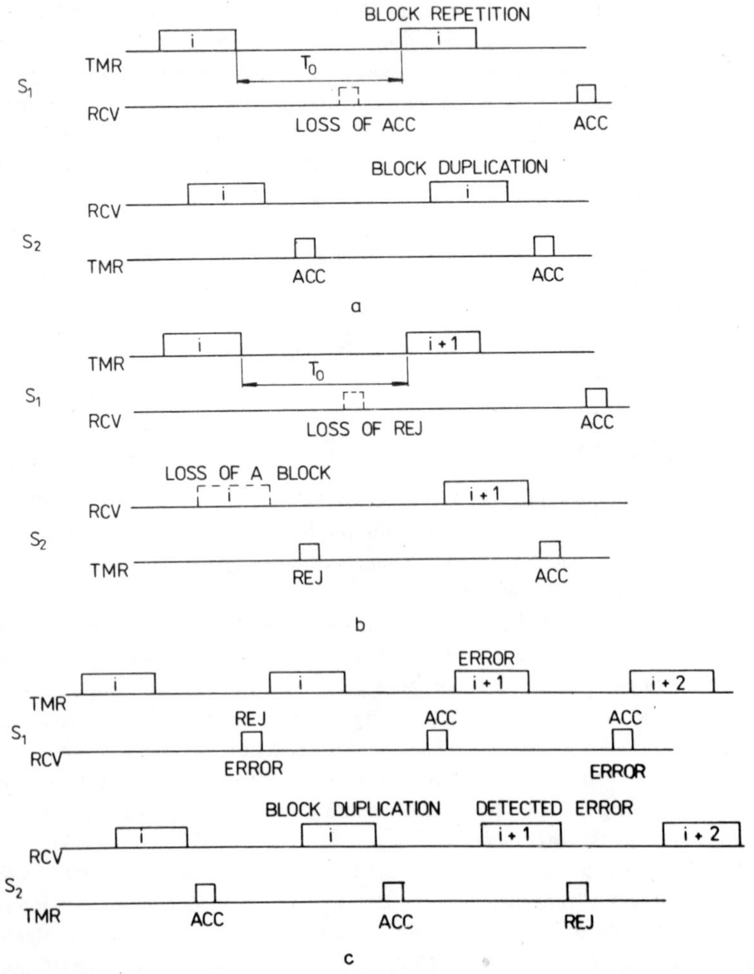

Figure 3.21 A comparison of several acknowledgment schemes with respect to the block losses and duplications

been lost during transfer. Let us therefore assume that time-out is markedly longer than T; then it is evident that, for a block error rate lower than 0.5, a higher throughput can be achieved with a P-scheme than with an N-scheme while the highest throughput is achieved with the A-scheme.

Let us study another performance criterion — RER in relation to the acknowledgment schemes dealt with — in greater detail. Here we shall put no restriction on the length of time-out.

Although in Section 3.4.5 we praised feedback methods, especially the ARQ method, as being very effective as far as error-detecting ability is concerned, we had been bearing in mind error resistance in the forward channel and we were not considering errors in the backward channel which can lead to mutilation of the backward command. Even undelivered blocks (more exactly undelivered data fields) must be included in the residual error rate and also duplicated blocks. This can have a much greater effect on the value of RER than a bit or several bits erroneously received.

Thus for the P-scheme block duplication occurs when an ACC command is not received (Figure 3.21a) whereas the loss of a REJ command for an N-scheme leads to the loss of a block (Figure 3.21b). Moreover, a further case has to be considered, although not a very probable one, i.e. block loss during transfer over the forward channel (e.g. because of drop-out or excessive noise). For the P-scheme this loss does not matter because the receiving station S_2 does not send an ACC and the sending station S_1 repeats the block after time-out producing. The block is, however, lost with the N-scheme because S_2 does not react by command REJ (it receives no block, not even an erroneous one), and therefore S_1 continues by transmitting the next block.

The A-scheme is resistant to block loss as well as to the loss of the command REJ (after time-out the station S_1 repeats the block), while the loss of the command ACC is the same as for the P-scheme (Figure 3.21a), i.e. it leads to block duplication. But interchanging commands ACC and REJ is risky: an interchange of REJ for ACC means the block is duplicated and interchanging ACC for REJ means block loss (Figure 3.21c). (Here the concept of command interchange means that the receiving station S_1 evaluates the transferred command ACC or REJ erroneously as REJ or ACC, respectively, due to noise in the backward channel.)

We can enter all the mentioned phenomena into a table (Table 3.7), where the consequences of these phenomena are stated against the individual acknowledgement schemes (a dash means the resistance of the scheme to the respective phenomenon). For the acknowledgement schemes to be comparable with each other with regard to the residual error rate it is necessary to know the probability of the occurrence of the individual phenomena. For instance, if block loss is hardly probable or almost impossible and if backward commands are error protected so that even an interchange is practically impossible, the A-scheme will obviously be the most advantageous with regard to RER. If we require that block loss should never occur, while block duplication can be protected (e.g. by the internal data structure) and removed during processing, the N-scheme is completely unacceptable and the P-scheme becomes most advantageous.

In link protocols we encounter the A-scheme most often; in higher layer protocols (e.g. in a transport protocol) P-schemes are beginning to assert themselves.

Table 3.7 Consequences of events for acknowledgment schemes

Scheme \ Event	Loss of a block	Loss of ACC	Loss of REJ	Mistake of REJ for ACC	Mistake of ACC for REJ
P	—	block duplication	—	block duplication	—
N	loss of a block	—	loss of a block	—	loss of a block
A	—	block duplication	—	block duplication	loss of a block

At the beginning of this section reasons have been presented for the necessity for a greater time-out length than the propagation delay and the delay necessary for reception (T). However, what happens if time-out is shorter than T? Then, at most, unnecessary repetition will occur, throughput will decrease, but on the other hand the total delay will decrease. With an increasing time-out length, the delay begins to grow, but the throughput increases. It is possible therefore to determine the optimum value of the time-out according to the requirements for performance.

Another criterion for classification mentioned in the preceding section is the possibility of transferring backward commands on their own or inserting them into data blocks (piggybacked). Finally the last choice of an acknowledgment scheme is the acknowledgment of every block or of whole series of blocks by a single command. We shall discuss this in more detail, because of its importance.

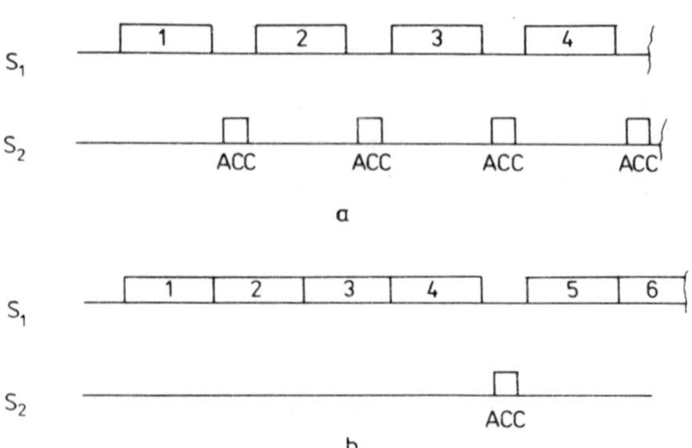

Figure 3.22 Acknowledgment after each block (a) and after a sequence of several blocks (b)

In Figure 3.22 two ways of acknowledging are shown: Figure 3.22a contains the traditional method of acknowledging each block, in Figure 3.22b a whole sequence of 4 blocks is acknowledged by a single command. From the time diagrams it is evident that method b) is far more effective, since it leads to a higher throughput. That is true not only for the simplex mode of transmission shown in Figure 3.22 but also for FDX transmission, because in case b) space for backward commands is saved in the data blocks.

The number of blocks which can be transmitted without acknowledgment (4 blocks in Figure 3.22b) is called window size, K. The first block is the left window edge, the last block forms the right window edge. The sending station then transmits one block after another up to the window size and, unless it receives a positive acknowledgment within a certain time interval (determined by the time-out agreed upon), retransmits all the blocks of the window. The receiving station can either acknowledge the last block of the window which was received (right edge) which means that all the preceding blocks of the window were received without an error being detected, or the first block of the following window (its left edge) can be acknowledged which means that a sequence of blocks of the following window is awaited.

The "window" method can also be combined with an N-scheme or with an A-scheme. In that case, when an error is detected in a received block of the window, either a repetition is requested (by command REJ) of the blocks in which the error was detected (selective ARQ), or a repetition is requested of all the blocks of the window, beginning with the block in which the first error was detected. Hence a window is not some sort of superblock which only adjusts the length of the original blocks to new transfer conditions, but is a mechanism permitting a throughput increase (provided certain transfer conditions are satisfied). It also serves for a flow control function (Chapter 3.5).

With selective acknowledgment the window size is unlimited, more precisely, it is limited by the buffer capacities at the sending and receiving ends. It is, however, dependent on the numbering modulus, for block loss or duplications not to occur. We shall return to this in the following section.

Acknowledging can also be carried out after a certain time, i.e. instead of transmitting blocks which fill a window determined in advance, blocks are transmitted in the scope of some time interval. The difference is that a window contains blocks that have actually been transmitted, whereas a time interval need not contain a whole number of blocks or need not even contain any block.

3.4.8 Numbering methods

To prevent block loss and duplication it is necessary to inform the receiving station whether the block being sent is a retransmitted block or a new one. For this one bit is sufficient, the value of which changes with each newly transferred block to the value opposite to the one in the last block received (that is why this bit is called an alternating bit).

The alternating bit is nothing more than differentiation between odd and even blocks, which means numbering them modulo 2. Thus we arrive at block numbering as another way of improving RER.

It would evidently be ideal to number all data blocks of a message serially; it would then, however, either be necessary to shorten the length of data messages or else sending and receipt (counting of block numbers) would be much more complicated, unless we put a limit on the message length. That is why cyclic numbering modulo some integer M is quite natural; thus blocks are numbered in succession 0, 1, 2, ..., M-2, M-1, 0, 1, 2, ..., etc.

Numbering is further information which must be part of the block envelope (header or trailer) and numbering modulus M is another parameter of the error control procedure, because its value is determined on the basis of the required performance. In the designed protocol the possibility of enlarging the numbering field and thus changing the value of M can be provided for.

If we want to fully utilize numbering for the prevention of block loss and duplication then M must be chosen to depend on the delay and the transmission rate. The smallest modulus is $M=2$ (if $M=1$, blocks are unnumbered) which, as has already been stated, takes up 1 bit of the format (0 or 1) and at the receiving end even (0) and odd (1) blocks are distinguished. Because of its simplicity it is used very often, as long as time delay between sending a block and receiving the corresponding backward command is not longer than the time of sending the next block, which is true e.g. for the "stop-and-wait" method (BSC link protocol). Otherwise the modulus has to be enlarged: e.g. to 3 (CCITT V.41 link protocol), 8 (basic HDLC format), 10, 16, or even many times larger, e.g. 128 (extended HDLC format) or 256. When the block number is expressed in binary form the length of the numbering field in the format must be at least $\lceil \log_2 M \rceil$.

It is possible to number only data blocks (for receiving station control purposes), only backward commands (for sending station control purposes), or data blocks and backward commands simultaneously. In the FDX mode on the one hand numbering concerns transmitted data blocks, on the other it is possible instead of backward commands to transmit the numbers of received (expected) blocks, which further enlarges transmission accuracy.

The numbering modulus is also dependent on subsequent error control procedure parameters, particularly on the number of blocks N, over which the sending station must return in the case of a negative command during the continuous ARQ method, and on the window size K.

Let us consider the link protocol as an example. Here the blocks are transmitted one after another and the blocks arrive at the receiving station in the same order. When an error is detected, the receiving station requests repetition of all the blocks, beginning with the erroneous one. Then, to avoid loss or duplication of numbered blocks, two sequences of K and N blocks, respectively, which begin with the same number, must never appear side by side. From this it follows that K and N must not be integer multiples of M. An example in which N (or K) equals 5 and $M=4$ is shown in Figure 3.23a. The first sequence (e.g. window) begins with block No. 0, followed by blocks 1, 2, 3, and 0, while the subsequent sequence contains blocks Nos. 1, 2, 3, 0, and 1.

If a further requirement is added, i.e. that the same block numbers should not appear in any sent and received sequence, which is necessary in a selective ARQ, the number M must moreover be greater than K or N, respectively (Figure 3.23b, where again $M=4$, but $N=3$). In the example in Figure 3.23b we can see that block numbers can become identical after four sequences of triples of blocks, which occurs with so small a probability (the receiving station would have to refuse block No. 0

three times and simultaneously a loss or erroneous transfer of the backward command REJ would have to take place), that it is unneccessary to consider such an event at all. If, however, we wish to achieve the highest non-repeatability, $M=N+1$ must hold and is quite often used in practice.

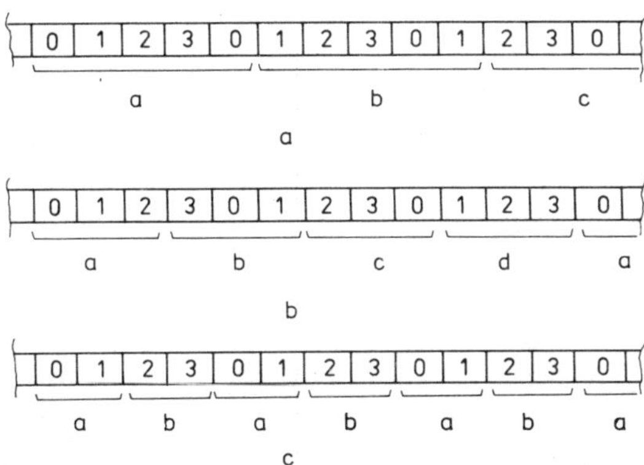

Figure 3.23 Examples of dependency between numbering modulus and window size

Let us now consider the case when the receiving station need not receive blocks in the order in which they were transmitted, which is the case of a packet layer in a virtual call service. Then it is necessary that the same block numbers should not appear in two sequences following each other. If this happened, then, during backward command loss and an unnecessary repetition or continuation of transmission, the receiving station may not, during the receipt of a block from the window, recognize whether the block is a new one or a repeated one. This is achieved by the condition $N(\mathrm{or} K) \leqq [M/2]$, where $[x]$ denotes the integer part of x. Hence for $M=4$, N (or K) must be $\leqq 2$. This is the example in Figure 3.23c. However, after two windows two identical block numbers are repeated. If we want to increase the number of windows after which this happens to, for example, q windows, we must require N or K to be less than or equal to $[M/q]$.

3.4.9 Historical and bibliographical notes

There are many books dealing with encoding and error control of information transmission by means of correction codes. Let us mention particularly Peterson—Weldon's book [183], which is the second revised edition of the book from 1961, today already considered classic, which can even be studied by readers without mathematics training. The possibility of utilizing a backward channel for achieving greater transmission accuracy was shown as far back as 1948 by C. Shannon but it was only later that Chang [38] analysed the practical utilization of decision and information feedback. Decision feedback (ARQ) as the most promising method of error control for data transmission over real channels was designed by Van Duuren in 1943 for telegraphic transfer (without calling it so), but ARQ was later analysed in greater detail in [17, 18, 252]. In [218] the relation between BCR and RER and the importance of optimum error-detecting codes was shown. Error-detecting codes are also the subject of a series of works on coding theory, but the very first analysis of cyclic codes for error detection was performed by Peterson [182]. Extremely good summaries, together with original results from the field of error detection by the most diverse feedback methods, are presented in [122, 229, 255, 256]. The possibility of increasing the throughput of the ARQ method and the "stop-and wait" method is mentioned in [7].

Combined feedback was first described by Schwartz in [252], its comparison with information and decision feedback in [229], and the first reference to the memory ARQ (MRQ) method using complementary check bits is made in [62] and using whole block repetitions in [260]; new encoding ways for these methods can be found, for example, in [31, 163]. The hybrid method was first described by Brayer in [30], and analysed in [236]; the use of burst-trapping codes is described in [246]. The comparison of different error control methods, especially feedback methods, from the error rate and throughput viewpoint is presented in [32], in relation to real channels and their models in [87, 121].

Sastry [246] proposed a continuous ARQ method for forward channels with a high error rate by means of s-fold repetition, [167] gives its modification which is similar to the selective ARQ, which increases the throughput.

A summary of error control and its procedure parameters used in link protocols is presented in [227], error control for transmission through satellite links is presented in [245].

[13, 95] and summarily [209] deal with continuous ARQ methods for FDX transmission. In [94] it has been proposed, on the basis of measurements, to use a format trailer instead of the usual header for an embedded backward command (see also [209]).

Even though acknowledgment is an integral part of the ARQ method, only recently has the influence of acknowledgment on error control procedure performance been studied in greater detail [11, 269], however, the analysis presented in Section 3.4.8 is due to authors. The A-scheme used most often, which has asserted itself in link protocols, is superseded by the P-scheme [35] on higher layers. Sunshine [269] carried out an analysis of the length of time-out with respect to throughput and delay and has also introduced the concept of a repetition interval rather than time-out while Petrenko [184] used Petri nets for determining necessary time-outs. The window method was first used in the ARPA network for remote HOSTs and in the CYCLADES network; it is, however, also designed for an internetwork protocol [35]. As far as the determination of the window size with regard to throughput is concerned, this is reflected upon to some extent in [181].

The method of numbering modulo 2 using an alternating bit was first proposed by Lynch [146] who also worked on two-way data interchange in the HDX mode and in the minimum necessary overhead involved in the transmission of backward commands and block numbers which, for independent transfer in both channels, amounts to 2 bits. In [13] is described the error control procedure developed at NPL which reduces overhead per bit while achieving the same results, provided that both channels are block synchronized. Numbering is treated generally in [65]; in [227] numbering methods in diverse link protocols are compared. The relation between the numbering modulus M and the window size K (the number of retransmitted blocks N) presented here, is due to authors; another derivation is in [66].

3.5 Flow Control and Congestion Avoidance

3.5.1 Contents, definitions, and mutual relations

Hardly any communication functions overlap so much, from the aspect of their contents, as flow control, congestion control, and routing, not to mention traffic control and access control. Although traffic control and access control are treated independently in the literature, they can be expressed in terms of the three other functions, which are more elementary from the point of view of the activities they perform.

The overlapping mentioned above follows from the joint aim of the three functions. This aim is to keep the communication network performance in the required limits even under large fluctuations of communication load and in the event of considerable changes of network internal characteristics (e.g. failures of lines and nodes). Because of the uniform terminology used in this book the communication subsystem (or network) will be called a subnetwork.

When we realize that the communication control in a subnetwork is synthesized from all the communication functions being realized in the subnetwork, and that the communication control as a whole constitutes one of four main components determining the resulting subnetwork performance (see Figure 3.24), then the joint, and also

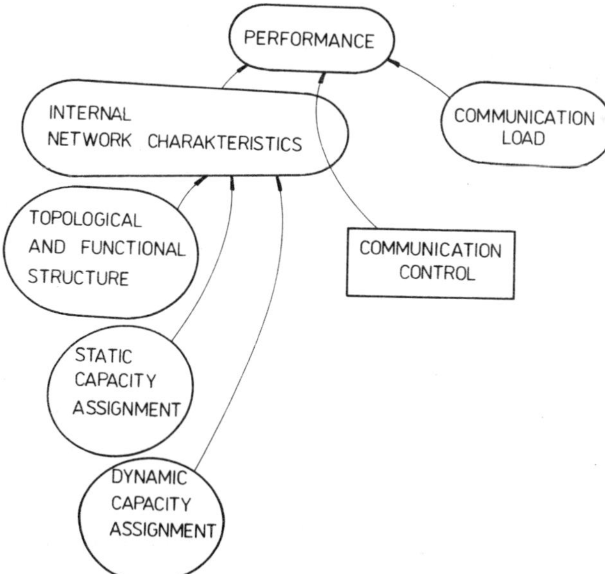

Figure 3.24 Factors determining the subnetwork performance

the final, aim mentioned above is quite obvious. But this was not so when early packet switching networks were designed. The development of the two communication functions described in this chapter proceeded from simple mechanisms capable of solving partial problems only to the complex ones that are used nowadays. The case is still more complex owing to the fact that subnetwork performance is not defined by a single variable, but by several performance measures. These measures may have different weights in various subnetworks and applications. So it is necessary to investigate the influence of individual methods of communication functions on each performance measure, e.g. on throughput, on average transit time (or data block delay), on degree of resources utilization, etc. In the design of actual subnetworks, the most important performance measure should be selected and then the subnetwork design should be optimized with respect to this performance measure. In other words, classes of services provided by the subnetwork should be defined and one of them should be selected, e.g. guaranteed transit delay, guaranteed throughput, guaranteed message delivery, etc. Of course, guaranteed here means only some high level of probability.

Among the agents determining the subnetwork performance values (Figure 3.24) communication control plays a special role.

Subnetwork topology, functional structure, and capacity assignment are fixed during the design of a subnetwork. Subnetwork resources are represented by line capacities (transmission rates, transmission powers), by memory capacities (sorts and numbers of buffers in subnetwork nodes) and by processing capacities (i.e. processing capabilities of CPUs in subnetwork nodes). Capacity assignment means selecting (according to estimation, calculation, and/or modelling and simulation) the corresponding numeric values of all subnetwork resources mentioned above.

The resources are quite often shared, in order that their utilization may be increased. Of course, sharing requires an adequate control to be implemented somewhere in the subnetwork in order to allocate individual shared resources to specified user classes. All the three components described until now, i.e. topology, functional structure, and capacity assignment, have to be selected for some expected traffic load (or for some required class of services). They represent, in principle, a sort of static design of the subnetwork, or the design with a small range of dynamics.

When a much wider range of dynamics is required (i.e. large traffic fluctuations and/or complete failures of some nodes and lines), special functions have to be implemented in the subnetwork. These are, as we already know, the communication functions. They constitute communication control and they exert such influence on the subnetwork elements that even the effect of large changes in both the subnetwork itself and in the traffic is smoothed down or made negligible. Two cases may be distinguished here. When the changes are not very great, communication functions may optimize the subnetwork performance, whereas with large changes the role of communication functions is not to optimize, but only to keep the resulting performance within prescribed limits.

From the point of view of one performance measure, namely that of resources utilization, the situation looks as follows. In a precise design of subnetwork, the expected traffic must be specified (by estimation, measuring and statistical evaluation of results, by modelling, etc.). The capacity is then assigned for this expected load. The resources should not be overrated because then they would not be sufficiently utilized. But we all know how difficult (if at all possible) it is to estimate the traffic. Therefore more communication control is built into the subnetwork providing for less stringent dimensioning of the subnetwork resources.

Of course, there may be a wide range of both traffic changes and failure occurrences which requires a corresponding range of communication functions and/or methods of their realization in order to achieve the aim described.

In the case of very large traffic increase, or that of failures of several nodes and lines, a catastrophic deterioration of subnetwork performance may occur. This takes the form of total overloading of a subnetwork, or of congestion of a subnetwork as a whole or of a substantial part. It also causes the subnetwork to stop transferring packets, at least for a subset of subscribers. Sometimes the subnetwork may not be capable of transfering the blocks between subscribers even when the traffic is not large, and, therefore, the subnetwork is not overloaded. In this case various deadlocks and lockups are the cause of worsening of subnetwork performance. We shall describe these briefly later in this chapter.

The subnetwork overloading in the case of packet switching networks shows in an increased number of packets in the subnetwork. More packets enter the subnetwork than it can transfer and output. Therefore packets occupy more and more buffers in the subnetwork nodes, thus overloading the network until there are no more free buffers, i.e. congestion occurs. Figure 3.25 illustrates this situation. The line of ideal transfer relates to a subnetwork with unlimited internal resources.

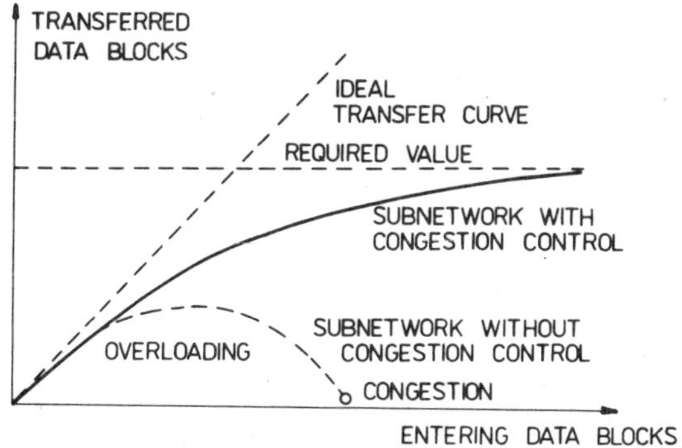

Figure 3.25 Subnetwork transfer curve

Overloading takes place in the circuit-switched networks as well. These show transfer curves similar to those of packet switching networks. As a matter of fact, the transfer curves of circuit-switched networks were known first.

In order to differentiate between flow control function and congestion control function, the subnetwork overloading and subnetwork congestion (i.e. the worsening and catastrophic deterioration of a subnetwork performance) should be clearly distinguished. The communication functions analysed here can lessen the deterioration in performance, or prevent catastropic deterioration, or both. Figure 3.26 shows how the differences mentioned above can serve to distinguish between the individual communication functions.

Routing essentially changes the communication load distribution in a subnetwork and by doing this improves (or optimizes) subnetwork performance. In a limited range routing can prevent subnetwork congestion from developing. This holds good for a node congestion as well.

AIMS / SUBJECT	PERFORMANCE IMPROVEMENT	CONGESTION AVOIDANCE
PAIR OF STATIONS	FLOW CONTROL	CONGESTION CONTROL (FLOW CONTROL)
ENTIRE SUBNETWORK	ROUTING (FLOW CONTROL)	CONGESTION CONTROL FLOW CONTROL (ROUTING)

Figure 3.26 Approach to distinguishing the routing, flow control and congestion control

Congestion control has only one aim: namely to avoid subnetwork congestion, or subnetwork node congestion. Buffer overflows will not be called congestion here, although it is clear that fully occupied (i.e. congested) buffers are the primary reason for any congestion occurring in the subnetwork.

Flow control primarily concerns pairs of stations. Essentially it relates to regulation of block frequency (or block occurrence) exerted by a receiving station on a sending station. Improved performance (or maintaining performance within prescribed limits) may be considered to be the direct aim of flow control. As will be shown later, flow control mechanisms can be utilized to perform the congestion control function. It is in this sense that congestion prevention may be regarded as an indirect aim of flow control.

Basic flow control mechanisms, which will be described later in this chapter, can be applied to different pairs of stations. Once we have the pair comprising the subscriber station and the subnetwork node, then by controlling flow between these two stations we can regulate the inputting traffic. So we have a sort of access control achieved by means of the flow control mechanism. By using this in all input places (i.e. on all subscriber-subnetwork node pairs) and by determining properly the criteria for starting these flow control mechanisms in individual pairs of stations, we may perform the traffic control. The aim of the traffic control may be either the optimization of the subnetwork operation, or just the improvement of larger performance deteriorations. In any case, flow control mechanisms provide for access control and, at the same time, for traffic control. This may be the explanation of the mutual relations among the above communication functions.

Figure 3.27 shows all basic pairs of stations as objects for communication protocols in general, and for flow control in particular. It should be recalled here that stations need not be identified with the network or subnetwork elements only. They may also be identified with protocol stations in individual layers of the network architecture (see Chapter 2.3). The basic pairs which are depicted in Figure 3.27 are detailed in Figure 3.29.

It follows from the brief characterization of the three communication functions analysed that the principle of redistribution of the communication load by means of route selection is typical for routing, whereas flow control is primarily concerned with the immediate aim: block generation frequency regulating. This immediate aim can be utilized for achieving the two basic aims, namely performance improvement and the avoidance of subnetwork or node congestion. As may be seen in Figure 3.27, flow control is present in all recognized cases. This means that flow control is a sort of basic (elementary) communication function that can act alone or in more complex schemes within the frame of a congestion control function. The mode of utilization of some flow control mechanisms has been already shown above. Because of its elementary nature, flow control will be described in more detail, but first some other general notes related to the three communication functions will be given, together with a sort of subnetwork reference model for the purposes of this and of the following chapter.

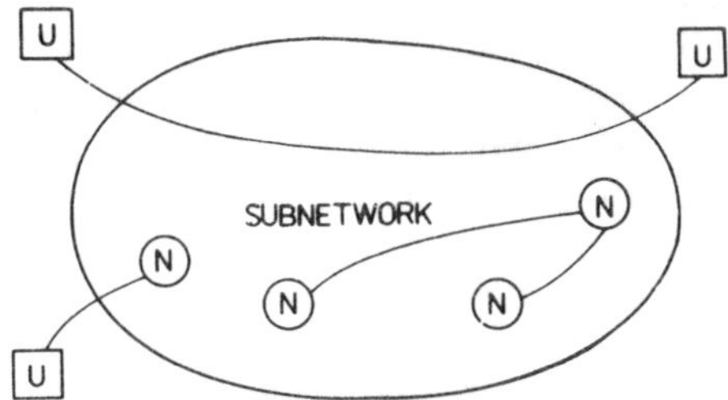

Figure 3.27 Various pairs of stations as subjects of the flow control
N—N = flow control
U—N = access control
U—U = end-to-end flow control
N = subnetwork node
U = user station, subscriber station

The difference between flow control for performance improvement and flow control for congestion avoidance may not lie only in different pairs of communicating stations, but in different criteria for starting flow control mechanisms and in different mechanisms themselves as well.

When congestion control is assigned with only such activities as needed for subnetwork congestion avoidance, and when flow control is concerned with only a pair of stations, then the question arises which communication function will regulate the amount of overall traffic in the subnetwork using all partial means. Such a communication function is sometimes explicitly distinguished, and sometimes not. In the first case it is most often called traffic control, as we have already mentioned. So traffic control may be regarded as the coordinated utilization of the common actions of flow control, congestion control, and routing. When not distinguished explicitly, it can take the form of differently structured criteria for starting the mechanisms of the three functions that may be regarded as more elementary. Because the mechanisms of communication functions are of primary interest in this book, traffic control will not be treated here explicitly. Moreover, some authors use flow control to denote the subject of traffic control as described above. In connection with this, the basis for differentiating between flow control and traffic control must be emphasized. Or, in other words, the aim, the means, and possibly the configuration of the communication functions being treated here should be clearly recognized and distinguished. This is often not simple because the same terms are often used for all the three aspects. When, for example, by flow control we denote both the means and the aim, the latter being congestion avoidance in this case, then ambiguites are very probable, because congestion control is also used to denote both the means and the aim. Facing these facts, the only way out of these ambiguities lies in analysing the context and assigning to the ambiguous term either the aim, or the means, This chapter could provide some background for such distinction.

The following points of view may be used when trying to differentiate clearly between the communication functions:

1. The aim, i.e. the expected result of relevant activities.

2. The mechanism, i.e. the means used to reach the aim. This point can be extended to cover the methods of realizing communication functions and the course of the corresponding control operation.

3. The subject, i.e. the configuration of a subnetwork in which the function is implemented and in which it exerts its influence and/or activities. All nodes and all parts of a subnetwork (even the whole subnetwork, if needed) should be included and clearly identified.

4. The subnetwork status information, i.e. a sort of feedback information that may be specified by the following considerations:
— what information to measure or to find out,
— where to measure or collect it,
— where to use it,
— in what way to transfer it from the place of origin to the place of utilization,
— whether, and where, to process it.

5. The start of a mechanism, i.e. the algorithm or the criterion (e.g. the limit value crossing — the crossing of a threshold value) for decision making resulting in the start of the relevant mechanism. The decision is based on the network status information mentioned in point 4.

Figure 3.28 presents the subnetwork reference model. The object communication takes place between subscribers U and it is mediated by the subnetwork containing nodes N. The subnetwork can represent the packet switching network, the communication subsystem, the data network, the data transmission system, etc. In keeping with most of the papers treating flow control, congestion control, and/or routing, it is assumed here that only one subscriber U is connected to each subnetwork node N. The communication path (from one subscriber to some other subscriber) may comprise either two nodes only (e.g. N_2 and N_3 in Figure 3.28), or more than two nodes (e.g. N_m, N_k, N_j, N_i). When considering one communication path, the end nodes and the intermediate nodes can be differentiated. The end nodes are connected with subscribers (in a given communication path), the intermediate nodes are not. The nodes N_2 and N_3 are both end nodes and there are no intermediate nodes in that communication path. When considering the direction of a transmission, the source nodes and destination nodes can be recognized.

The end nodes and intermediate nodes are not absolute, but they are determined by the relevant communication path. Certain nodes may function as the end node in one communication path and as an intermediate node in a different communication path. When both communication paths are active at the same time, then the corresponding node is both end node and intermediate node simultaneously. Because essentially any communication path may be created in the subnetwork, all nodes have to be capable of acting universally.

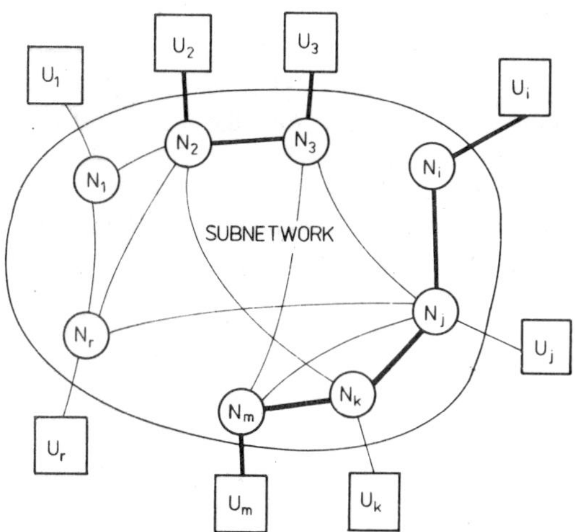

Figure 3.28 Reference model of the subnetwork
U = user station, subscriber
N = node

It should be recalled that there is no subnetwork node such that no subscriber is connected to it (i.e. intermediate node only). To each node N just one subscriber U is connected. Such models are used commonly in routing.

3.5.2 Flow control

Flow control, as described in this book, essentially concerns the regulation of the number of blocks generated by a sending station, transferred over any communication medium, and then entering a receiving station. Let us recall that the station represents either the whole network element, or a software module, or a protocol station. In the case of the N—N pair of neighbouring nodes (see Figure 3.27) the receiving station limits the generation speed of blocks being transmitted by the sending station. The limiting may be based on the state of the receiving station alone, or include also the knowledge of the status of neighbouring nodes, or even the status of the whole subnetwork. Status concerns primarily the readiness of buffers in the sense of buffer allocation and management strategy used.

When the *U—N* pair of stations (see Figure 3.27) is considered, the station *N* limits the block generation speed in the station *U* if the subnetwork starts to become overloaded or if the subnetwork performance starts to worsen. The crossing of a threshold may also be utilized as the criterion for starting the relevant limiting mechanism. The maximum permitted number of occupied buffers can serve as the threshold variable, just as in the case of the *N—N* pair of stations.

Flow control related to the *U—U* pair of stations features a different criterion for starting the speed limiting mechanism. This criterion is based on the availability of resources of the station *U* alone, i.e. it does not depend on the subnetwork. As we know, resources of the station *U* may be the resources of a host computer, of a concentrator, of a terminal controller, etc. But the communication path for communication of the *U—U* pair of stations possibly consists of several of the pairs *U—N*, *N—U*, and *N—N*. This only emphasizes the well known fact that blocks exchanged between the *U* stations travel over the subnetwork and add to its traffic. This partial traffic is, of course, influenced by the *U—U* stations' flow control (i.e. by the end-to-end flow control). But in order to have a traffic control mechanism, the feedback from the subnetwork to the *U* stations has to be provided, as an additional criterion for exerting the end-to-end flow control. This feedback information could be transferred from the subnetwork to *U* situations by means of the communication protocol assigned to the *U—N* basic communication element. Without this feedback, the flow control between the *U* stations can only act on changing load conditions in the subnetwork by tracing and evaluating the transit delay.

Summarizing the examples and explanation presented both in Section 3.5.1 and at the beginning of this section, the aim and means of flow control may be stated as follows. There are two aims of the flow control function: performance improvement or optimization, and congestion avoidance.

The basic means is the limiting of block generation speed. Several flow control mechanisms are available. The criteria for starting these mechanisms cover both internal states of the subnetwork, or the state of nodes or stations, and the external behaviour of the communication medium used. The values of some performance measures serve the purpose in the latter case.

First, various flow control mechanisms (or techniques, or algorithms, or methods) will be explained and then criteria for starting the mechanisms will be treated.

When analysing various flow control schemes four basic principles may be distinguished, namely speed modification, rejection, single permission, and multiple permission.

Block generation speed is characterized by block interarrival intervals. By changing an average value of this interval the speed modification is achieved.

In the case of rejection, the receiving station either refuses to receive the transferred block (after the block arrives at the station), or the receiving station informs the sending station about its temporary inability to receive blocks. So in the first case we have rejection after the transmission and in the second case rejection before the transmission. Of course, releasing of such rejection status must be announced to the sending station. This announcement has the character of infinite permission, i.e. it permits the sending station to send theoretically an infinite number of blocks. Rejection can also be regarded as a temporary interruption of block transmission.

Single permission is in a way similar to rejection, from one special point of view. Permanent rejection is present in this case and releasing of this rejection has the form of permission for a single block transfer. The sending station may wait until such permission arrives, or it may be active and ask for permission to send one block. In any case, the block may be sent only when the sending station has received the permission. The criteria for sending such permission can be various including, for example, the preallocation of a buffer.

Multiple permission concerns the whole group of blocks. The number of blocks allowed to be sent to the receiving station may be fixed (i.e. static), or variable (i.e. dynamic). In the first case, each permission allows the same (agreed beforehand) number of blocks to be transmitted, while in the latter case each permission must contain this number. A typical example of this principle is the well known window mechanism.

Now some of the best-known mechanisms will be assigned to the four principles.

The throttling mechanism represents the realization of the speed modification principle. An example of one form of this mechanism which uses the so called choke packets and which was developed for the CIGALE subnetwork of the CYCLADE computer network will be described here.

The choke packet is a request for decreased speed. It is sent by the receiving station when the degree of line utilization reaches some agreed value. Other criteria may be used as well, though. After receiving the choke packet, the sending station lowers the speed (e.g. by increasing the minimum time interval between successive packets), and at the same time it starts the timer. When no further choke packet arrives during the time-out interval, the sending station increases the speed to the original value. But if a further choke packet comes during the time-out interval, further decreasing of the speed follows. Generally, each choke packet causes one step of decreased speed and each expired time-out interval causes one step of increased speed. Of course, there should be some reasonable limits.

The receiving station generates choke packets by using the other timer. If the degree of line utilization is still higher than the agreed lower threshold at the expiration of the time-out interval, then an additional choke packet is sent. This operation may be repeated, but only within reasonable limits.

The choke packet can be also regarded as a special command. It can have higher priority in order to pass over the subnetwork without the delays to which data packets are prone. Or it can have no special priority, but being short (i.e. not being piggybacked) it still can be transferred quickly over the subnetwork. Of course, the generation and evaluation of choke packets (i.e. of the corresponding commands) is the task of the relevant protocol stations.

In connection with the rejecting principle, two basic mechanisms will be mentioned here, namely the discard mechanism and the stop-and-go mechanism. The discard mechanism first sends and only then rejects a data block. It discards, i.e. doesn't process, the blocks arriving in the receiving station from the sending station when the criterion used has been fulfilled. It is this criterion that determines if this mechanism is for flow control or for congestion control, as will be explained later.

The stop-and-go mechanism belongs to the rejection before transmission principle. Normally the sending station keeps on sending until some stop command comes from the receiving station. This means that the receiving station is not capable of receiving further blocks. The receiving station knows the reasons for that. The sending station must stop sending blocks and it must wait for a go command to arrive. The go command is a permission for the sending station to go on sending blocks to the receiving station.

The wait-before-go mechanism is an example of the implementation of the single permission principle. The sending station waits passively until some kind of permission comes from the receiving station. Only then may the transmission be performed and then only one block may be transmitted.

Another mechanism using the same principle could be denoted the ask-and-wait mechanism. Here the sending station is active in that it requests permission from the receiving station by notifying it of the existence of a block to be transmitted. Again the block is transferred only after the permission arrives. The request for permission can serve as the allocation request as well.

The last two mechanisms differ in which station is active. In both cases time-out can be used to determine the repetition of commands representing the active steps.

In the latter mechanism the activity assignement may be flexible in such a way that only one request is sent from the sending station. Then, instead of repetition of the request when no permission is coming from the receiving station, the receiving station takes the initiative and at the first opportunity sends the permission. This means that the receiving station becomes active by remembering the request for permission and by sending the permission automatically.

The window mechanism, which is a realization of the multiple permission principle, has been already explained in Chapter 3.4 in connection with error control and so will not be described here. The difference between using the window mechanism with two different communication functions lies in the different circumstances of its use. It is the error-free reception of a block that shifts the window edge in the case of the error control function, and it is the internal condition occurrence (i.e. freeing of buffers) that does it in the case of flow control. As far as flow control windowing is concerned, the window width may be either static (e.g. HDLC protocol) or dynamic, i.e. adjustable (e.g. credits in the INWG 96 protocol).

When comparing the single permission mechanisms with the window mechanism, the latter features higher throughput and higher line capacity utilization, but it needs more buffers and more processing as well. In each subnetwork design the analysis of the requirements and properties and prices of lines and nodes is to be made in order to make a proper trade-off and to select a suitable approach.

Flow control, as well as any other communication function, requires exchange of control information between the two communicating stations. Until now, only the basic communication element was considered. But in real networks more complex configurations exist. We present here only one sort of such configuration, namely the tandem network. Some patterns expressing typical flow control situations or schemes in tandem networks are depicted in Figure 3.29. The labelling of individual nodes used in Figure 3.29 is that of Figure 3.28. Sometimes the mediating stations (see Figure 3.29) are not only supporting the transfers between two basic communication elements (or between two communication protocols), but they also may actively contribute to the flow control proper by providing additional status information.

Now let us come back to the criteria that express conditions for starting of individual flow control mechanisms. Basically these conditions relate to either threshold values, or to the existence of preallocated resources (buffers mostly).

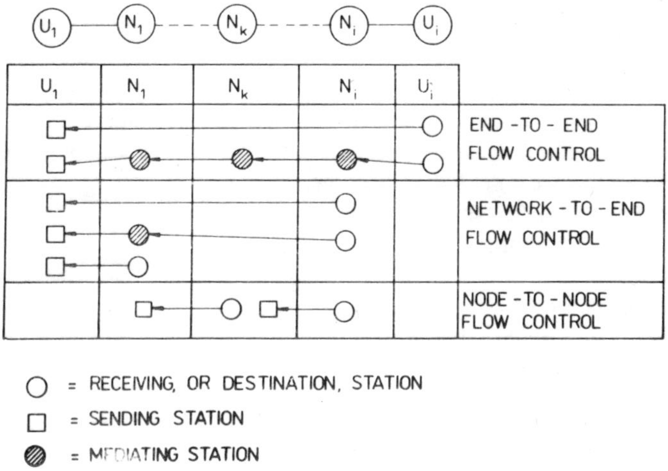

U_1 — N_1 - - - N_k - - - N_i — U_i

END-TO-END FLOW CONTROL

NETWORK-TO-END FLOW CONTROL

NODE-TO-NODE FLOW CONTROL

○ = RECEIVING, OR DESTINATION, STATION

□ = SENDING STATION

● = MEDIATING STATION

Figure 3.29 Configurations for the flow control

Thresholds concern various critical numbers of buffers. These numbers may be for buffers in queues, or in nodes, or in a subnetwork as a whole. Also some other resources and/or variables may be analysed for crossing thresholds, i.e. for fulfilling the relevant criterion. The satisfying of a criterion condition leads each time to a corresponding change of the state of a station and sometimes to automatic notification of some or all of the other stations (nodes) about the event.

Preallocation expresses an essentially different approach to creating necessary conditions for the transfer of one block, or of a group of blocks (sequence of blocks).

Thresholds can express, for example:

— the maximum allowed number of occupied buffers in a node,
— the maximum allowed number of occupied buffers in a whole subnetwork,
— the maximum allowed number of occupied places in an output queue (or in several output queues),
— the minimum required number of free buffers,
— the maximum allowed number of occupied buffers both in the node and in the neighbouring nodes.

This is not a complete list of all possible (nor of used) thresholds. For example, in the throttling mechanism with choke packets the degree of line utilization was used as the threshold.

As can be seen, the conditions for starting the flow control mechanism concern either one node or more than one node (including the whole subnetwork, i.e. all nodes). As soon as the condition selected relates to more than one node, status information transfers have to be carried out (using the same subnetwork). These transfers are to be built into corresponding communication protocols. This means that adequate commands should be available and an appropriate field for status information has to be reserved in formats. The structure, or coding, of status information has to be specified as well.

Buffer preallocation also has several forms. Reserved buffers may be assigned:

— to a message (i.e. to the group of blocks),
— to a logical channel,
— to a session (or to a call),
— to a subscriber station.

We also distinguish various overall strategies used in communication systems. For example, we can differentiate between datagram service and virtual circuit service. From this point of view the buffers may be located:

— in nodes of the logical channel (of the communication path),
— in a subscriber station,
— in end nodes,
— in intermediate nodes,
— in nodes of the whole subnetwork.

Of course, there is a close relation between the location of buffers and the network topology.

Some examples of flow control implementation in the frame of communication protocols will be given in Appendices.

3.5.3 Congestion control

We start by emphasizing here that a communication subnetwork is designed usually for some communication load. When, in the case of packet switching networks, the number of packets (average number) entering the subnetwork is larger than would correspond to the supposed communication load, especially when the number of packets increases in a short time interval (surge traffic), then the subnetwork is normally not able to process such traffic. The subnetwork may be either overloaded or congested in such a case and the performance is accordingly either deteriorated or zeroed.

Packets begin to accumulate in nodes (in corresponding buffers in the nodes), because the subnetwork cannot transfer them quickly enough and pass them over to destination subscribers. Such a packet accumulation first occurs locally, in the neighbourhood of such end nodes as are input nodes for excess traffic. The number of free buffers decreases, first slowly and in local areas of the subnetwork, then very quickly and in the whole subnetwork. Without any precautions present, the situation may arise when all buffers are occupied and no transfer of packets is possible at all. This is the congestion marked by G in Figure 3.30. A similar situation can appear when the traffic is not so high as to reach the point of no transmission but when large failures occur.

Figure 3.30 is only an extension of Figure 3.25, i.e. the influence of the number of buffers used is shown. Dashed lines depict the ideal throughput curve corresponding to asymptotic conditions (unlimited number of buffers up to the expected maximum load, and no interrelations). The dashed curve is assigned to the subnetwork with congestion control built in. Full line curves marked A and B both correspond to subnetworks without congestion control, and to the optimum and a small number of buffers respectively. The overloading and congesting points are shown in Figure 3.30.

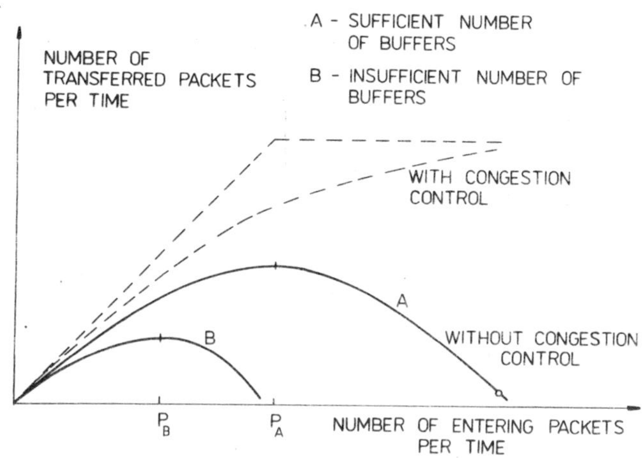

Figure 3.30 Transfer curve for a packet switching network

The first one is determined by the value p of the difference between the ideal and real throughput. The congesting point does not belong to the traffic yielding the congestion of subnetwork, but rather it corresponds to the top of the throughput curve (without congestion control being present). After this point the output traffic decreases. When the subnetwork is designed optimally with respect to the number of buffers selected, the overloading point may be identical with the congesting point. Such optimal design makes other performance measures optimal as well, as is shown for packet transit times by curves A and B, in Figure 3.31. As can be seen, the packet transit time begins to rise quickly just in the vicinity of the congesting point.

As we have already mentioned, congestion is created step by step. First, the area of failure occurrence or of excess input traffic is affected, followed by the whole subnetwork. The time and space course of this congestion or spread overloading depends on the extent of the changes that caused it. When the changes are not great, even without congestion control built in the subnetwork may accomodate them; the performance will be worsened, but not totally degraded. The deterioration of services for users may develop selectively for different groups of users. Of course, equal service for all users is required in public data networks. Therefore this situation has to be improved.

When the conditions for developing congestion are recognized early, the congestion can be avoided. This is the aim of the congestion control communication function.

Let us recall that congestion may concern the whole subnetwork (total congestion), some nodes only (local congestion), only one node (node congestion), and several buffers only (buffer overflow).

Each of the four kinds of congestion can be avoided by means of an appropriate congestion control mechanisms. But it is total congestion and local congestion (i.e. congestion concerning the subnetwork) that are to be avoided primarily; this is the main aim of the congestion control function.

Preventing of buffer overflow and/or node congestion is more a flow control task (see Figure 3.26).

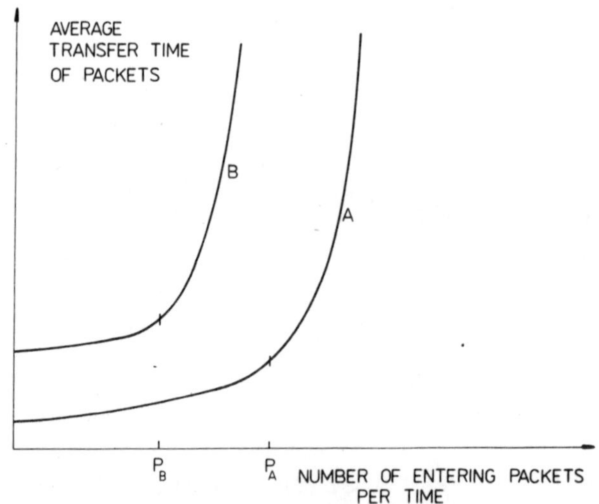

Figure 3.31 Delay curves for a packet switching network
(for A, B see Figure 3.30)

The catastrophic deterioration of the subnetwork performance may also develop discontinuously. Various deadlocks and lockups are examples of this. When the traffic level is higher (but can still be far from the critical value) a situation may arise in which mutual blocking of resources appears in the subnetwork with no transfer being allowed in the blocked area. Depending on how large an area of the subnetwork is affected, local or global congestion may occur.

Deadlocks and lockups are often consequences of communication protocol flaws, but sometimes they can be improved or avoided by means of a congestion control mechanism. That is why they are mentioned here.

In what ways can congestion be avoided? Basically there are three ways to do it:

a) by limiting input traffic (into a subnetwork, or node),

b) by decreasing the existing load in the subnetwork,

c) by locally redistributing the existing traffic.

The last way, which may be realized by means of routing, serves to avoid local congestion only, or to deal with local surge traffic.

The first way is inherently the most powerful. When applied to the communication element with one station in a subnetwork and the other identified with a subscriber, it is naturally called access control. The *U—N* pair of stations of Figure 3.27 can serve as an example.

The second way involves discarding some packets (or blocks, generally). Several criteria can be used to determine which blocks are to be discarded. They will be described later.

One special access control method, which was developed at the National Physical Laboratory in England, will be explained. It is known as isarithmic flow control, and is based on the fact that the degree of overloading (or congesting) depends on the number of packets residing in the subnetwork at the moment. Limiting this number artificially to some reasonable value means preventing congestion. Later on the mechanism used will be treated in some detail.

Discarding of blocks utilizes the mechanism that was described among flow control mechanisms. The mechanism is based on the rejection principle. The variant used features no notifying of the sending station about the discarded packet, so the basic mechanism is the same both in the case of flow control and of congestion control. The difference is primarily in the criteria used for starting the mechanism and secondarily in the different configurations. Flow control mostly relates to two stations and the criterion is derived from the state of one station only. Congestion control concerns the whole subnetwork and the criteria used correspond to this wider range. For example, the "life time" of a packet in the subnetwork, or the number of nodes through which the packet has already passed, are used as such criteria.

Discarding packets without notifying sending stations requires that subscribers (sending stations) be informed about it, of course, and see to it themselves, e.g. in the scope of some end-to-end protocol. This way of decreasing traffic already existing in the subnetwork is quite typical for datagram networks (or networks with datagram service).

So, after all, the only mechanism of congestion control is the mechanism of permits. This mechanism realizes the isarithmic flow control method and is used for access control, as we have already explained.

The so called "permits" are the basis of this mechanism. Each permit allows one packet to enter the subnetwork (so it is subnetwork based), so the number of permits present in the subnetwork determines the maximum possible number of packets that can reside in the subnetwork. In reality, the number of permits is generally smaller than the maximum allowed. A packet may only enter the subnetwork when it finds a free permit in the input node. If there is no such permit in the input node, the packet must wait until some arrive. When finding a free permit, the packet occupies it and takes it with him. After reaching the destination node the permit is freed. It either waits there for another entering packet, or, when no such packet arrives, is transferred to another node of the subnetwork. So the permits travel through the subnetwork either with packets or alone when they are redistributed. It could happen that permits begin to accumulate in several nodes, neglecting the other nodes. In order to prevent this situation, proper redistribution algorithms are to be used. But, because such algorithms are deterministic and the movement of permits in the subnetwork is random, some permits will remain unused. However, the number of such permits should be substantially smaller than in the case when the algorithms are not used.

From this, two critical variables follow as influencing the resulting properties (characteristics) of the packet switching network significantly. These variables are:

a) the number of permits in a subnetwork,

b) the redistribution algorithms used.

This method is not able to solve local congestions that may occur as a result of unevenly distributed input traffic.

We can regard the isarithmic method to be a flow control method using the rejection mechanism where the condition for starting this mechanism is the lack of permits in the relevant input node.

At first sight the isarithmic method does not look like a control method in the sense of control theory, because it does not measure the subnetwork (so that there is no feedback). But this is not quite so, because the redistribution of permits may be based on measuring the state of the subnetwork.

Permits need one bit only. Whatever the coding of permits may be, there should be a place for them in formats of corresponding communication protocol and manipulation with permits must be, of course, included among the tasks of the corresponding protocol stations.

3.5.4 Bibliographical notes

An overview of flow and congestion control problems and approaches may be found in surveys of Davies [64], Pouzin [207], Chou and Gerla [41], Inose [115], and Rudin [240]. The subject is also dealt with, in the following books: [126, 256, 253].

Many valuable papers devoted to flow and congestion control, as well as to routing, have been presented in the proceedings of the first monothematic international symposium on flow control which took place in Versailles, in February 1979; see references [69, 136, 155, 176, 241, 254, 291].

Congestion control is dealt with, for example, in [63, 140, 180, 254] and flow control in [69, 120, 240, 272]. Flow control in ARPANET is treated in [109] and in the X.25 environment in [136]. Isarithmic methods may be found in [63, 211].

Routing and flow control is dealt with in [43, 241], flow and congestion control in [64], and routing and congestion control in [155].

Experience with practical use of several methods is described in [127].

There has been a lot of work done on the modelling of various flow and congestion control methods in different types of networks. From among the great number of these models some results of simulation may be given as examples [116, 117, 211, 213, 99].

3.6 Routing

3.6.1 Principles of routing

Routing means finding and assigning to each block that enters a node N_k (see Figure 3.28) the output line or the next neighbouring node on the route to the destination node, aiming at the following:

a) Performance optimization, or maintaining within prescribed bounds (e.g. minimization of average packet transit time, maximization of subnetwork resources).

b) Congestion avoidance, concerning the whole subnetwork or only parts of it.

c) Reliability increase (of the subnetwork) by means of utilizing inherent redundancy of the polygonal network topology.

Of course, finding a route for packets concerns only those packets which have not yet reached their destination, i.e. for which the node N is not an end node. A further route is primarily determined by the decision-making node N_k and by the destination node N_j.

Let us recall that subnetwork performance is derived from the internal characteristics of the designed subnetwork and from the pattern and scope of the communication load. The performance also depends on how the entering traffic is distributed among individual subnetwork input nodes. The subnetwork performance may be quite sensitive to changes of assignment of input traffic to different input nodes. Both traffic and the subnetwork state change during the operation. The first because of the inherently random character of user demands and the second owing to failures and errors that may not be so very frequent but nevertheless do occur.

In the design of the subnetwork the procedure is such that first the traffic is estimated (or determined by more precise and sophisticated methods) and the network topology is selected, and then the initial fixed routing is calculated by means of some known methods of flow assignment optimization. Various methods of mathematical programming are used for the purpose. So some optimization is made even during the initial design of the subnetwork, yielding a sort of static solution or a static route assignment. Of course this static route assignment is not the subject of a routing communication function, this being a part of a dynamically active communication control.

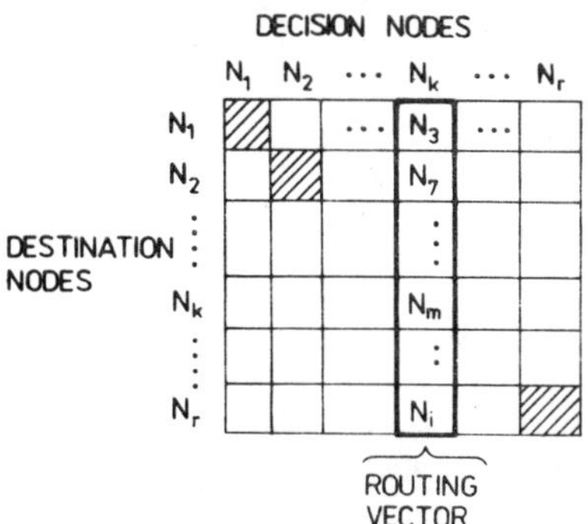

Figure 3.32 Routing table

Routing vectors are primarily of the static flow assignment and they represent the basic formal tool. The routing vector, being one column of the routing table (see Figure 3.32), contains for each destination node the corresponding neighbouring node through which the block should be transferred on its way to the destination. Fixed routing vectors, determining block flow distribution in the subnetwork, are assigned to each subnetwork node. The controller part of the routing communication function is devoted to the vector look-up and to the corresponding new address assignement, this being done for each block passing through the node. This activity is nothing more than ordinary switching that also may be regarded as routing. But the control part of the routing function is basically a dynamic one.

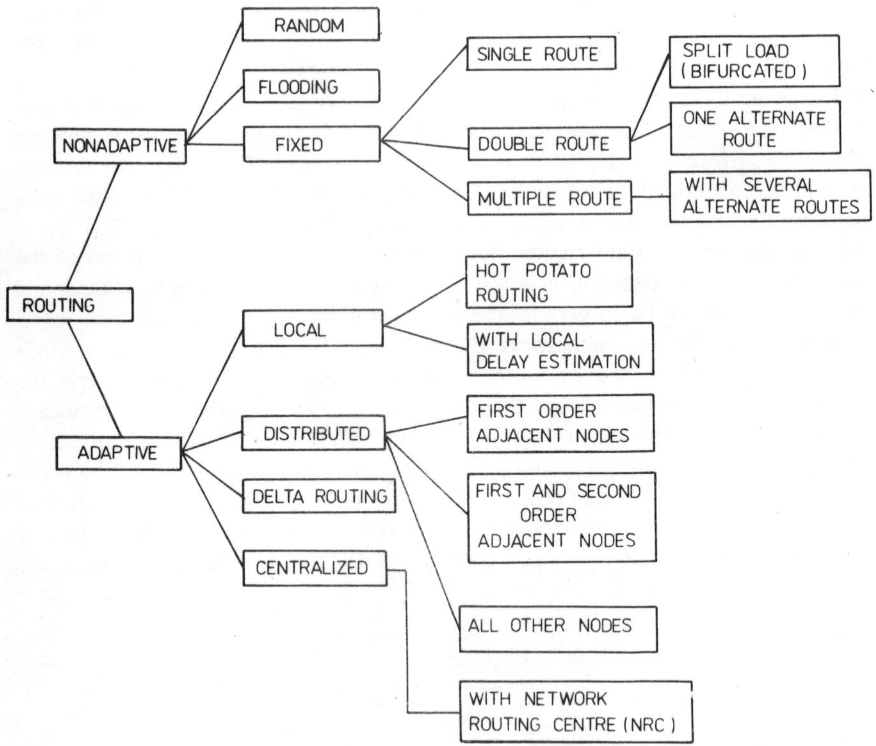

Figure 3.33 Overview of routing methods

Two basic groups of routing methods can be differentiated: adaptive methods and nonadaptive methods (see Figure 3.33). Adaptivity relates to the built-in capability of reacting to changing traffic characteristics and/or to changing network configuration, the latter being changed owing to failures or to some other reason (e.g. management). Based on measured, collected, and processed knowledge concerning the changes mentioned above the decisions have to be taken regarding the further route of blocks in a subnetwork. All these activities belong to routing. Adaptive routing methods used to be called also dynamic methods.

Nonadaptive routing methods (or algorithms, or doctrines, or protocols, etc.) do not react to traffic changes, or apart from some exceptions, to subnetwork changes. They are also called permanent, deterministic (some of them only), or static routing methods.

Adaptive routing methods change the distribution of communication load in a subnetwork. By means of adaptive routing instantaneous traffic changes and failures of nodes and/or lines may be recognized and suitably dealt with by deviating the block stream from the congested or failed parts of the subnetwork to less occupied (and, of course, not disturbed) parts. In this way traffic distribution can be optimized. The dynamic flow assignment optimization requires the performance of similar calculations as in the case of static optimization having been performed during the subnetwork design. In the case of adaptive routing these calculations have to be done quickly, because they have to provide input values for communication control.

Such dynamic treatment of the changing situation in the subnetwork can be performed in many ways. A survey of them is given in Figure 3.33. Before explaining the principles of the individual adaptive routing methods we shall present some basic activities that are needed for most of the above adaptive methods. These background activities are the following:

a) Measuring, or, generally, finding out the state of individual subnetwork elements (e.g. queue lengths, numbers of occupied buffers, various delays, number of retransmissions, etc.).

b) Notifying several (e.g. neighbouring) or all other nodes about the measured or found states, i.e. spreading the routing information.

c) Calculating the global subnetwork state required for proper traffic distribution.

d) Calculation of optimal routes based on the accumulated information about the subnetwork.

e) Transferring the calculated results into the relevant nodes.

f) Updating of routing tables (or routing vectors, or other tables) in the nodes of the subnetwork.

This is a comprehensive list of basic activities, i.e. not all of them are present in individual routing methods, because sometimes some of them are inherently unnecessary.

Nonadaptive routing methods either do not perform any of the activities listed above, or they only perform the last one (in a way which will be described later).

Adaptive routing methods usually perform several of the above activities, and sometimes all of them. The adaptive methods can even be identified by means of the above listed activities. The following criteria can be used:

1. The subnetwork elements in which the individual activities are performed.

2. The algorithm used for determining the subnetwork global state and the algorithm used for determining the optimal routes.

3. The frequency (periodical, or event-driven) with which the individual activities are started and/or performed (i.e. when to measure states, transfer results, calculate delays and routes, update routing tables).

The network shown in Figure 3.28 will be used as a reference for defining the routing table. In this network all subnetwork nodes may be either source nodes, or destination nodes, or intermediate nodes (of course, not simultaneously). Therefore the routing table, which is shown in Figure 3.32, has r rows and r columns (r being the number of nodes).

Each entry of the routing table generally contains one neighbouring node (i.e. the index of that node). To this node the block passing over the decision node will be routed on its way to the destination node. This is the single-route routing.

When alternate or bifurcated routing is used, then two or more neighbouring nodes provide the corresponding entry of the routing table. These are examples of multiple route routing methods. Of course, numbers of lines may be utilized instead of numbers of nodes in routing table entries.

Each decision node must contain at least the corresponding column of the routing table. Of course, this column must be updated in order to be capable of serving as a routing vector. Each entry of the routing vector is assigned to some destination node and each entry contains the neighbouring node selected by means of the routing algorithm.

3.6.2 Routing methods

Now the principles of individual routing methods will be described, with reference to the survey illustrated in Figure 3.33.

Random, or broadcast, routing selects the next node in a random way, without considering the real state of a subnetwork. All routes (i.e. all outgoing lines) may have equal probabilities assigned, or the probability assignment may prefer some output lines. The principles of block movement in a subnetwork were explained in Chapter 3.3 in connection with broadcast addressing. Therefore, we shall remind the reader that loops are to be prevented (block passing several times through the same node) and that this routing method is of advantage when information concerning subnetwork state is to be disseminated efficiently.

Flooding may be regarded as a special case of multiple route routing, and also relates to the flooding addressing described in Chapter 3.3. Let us recall that in each node copies of the block being transferred over a subnetwork are sent in all directions except the one from which the block has arrived. Again blocks may be sent over the subnetwork in loops if no measures for preventing this are taken. An example of such measures is described in Chapter 3.3. This routing method produces relatively large internal traffic and, as we have already explained, is advantageous in special applications only, these being similar to those mentioned with the previous broadcast routing method. For example, flooding is very suitable when the number of blocks being transferred is small and a high degree of reliability is required from the delivery.

Fixed routing is the typical kind of nonadaptive routing. It can be either single route (only one neighbouring node N_m is assigned to each pair of nodes N_k and N_j, where N_k is the decision node and N_j is the destination node), or multiple route. The neighbouring nodes are determined according to the results of static optimization and they are not changed during the subnetwork operation, whatever the traffic or subnetwork changes.

First the single route fixed routing will be treated in more detail. The realization of this method is simple and subnetwork performance is good, especially with larger traffic, therefore this method is widely used. When compared with flooding, it features opposite properties: it is suitable for large traffic (i.e. many blocks being transferred), but, on the other hand, it is very vulnerable. The failure of one node or one line results in a complete interruption of all paths that contain either the line or the node (or both). It is clear then that fixed single route routing does not allow the utilization of the most significant advantage of the polygonal topology: the possibility of a substantial increase in reliability by means of redundancy. But single route fixed routing does exclude loops.

A natural approach to the above-mentioned disadvantage lies in the addition of at least one alternative, or by-pass, link (i.e. having at least two entries in each routing vector field). In other words, single route routing should be replaced by bifurcated routing when necessary (or when it is more suitable). When two directions are assigned, one should decide between them. This decision may be either deterministic, or random. When selecting one of the two directions (nodes, lines) at random, probabilities p and $(1-p)$ are assigned to each of them. The mechanism needed to realize this principle must be implemented in nodes. Using probabilities means that there is no feedback from the node or from the subnetwork utilized. The output line may be selected according to the random selection principle even when it is down and so not capable of transferring blocks. But this routing method, not being adaptive, will continue to send blocks into such a line. Of course, excess traffic will occur caused by retransmissions being effected over the other, correct line. This routing method differs from random routing in that only two output lines are used, i.e. there is only one alternative approach.

The disadvantage of the previously described method can be removed, of course, when the states of a node or of outgoing lines are measured and evaluated. Then normally the first direction (line, node) is selected and all blocks are sent in this direction until a failure appears. The node, after finding out that the line or the neighbouring node is down, will switch the block stream to the alternate line. It is obvious that this is also a basic mechanism for increasing reliability.

The switching to the alternate route can be caused by another reason, namely the number of blocks waiting in the output queue (i.e. a threshold value). When the node finds out that the number of blocks in the queue of the first line is equal to some critical value, a switch-over occurs. This method is sometimes called overflow routing, because overflowing of output line buffers is monitored.

Both of the last methods are partially adaptive, i.e. hybrid. They find out the state of a node or line (which is one of the basic activities featured by adaptive routing methods), but they do not calculate the resulting route. Instead, they utilize fixed routes, determined beforehand and, therefore, not reflecting the real state of a subnetwork. They only choose between these fixed routes, or they select one of several possible fixed routes. Nevertheless, they are very useful and are able to improve the performance remarkably. Adaptive routing methods utilize the information about the subnetwork state (which can concern one node, neighbouring nodes, or all nodes) in a different way. They do not use any precalculated routes, but each time they evaluate the information about the state and calculate the optimal routes according to the algorithms used. They also disseminate the calculated results at reasonably short time intervals in the form of routing vector updates throughout the subnetwork. Of course, the realization of adaptive methods is much more complex and the overhead (in terms of CPU time, memory space, and line capacity) is obviously higher than in the case of nonadaptive routing methods.

In the survey presented in Figure 3.33, adaptive routing methods are classified according to the place where subnetwork status information is processed and routing vectors are calculated, and also according to the subnetwork area involved (i.e. one node, several nodes, the whole subnetwork).

The most often used measure of optimality is minimum delay (or transit time). Therefore a basic tool for most adaptive routing methods is the so called delay table (or network delay table), which formally resembles the routing table but whose entries are not output lines (directions) but delay estimates related to pairs N_k, N_j. The entry $T_k(m, j)$ of the delay table denotes the transit time estimate for the block travelling from the node N_k to N_j through N_m.

Various adaptive routing algorithms differ in the way the $T_k(m, j)$ entries are derived (or calculated), how often the calculated values are updated, and how often the $T_k(m, j)$ values are utilized to calculate the entries of the routing table.

The delay table represents the most often used means of expressing the global state of a subnetwork.

A brief characteristic of each kind of adaptive routing method will be presented here.

Local, or isolated, adaptive routing methods are based on capabilities of isolated nodes, i.e. on the subnetwork status information which one isolated node can acquire. Such information is utilized by the node itself, and is not transferred to any other nodes. This means that all calculations needed for determining the routing vector are performed in the node. Several methods belong to this group: two of them will be mentioned here.

The shortest queue routing method selects the output line with the shortest queue at the moment the block is sent out of the node (without regard to the destination node). It is certainly an effective method when the primary criterion is sending blocks out of the node. It is also called "hot-potato routing", which illustrates the principle. But, disregarding the destination node, it results in worse overall performance.

The other method is the so called local delay estimate method, which is the method with backward learning. It has a wider "range of vision" than the previous one. It appraises the state of a larger area of a subnetwork, though not completely and with a relatively great delay. Therefore the decisions concerning route selection may either lack precision or be out of date. In this method the $T_k(m, j)$ entries are calculated by using the measured values of block transit time in the opposite direction, i.e. when the block travels from node N_j to node N_k through node N_m. So the basic assumption of this method is that transit times in a backward direction (on the same path) do not differ substantially from those in a forward direction. It is because of this backward direction transit time that the method is also called "backward routing". The frequency of updating is random and is given by the occurrence of blocks coming in the backward direction. When N_j sends no blocks to N_k, there is no update (i.e. the delay estimate is not changed; it remains fixed for a while).

In order to measure the transit time special means have to be used and built into both nodes and protocol. Some kind of network time has to be built into the subnetwork; each block is provided with the so-called "time stamp" when it leaves the sending node. There should be some place for these time stamps in the formats of the protocol used.

Other distributed adaptive routing methods will be treated briefly. A typical example of this group of routing methods is the method which was utilized in the ARPANET computer network in the early stage of its operation. Only the basic idea of this method will be described here: this uses the fact that routing information is exchanged between neighbouring nodes only. In each node the delay table of limited size is maintained. This is so because only rows corresponding to output lines, i.e. to neighbouring nodes, are considered. The minimum delay vector is maintained in each node containing the minimum transit time for each destination node N_i. Minimum delay vectors are exchanged periodically (e.g. every 2/3 s in ARPANET) between the neighbouring nodes. The values of network delay table entries are recalculated after each such exchange. Of course, to each minimum delay vector a routing vector is assigned containing numbers of those lines which correspond to minimum delays.

Indirectly, the state of the whole subnetwork (as far as delays are concerned) is reflected in each routing vector. But the routing information propagation time may be quite long, because of the indirect way mentioned above.

Generally, there are several methods of initializing the routing information (minimum delay vectors) transfer, viz. a periodical transfer, event-driven transfer (e.g. when some specified kind of failure occurs), or event-driven transfer caused by reaching some threshold value.

The number of hops, i.e. the number of pairs of nodes between the node N_k and the destination node N_j, is also used as an optimization measure (e.g. in ARPANET). The metric used can serve as an auxiliary classification criterion.

Centralized routing methods are characterized by the existence of the so-called network routing centre — NRC. In this centre most of the activities of adaptive routing are performed. All nodes send status routing information into this NRC, which processes the incoming data, calculates the routing vectors, and sends them to individual nodes as updates. So nodes can be nearly as simple as in the case of fixed routing, except that they must know how to pick up the routing information from the blocks received and how to replace the old routing vector with the updated one.

There are several variants of centralized routing methods. They differ in the routing information being collected, in the type of processing of routing information, and in the frequencies of entering and distributing of routing information. All these methods have one thing in common, that is that the whole subnetwork is covered and, as a result, that large delays occur.

When comparing the distributed routing with centralized routing, we find that distributed routing methods have opposite characteristics; namely they are concerned with a small part of a subnetwork, and they react quickly.

By combining both these methods one can utilize advantages of both of them and reach an overall improvement of routing characteristics. The example of such a compromise solution is the so called "delta" routing. There is centralized routing in the delta routing intended to produce a routing strategy based on the coverage of the subnetwork as a whole. Such strategy need not change either often or quickly. The centralized routing also smooths down the influence of local changes. The strategy is transferred to all nodes and the latter use it to combine it with local environment status information and for calculating the required routing vectors. These calculations can be done quickly enough.

Two considerations are important from the point of view of global communication control.

The first concerns the time relations connected with communication control. Routing is one of the communication functions, i.e. a part of communication control. Various routing methods used have various inertia. When traffic and subnetwork change too quickly, it may happen that the routing method used is slower, or its implementation in the subnetwork is, and that it is not able to react in time. Delayed reactions may have very unpleasant consequences which are known from the control theory (e.g. instability, slowness, overshoots, etc.).

The second consideration emphasizes the fact that routing is only one of several communication functions and that communication control synthetizes the activities of all communication functions implemented. Flow control and congestion control are the most important ones from the above viewpoint. There is an interplay between the three functions. Therefore complex modelling of communication subnetwork is necessary. And similar completeness has to be applied to evaluation of measurement results as well.

As far as the relation of routing and communication protocols is concerned, it depends largely on the routing method used. Nonadaptive methods do not require status information exchange and, therefore, there is no need to include them in communication protocols. They are realized in layers, in relevant modules, but not in protocol stations.

The situation is different with adaptive routing. Here the exchange of status information between nodes is necessary. Such exchange, of course, must be part of the corresponding communication protocol. Stations exchanging routing information have to generate blocks containing the routing information and to recognize this routing information in the blocks received. This means that all kinds of routing information (both status and updating) must be included into format and command definitions. Moreover, the reactions of corresponding protocol stations have to be expressed in relevant sequences of commands and responses.

Though the protocol evaluation is the subject of Chapter 4.5, it may also be useful to mention here that we have routing method, realization of the routing method by means of communication protocol used, and implementation of this communication protocol in corresponding network elements. Performance is influenced, more or less, by all the three agents, i.e. by the method, by the protocol, and also by the implementation. This means that even using the effective routing method does not guarantee the expected performance, because the protocol may not be the most suitable (e.g. it may introduce unnecessary delays) or the implementation may have a negative influence.

3.6.3 Bibliographical notes

Mathematical background and principles of static routing and of various routing method may be found in books of Kleinrock [126], Seidler [256], Schwartz [253], and in the survey of Inose [115].

Well-written surveys of routing methods (or techniques, or doctrines, or algorithms, or protocols) are, for example, those of McQuillan [153], Rudin [239], Fratta [86], Gerla [88].

The following are some references to several routing methods: adaptive routing [16, 156, 212], bifurcated routing [210, 212], delta routing [239], local distribution routing [107].

Comparison of adaptive and nonadaptive routing methods is, for example, in [31], and evaluation of several routing methods in the performance context is in [127, 213].

Routing and flow control together are dealt with in [43, 241], and routing and congestion in [155].

From among many other publications the following may also be mentioned [29, 40, 243].

3.7 Link Capacity Sharing

3.7.1 Frequency and time-division multiplexing

As the economic analysis of computer networks and of complete systems of teleprocessing show, and as we have also pointed out several times, the communication means constitute the most expensive part and this price can be supposed to rise constantly, thus representing an ever increasing portion of the total cost of computer systems. We shall not analyse the reasons, since they are not directly related to our problems, but we should realize that communication means must be handled with the highest possible economy.

In this chapter we shall deal with link and channel capacities which in statistical information theory acquires a precisely defined value depending on the amount and the character of noise which causes an erroneous receipt of information. The capacity represents the maximal information which can be transmitted from a sender to a receiver over a noisy channel with an arbitrarily low error probability (residual error rate). It is possible to achieve the channel capacity (at least theoretically) by optimal transmission and reception methods (modulation and coding, demodulation and decoding). These values are not achieved in practice: in most cases the channels are utilized far below such a limit. As we are unable to influence the amount of transmitted information in the above sense by means of communication control and protocols, we shall not deal with this capacity and its utilization.

Let us start with the situation with which we are concerned, namely with data links characterized by their transmission rates. The rate is determined by the communication and coding methods, and to increase this rate without changing these methods is practically impossible. For the purposes of communication control we may consider the transmission rate as a practical link or channel capacity (remember the difference between a link and a channel from Chapter 1.2), and find within the frame of protocols the methods of sharing this capacity among several participant stations.

In this chapter we shall deal with two basic models: a two-station model and a multistation model. Both models are shown in Figure 3.34.

In the first model the link capacity is shared between two stations that wish to work in the HDX mode (e.g. in a dialogue) and it is therefore necessary to build a channel from station S_1 to station S_2' and vice versa. A second model, a more universal one, is expected to utilize a common link by more stations on both sites. This model includes a multiaccess, if $u>1$ and $v=1$ (one station receives and other stations intend to send data), and a broadcasting and a group calling service, if $u=1$ and $v>1$ (one station sends data to several stations simultaneously). In both cases there is supposed to be an SX operation from the station S to the station S'; for a HDX operation the same model with the help of the two-station modification is to be used. An FDX communication mode demands two equal models, each for one direction of transmission.

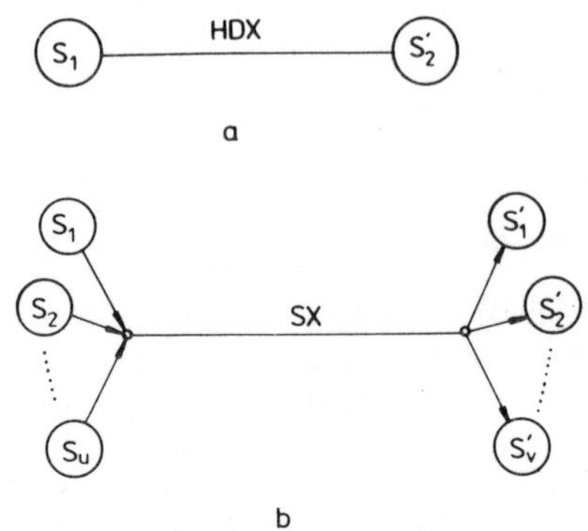

Figure 3.34 Basic models for channel capacity sharing
a) two-station model
b) general model

The reason for sharing the link capacity among more stations is partly the high cost of communication but especially the low utilization of the link whenever it serves for a pair of stations only. For example, in a conversational mode it has been estimated that only 2 to 5 per cent of the time during which the stations are joined to a link is usable for data transmission. For a great deal of time the link is inactive: stations process data, wait for a response, prepare information for transmission, etc. It is therefore quite natural that it appears advantageous to offer the transmission capacity to stations being prepared to exchange data whenever the station which occupied it before terminates its session.

Some remarks on terminology. We have used the term "capacity sharing", since it best expresses the reality even though it is used more often for dividing the processing and storage capacities. In the literature the term "multiplex" is frequently used but as we shall see later this means only one, the least economical, method of sharing. The comprehensive term "channel capacity assignment" already has its firm place in topological network design where the problem of allocation of channels of different capacities in the network is being solved provided that the constraints on throughput and the minimal costs of the network are fulfilled.

Before we demonstrate the basic methods of providing channels on one common link, which forms the ground for assigning these channels to the stations in operation, let us briefly explain the two main methods — that of frequency division and that of time-division. In spite of the fact that both methods are well known to most readers let us repeat their main feature.

The frequency division multiplexing (FDM) results from the fact that where a link is characterized by a frequency bandwidth, it is possible to transmit only signals within this bandwidth, which itself is related to the transmission (more precisely signalling) rate. If the rate is lower the bandwidth is not fully utilized so that a portion of it remains free for the transmission of other signals. Thus, the band may be divided with separating filters in order to create several subbands — subchannels. For practical reasons it is necessary for certain portions of the bandwidth to remain unused: this is the price we have to pay for such a division. FDM is applied, for example, in modems for creating two independent channels (e.g. a 75 bit/s channel and a 1200 bit/s channel in voice band modems), and in the same way voice-frequency telegraphy is performed (each telegraph subchannel with the rate of 50 bit/s occupies the bandwidth of 120 c/s including necessary guard bands for the separation with filters).

As there is a relation between frequency and time it is possible to transform the FDM technique into the time-division multiplexing (TDM) one by dividing the reserved time into short time slots and by assigning each slot to one subchannel. The number of subchannels depends, as in FDM, on the transmission rate in every subchannel and on the total rate of the common channel. It is again necessary to take into account a certain overhead (in this case a time overhead), as in the FDM technique, needed for synchronization and phasing.

One would expect that there is no great difference between both methods and that they differ in their realization only (TDM is built of a digital circuitry, the price of which is decreasing, while the cost of LC filters for FDM remains practically unchanged). This is not quite true, although the frequency and the time are mutually interchangeable variables. It suffices to compare the two methods with regard to time delay.

Suppose the same initial conditions: the equal number of stations (subchannels) u independently generate data blocks of n bits long with the traffic intensity λ in block/s according to the Poisson distribution, the transmission rate is equal to R bit/s, and the same utilization factor $\varrho = \frac{\lambda n}{R}$ (remember the utilization factor designates the degree of channel utilization, which under perfect scheduling achieves 1 and we may therefore call it a capacity, too). Let us neglect otherwise unavoidable frequency and time gaps for FDM and TDM, respectively. It can be shown that the waiting time in buffers under the same conditions is the same so it is sufficient only to deal with the time needed for sending a block from a buffer. For FDM it equals $u \cdot \frac{n}{R}$ because only one subchannel is available while in TDM it is n-times shorter due to the larger transmission rate R, but in the latter case we must add the time necessary to find out the corresponding slot, which represents on average $\frac{nu}{2R}$. By comparing we finally find that TDM gives smaller mean time delay than FDM. From that it follows, with the constant delay assumption, that TDM will serve more stations (it allows more subchannels to be formed) than the FDM method.

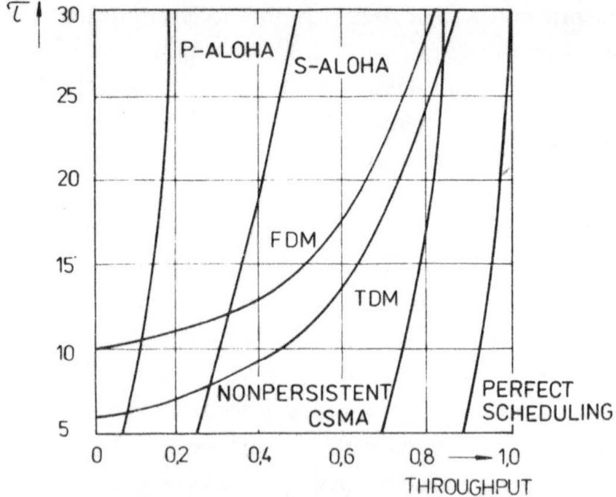

Figure 3.35 Mean normalized (with respect to n/R) delay τ vs. throughput

We may represent our results graphically. The dependence between the mean delay, related for easier comparison to $\frac{n}{R}$, and the total throughput is depicted in Fig. 3.35. We see that TDM affords better capacity utilization than FDM and therefore we shall not deal with FDM any more and TDM will be the subject of the rest of this chapter.

3.7.2 Methods of time assignment

Time division multiplexing means that a certain time slot is to be assigned for a station for the time during which it can exchange data with another station. Let us consider the model of multiaccess where a certain number of stations (say u) wish to correspond with the station S_0 (see Fig. 3.45b, where S' is replaced by S_0). We can recognize three cases.

In the first case the whole link capacity is occupied by the station S_0 which opens a transmission with one of the other stations, say S_i, sends data, waits for an acknowledgment, and eventually receives data from it. Finally, S_0 terminates the transmission. It is not important which station is initiating and which controls the communication. As soon as the link becomes free, S_0 may open a transmission with another station S_j (Figure 3.36a). It is clear that during a session (from the transmission opening up to the transmission termination) the whole link capacity is assigned to one pair of stations. Such an assignment method is essentially the same as the well known circuit switching even though it is not a matter of space division among several links (see Chapter 1.2) but of time division among slots. The slots are, however, assigned for entire sessions.

Now let us suppose S_0 wants to exchange data with several station (say S_i, S_j, and S_k). For the sake of shortening the mean delay all pairs of station will take turns according to messages, i.e. first the station S_0 sends a message to the station S_i and without waiting for a response it passes the link capacity to another station (S_i), of course for one message only, etc. It is apparent that data messages may be of different lengths and some of the stations will wait for their sessions longer than others. Nevertheless, the mean waiting time is shorter than in the case of line switching.

The changing in utilization of link capacity for separate messages is called message switching, although the messages cannot quit the station S_0 on different links, but do so in different time intervals — slots.

Message switching may give longer delay within a session than circuit switching, in particular in a conversational mode, because one station has to wait for a response until all messages to other stations are sent (remember that there are no bounds to the message lengths). A way of improving the chances of all stations is to give the link capacity of shorter slots than of full messages. Therefore, each data message must be divided into fragments (enveloped in blocks as for error control purposes) and the link capacity is consecutively accorded by embedding them into fixed length slots. The time course appears as represented in Figure 3.36c. To each pair of stations a fixed length slot is assigned and is filled with commands, responses and data fragments. As the blocks rather than the messages are switched, we may call such a capacity sharing method block switching or, according to the widely used notion, packet switching. The blocks (packets) are not, however, split in many directions as we are accustomed to in the packet switching networks but the essence is the same.

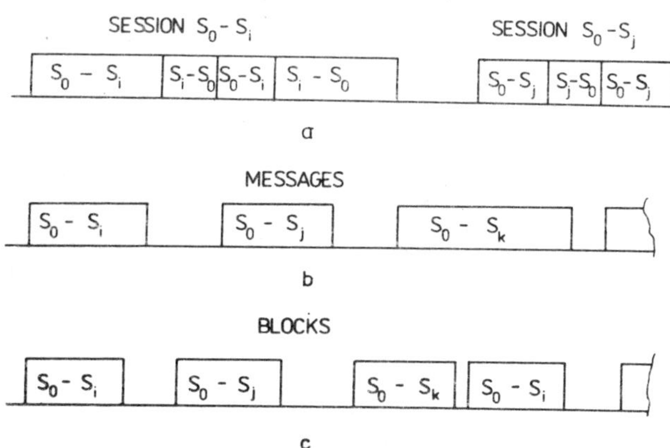

Figure 3.36 Types of unslotted time division
a) circuit switching (according to sessions)
b) message switching
c) packet switching (according to blocks)

All the methods dealt with so far suffer from a common disadvantage. It is impossible to fully utilize the link capacity because between sessions (in circuit switching), messages (in message switching), and blocks (in packet switching) the gaps are required for passing the link from one pair of stations to another. Moreover, collisions may occur (in practice very often) when a station begins to send data at the same time as another one uses a link. In that case the signals transmitted are thrown into confusion and the receivers cannot separate them accurately. There exist two ways of avoiding or at least reducing collisions. One method consists in a special control either from outside or by one of the stations (central control), the other is to synchronize all slots. Besides the methods described above, which we can commonly call unsynchronized or unslotted, synchronized or slotted methods are in use.

The slotted sharing methods need the division of the time for which the link is to be utilized into consecutive fixed length slots without any gaps, and permit the stations to begin sending only at the starting instant of slots (Figure 3.37). This measure leads to a reduction in the number of collisions even they cannot be entirely suppressed without additional control, as we shall see in Section 3.7.5.

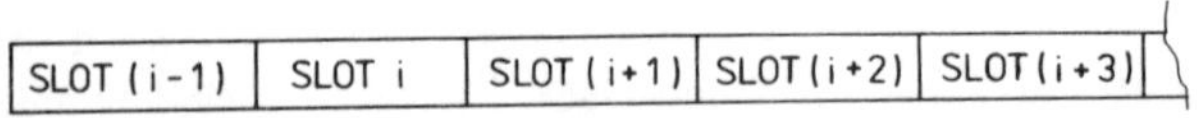

Figure 3.37 An example of slotted time division

It might seem that slotted methods are suitable only for packet switching because every packet fits just in exactly one slot, but this is not quite true. Sessions as well as long messages may be put into several consecutive or nonconsecutive slots and thus utilize the advantages of slotting. Naturally, slotting methods demand synchronization between stations and therefore it is correct to call them synchronized.

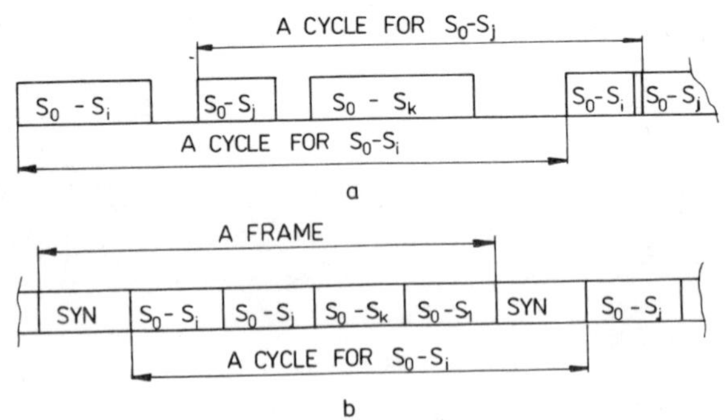

Figure 3.38 Determination of cycles and frames
a) the case of unslotted TDM
b) the case of slotted TDM

In the time division technique, besides a slot the notion of a cycle will be suitable. We shall define this as a time interval between the beginning of the slot assigned to the station (session) and the beginning of the nearest slot assigned to the same station (session). An example of cycles is shown in Figure 3.38: Figure 3.38a illustrates a case of an unslotted TDM and two cycles of various length (the cycle length depends upon the station or the session in question), the fixed length cycles are depicted in Figure 3.38b for the slotted TDM.

All slotted methods require synchronization and phasing so that every station might utilize a predetermined slot. Therefore after a certain number of consecutive slots devoted to station purposes (data slots) the synchronization (phasing) slot must be inserted. The time interval between the beginnings of two consecutive synchronization slots which embeds only data slots is called a frame (not to be confused with the block, also called a frame in the HDLC protocol). An example of a frame is in Figure 3.38b, where the synchronization slot is designated by the abbreviation SYN.

All the methods we have just described use only the method of dividing time into slots (of equal or unequal length, slotted or unslotted) but they do not control the assignment of slots to stations or pairs of stations. This is the task of capacity sharing control, or, more precisely, of slot assignment control.

We should try to classify the assignment methods but, as we shall see later, this is hardly possible because various methods exist, so that to place them in a certain class is very difficult. We attempt at least to specify the basic classes of assignment control, which will help us further in our interpretation.

FDM and TDM methods, and others, in which the subchannels (in TDM time slots) are permanently assigned are called static, fixed, or deterministic. It does not follow that every station has to be assigned to one or several slots regardless of the requirement to exchange data. There are methods giving a slot (subchannel) only to a station in operation but in which such a slot (subchannel) remains assigned to that station until it terminates its transmission. Such methods may also be assumed to be deterministic.

Another method is dynamic or adaptive assignment: the capacity is divided between the stations which are prepared to exchange data. We endeavour to let no station wait long for a release of the link capacity, so have appropriate buffer sizes, and at the same time allow it to reach a capacity as high as possible. It is clear that the dynamic assignment control will be much more complicated than the static one. The dynamic assignment may be centralized or decentralized (distributed).

Finally, the assignment need not be controlled at all; in spite of this fact we can obtain in several cases quite satisfactory utilization by the link capacity of many stations. This is not so peculiar: we have met a similar approach in the preceding chapter on routing. Such uncontrolled methods use random mechanisms and therefore we may call them random.

Table 3.8 The price of channel capacity sharing controls

Type of control	Errors due to collisions	Idle capacity	Overhead
no control	yes	no	no
static control	no	yes	no
dynamic control	no	no	yes

For better illustration the main classes of link capacity sharing and assignment are schematically shown in Figure 3.38. In order to let the reader see the advantages and disadvantages of control modes, in Table 3.8 they are compared with respect to the possibility of a collision occurrence, to the unused link capacity, and to the overhead needed for control. The comparison is very rough but it suffices for the purpose of this section; in further sections we shall make the differences and features of link capacity sharing methods more precise.

3.7.3 Unslotted methods

Unslotted sharing methods do not assume a timing, i.e. the assignment of link capacity may occur at any instant. First of all we shall deal with the controlled assignment, central or distributed. Distinguishing the static and the dynamic assignment is possible in principle, too, but for the time being we shall suppose the assignment is dynamic. Let us begin with the point-to-point HDX link.

As soon as the data exchange is provided on the HDX line between two stations it is necessary to take care of the alternating of transmission directions. In order to avoid collisions it is advantageous to appoint one station as a control station and the other as a tributary station, either permanently or for a given session. The control station then has among others a right to dispose of the link capacity and may assign it in accordance with the requirements of the tributary station. If the roles of stations are not decided in advance a mechanism must be given telling how and when to appoint a station to be a control. The control function can be shouldered by the station which established the connection, which opened the transmission, or which is intended to send data. For the sake of brevity we shall call the station which is just sending data a master station, and the station receiving data a slave station. We remind readers who deal with data transmission and its control that the terminology is not yet stabilized, e.g. a couple master-slave may in some cases indicate the relation of superiority and subordination while in the HDLC protocol the same relation is called primary-secondary (see Appendix C). We emphasize this as we had to decide on a uniform terminology for this book and we do not want to devise a new one for the reason that till now its usage is not consistent enough.

If neither station is appointed for the control then collisions clearly cannot be eliminated. Such cases where both stations mutually start to establish the connection, both stations open the transmission at the same time, or both stations are intended to send data (they become master), lead to unsuccessful operation. These exceptional situations must be anticipated and allowed for by a sophisticated control mechanism (e.g. exceptional state recovery, which is the subject of Chapter 3.8).

Suppose the control station is at the same time a master one. Then it has the right to profit from its position and to keep the link capacity for sending a data message. It is obliged, however, to pass over the capacity to the tributary station because it needs an answer from it and, moreover, it does not know if the tributary station will then send data (it becomes master and the control station changes its position to slave). The moment of passing over the capacity is indicated by the end of a message (of all the blocks or at least of the last block of the message), or by a special command, or, of course, by an appropriate time-out.

As the control station hands a link capacity to the tributary one, so the tributary station does to the control station. The difference consists in a latitude: the control station has the right to take away the capacity from the tributary one regardless of whether the tributary station utilizes it or not, but the tributary has no such right.

Let us now consider a more complicated case — the data exchange over a multipoint link. Such a link is two-way either alternate (HDX) or simultaneous (FDX) and in both cases the link capacity has to tocared about the assignment to pairs stations. First of all, we appoint a control station so that the others remain tributary. In general, there are four cases. The control station is at the same time either master or slave, and the same holds for the tributary one (it becomes either slave or master). If the control station wishes to send data to a tributary we speak about the discipline of selecting. Otherwise (the control station will receive only) we speak of polling.

In the conversational mode the two disciplines alternate and if only short messages are exchanged, even very frequently, the waiting times for releasing the link capacity for any pair of stations are not long. If, however, a tributary station had sent a long data message, access to the link would be locked up to other tributary stations. Such a situation has to be recovered from the side of the control station, e.g. it interrupts the communication for a certain time and passes the link over to another station. It may again revert to the original station in a short time.

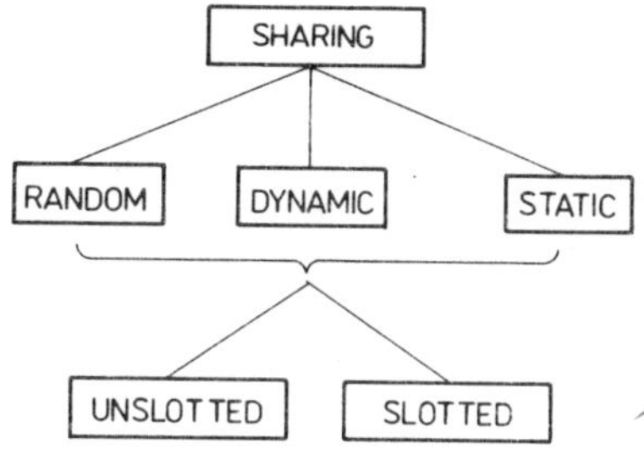

Figure 3.39 Methods of link capacity sharing and assignment

Now suppose that some tributary station sends data at a low traffic intensity (once in a long time) and the control station has no other means of recognizing the moment when the tributary station is prepared for sending than by permanently checking the poll. An unsuccessful polling consists in connecting the control station with a tributary one (in addressing) and in waiting for a negative response which requires a certain time which is missing for other tributary stations. It is possible, however, not to ask such a station but to wait for its announcement. This is the third case, which is called a contention, and which means in the centralized control of link capacity sharing that a tributary station (or several tributary stations) may make a claim during a pause in a transmission, and call the control station's attention to the fact that the tributary one is ready to transmit. The control station must take into account certain pauses (idle states), i.e. let the link be unused for a short time without reacting by polling. Thus the control remains centralized.

The last case when the tributary station is at the same time slave is performed by selecting and does not carry any special indication.

All the three cases are illustrated in Table 3.9.

The selecting in the centralized control enables the control station to assign the station to which data will be sent, e.g. by means of its address and the corresponding command. In addition to this, the selecting allows the performance of a group calling service in a multipoint, i.e. the emission of data simultaneously to a group of slave stations. First, all stations for which data are intended need to be designated by means of consecutive transmission openings or of a special group calling command to which only the station being appointed in advance (or during the transmission opening by its address in the command) will react. The same procedure is of use for the message confirmation: the accepted message is acknowledged by all stations in a group or by one of them (usually this is a strategically important one, perhaps the one furthest away from the control station).

Table 3.9 Types of operation

Station	master	slave
control	selecting	polling
tributary	contention	

When the control station polls tributary ones, it does not know which station is prepared to send data. It must, before assigning the link capacity, discover the master station by some mechanism. The simplest way is by means of a cyclic interrogation in a predetermined order, in other words a static probing. If each station is interrogated once within a polling cycle (do not confuse this with a station cycle, defined in Section 3.7.1, because now the cycle is related to the control station and denotes the time interval within which the control station turns to a multipoint link), then its duration is equal to the duration of a station cycle and every tributary station must wait, on average, half of that duration before it is polled. It is of course possible to shorten the waiting time, at least for a few stations, by shortening their cycle by polling the stations more than once within a polling cycle (for details see Section 3.7.5). In all cases, however, the number and the order of inquiries is predetermined in a round-robin fashion and therefore this polling discipline is called roll-call or bus polling.

As in roll-call polling, each successive poll and poll-acknowledged message and command must flow back and forth between the central station and the tributary ones, the waiting time and therefore the round-trip delay is substantially long. In order to shorten the overall delay the tributary station furthest away is interrogated first. This station, having no data to send, in turn polls the next tributary station down the link, etc., until the polled tributary station becomes master. Then the polling control is passed back to the control station and the roll-call polling follows.

Such a discipline, known as hub or distributed polling (the latter term is more appropriate since in fact the control is distributed over all stations), needs the tributary stations to be more elaborate because they must be able to interchange their own addresses with the addresses of the next stations. In addition to this, they must recover the failure situations when the next station cannot react to a poll (e.g. it is out of order). In that case the polling cycle is interrupted and the control station, after an appropriate time-out, must try to find the broken link by means of the roll-call polling. When the station having a failure is found out the control station commands the preceding station to change permanently the address of the sending poll command.

Hub polling is depicted in Figure 3.40. Case a) shows the failure-free operation; in case b) station S_2 is out of order and station S_3 changes the address of S_2 to the address of S_1.

The hub polling discipline shortens the cycle length and compensates for the time delay on long links (in particular satellites) but does not decrease the access time to links with small propagation delay. The contention leads to a decrease in the mean waiting time when there are more stations with a low traffic intensity, but it allows collision occurrence. It is possible, however, to control the polling from the control station side in such a way that tributary stations being ready for sending will access to the link capacity sooner.

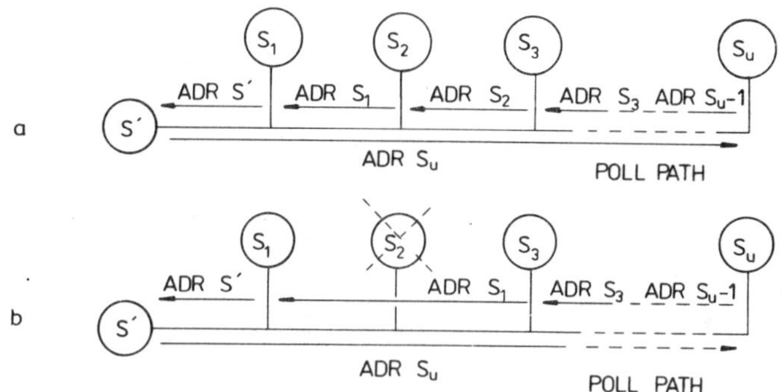

Figure 3.40 Hub polling system
a) all stations are ready
b) the case of the station S_2 being in a failure

Instead of interrogating consecutively or according to the predetermined program the control station may probe the whole group of stations. If there are more stations in a polled group which are sending the contention inquiry the control station hears it as a "noise" (collision occurs) and judges from it that at least two stations in the group want to transmit data. If in the polled group there is no such station the control station proceeds to the next group. (The case when exactly one station announces is handled by the normal contention and polling discipline.)

The appropriate division of all tributary stations into groups may substantially shorten the mean access time of master stations to a link. The best way is to divide all stations consecutively into halves: first, the half of all stations and its complement is interrogated, then each group is narrowed in two halves, etc., until all ready stations are polled. As a consequence, the number of interrogations as well as the length of station addresses is reduced (the latter needs an appropriate coding of addresses), which influences the amount of overhead.

Figure 3.41 shows the dependency between the mean cycle time and the probability, that tributary stations have prepared at least one data message, for the roll-call polling (this is constant regardless of the traffic intensity of stations) and for the probing, discipline just described which may be called, for our purposes, a binary searching.

As the figure shows, the mean searching time of binary searching depends on the traffic intensity of polled stations and there exists the probability p (a utilization factor) above which binary searching is worse than the roll-call polling. Binary searching may be improved if we have knowledge about the traffic intensity or if we remember the length of the last searching action. Then the starting moment should be determined when the control station must change from binary searching into roll-call polling.

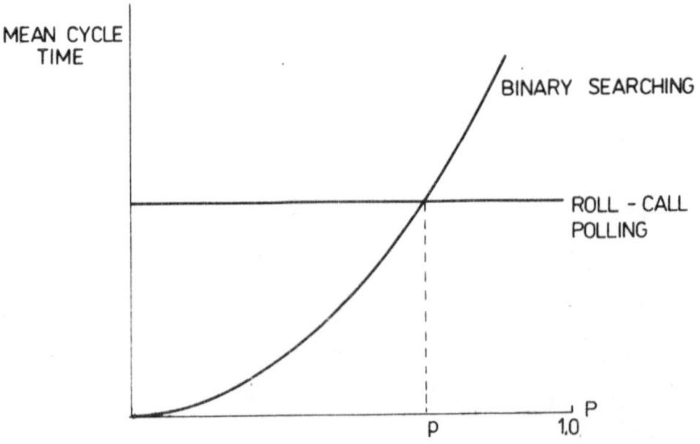

Figure 3.41 Comparison of roll-call polling and binary searching. (P = prob{at least one message at the beginning of a cycle})

Let us return to slot sizes which were dealt with in the preceding section (see also Figure 3.36). In spite of all the lengths which may be used in any polling/selecting disciplines, the operation on a multipoint link prefers sharing according to sessions, i.e. the control station turns to a tributary one for the whole duration of a session. If the control station, however, exchanges data with tributary stations via a concentrator, capacity sharing according to messages or blocks shortens the polling cycle because during the time, when the control station waits for a response from the tributary station it may contact another station (it is understood for a message or for a block). When the contention discipline is used the capacity is shared among many stations according to short messages or blocks (see the next section).

3.7.4 Contention methods (multiaccess)

In the previous section we have dealt with the contention discipline when one station has been put in charge of control. In this section we shall go further and consider the case when no station is control and master stations want to send a message to the slave one over a common channel (see the multiaccess model in Figure 3.34b). Moreover, suppose that each master station has a backward channel from the slave station at its disposal.

The action of master stations to a slave one is very similar to centrally controlled searching. The only difference is in the inability to perform collisions by means of the slave station (at that time control station) because the control is now distributed. The master stations have to take care of successful data transfer in spite of collisions.

Suppose a station began to transmit and during the transmission another station also opened its transmission. As soon as two or more signals overlap the slave station receives a noise and therefore it cannot acknowledge in affirmative over a backward channel. It either responds by a negative acknowledgment or does not respond at all. In the latter case the P-acknowledgment scheme is used (for details see Chapter 3.4) so that the time-out is needed during which the master station waits for the reply and after time-out elapsing it may repeat the message.

If, after the negative reply or time-out elapsing, the master stations began to transmit again, the signals would collide for sure. To avoid the repeated collisions two methods, deterministic and stochastic, can be used. The former consists of assigning to each station different lengths of time-outs so no pair of stations can begin to transmit at the same time. The time differences, however, must be so great that each message, regardless of its length, may reach the destination without any collision. Such a method is very cumbersome and therefore the stochastic lengths of time-out are preferred. In that case the master station retransmits a previously collided message at random, i.e. it chooses the length of time-out according to some probability distribution (say uniform) and after it expires the message is sent again. It must be admitted that the collisions are not fully suppressed but, as analytical and experimental results show, the random method is surprisingly efficient.

As the random contention (from this moment we shall call it random multiaccess method) with random waiting after a collision was implemented for the first time in radio network ALOHA, it is called very often a method of "pure ALOHA" or "unslotted ALOHA" (abbreviated P-ALOHA). The maximal relative throughput of P-ALOHA is $\frac{1}{2e} = 0.184$ and it does not require any control and any "intelligence" in terminal stations. Also no overhead is consumed with the exception of, say, necessary addressing.

Provided the channel utilization of 18 per cent seems to be very low, let us show a simple example. Consider a radio channel with the transmission rate of 24 kbit/s and master stations that transmit data messages of 1000 bits length. If only one master station used this channel it would emit, on average, 24 messages per second. Suppose a terminal station is able to emit on average one message per minute. Then the method of pure ALOHA enables a common radio channel to be shared by at most 265 stations with the mean transmission rate 4416 bit/s. And it already forms a very extensive terminal network.

The dependency between the normalized delay and the relative throughput is depicted in Figure 3.35 for several capacity sharing methods, among others for the P-ALOHA method. We see that P-ALOHA is much better for low traffic intensity not only than FDM but also than TDM. We must add, however, that the variable length of messages decreases the throughput and increases the delay (up to 25 per cent).

We have, for the present, considered that all master stations are "deaf" to signals in a common channel (they listen only to signals in the backward one) and that they announce at any moment when they have a message prepared, regardless of the state of a common channel. Let us give them the ability to sense the carrier due to another station transmission. It is understood, however, that the propagation delay of the backward channel is very small compared to the message transmission time.

The carrier-sense multiple-access method (or multiple access with side information), abbreviated CSMA, enables the ready stations to learn whether the common channel is free or busy. As soon as they are sure the channel is free (no carrier is heard) they occupy it by sending their message. There are two actions to be taken by the station if the channel is busy.

One extreme case occurs if, after the common channel is sensed busy, the station permanently listens to it and waits until the channel goes idle, and only then transmits a message. As the station persists in transmitting, the method is called persistent or, more precisely, 1-persistent (the master station transmits with probability one). The 1-persistent CSMA achieves greater throughput than the P-ALOHA but among other CSMA methods is the least effective.

Another extreme case is the nonpersistent CSMA. A ready station senses the common channel and transmits a message if the channel is idle, otherwise it schedules the new sensing to some later time. At this new point in time, it returns to sensing the channel and repeats the action described above. The nonpersistent CSMA gives much better performance (higher throughput) than the 1-persistent CSMA.

The two CSMA methods differ by the probability (one or zero) of not rescheduling a message which upon arrival finds the channel busy. In fact, both methods are deterministic (unless the new point in time is randomized) but we anticipate that due to differences in throughputs and delays some interjacent methods need to be available.

In the case of a 1-persistent CSMA whenever two or more stations become ready, they wait for the channel to become idle and then they all begin to transmit at once. So a collision will occur with probability one. The modification of 1-persistent CSMA consists in including an additional parameter p, the probability that a ready station persists, $1-p$ being the probability of delaying transmission by a certain time. This gives rise to the p-persistent CSMA, which is a generalization of the 1-persistent CSMA.

The parameter p will be chosen so as to increase the throughput as much as possible for different numbers of stations and various traffic intensities. While the throughput of the P-ALOHA method does not depend on the propagation delay, the throughput of CSMA does. An increase in the ratio of propagation delay to message transmission time results in older channel state information from sensing. The throughputs for nonpersistent and p-persistent CSMA are more sensitive to increases in this ratio, as compared to the 1-persistent CSMA. For larger ratios, optimum p-persistent is lower-bounded by 1-persistent, while for smaller ratios the nonpersistent and the optimal p-persistent CSMAs are nearly equivalent with respect to the throughput and the delay.

The relative throughputs for several CSMA methods, for the ratio of propagation delay to message transmission time equal to 0.01, range from 0.184 for pure ALOHA to 0.857 for slotted nonpersistent CSMA. We note that the optimal value of p is 0.03 giving the relative throughput of 0.827, and that the nonpersistent CSMA is only a little poorer.

There is a situation, in particular in networks with mobile terminals connected with radio channels, when some stations may not be able to hear all the other station traffic and cannot effectively use any CSMA method. This gives rise to the so-called "hidden terminal" problem mentioned in Chapter 1.2. If all stations are in line-of-sight of at least one station (say satellite) the hidden-terminal problem can be eliminated by dividing the common channel into two subchannels; one of them is assigned to the busy tone (hence the term busy-tone multiple-access or BTMA method). As long as the station is receiving a message on the data subchannel, it transmits a busy tone signal on the other subchannel which is sensed by the other stations, so any CSMA methods is usable.

3.7.5 Slotted methods

As has been stated in Section 3.7.2 the slotted time division multiplexing consists in forming a frame divided into fixed lenght slots. In that case no station may access to a common channel except at the beginning of a slot. This, on one hand, leads to reducing the number of collisions (a collision takes place only if two or more whole full slots overlap while unslotted method admits collisions even if the last bit of one message overlaps the first bit of another message), on the other hand, the synchronization and the phasing have to be ensured and actions of all stations must be put under a channel synchronization control. Besides less collisions the slotting yields higher channel utilization, particularly in the decentralized control of capacity assignment, because idle and unused time intervals between slots are eliminated (cf. Figure 3.38a and 3.38b).

The increasing in throughput and the decreasing in delay is especially remarkable with the synchronized or slotted multiple access (S-ALOHA). Due to reduction of collisions the relative throughput of S-ALOHA is two times higher than of P-ALOHA, i.e. $\frac{1}{e} = 0.368$ (Figure 3.35). Similarly, the introduction of slotting into other multiaccess methods increases their throughput (for example slotted one persistent and nonpersistent CSMA method a chieves 0.531 and 0.857, respectively).

In general, it is not necessary to put a station in charge of a control, excluding such cases as to perform exceptional situations when a control station may play its important part. Otherwise each station may, of course, catch a corresponding slot and use it for transmission according to an assignment method. The slotted methods are most interesting with respect to the methods of assignment which we have divided in Section 3.7.2 into static and dynamic. We begin with static methods.

The simplest approach is to assign each slot (with the exclusion, say, of the slot needed for synchronization and phasing of slots and frames) to exactly one station (one session) in a frame on fixed predetermined basis. If a frame contains u slots designated for the data transfer (data slots), up to u stations can share the common link capacity. Each station then occupies one slot on *a priori* position in a frame so that the control mechanism only cyclically scans the set of u stations, in a round-robin fashion, similarly as in the polling. While the polling can operate with sessions or with messages owing to the variable duration of time slots, multiplexing needs message fragmentation into fragments of fixed length. Since the allocation of stations in slots in a frame is fixed or synchronized (phased), the term synchronous time division multiplexing (STDM) is often used in order to distinguish it from the asynchronous time division multiplexing (ATDM) which will be described below.

Figure 3.42a shows an example of the division of link capacity among five stations by means of STDM. The frame is divided into six slots, one of which serves for synchronization purposes (SYN), the other 5 slots are once and for all assigned to the stations S_1 to S_5 to exchange data between each other or with the station S_0. No overhead information (e.g. addressing) is needed for such an access control because both sides of the communication system being synchronized identify exactly the positions of all sessions in slots within a frame. This is a substantial advantage of STDM.

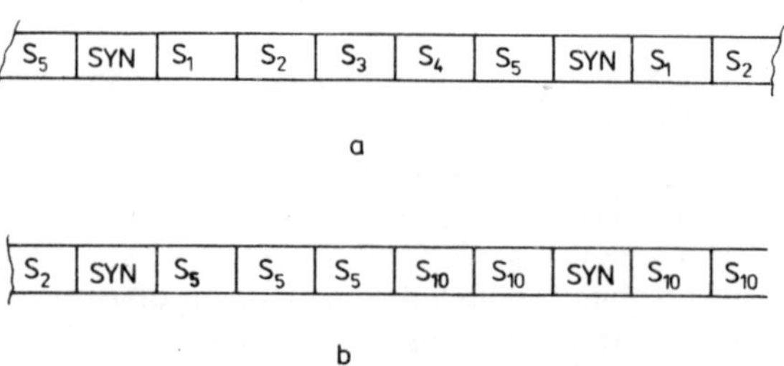

Figure 3.42 An example of STDM (a) and ATDM (b) techniques

Deeper analysis of data traffic reveals that during a session (from the transmission opening up to the transmission termination) the computer station is active no more than 30 per cent of the time and the terminal stations have much lower efficiency, about 5 per cent. As a consequence, the channel is idle for a significant portion of the holding time. Thus, most of the data slots remain unutilized even during the high traffic period, and this is a penalty we pay for the simplicity of synchronous access control.

In order to increase the link utilization, another allocation scheme has been suggested. The slots are not dedicated to all stations regardless of their activity but only to those which are ready to transmit data. As soon as the active station terminates its transmission, consecutive empty slots are given not at random but only to the stations in whose buffer the data are already prepared. The station therefore asynchronously or statistically may use time slots according to their traffic, so that the term statistical or ATDM is quite appropriate.

Because of lower traffic intensity fewer data slots than the number of required sessions in a frame are necessary, i.e. the same frame as used for STDM can cover more sessions (it is estimated 2- to 4-times). Such a case is depicted in Figure 3.42b. The frame with 5 data slots is shared among 10 stations S_1 to S_{10}. At the moment corresponding to the frame depicted, only S_2, S_5 and S_{10} are in operation and are using the free slots. The station S_2 transmits a short block message holding in one slot while the stations S_5 and S_{10} require more than one slot for their messages. (S_5 transmits a three-slot message, S_{10} transmits a four-slot message.)

The ATDM technique suffers from two substantial shortcomings. First, it is necessary to indicate the position of each session in a frame, e.g. by addressing, which constitutes a not negligible part of the data slot and increases the overhead. Second, buffering is required to handle statistical fluctuations in the input traffic. But the advantages of ATDM are so great that this technique surpasses that of STDM with respect to the channel capacity utilization.

It is clear that ATDM belongs to dynamic sharing methods as they have already been discussed in Section 3.7.2 because it dynamically allocates the time slots to the currently active stations, in contrast to STDM which operates statically.

The performance of STDM can be improved, however, if the behaviour of the station served is known in advance. Suppose that among five stations there are two (say S_1 and S_2) with considerably higher traffic intensity than that of the three remaining ones. In a classical solution by means of STDM the two first data slots will be almost always busy and, in addition, the buffers of S_1 and S_2 may overflow, while the three other data slots remain unutilized. It is possible to find a solution to this problem even within the STDM principle by a slightly different allocation of stations in a frame. We can either lengthen the slots or shorten the cycle. The first solution termed contiguous fixed assignment works as follows (see Figure 3.43a): the stations with heavy traffic will occupy several consecutive slots (two in our example) so that for these stations more room for data in each frame is available. To shorten a cycle for stations with heavy traffic means that two or more nonconsecutive data slots in a frame are assigned to them (Figure 3.43b). The latter method is occasionally called a distributed fixed assignment.

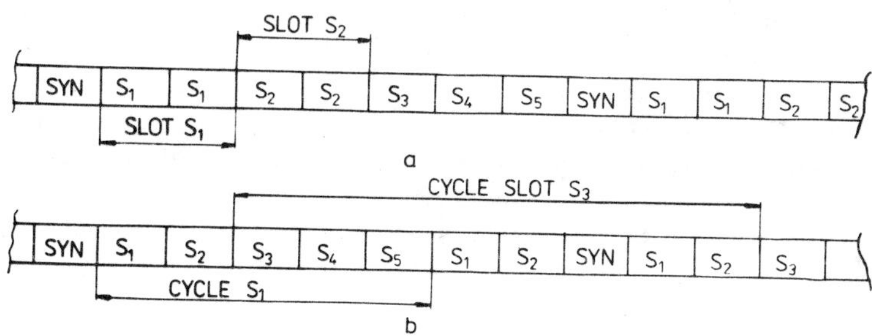

Figure 3.43 An example of contiguous (a) and distributed (b) fixed assignment

There does not seem to be any difference between the two methods, but deeper analysis shows that the performance depends on the sharing overhead (idle slots, safeguard time intervals). For large overhead the contiguous fixed assignment method is superior to the distributed one and vice versa (when the sharing overhead is small, distributed fixed assignment provides slightly better performance).

The above assignment techniques (and many others) are associated with two parameters: the cycle length and the slot length, both being integer multiple of the elementary slot.

Let us return to dynamic assignment. The necessary penalty which must be paid if it is used is a certain but nonzero overhead of each data slot. The overhead bits are needed not only for addressing but also for the free/busy status indication, for priority degrees, etc.

The free/busy status may be implemented by one bit, e.g. 1 indicates that the slot is busy while 0 means it is free (the first bit in a slot is most convenient for that purpose as the free/busy status is then recognized immediately at the beginning of reading a slot). The one bit indication substantially economizes the overhead but it is less resistent to the occurrence of an error.

The addressing of u stations requires $\lceil \log_2 u \rceil$[1]) bits (in binary coding). If $\lceil \log_2 (u + 1) \rceil < \lceil \log_2 u \rceil + 1$ then it is more convenient to represent the free/busy status in an unused address combination.

The dynamic allocation technique can be used regardless of the communication media. In particular, it suits the sharing control in loop or ring links. If we recall the topology and the transmission technique of such links from Chapter 1.2, we can easily apply our consideration to that case. For example, the notion of a frame acquires a physical meaning: it is formed by all the bit signals present on a loop at a given instant of time. A special loop controller generates phasing slots and repeats and regenerates, if necessary, a loop signal.

If the sharing is centrally controlled, one station is prescribed to govern the sharing and the assignment, i.e. it has a priority to handle all data slots. It need not leave any busy slot but it may fill it with its data. Thus, besides packet switching we find message switching in centrally controlled loops (a data message is divided into fragments, but they are inserted into consecutive data slots).

It is understood that the control station cannot use all data slots only for its data; it is obliged to enable a transmission to other tributary stations. In the case of message switching the end of message needs to be indicated and then a sufficient amount of free slots must be released. If the control station does not indicate in free slots the address of the destination to which the slots are assigned, all far stations in a loop have a disadvantage over the near ones because the latter are automatically given priority in filling the slots. This method can be improved by passing control to the well designated station (as in hub polling), or by reserving free slots for a station specified in advance. We shall return to reservation schemes in more details in the next section.

Regardless of the control (centralized or distributed) there are two methods of occupying free slots. In the first one the station, upon data receipt, copies the content of the slot into its buffer and does not delete it. Data in the slot runs to the control or master station which is responsible for deletion. In the second method the intended station takes the message and deletes the content of the slot so that it can re-use this slot itself, or another station in the loop can use it.

We call these methods "slot no deletion" (without slot release) and "slot deletion" (with slot release), respectively. The slot deletion method seems to be more efficient than that of slot no deletion because busy slots do not unavailingly travel around the loop but the necessary delay must be taken into account. The station must delay the slot by at least $\lceil \log_2 (u + 1) \rceil$ or $\lceil \log_2 u \rceil + 1$ bits in order to hold and delete the slot status, the destination address, and the slot content as the slot passes by. If slots are not released the station need only delay the slot by one bit to determine if the slot is empty or full. If we compare the two methods in more detail from the viewpoint of the

---

[1]) We recall that the symbol $\lceil x \rceil$ means the least integer greater than or equal to x.

mean total delay we find that the delay depends on the length of messages which are fragmented and inserted into slots. For short messages the slot no deletion method is more advantageous while with increasing length the slot deletion methods prevail.

We have already mentioned the priorities as a tool for reducing the delay for the farthest stations from the control one. In principle, the priority can be appropriated either only to stations, or only to messages (data slots), or to both. In centrally controlled loops the farthest station usually has the highest priority degree, namely in the direction both from the control station and from the tributary one. In distributed controlled loops the priorities can be assigned to stations, too, e.g. according to their traffic intensity: the lower the intensity, the higher the priority. Such a priority discipline is a sufficient condition for maximizing the mean percentage of slots able to deliver data at the station, and a necessary condition for minimizing the mean response time. Or, the priority degrees are given only to data slots according to, e.g. the following rules: the data slot transmitted to more distant stations has higher priority and among the slots having the same destination the slot sent by a more distant station has higher priority. If we come back to Figure 1.15b on page 29 the slot sent by the station S_0 to the station S_3 is prefered to the slot destined for S_1, and among slots being directed to the station S_3 the slot from S_0 has higher priority to the slot from S_2.

The operation with priorities may proceed as follows. Each station having prepared data in its buffer captures the first free or unreserved slot and designates it according to its own priority degree. If this slot passes another station with a higher priority degree, its content is either destroyed or kept in the buffer and replaced by new data and, of course, by a new (higher) priority degree. In the first case the original data slot will not reach the destination and must be retransmitted. In the latter case the bufferred data is only delayed and sent into the nearest free slot or into the slot carrying data with a still lower priority degree. The bufferring of lower priority data gives better performance but it requires a larger storage capacity.

Note that the priority indication in slot formats must lead the header in order to determine the action of the station as soon as possible. The priority indication as well as the addressing and status indication form the slot overhead.

Let us further complete this section with one task of the control station: to prevent the buildup of traffic in the loop due to station failures and thus to undelivered data slots. If an addressee of a data slot could not receive, such a slot would run around the loop and occupy it uselessly. The control station has to watch for such slots and after their passing several times through the control station (the number of passages may be a parameter of the procedure) they are cancelled or sent back to the sender, e.g. by replacing the destination address with that of the sender.

3.7.6 Slot reservation methods

Up to now we have dealt with the case when stations occupy free slots themselves or replace the content of busy slots. There exist, however, several methods of reserving some free slots in order to use them later, e.g. during the next pass. The simplest reservation method is a combination of the pure slotted allocation technique depicted in Figure 3.42b and the static allocation which gives rise to virtual channels.

As soon as a station is prepared to transmit data it captures the first free slot and occupies it with the address of destination and with data. If more than one slot is necessary to carry the data message, the other slots are assigned in consecutive frames at the same position as the first opening slot. Hence, after a dynamic allocation of the first slot the system behaves as STDM. A virtual channel consisting of several slots which are in the same position in each frame is released after an entire data message is transmitted or a session terminates.

The concept of such an allocation technique (we shall call it dynamic channel allocation) is illustrated in Figure 3.44, where the station S_2 uses the virtual channel set up of the first data slots in a frame. Station S_7 initiates the access slightly later than S_2 so that it may use the virtual channel consisting of the second data slots.

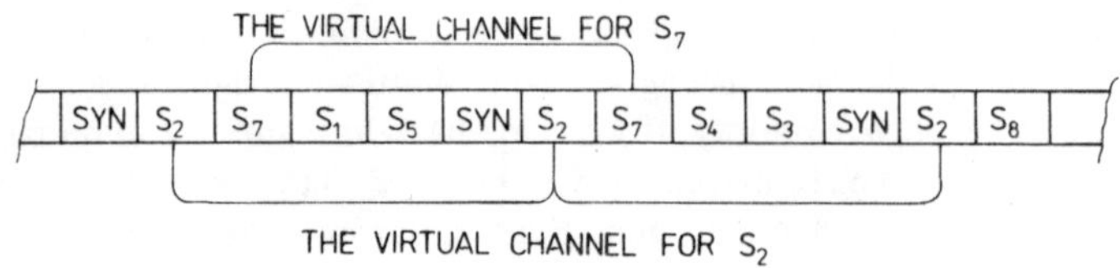

Figure 3.44 Dynamic assignment and virtual channels forming

The main feature of the dynamic channel allocation technique is a significantly lower overhead with respect to the pure dynamic slot allocation, in particular for long data messages. This is due to the fact that only the first slot needs to be addressed; the consecutive slots are fixed allocated for maintaining the virtual channel.

The time duration of virtual channels is variable and depends on the length of data message (on the number of its fragments). The end-of-use of a virtual channel (its last slot) is either indicated by a special flag so that other stations know the slot with the same position in the next frame should be free, or unindicated. In the latter case the next slot is wasted (unless it carries a free indication) or the control station must take care of its releasing (if the control is centralized).

The performance of the allocation techniques described generally depends on the station traffic intensity and on the length of the data messages (obviously the delay and the throughput of these techniques vary with the number of stations and with the transmission rate). Without going deeply into mathematical considerations (for reference see Section 3.7.7) some remarks will be of use.

As we have already mentioned, slot allocation is superior to channel allocation if short data messages are emitted with a high traffic intensity. On the other hand, channel allocation gives better performance for long and rare data messages. Hence, for two-way communication between a computer and a terminal when the computer responds with long messages to short inquiries from the terminal, a combined technique sometimes called a limited assignment will be most convenient. Limited assignment gives the computer the possibility to form the required virtual channels while the terminals capture free slots for their inquiries on the dynamic slot allocation basis. Moreover, the computer, being a control station, may transmit many free slots to enable continual conversation.

The mere generating of free slots as in the limited assignment does not give the same chance to all tributary stations to get these slots because the "closest" tributary stations are being preferred. To enable all tributary stations to obtain an amount of free slots regardless of their distance from the control station, a reservation technique should be elaborated. We shall briefly sketch some.

The slots may be reserved either from the control station site or upon request of the tributary stations. Thus, the reservation decomposes into two actions: the addressing of a free slot to a certain session and a successful request for a reservation. The reader can find a resemblance to selecting and contention and he will not be far from the truth.

The reservation as well as the free/busy status indication can be performed by a binary combination (of an unused adress) or by one bit. In the latter case, to reduce the influence of noise which may cause an error, an alternating bit is used rather than the fixed one, which means that a control station modifies the first bit value of a free slot regardless of whether it had the value 0 or 1. Each station searches for a free slot by monitoring the reservation bit and comparing it with the value that has been observed in the previous frame. In order to avoid misunderstandings due to noise the reserved slot must run several times through all stations and whenever it passes through the control station its reservation bit is alternated. Only slots without any first bit modifications during several (two, three or more) consecutive frames are considered to be free (unreserved). The ensuing penalty is a larger transmission opening phase.

There are several schemes to reserve free slots from the tributary station site. Dynamic channel allocation is one of them. After the first slot is captured by a tributary station without collision the entire channel of required duration may be maintained.

Another reservation scheme has been proposed for multiaccess to radio channels. The frame is divided into $u+1$ slots rather than into u slots (we are omitting the phasing slot for this moment). The first u slots are dynamically assigned to tributary stations and the last slot is partitioned into w smaller subslots. Each station wishing to transmit a data message attempts to emit first a request to the control station in one of the w subslots on the contention basis. The control station responds with an acknowledgment whenever it receives the ungarbled reservation-request subslot, otherwise no acknowledgment is transmitted and the tributary station in question retransmits its request in another frame. All stations listen for the acknowledgment and all update their reservation queue counters so that they know the particular slots allocated to their own messages.

This reservation scheme substantially improves performance, approaching almost perfect scheduling (see Figure 3.35). For example, the dynamic reservation method gives less delay than the S-ALOHA beginning from the value 0.15 of relative throughput.

There exist other reservation methods, more or less efficient. For details we refer the reader to the bibliography mentioned in the next section.

3.7.7 Historical and bibliographical notes

The question of how to utilize the communication link capacity to the highest possible degree has grown in importance with the development of telecommunications. For example, the methods of FDM and TDM have been known for a long time both for telegraphy and for telephony, but a general comparison of the two sharing methods with respect to message delays and buffer sizes for data transmission has been made only rather recently [238].

Circuit switching became a basis for the commutation in telephone and telegraph networks; the beginning of message switching use is tied together with the public telegraph service (gentex). It is very difficult to find in the literature the author of the idea of block-oriented dynamic sharing, though the analysis of such a method is in [250]; it was Roberts [233] and Davies, et al. [67] who independently proposed packet switching in its present form although the original idea was published by Baran in August, 1964. The possibility of random sharing was first advanced by Abramson [1], and this method has been practically verified in the ALOHA network of Hawaii University for the access of mobile terminals to a radio channel [2]. Besides pure switching techniques also several hybrid methods were proposed and put into operation (see, for example, [125]).

The unslotted capacity sharing is widely used for multipoint links in all its forms (polling and selecting or contention). It is possible to apply it in loop links (e.g. so-called Newhall's procedure [81]). The notions polling, selecting (in [149] referred to as selective calling), and contention, as well as control-tributary and master-slave, which we have used in our explanation, are taken from the BSC/ISO link protocol terminology (see Appendix A). The described methods of multiple station selection are also subjects of the ISO link protocol. Hub polling was first used in the IBM PARS system: for more details see [133] where its advantages compared with the roll-call polling system are discussed. The reader can find a more detailed description of hub polling with many examples in [149, 197, 253]; in [149] the synonym hub go-ahead polling is also used. A similar sharing method as hub polling called mini-slotted alternating priority, abbreviated MSAP, was first proposed by Scholl in 1976 (see [131]).

Methods of binary searching were first suggested in [166], deeper analysis as well as simulation results are in [107] (the notion adaptive polling used there does better justice to the essence of choosing between polling and probing).

The idea of ATDM also stemmed from the necessity to increase the link utilization for analog speech transmission. An operating example of such an ATDM system is TASI (Time Assignment Speech Interpolation) which has been in use on the Atlantic ocean cable since 1959. But ATDM for computer communication was proposed later, in 1969 [42]; a survey of almost all multiplexing techniques is in [74], where the reader can also find many other references concerning this topic.

An analysis of fixed assignment techniques (contiguous and distributed) is in [135].

The loop link control, in particular its capacity sharing control, is associated with two groups of names: Farmer-Newhall whose mechanism has been mentioned above [81] and Pierce et al. who has proposed a buffered distributed control with the slot no deletion mechanism [189]. The comparison of the two methods with the slot deletion/no deletion modifications is in [232]. The classification of assignment methods of the loop link centralized control having, of course, more general applications, is in [284], another classification is in [171], where in addition to the link capacity sharing, routing by means of bypasses in loop links is proposed to increase the throughput. Decentralized or distributed access control in loop systems is discussed in [292] where also an alternating bit for the slot reservation is suggested. Decentralized control with priorities is also a subject of [292], while a mechanism of replacing data of lower priority by data of higher priority in busy slots has been proposed by Katz and Konheim [123]; further improvement of performance is due to Pawlikowski [179]. Many examples of sharing control in loop links may be found in [197].

Because of lack of space we cannot mention even the most important papers concerning this topic. The reader is referred to the excellent survey [134] where many sharing and access methods and techniques are dealt with along with results of queueing theory. The appended list of more than 150 references is recommended for further study. The books [66, 126, 253, 256] may be also of great assistance.

As soon as the multiaccess by means of P-ALOHA was practically verified by implementation in 1970, many other papers on this topic began to appear. They have dealt both with new and more efficient multiaccess methods and with the analytical and experimental comparisons of their performance (throughput, delay, buffer capacity). Thus, S-ALOHA was proposed two years later (a reprint of the corresponding research paper is in [235]). Although the principle of CSMA is well known from military aircraft, for data transmission it was suggested by D. Wax in 1971 and analyzed in detail by Kleinrock and Tobagi (with all aspects and modifications) in [132] who also solved the hidden terminal problem by means of BTMA [274].

A general and very interesting approach to the multiaccess is in [291].

The reservation upon request on the dynamic channel allocation basis for multiaccess to radio channels has been suggested in [49], its variants according to the end-of-use flag are mentioned in [137] where also a survey of many other methods (with or without reservation) is included. The reservation using a predetermined slot is called also the Robert's Reservation ALOHA because it was again Roberts who has first proposed it [234]. Decentralized reservation methods are in [19] while in [169] the centralized method using an intelligent satellite is suggested.

Other sharing methods have been proposed in [52, 148, 278]. The reader can find more about this topic in surveys [3, 20, 66, 138, 277], in Schwartz's [253] and Seidler's [256] book, and in the excellent monograph [126] where the performance of many sharing methods is calculated.

3.8 Exceptional States Recovery

As we have already seen earlier (Part 2) the communication system of two or more stations is not a simple deterministic system; its behaviour is, to a great extent, dependent on such random (stochastic) influences as noise, breakdowns, failures, and randomly varying data traffic. Hence if we wish to design the control of a system of this kind by such deterministic devices as protocols, we must consider in the protocols all the situations which can arise during communication. The situations may be of a nature we would not regard possible, e.g. destruction of the whole communication system or such a prolonged occurrence of errors that the phasing sequence is continuously interfered with so that the receiving station cannot be phased.

When controlling communication we can proceed in two ways. Either we find all situations and decide on the appropriate procedures for them, if need be solving these situations within some communication function, or the protocol is designed for the situations which occur most often and all the others which need not be precisely determined are regarded as exceptional situations and are solved by a common algorithm. The first way is more exact and efficient, it does not decrease throughput or enlarge delay very much, but is very complicated. If, however, some exceptional situation should be forgotten and unluckily it should occur it could have a negative effect on the performance of the activity of the network. Let us here remember the well-known "Christmas lockup" in the ARPA network of the end of 1973, when a situation occurred which the flow control procedure had not taken into account and so it had to be revised.

The second way is much more simple, but due to the common solution algorithm it enlarges the average delay and reduces the throughput because it would be possible to solve some exceptional situations much more quickly if we used a special algorithm to solve them. We shall discuss the latter method in more detail, since it is given preference because of the complexity of behaviour of the communication system.

Exceptional states recovery control uses a procedure which recognizes and exceptional situation (state) and transforms it into another situation (another state) from which another procedure begins to work. We must first define the concept of an exceptional situation. For us they shall be in particular such situations which are in no direct relation to data transfer proper. For instance the occurrence of errors in the transmitted data is certainly an exceptional situation when we use reliable data links. Since, however, we are interested in data transmission we solve the situation within error control. Similarly, in control procedures we recover errors in numbering, in backward commands to repeat an erronous block, etc. (see Chapter 3.4). The same holds also for overflow of input buffers, which is governed by the flow control procedure (Chapter 3.5). We call attention to it because in many protocol descriptions even some situations occurring within the error and flow control are considered as exceptional states.

Hence as an exceptional situation we shall regard an error which is concerned with the phases which accompany the data transfer phase (introducing a link establishment, synchronization and phasing, establishment and maintenance transmission opening, etc.). Examples which have already been mentioned are interference with the phasing sequences, an erronous transmission opening, an unexpected failure in a station, and even multiple repetition of one and the same block can be exceptional situations. The exceptional states recovery control procedure is then applied to them.

According to the definition of this procedure exceptional states recovery comprises two activities: recognition of the exceptional state and the algorithm of changing this state into another one. Let us begin with the identification.

For identification the protocol parameters are used, particularly the number of repetitions E and time-out T_0, which it is possible to combine with further characteristics by which some situations are differentiated between. As has been stated in previous chapters, several different time-outs and a few repetition limitations can be defined in the protocol for different procedures.

Let us show in examples the identification of an exceptional state by the protocol parameters. In Table 3.10 three cases of sending transmission command C from station S_1 are shown. In the example in Table 3.10a a maximum number of repetitions $E=2$ is chosen and as soon as the command is repeated twice, station S_1 realizes that an exceptional state has occurred and changes to the recovery phase. In Table 3.10b time-out T_0 is used for the identification of this state: unless the answer is received during the given time-out, the recovery procedure follows. And the last Table 3.10c shows a combination of both methods and no explanatory note is needed.

Table 3.10 Examples of exceptional state identification

a) by means of the maximum number of repetitions ($E=2$)

Station S_1	Station S_2	Note
C		command
	REJ	
C		repetition
	REJ	
C		last repetition
	REJ	
		S_1 recovers

b) by means of the timeout

Station S_1	Station S_2	Note
C		command no reply after time-out S_1 recovers

c) by means of both parameters

Station S_1	Station S_2	Note
C		command
C		no reply within the time-out repetition
C		no reply within the time-out last repetition
		no reply within the time-out S_1 recovers

As soon as the exceptional state is registered a method has to be found of how to pass from this state and where to go. Within the scope of the given protocol we can theoretically pass to its initial state, or the initial state of a procedure, to its final state or to another state, well defined beforehand and of course so chosen that the operation of the communication system cannot reach a lockup and that the data are not lost. When an exceptional state is being solved in a protocol, above which there is a higher layer protocol in the architecture, even passing the control to this protocol is a solution. Calling the operator by an acoustic and/or optical signal also belongs to this solution. It is exceptionally used in some rather simple link protocols, as the chief aim of communication control is its automation.

If we represent the communication by a state diagram, we obtain the above mentioned methods of transition as sketched diagrammatically in Figure 3.45.

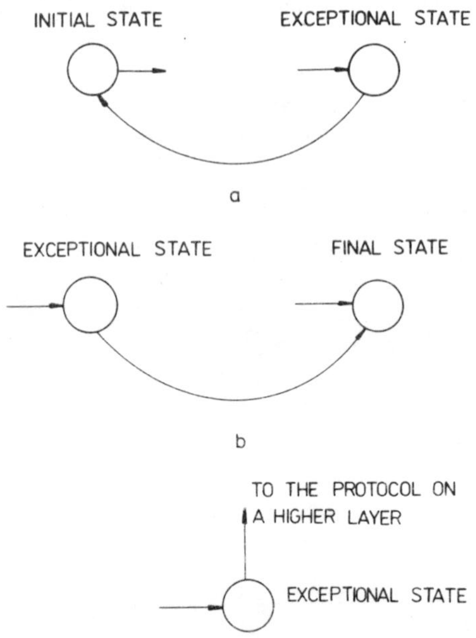

Figure 3.45 Exceptional state recovery
a) Transition to the initial state
b) Transition to the final state
c) Transition to the protocol on a higher layer

In the appendices, where the most important protocols are described, most of the appropriate methods of recovery control are touched upon. Here let us only look at the exceptional state recovery of lesser-used protocols. So, for example, in the SELEX link protocol, which works over the telex network using the 5 unit code ITA 2, an exceptional state is identified by a time-out and is recovered by calling the operator. A combined identification of an exceptional state according to Table 3.10c is used in the STR IBM protocol for a time-out duration of 3 seconds and 2 repetitions, after which the operator is called. The DDCMP link protocol, besides passage into another state, recovers, in the case of improper block length or an error in the block header, by passing to a protocol on a higher layer, since the format has to be changed.

Part 4
Communication Protocols

4.1 Design of Communication Protocols

4.1.1 The place of protocols in the communication system design

The design of communication protocols is a suitable common basis for the investigation and explanation of many details of the communication protocols. In the design and realization of communication protocols several disciplines and tools are used, e.g. models of the protocols, various protocol verification or validation methods, different approaches to protocol implementation, methods and tools for finding out the actual characteristics of the protocols designed and implemented, and various protocol evaluation approaches.

The communication protocol design, considering the interpretation of the communication protocol as described in Chapter 2.1 and 2.4, can be defined essentially in three ways: as the overall design of the communication system (or the communication subnetwork), as the selection of one or several communication functions methods, and, finally, as the implementation of the selected communication function methods. When regarding the communication protocol as the formal tool intended for the implementation of the communication function methods, we can consider the protocol design as the design of the protocol stations. Of course, input requirements for such a design must be acquired as the result of the communication subnetwork design (even not regarding the protocol as identical with the entire communication control in a network). Therefore the outline of the communication system design is given in Figure 4.1. The communication system performance is influenced by many internal design variables, which in Figure 4.1 are grouped into four basic variables referred to as network topology, communication control, network elements design, and capacity and flow assignment. As one can see in Figure 4.1, communication protocols represent only a part of the communication control.

The communication protocols' design must, of course, include the final objective, i.e. the reaching (and maintaining) of the required values of the performance measures (or performance criteria, or user requirements — see Figures 4.1 and 4.2).

In the above sense the protocol design is inherently included in the entire communication system design. One can see in Figure 4.1 that communication control is only one of the four basic design variables and that the communication protocols

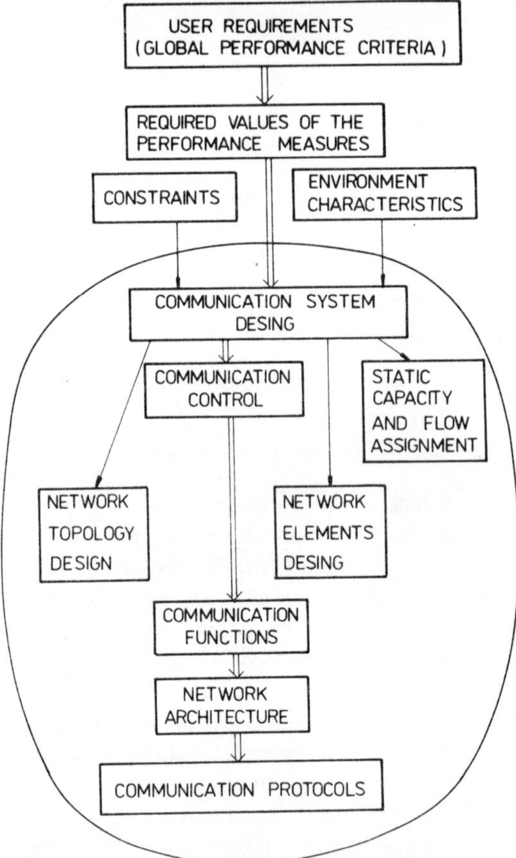

Figure 4.1 Outline of a communication system design

are only a part of the communication control supporting both network architecture and communication functions. Therefore, it is quite clear that the impact of the communication protocols, as defined in this book, on the resulting values of the performance measures is not great. Of course, the resulting values of the performance measures (transfer time, throughput, residual error rate, reliability, etc.) are determined not only by the characteristics of the communication system (subnetwork) designed, but also by the characteristics of the communication load, as outlined in Figure 4.2.

The communication protocols' design will be regarded as the design of the individual protocols, not as the design of the communication control as a whole. But the latter, containing both the selection of the communication functions methods and the design of suitable network architecture, is necessary for yielding the requirements on the properties of the individual protocols.

Thus the communication protocols' design concerns the communication controllers by which the entire communication control in a network is performed, but it does not

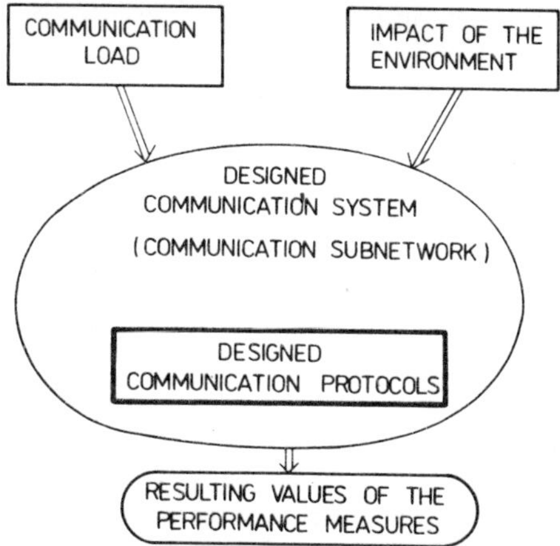

Figure 4.2 Position of protocols in relation to performance measures

concern the design of the communication control in the sense of the control theory. This is so because the communication protocol design generally does not comprise the entire communication subnetwork and is not focused (at least, not directly) on the performance.

4.1.2 Design and realization of protocols

The requirements on the individual communication protocols must be derived within the scope of the network architecture design, the communication functions methods selection, and the entire communication subnetwork design. As this derivation is not included in the protocol design, the main points of the protocol design, protocol implementation, and protocol evaluation can be expressed as shown in Table 4.1.

We consider it important to remind the reader that the contents and scope of all activities given in Table 4.1 substantially depend on the definition of the communication protocol as used.

The protocol evaluation is described in Chapter 4.4. The implementation of communication protocols, considered to be formal tools for the implementation of the communication functions methods, consists essentially of two parts:

a) the implementation medium selection (i.e. hardware, or software, or a combination of both; when hardware, then logical circuits, or microprocessors; when software, then the programming language, or the set of software primitives, etc.),

b) the incorporation of the protocol implemented into the overall network element design (e.g. into the node computer software), and especially into the overall control of the network element.

Because protocol implementation is basically transformed into the logical circuits design and the utilization of microprocesors, or into the real time software design, it will not be dealt with in this book. As far as the hardware implementation of protocols

Table 4.1 Main steps of the protocol design, implementation, and evaluation

Protocol realization steps	Protocol realization phases
overall design (word definition) specification (formal definition) verification (validation)	protocol DESIGN
implementation testing documentation	protocol IMPLEMENTATION
measurement evaluation	protocol EVALUATION

is concerned, one can find several LSI circuits on the market implementing some data link control protocols. The following are examples of such LSI circuits: Signetics multi-protocol communications circuit (MPCC/SDLC) 2652, Synchronous data link controller SD 1933 of Western Digital Corp.

The algorithms defining the contents (or semantics) of the communication protocol are determined by the methods of communication functions selected. Thus the subject of the protocol design is the selection of the protocol elements (above all, of the protocol words and the protocol station reactions to the individual protocol words) such as are suitable for the formal transformation of the above algorithms.

The communication protocol design proper consists of the first three points given in Table 4.1, i.e. of the elaboration of the overall design comprising the suitable transformation of the requirements into the protocol definition, then of the precision and completion of the above overall design, by using some formal model of protocol (see Chapter 4.2), and, finally, of the verification of the protocol designed, using the same or some other formal model (see Chapter 4.3).

As one can see, the formal models of protocols play an important role in the design of the communication protocols, because they help to find out various design errors and enable investigation of several properties of the protocols even before the protocols are implemented. Thus, the usefulness of such a formal specification and of protocol verification is quite clear. By including the specification and verification in the protocol design procedure, i.e. by differentiating between the protocol design and implementation (and by using the suitable formal models of protocols), the protocol design and implementation can be made not only more quickly, but also more effectively. Therefore, the communication protocol design should provide a formal specification and verification of the protocol designed.

4.1.3 Bibliographical notes

Protocol design comprises, for example, protocol modelling and protocol verification. Therefore, it is mostly treated in connection with these partial problems.

The following are examples of more explicit or independent treatment of the protocol design [10, 22, 56, 57, 66, 104, 226, 269, 270, 271].

Of course, from the point of view of performance the design of the whole communication subnetwork must be considered. Various aspects of such a design may be found in [115, 127, 157, 165, 196, 208, 222, 225].

4.2 Models of Communication Protocols

4.2.1 Subject and purpose of protocol models

As the models should express the contents of communication protocols, it is appropriate to recall the various meanings the communication protocol can have and to repeat again the meaning used in this book. Only after doing this can we determine the purposes and principles of the individual types of communication protocol models.

A communication protocol (see Chapter 2.4) may be regarded as representative of the whole communication control in a network (rare interpretation), or it may be identified with one communication function (frequent interpretation), or it may be considered as the formal tool equipped with everything that is necessary for implementation of the protocol communication functions.

The third alternative was chosen for the purposes of this book. Incidentally, it agrees very well with most of the formal models of communication protocols.

Models for the first two interpretations of communication protocols will be treated briefly here.

When a communication protocol expresses the overall communication control in a network, or in a substantial part of the network, then the purpose of such a model is to express and investigate the relations among the individual components of the communication control in a network. Because the overall communication control cannot be analysed without the consideration of a topological structure and capacity assignment to all network elements used, the model must cover the entire communication subnetwork. Queueing models are typically used in this case. This type of model will not be dealt with in this book, because we want to analyse communication protocols themselves and not the entire communication systems.

When a communication protocol is identified with some communication function, we have a partial case of the preceding communication system model. Again, the resulting model does not express the protocol in the sense used here, but it expresses the relevant communication function. As examples, the models of flow control or congestion may be mentioned. The purpose of such models is to investigate the influence of various communication functions methods on individual performance measures, i.e. on throughput, delay, utilization of network resources, etc. These models will not be treated in this chapter, except to the extent necessary to support the analysis of the influence on performance of protocol parameters.

So this chapter will deal with models which interpret a communication protocol as a formal tool intended to implement the prescribed subset of protocol communication functions. Such models also ensure the precise, complete and adequate formal description of communication protocols. Therefore they are often called formal models of communication protocols.

It follows from the above, that the models chosen are connected primarily with the implementation approach to communication control in networks.

The purposes of the communication protocol modelling are:

a) to find out the impact of the protocol (or of its parameters) on subnetwork performance,

b) to provide for an exact and complete description of the protocol, or for its specification, or definition,

c) to support the verification of the protocol,

d) to support the various types of analysis of communication protocols, i.e. investigation of various relations, sensitivity, stability, etc.

The aims expressed under a) and, partly, under d) require the model of the entire communication system, because protocol parameters manifest themselves clearly only in such models. Of course, the impact of the protocol parameters must be clearly differentiated from that of the methods of communication functions.

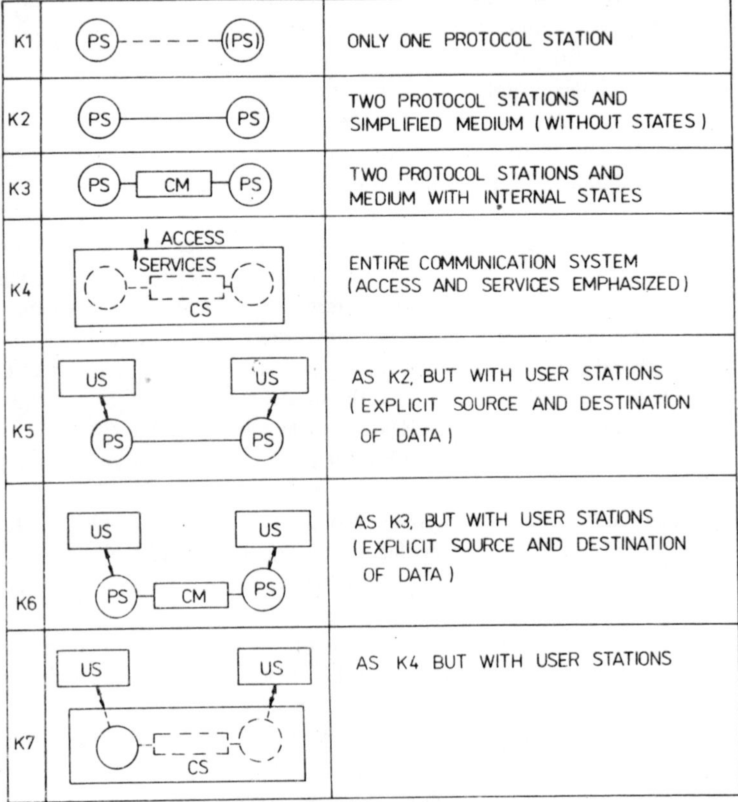

Figure 4.3 Configurations for communication protocol models
PS = Protocol station
CM = communication medium
CS = communication system
US = user station

The aims expressed under b) and c) may be investigated by means of the formal models of protocols.

But let us come back to the subject of modelling. Various configurations of stations and of communication media may be used (and are actually used) as subjects of modelling. Figure 4.3 shows a survey of them. All configurations that are included in the survey can be found in various publications dealing with communication protocol models, protocol verification, etc. It can be seen in Figure 4.3 that even the subject of formal models of protocol may be different and so, of course, are then the corresponding models. Hence, for each formal model of a communication protocol the corresponding subject configuration must be specified.

Now some remarks concerning the survey shown in Figure 4.3. The configuration K1 is rather incomplete, because the communication protocol requires the presence of two stations. However, we may assume that the configuration K1 express the case of two identical protocol stations. Some models cover only one protocol station (e.g. an interlocutor) and the influence of the other station is expressed by appropriate inputs and outputs.

The difference between the configurations K2 and K3 lies in the communication medium which has no internal states in the K2 configuration and which exhibits internal states in the K3 configuration. The K4 configuration is more related to subnetwork modelling.

User (or subscriber) stations are used in configurations primarily for expressing the coupling with the adjacent higher layer of network architecture. In the reference to network architecture such a coupling may be expressed by an interlayer communication protocol (see Chapter 2.3). However, this is not so generally, chiefly because the interlayer couplings (or communication) are implemented inside one network element and are not to be distinguished in the overall software design. In existing protocol models an interlayer communication is generally included in protocol stations and expressed by means of the relation between the protocol station and the user station (configurations K5 and K6). Sometimes an access protocol is defined, specifying the access of the user stations (i.e. of the adjacent higher layer stations) to the whole subnetwork, as is shown in configurations K4 and K7.

Some of these configurations will be dealt with later, when correspondent models are explained.

The internal states of a communication medium deserve special notice. These states are introduced in order to allow several data blocks to be transferred via the medium simultaneously. Thus a different number of data blocks transferred means a different internal state. The packet switching network is a typical example of a medium with internal states. Of course, we can distinguish several internal states even in the case when only one data block is transferred by considering the various errors and failures that may occur.

When modelling communication protocols one should realize firstly that communication elements are essentially modelled and secondly that the variety of protocol stations and/or communication media is much greater than Figure 4.3 may depict. Therefore the analysis of the communication control element to which the communication protocol investigated is assigned, i.e. the analysis of the subject of the communication protocol, is the natural first step in constructing the model of a communication protocol.

4.2.2 Formal means of modelling of protocols

Formal models of communication protocols are designed by using the following formal means: finite state automata, state diagrams, flow tables, Petri nets and timed Petri nets, evaluation nets, flow diagrams, formal grammars and languages, higher level programming languages (especially the Pascal language), regular expressions, flowcharts, etc. Some of them will be briefly characterized in this section. More detailed description of some of these formal means and examples of their application will be presented later within the scope of the description of selected protocol models.

The above formal means may be classified according to their principles, or according to the subject they are focused on. This subject can be:

a) states,
b) transitions, and conditions for starting the transition,
c) decision making and branching,
d) sequences (or strings) of words,
e) formalized algorithms.

Formal means focusing on states have a common background, namely finite automata. The formal definition of the finite automaton is as follows:

$$FA = (V, W, S, \lambda, \varkappa, s_0)$$

where V and W are input and output alphabets (or V is a set of input states and W is a set of output states), S is an internal alphabet (or a set of internal states), $\lambda = (V \times S) \rightarrow S$ is a transition function (or mapping) and $\varkappa = (V \times S) \rightarrow W$ is an output function (for a Mealy automaton), or $\varkappa = S \rightarrow W$ is an output function for a Moore automaton, and $s_0 \in S$ is an initial state.

The automaton is finite because the sets V, W, and expecially S are finite. There are no time intervals or time relations in the formal definition of the finite automaton: they are not necessary for lengthy theoretical considerations, but are needed when actual systems must be described completely.

The finite automaton represents the action of the system described in steps, i.e. the time axis is divided into time intervals (not necessarily equal) and then the entire time interval is replaced by one point and all the components of the system action are related to this point. It is typical for finite automata that the transitions concerns two adjacent points, i.e. the next internal state (or the next output state) depends only on the immediately preceding state and input. Each step involves the change of the internal state (assuming that the next state is not the same as the preceding one). The pair (v, s), $v \in V$, $s \in S$ defines (by means of the function λ) a new internal state $s' \in S$ regardless of the other preceding inputs and internal states. The finite automaton does not consider the input and internal history directly; it only reacts one step backwards. The system history must be transformed into the last internal state.

The properties described qualify the usage of finite automata for expressing such systems the action of which may be divided into elementary steps and in which the relations between the present states and next states may be transformed into two steps.

The decomposition into elementary steps is advantageous as far as the sensitivity of the resulting insight is concerned. But when the system is large, the number of internal states and, even more, the number of elementary steps, is so great that no practical manipulation is possible (even the computer will not be of much help here).

The number of pairs (s, v), which is given by the product of a number of elements of the set V and a number of elements of the set S, may be kept within practical limits by appropriate definition of individual inputs and internal states. There is no need to distinguish too many input and internal states in the system modelled. Of course, such an approach is only permissible when the number of distinguishable states is inherently small. When it is large then the only way out of the difficulty is to decompose the whole system into suitable blocks and to assign, say, subautomata to the individual blocks. There is no general solution to the problem. The decomposition may be different in each actual system.

Here we have touched upon one general point, namely the adequate and correct interpretation of the actual system by the formal means selected. The transition from the actual system to the system modelled represents the most critical phase in the application of formal means. The above transition, or transformation, may be performed in many ways. In order to select a good way (or even the best way) one must have a good knowledge of the properties of the formal means used and of the characteristics and particularities of the system modelled.

Therefore, the individual formal means will be described first, and the communication protocols or communication elements as subjects of modelling will be investigated generally before the individual models of communication protocols are explained.

The finite automaton may be specified by listing all elements of the alphabets V, W, and S and all terms of the mappings λ and $\varkappa$.

A convenient form of specifying the functions λ and $\varkappa$ is a table. In the case of the transition function the so called flow table is used. In this table columns correspond to inputs $v_j \in V$ and lines to internal states $s_i \in S$. The entries of a flow table correspond to pairs (v_j, s_i) and express next internal states $s'_k \in S$.

The table is particularly suitable for expressing the operation of a finite automaton for all possible combinations of inputs and internal states (i.e. for all pairs). The table does not in practice permit the omission of any combination. Further, it is not capable of depicting dynamic operation or of expressing the sequences of transitions: it is inherently static.

The properties opposite to those of a table are featured by graphs. The graph is generally defined as a set of nodes and a set of arcs connecting the nodes. Graphs may be used instead of tables to specify the finite automata. The graph equivalent to the flow table is the state diagram. In the terminology of graph theory it is an oriented and evaluated graph. The set of nodes is identical with the set of internal states and the set of arcs is identical with the set of transitions used, i.e. with the set of selected pairs of states. The arcs are evaluated by corresponding inputs v_j (see Figure 4.4).

The state diagrams and corresponding results of graph theory provide for the investigation of the occurrence of deadlocks, loops, cycles, etc. Moreover, they enable one to analyse the possible attainment (or reachability) of individual selected internal states, recoverability (i.e. the ability to return to normal operation after the occurrence of specified errors or failures), transition path lengths (i.e. the numbers of intermediate states between the first and the last states of some multistep transition), etc.

In each case their expression depends on the definition of input and internal states. Thus again we can see that the transformation of the actual system into its model is the most critical part of the modelling process.

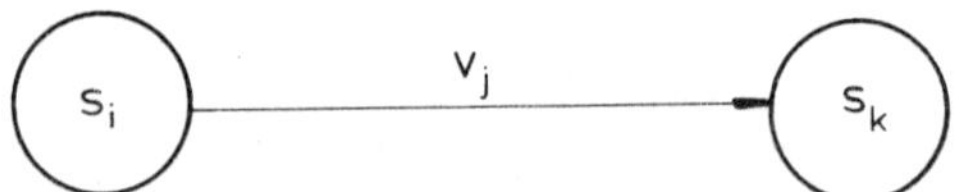

Figure 4.4 Principle of expressing the relation $(v_j, s_i) \rightarrow s_k$ in state diagrams

State diagrams are often used, because they provide specific patterns for specific types of system operation, they clearly express the possibilities and locations of branching, and they enable, as we have already said, us to use various theorems from graph theory for specific types of analysis.

They are not suitable when the number of input and internal states is high, because then they are not easy to follow and they cannot be checked completely. This is because state diagrams are primarily intended to be used by man, not by a computer. And for man, tens of states are already too many to be dealt with effectively.

In a complex system it is often difficult to find the most suitable, or even a good, way of distinguishing states and inputs. States consist very often of several components, and these components may occur in other states too. The same holds for inputs. The components may be active in several global states simultaneously, or successively. Sometimes it is not enough to know the transitions between the global states (i.e. between the states containing several components which are not expressed by the finite automaton representation of the system modelled), but detailed conditions for individual transitions must be specified as well. Finally, it may be very useful to have a means of investigating the system dynamics in the form of movement of "irritations" in the static model of a system (i.e. in a state diagram).

The above requirements are met in the next formal means, which is the Petri net. Again, it is a directed graph which has two types of nodes, namely the so called locations and transitions, and which has no evaluated arcs — see Figure 4.5. Each location (a circle) corresponds to one condition needed for allowing the transition (bar). Arcs connect locations with transitions and transitions with locations.

In a Petri net the fulfilling of a condition is marked by a token (dot) which is drawn inside the circle assigned to the condition. In the sense of the above considerations conditions may be regarded as components of global states.

All locations from which arcs direct to some transition bar are input locations of the transition, and all locations to which arcs direct from some transition bar are output locations of the transition. Output arcs may branch.

We have mentioned that it would be desirable to express explicitly when a certain event occurs and what it can cause. Transitions serve this purpose in Petri nets. An event occurs, or, in the terminology of Petri nets, a transition fires, when tokens are in all input locations (or when the token comes into the last nonoccupied location). When the transition fires, it removes one token from each input location and simultaneously inserts one token into each output location. Tokens represent the "irritation". So by the movement of tokens in a Petri net the propagation of "irritations" may be investigated. Various patterns of the above movement can be identified and classified, and various formal rules, procedures, and criteria are defined within the scope of Petri nets.

The Petri net, as a graph, is a kind of static model. However, it is changed into a dynamic model by tokens and rules introduced, the latter specifying the movement of the tokens in the graph.

The state of a Petri net (and, therefore, of the whole system modelled) is determined at any moment by the set of all locations which contain at least one token.

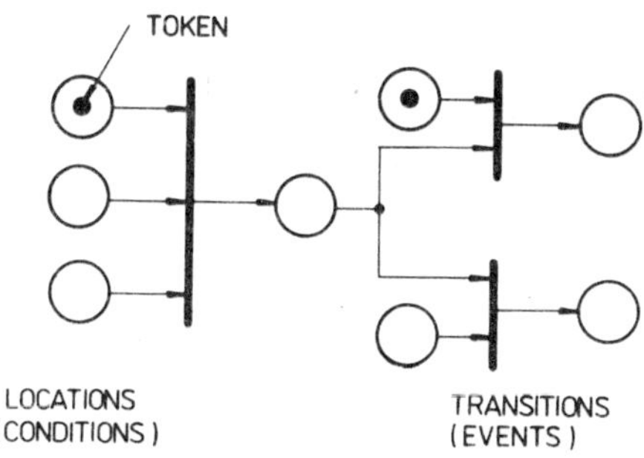

Figure 4.5 Example of a Petri net

The state defined as specified above illustrates one of the principle of the Petri net, i.e. the explicit representation of multiple influence of the components of global states. The components are identified with conditions (locations), so it is clear that the combinations of conditions correspond to states. Because the components (conditions) can generally be much more easily distinguished in a complex system, than can the global state, it is clear why Petri nets are suitable for interpreting complex systems. It should also be noted that only one or a few components change when the global state is changed.

When comparing Petri nets with state diagrams (i.e. with finite automata representation), we can see that in a state diagram the internal (global) state is expressed by one node, but in a Petri net by a set of nodes (locations). Transitions are expressed by arcs in a state diagram and arcs determine the pairs of states between which the transition occurs, but the conditions necessary for the transition to occur are not explicitly expressed in a state diagram. They are expressed in Petri nets, however, namely by means of transition bars (i.e. by means of special nodes). We can follow the successive fulfilling of individual conditions in a Petri net, which is not possible in a state diagram.

This means that Petri nets provide a better structured representation of the system modelled. Of course, the Petri net is not suitable in all cases, but for many actual systems it is more convenient than finite automata.

By extending the principles of Petri nets new formal means have been elaborated, namely the so-called evaluation nets (E-nets). The extension consists in: introducing additional types of nodes, attribute tokens, and blocking of transitions by logical conditions.

The additional types of node consist of one new type of location, namely of the so-called decision location (a graphical symbol: hexagon) and of several new types of transition, namely T-transitions, F-transitions, I-transitions, X-transitions, and Y-transitions. A transition time may be asigned to each type of transition. By this feature evaluation nets differ substantially from Petri nets and become more suitable for modelling actual systems.

The blocking of transitions by logical conditions is made by the decision location that may contain either 1, 0, or Ø, i.e. its contents can be unspecified. In the last case, two logical functions, p_0 and p_1, which are assigned to each decision location, may act. These functions are evaluated during the operation of a system. If $p_0 = 1$, then 0 is inserted into the decision location. When $p_1 = 1$, then 1 replaces the unspecified symbol Ø.

In evaluation nets either single tokens are used (as in the Petri nets), or attribute tokens are used. The attribute tokens have an attribute vector assigned to them. When the attribute token moves through the net, values of individual attributes (terms of the attribute vector) are both evaluated and changed.

Besides attribute tokens and attribute vectors, a vector of global variables can also be introduced. This is accessible from all transitions, and its terms may also be evaluated and changed.

Even from this very brief description of evaluation nets one can see that they are focused on actual systems and on complex systems.

Well-known flowcharts may also be regarded as special graph models, namely ones that are capable of expressing the sequences of actions and decisions. In particular, branchings and repetitions involving cycles are well suited for representation by flowcharts. The states of a system are represented by flowcharts indirectly and incompletely, namely by expressing which conditions assigned to decision nodes are fulfilled and which are not. Because they are quite commonly used for the description of various programs, and because communication protocols are often implemented in the form of programs, flowcharts may be used for descriptions of protocols, i.e. as a kind of protocols model.

Communication protocols are mostly assigned to a pair of communication stations. Let us recall that the communication between the stations in such a pair may be interpreted as a kind of a talk, in which the language agreed upon is used. This is one of the considerations that led to the utilization of formal languages for protocol modelling.

Before describing the principles of formal languages we must note that programming languages of the higher level are used for protocol modelling too. They provide for more precise and detailed and, sometimes, for better structured specification of communication protocols and/or protocol stations. They can specify the algorithms used more precisely than would be possible by definitions using normal language. On the other hand, they ensure more comprehensible descriptions than assembly languages and machine codes. The specifications of protocols using high-level programming languages may be considered to represent the highest level of protocol implementation as well.

Several high-level programming languages have been used for protocol modelling. It seems that the most appropriate are various versions of the Pascal language, especially the concurrent Pascal.

Now let us return to formal languages and grammars. The formal language L is defined as any (even infinite) set of words being defined on some alphabet A. The alphabet is a finite set of symbols and the word defined on the set A is any finite string of symbols from the alphabet A.

A formal grammar represents a finite means of generating both finite and infinite languages. From the practical point of view it is important that a grammar makes possible substantially shortened notations which correspond to many long strings (or sequences) of words belonging to some language.

The formal grammar may be defined as follows:

$$G = (V_N, V_T, R, S)$$

where G is a formal grammar, V_N is a finite set of the so-called nonterminal symbols, V_T is a set of terminal symbols, R is a set of rules, and $S \in V_N$ is an initial symbol.

The union $V_N \cup V_T$ will be denoted by V. The set of all words on the alphabet V including the empty word ε will be denoted by V^*. The set of all words on the alphabet V but without the empty word ε will be denoted by V^+.

The rules have the form of $\alpha \to \beta$, where $\alpha \in V^+$ and $\beta \in V^*$. The language generated by a grammar G will be written as $L(G)$. Such a language contains all words w for which the following holds:

a) words w consist of the terminal symbols only, i.e. $w \in V_T^*$,

b) words w may be derived from the initial symbol S.

When it is true for some grammar G that for each rule $\alpha \to \beta$ from R the following conditions are fulfilled:

a) α is the only nonterminal symbol,

b) β is a string (word) different from the empty word ε,

then the grammar is called context free.

When each rule from R has the form of $A \to \alpha B$ or $A \to \alpha$, where A and B are nonterminal symbols and α is a terminal symbol, then the corresponding grammar is regular.

Languages generated by regular grammars are called regular languages. They feature one property, namely that they can be recognized by finite automata. This means that when various words come at the input of the finite automaton, it is capable of selecting those words which belong to the regular language.

A useful notion in connection with protocols is that of concatenation of two languages, which is defined as follows. The concatenation UV of the two languages U and V is the set in which each element of this set is created by the concatenation of some word from U and some word from V and all possible concatenations of words from the two languages are present.

4.2.3 Basic features of formal models of protocols

Formal models of communication protocols are essentially determined by the configurations (see Figure 4.3) and by the aims. Two aims are typical for the formal models, namely those of exact description (focused on protocol implementation) and verification. The exact description concerns the K1 configuration, because the protocol implementation means the implementation of individual protocol stations. Verification generally requires the consideration of two protocol stations and often also of a communication medium, i.e. it relates to the configurations from K2 to K6.

In the sense indicated above one should differentiate between a protocol station model and a protocol model.

The protocol model must involve two protocol stations and, either directly or indirectly, the communication medium.

Already (Chapter 2.4) two basic dual approaches to protocol definition have been touched upon. The first approach lies in enumerating (listing) all usable or meaningful sequences of commands and responses, or of protocol words (according to the terminology used here) which may be exchanged between the two protocol stations. It has also been said that the protocol words may express errors and results of failures too. Of course, the corresponding recovery procedures (if any) must also be formally expressed by appropriate protocol words belonging to the corresponding sequences.

This approach can be regarded as primary when a top down procedure of the protocol design is used. This procedure consists of first selecting the communication function method for each communication function used, then of designing the set of protocol words and the set of meaningful sequences of the protocol words. As we have already learned each such sequence corresponds to one communication method or to some part of the method, called a mechanism. The sequences of protocol words interpreted in the above sense represent the first level of the implementation of the corresponding communication functions and, therefore, they are the natural basis for the next step which consists of the design and implementation of protocol stations, or the precise specification of protocol stations by some adequate formal model.

This next step already belongs to the second approach to a protocol definition, which is characterized by the use of some state models, e.g. finite automata.

The basic problem in using the state models is in interpreting the states. The states of the state model used may represent the states of individual protocol stations, or the states of both the protocol stations together, or the states of the communication medium used, or the states of both protocol stations and communication medium together, i.e. the states of the communication element as a whole. The states of this last case are referred to as global states. Sometimes the states of an environment and those of user (or subscriber) stations may be considered too. Hence, the interpretation of states is not unequivocal and it must be clearly defined in each application of the state models.

The main feature of the communication protocol modelling is the existence of two stations (not one station only). The cooperation of the two communicating stations requires the remote exchange of commands and status information. This exchange must be reliable, and it is this reliability that is the main subject of protocol modelling (as far as formal models are concerned). We may repeat that each protocol station reacts, or acts, according to its image of the other protocol station status. If this image does not correspond to reality, the action taken is incorrect. Because the protocol stations are generally remote and the communication medium used is generally far from being reliable, i.e. it may introduce various distortions and even losses of data blocks transferred, the communication protocol must be designed so that it can cope with the situation described. The formal models of communication protocols are very important tools ensuring the analysis and verification of communication protocol properties under the above conditions.

The problem described may be interpreted as the problem of general synchronization of the two stations, primarily at the beginning of system operation, establishment of a data link and opening of the data transfer, and finally at the occurrence of various errors and failures that may to different extents influence the normal, i.e. assumed, operation.

So we may conclude that the main feature of the communication protocol modelling consists in the need to model the simultaneous (concurrent) operation of two independent protocol stations, not the operation of one station only. But modelling of one protocol station is the necessary partial approach to the modelling of the protocol as a whole. The modelling of one station is more focused on implementation than on verification of protocols.

4.2.4 Selected models of communication protocols

A survey of various formal models of communication protocols is given in Table 4.2. Some of them will be explained here, some others in Chapter 4.3.

Interlocutors and Communication Devices

The so-called communication device comprising two interlocutors, i.e. the special models of protocol stations, is the model especially suitable for protocol implementation and network architecture description.

The interlocutor (see Figure 4.6) has three inputs: τ, μ, η and three outputs: t, m, c. Its simpified form (see Figure 4.6b) is suitable for expressing the formal manipula-

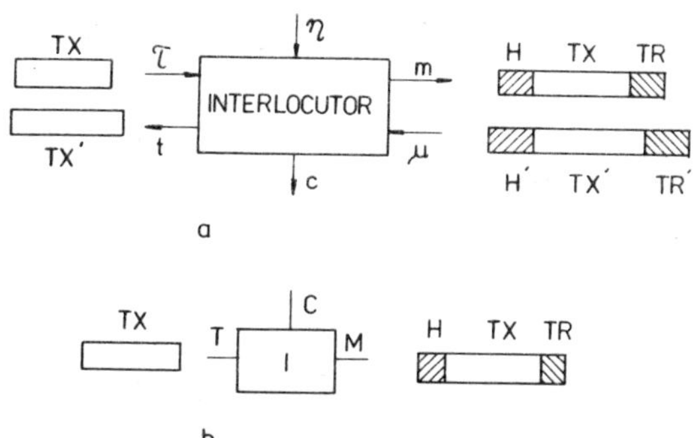

Figure 4.6 Scheme of the interlocutor: a) basic, b) symbolic (TX = text, H = header, TR = trailer)

Table 4.2 Survey of communication protocol formal models and modelling techniques

No.	Name of the formal model or technique	authors	purpose
1	finite state machines	Bjørner Danthine Bochmann	specification verification
2	interlocutors	Le Moli	spec., verif.
3	decomposed finite automata	Danthine	spec., verif.
4	Petri nets	Merlin	spec., verif.
5	timed Petri nets	Merlin	spec., verif.
6	evaluation nets	Danthine	spec., verif.
7	Pascal language	Bochmann Stenning	spec., verif.
8	UCLA graphs	Postel	specification
9	state diagrams	Bjørner Lynch	spec., verif.
10	assertions	Bochmann	verification
11	transition matrices	Bjørner Danthine	specification
12	global state model	Cerf Sunshine	spec., verif.
13	formal grammars	Bjørner Harangozo	specification
14	variable structure automata	Mezzalira	specification
15	flowcharts	Lynch	specification
16	programming languages	Hajek	spec., verif.
17	duologues, phase diagrams	Rudin, West Zafiropulo	verification

tion with transferred data blocks, i.e. adding, removing, and converting headers of data blocks.

The text (or message, or fragment of a message to be transferred) enters through the input τ. The interlocutor adds a header (H), and/or a trailer (TR), to the text. The header and the trailer create an envelope. The envelope and the text constitute the data block which is then outputed from the output m and transferred to another interlocutor. The data block enters the interlocutor through the input μ. The interlocutor then separates the text from the envelope, evaluates the envelope, and shifts the text to the output t and further on towards its destination. It is assumed that the text may be buffered in the interlocutor until the envelope is processed and then sent out, with another envelope, through the output m.

The interlocutor not only adds and removes the envelopes, but it also evaluates the contents of envelopes received and generates the contents of the envelopes sent. The method and rules for this evaluating and generating are defined by the corresponding communication protocol. The protocol is assigned to the communication device, i.e. to the pair of interlocutors, as shown in Figure 4.7.

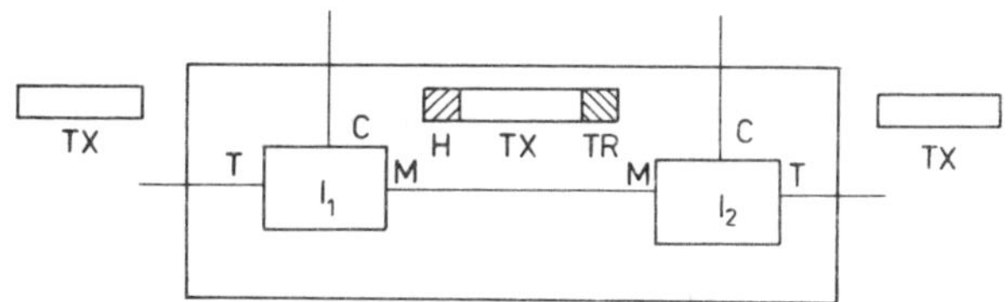

Figure 4.7 Scheme of the communication device

The interlocutor is not isolated, but has contact with, say, the environment by the input η and the output c which are intended for control and status information. The input η exerts its influence on the generation of envelopes. As can be seen from Figure 4.6 the interlocutor supports a two-way communication.

The interlocutor can be used as a basis element for the analysis and synthesis of the communication control structure in networks. Two interlocutors may be interconnected in three basic ways. One of them leads to the communication device. Chains of interlocutors can be created or recognized. They contain the above basic pairs of interlocutors. Chains of interlocutors are capable of expressing various complex structures of communication control in networks. From the point of view of communication protocols, the most important pair of interlocutors is that of the communication device, which is a model of the communication element. This also means that the interlocutor may be regarded as the model of one protocol station.

Figure 4.8 shows how the layered structure of communication control in networks can be expressed by interlocutors and by communication devices. We can see that for each layer of communication control structure one communication device may be assigned. Of course, a communication protocol and a corresponding envelope (or header) are assigned to the layer too. In this way may be modelled not only the protocol, but also a logical network architecture.

There are no interlayer communication protocols drawn in Figure 4.8. Instead, a parallel interface between the layers is used and is marked by the interconnection of C terminals of interlocutors separately on the left and right of the scheme, which corresponds to the idea of separated (and remote) network elements. There are three interlocutors in each network element in Figure 4.8, namely the I_1, I_2, I_3 in the left-hand-side element and the I_4, I_5, I_6 in the right-hand-side element. The adding and removing of envelopes (headers) is also illustrated in Figure 4.8.

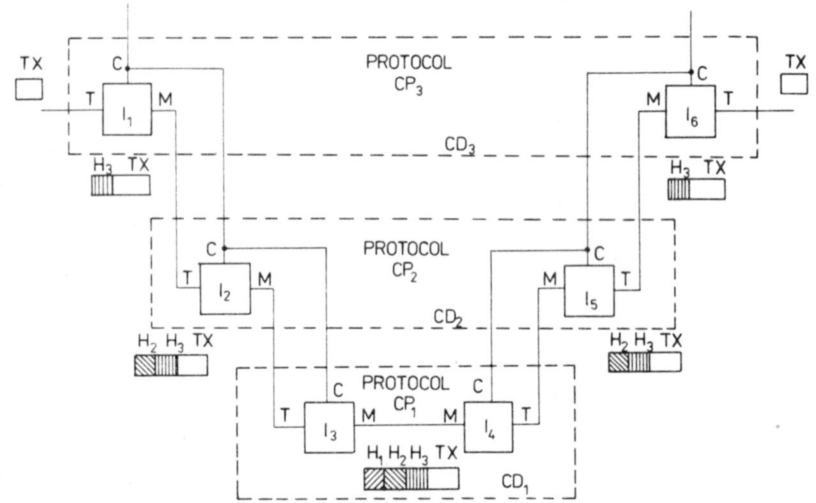

Figure 4.8 Expressing the logical network architecture by interlocutors (I) and communication devices (CD)

The formal definition of the interlocutor contains many additional details, of which only some especially important ones will be explained here. They all will concern the interpretation of the interlocutor as a special finite automaton.

The input dictionary is defined, assigned to the input μ, containing all envelopes (or headers) used. Similarly, the output dictionary is defined, containing all envelopes (or headers) used and assigned to the output m.

The internal states of interlocutors may be recognized: these can be present and next. The next internal state depends on the present one and on both inputs μ and η, similarly, the output c is also determined by the present internal state and by both inputs μ and η. So we can see that the interlocutor may be regarded as the finite automaton which has one set of internal states, but two sets of inputs (two input alphabets), namely μ and η, and two sets of outputs, namely m and c.

Applying the symbols used for the definition of a finite automaton in Section 4.2.2, the interlocutor definition may be written formally in the following way:

$$I = (V_\mu, V_\eta, W_m, W_c, S, \lambda, \varkappa_m, \varkappa_c, s_0)$$

It holds that $V_\mu \cup V_\eta = V$ and $W_m \cup W_c = W$. The decomposition of the input and output alphabets and that of the output function (output mapping) indicates the way to remove or decrease the basic disadvantage of finite automata, which is the unbearable increase of complexity in the case of a high number of internal states. With newer communication protocols (using numbering schemes) the number of internal states may be higher than one hundred. In such a case the only efficient approach lies in the decomposition of the set of internal states, or in the decomposition of the corresponding finite automaton into appropriate blocks (subautomata).

An example of a possible decomposition is given in Figure 4.9. The text parts are left out in this scheme, because they do not affect the communication control represented by interlocutors.

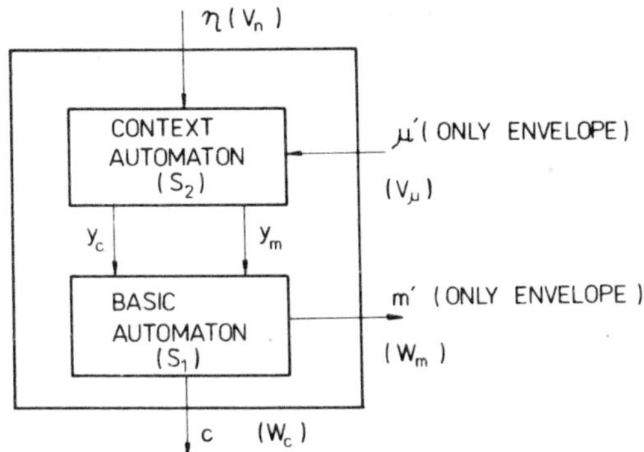

Figure 4.9 Decomposition of the interlocutor automaton into two subautomata

The basic idea of the decomposition shown in Figure 4.9 consists in dividing the operation into two stages. Only inputs η and μ' are processed in the scope of the first stage and they affect only the states of the so called context automaton (the set S_2 of internal states) and specify the auxiliary output y (the set of auxiliary output symbols Y). The set Y may be decomposed into two subsets Y_c and Y_m assigned to the outputs c and m'.

The output y, or the two separated outputs y_m and y_c, enter the so called basic automaton (the set S_1 of internal states) and affect both its internal state and resulting outputs c and m'.

The basic automaton may be further decomposed as follows:

$$S_1 \subset (cS_1 \times \mu S_1)$$

where cS_1 is the set of the so called user partial states and μS_1 is the set of the so called network partial states. The user partial states are changed only by inputs belonging to the set Y_c. The network partial states are changed only by inputs belonging to the set Y_m. In both cases all internal states of the basic automaton exert their influence. Additional details may be found in the publications referenced in the bibliography.

Petri nets

The well-known example of the communication protocol model using the Petri net is given in Figure 4.10. The protocol modelled is very simple. The Petri net shown in

Figure 4.10 expresses the global states, i.e. the states of both the protocol stations together.

The individual locations of the Petri net are assigned by the following conditions:

A — the process P_1 is prepared to send a data block (and it tells this to station S_1)
M — the station S_1 has sent a data block
B — the station S_2 is prepared to receive a data block
C — the station S_2 has received a data block
W — the station S_1 expects the acknowledgement of the data block received by the station S_2
E — the station S_2 has informed the process P_2 that the data block has been received
K — the station S_2 has sent the acknowledgment of the data block to the station S_1
D — the station S_1 has informed the process P_1 that the data block was transferred.

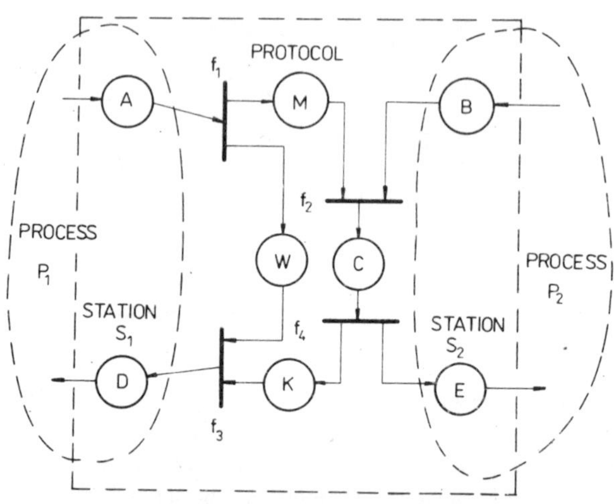

Figure 4.10 Petri net model of a simple protocol

The operation described by the Petri net follows from the meaning of the locations and from the graph itself.

The corresponding token machine, which expresses the sequence of the Petri net states, is given in Figure 4.11. The arcs of the token machine are assigned by individual transitions and the rectangles of token machine correspond, as mentioned above, to the Petri net states, i.e. to the so called markings. This means that the firing of a transition is associated with the corresponding marking.

The normal operation of the two communicating stations is represented by the vertical part of the token machine, i.e. the A—DE part. The marking WB, which is connected with the marking WMB by a horizontal arc labelled M, expresses the loss of a data block. This corresponds to the situation when the station S_1 has sent the data block (the token in the location M) but the data block has not arrived at the input of the station S_2. So the loss of a data block may be expressed by the removal of the token from the location M. In such a case the new marking, namely that of WB, may be recognized and drawn as shown in Figure 4.11. It is clear that the protocol modelled will not operate correctly in this case, because it will be locked up in the marking *WB* (*WB* is a final marking).

The above example only illustrates the principle of finding some errors, or imperfections, of communication protocols, which is the main task of the protocol verification. This means that Petri nets may serve as a good means of visualizing and clean-cutting some errors. Ways of removing such errors are described in the literature given in the bibliography.

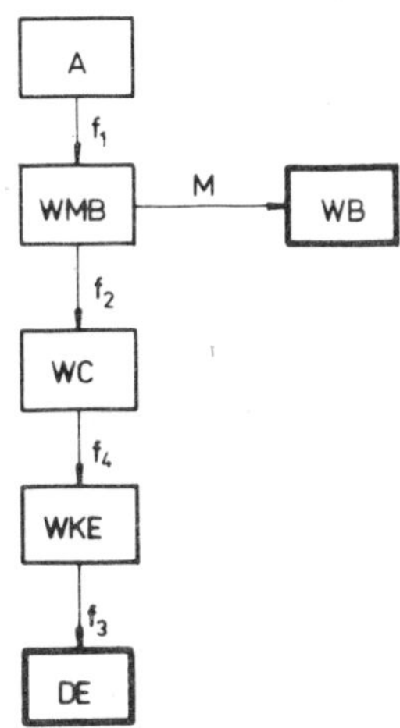

Figure 4.11 Token machine for the Petri net shown in Figure 4.10

The token machines with additional error markings are called error token machines. The additional markings are called illegal.

The Petri nets may be used for the investigation of the so called recoverability of communication protocols. The recoverability denotes the ability of protocols to return from an illegal marking to some legal marking after a finite number of steps and to continue in normal operation.

The protocol is said to be recoverable from the consequences of the failure *F* if and only if the following holds for the corresponding error token machine:

a) the number of illegal markings is finite,

b) no illegal marking is a final one,

c) there exists no oriented loop containing only illegal markings.

Additional explanation of Petri net models of protocols and the description of the design of recoverable Petri nets, i.e. protocols, may be found in the literature.

Time Petri net

Common Petri nets do not express time intervals assigned to the durations of various operations, e.g. time-out intervals. However, the definition of a Petri net can be extended by the assignment of two time intervals, the min t_i and max t_i, to each transition f_i. The time intervals are defined in the following way:

a) the transition f_i may fire not sooner than after the time min t_i (i.e. delay) measured from the arrival of the token to the last free input location of the transition f_i,

b) the transition f_i must fire not later than the time max t_i, measured from the arrival of the token into the last free input location of the transition f_i (time-outs).

In this way delays are assigned to transitions: either required delays (i.e. time-outs) or unwanted delays (e.g. time-outs, propagation times, processing times, etc.). When only one type of delay is to be investigated, it is enough to use only one time interval.

Petri nets with time intervals assigned to the transitions are called time Petri nets (or, also, timed Petri nets).

Two time intervals are used when more complex situations are analysed. Logical circuits and parallel processes may serve as examples.

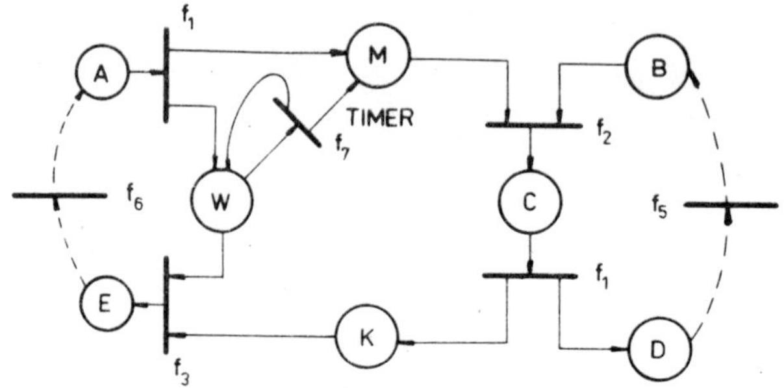

Figure 4.12 Time Petri net for the protocol shown in Figure 4.10

The removal of imperfections of the protocol shown in Figure 4.10 by means of the timer is illustrated in Figure 4.12, where the time Petri net is used. The timer is expressed by the transition f_7. Formally there is no difference between the common Petri nets and time Petri nets. However, of course, the corresponding token machines will be different.

If the network modelled by the time Petri net shown in Figure 4.12 is to be recoverable, then the following condition must hold:

$$\min t_7 > \max t_2 + \max t_3 + \max t_4$$

This condition essentially states that the minimum time-out interval used must be greater than the sum of the maximum transfer time required for transferring a data block from the station S_1 to the station S_2 (the stations S_1 and S_2 are remote), the maximum reception time (the generation of the corresponding acknowledgment need not be immediate), and the maximum transfer time required for transferring the acknowledgment back to the station S_1 (this may be shorter then max t_2, because the acknowledgment may have higher priority, or it may be transferred alone, not piggy-backed with data).

Formal languages and grammars

Again an application will be described, namely that of one version of half-duplex, NRM mode HDLC protocol (see Appendix C).

The formal grammar describing such a protocol is defined in the following way:

$$G(\text{HDLC}) = (V_N, V_T, R, S)$$

$$V_T = V_{T1} \cup V_{T2}$$

where $V_{T1} = \{\overrightarrow{\text{snrm}}, \overrightarrow{\text{disc}}, \overrightarrow{\text{i}}, \overrightarrow{\text{rr}}, \overrightarrow{\text{rnr}}\}$ is the subset of terminal symbols containing the symbols assigned to the commands, i.e. to the protocol words sent by a primary station to a secondary station (see Appendix C), and where $V_{T2} = \{\overleftarrow{\text{ua}}, \overleftarrow{\text{cmdr}}, \overleftarrow{\text{i}}, \overleftarrow{\text{rr}}, \overleftarrow{\text{rnr}}\}$ is the subset of terminal symbols containing the symbols assigned to the responses, i.e. to the protocol words sent by a secondary station to a primary station, R is the set of rules defined by Table 4.3, and S is the initial symbol.

Table 4.3 defines a sort of finite state transducer, essentially the flow table with nonterminal symbols assigned to rows and with terminal symbols assigned to columns.

Table 4.3 Definition of rules for the formal grammar G(HDLC)

Nonterminal symbols	Terminal symbols									
	$\overrightarrow{\text{snrm}}$	$\overrightarrow{\text{disc}}$	$\overrightarrow{\text{i}}$	$\overrightarrow{\text{rr}}$	$\overrightarrow{\text{rnr}}$	$\overleftarrow{\text{ua}}$	$\overleftarrow{\text{cmdr}}$	$\overleftarrow{\text{i}}$	$\overleftarrow{\text{rr}}$	$\overleftarrow{\text{rnr}}$
S	A	—	—	—	—	—	—	—	—	—
A	—	—	—	—	—	B	C	M	M	M
B	A	H	D	E	F	—	—	—	—	—
C	A	H	—	—	—	—	—	—	—	—
D	—	—	D	E	F	M	C	J	K	L
E	—	—	D	E	—	M	C	J	K	L
F	—	—	D	—	F	M	C	N	K	L
H	—	—	—	—	—	Ø	C	M	M	M
J	A	H	D	E	F	—	—	J	K	L
K	A	H	D	E	F	—	—	J	K	—
L	A	H	O	E	F	—	—	J	—	L
M	A	H	—	—	—	—	—	—	—	—
N	A	H	D	E	F	—	—	N	N	N
O	—	—	O	O	O	M	C	J	K	L

The definitions of the formats used and that of binary coding of individual commands and respondes by means of formal grammars can all be found in the literature.

The description given of the HDLC protocol by a formal grammar does not contain errors and failures. Neither does it include the operation of timers. Only the basic operation of the communication element governed by the modelled protocol is covered, but this does not mean that the missing aspects of protocol operation may not be expressed by formal grammars. Again, examples may be found in the literature.

4.2.5 Bibliographical notes

Overall views of formal models of protocols can be found in [10, 104, 194]. More general models of protocols are surveyed, for example, in [14].

Interlocutors introduced by Le Moli [142, 143, 144] within the scope of a theory of colloquies [164] have been further developed by Danthine and Bremer [55], who have defined and decomposed the automaton for the interlocutor [55, 57].

In order to give at least some examples of various modelling techniques used, the following brief outline is presented: Petri nets [187] models [53, 159, 160, 185], evaluation nets models [5, 53, 173], graph models [10, 199, 201], finite state machines models [21, 24, 25, 55, 56, 143], formal grammar models [21, 105, 110], flowchart models [17, 146, 186, 268], high-level languages models [22, 28, 100, 262], state diagrams models [13, 24, 51, 100, 242], state models [262, 268], transition matrices models [55, 57], etc. All these different models are formal models. Here we do not deal with models of protocols which are models of individual communication functions or of entire communication control. For probabilistic models see, for example, [150, 221]. The principles of modelling of a software implementation of protocols are dealt with in [102, 103].

4.3 Verification of Communication Protocols

4.3.1 Role of protocol verification

The verification of communication protocols can concern any of the three basic meanings of the term "protocol". But most of the publications describing protocol verification, or validation, deal with formal properties of protocols, i.e. it is the logical verification of protocols. Such an interpretation of protocol verification corresponds well with the notion of communication protocol used in this book.

Referring to the scheme of the protocol design procedure (see Table 4.1) we can consider the investigation of correctness, completeness, and adequacy of the formal specification of the designed protocol as the substance of protocol verification. The verification is based on such techniques of usage of formal models of protocols which take advantage of the specific properties of the individual kinds of formal models and provide for the identification of the individual protocol errors and imperfections. When no formal model of protocol is designed in the course of the protocol design, it must be designed later for the purposes of verification. Adequate selection of the formal model, together with appropriate verification techniques, make the individual protocol errors "visible".

Figure 4.13, showing the place of the protocol verification, testing, measurement, and evaluation, supplements the overall view given in Figure 4.1 and in Table 4.1. As one can see in Figure 4.13, four transformations form the subject of the verification of communication protocols, namely, the transformation of the word specification into

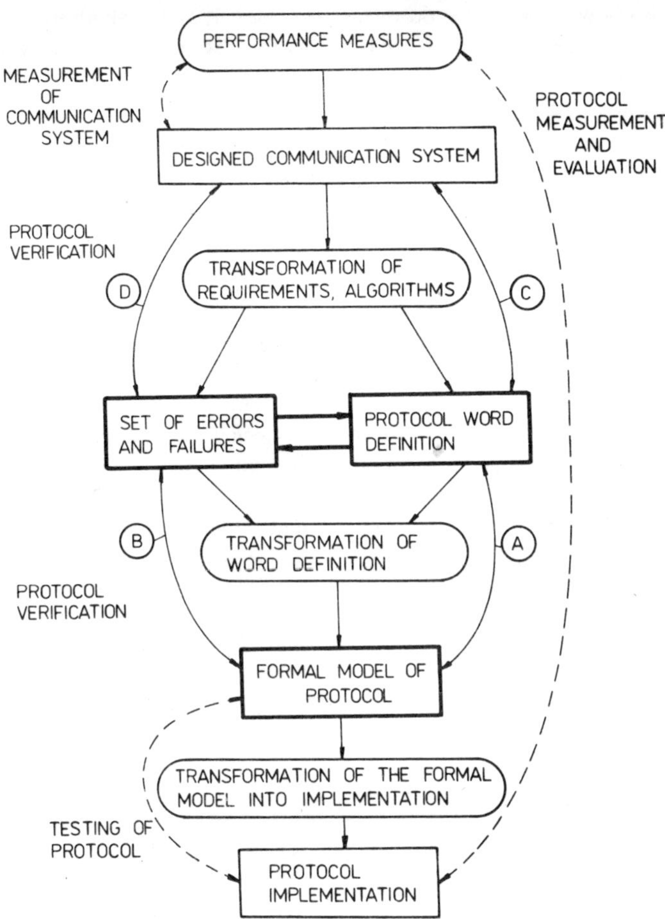

Figure 4.13 Location of protocol verification, testing, and evaluation

formal specification (pointer A in Figure 4.13), the transformation of the set of errors and failures of the medium and stations into the formal model of the protocol (pointer B), the transformation of the requirements and communication functions algorithms into the word specification of the protocol (pointer C), and, finally, the transformation of the properties of the communication medium used and of the communicating stations into the set of errors and failures (pointer D). Pointers A and B represent the investigation of the protocol design errors, whereas pointers C and D represent the investigation of the completeness and adequacy of the basic specification of the protocol and of the set of error and failures.

The verification does not concern the implementation of protocols. The errors due to implementation are traced by testing, i.e. by the measurement focused entirely on finding this type of error (diagnostic measurement).

Figure 4.13 also illustrates the place of measurement and evaluation of protocols.

As one can see in Figure 4.13, protocol measurement and evaluation relates to the values of performance measures used, not to the comparison of the two forms of protocol specification.

To verify the communication protocol as a whole is fairly complicated, so the verifications of only parts of communication protocols are described in the literature. These are mostly the individual communication phases.

4.3.2 Errors investigated by verification

The overall view of the protocol errors and imperfections is given in Table 4.4. The individual errors, or groups of errors, are explained in Section 4.3.3. Two columns of Table 4.4 are assigned to essential sources of protocol errors which are poor protocol design (pointers A and B in Figure 4.13) and inadequacy of the word specification and of the set of errors and failures (pointers C and D).

In the last column those errors are included which may be regarded as protocol imperfections, i.e. as some protocol properties not being adhered to, because of unexpected errors or failures.

For example, the protocol can distinguish and remove duplicated data blocks (by

Table 4.4 Overview of errors investigated by the verification

No.	Protocol errors and imperfections	faulty design	incomplete set of errors	protocol property
1	improper continuation		●	
2	improper initialization		●	
3	improper termination		●	
4	lacking of liveness	○	●	○
5	protocol failures	○	●	○
6	incompleteness	●		
7	deadlocks	●	○	○
8	looping	●		○
9	tempo-blocking	●	○	○
10	race conditions	●	○	○
11	time-out errors	○	●	
12	sequence number ambiguity	○	●	
13	loss		●	●
14	duplication		●	●
15	distortion		●	●
16	out-of-order reception		●	●

○ = possible occurrence
● = typical occurrence

implementing some mechanisms described in Chapter 3.4). This ability is a protocol property. Some protocols have this property, some not. But even a protocol having this property may not be able to apply it if the set of real errors and failures of both communication medium and protocol stations is different from the set assumed. When the real set (pointer D) is different, duplication (pointer B) may occur.

In Table 4.4 the dots stand for common occurrence or for strong context, the circles stand for rare occurrence or for weak context.

As can be seen in Table 4.4, almost all protocol errors and imperfections are caused by unexpected communication medium and protocol station errors and failures, though some of them may be caused by poor design.

Table 4.4 also suggests the classification of protocol errors and imperfections. Altogether four groups of errors and three single errors can be differentiated.

The first group of errors (1, 2, 3) comprises the errors characterized by the loss of synchronization in the various phases of a communication.

The errors assigned to the second group (4, 5) may occur when large extent failures take place. These errors can be interpreted as inability of the protocol to cope with such extensive failures.

The errors of the third group (6, 7, 8, 9) may occur even when the real set of errors and failures coincides with the assumed set, i.e. they may be caused by poor protocol design, or by poor transformation of word specification into formal specification.

The fourth group (13, 14, 15, 16) contains the errors which are closely related to the properties of protocols.

The uncertainty under simultaneous inputs [10] also reflects the property of a protocol. Apart from that, uncertainty does not depend on failures, but only on the internal structure of the protocol stations.

The errors caused by the improper time-outs [11] are typical examples of time-dependent errors.

Finally, the sequence numbers ambiguity [12], caused by the selection of too small modulus of numbering, is another example of the error brought by the improper selection of the protocol parameter value.

4.3.3 Description of individual protocol errors

Loss of protocol synchronization (errors 1, 2, 3).

This occurs when some data blocks with important control information are either lost or too much delayed, causing an improper continuation, an improper initialization, and an improper termination. We know that the protocol stations act according to the internal events and according to the entering inputs, namely the protocol words (i.e. inputs coming from the opposite station). We also know that the sequence of the internal events and inputs is of great importance. Now, when some protocol word is lost or too much delayed, the proper sequence may be destroyed and the reaction of the protocol station may be quite different from the one assumed by the first protocol station. Hence, the further action of the protocol station (if any) will be out of synchronization. Synchronization is also dealt with in Chapter 3.2.

Liveness and protocol failures (errors 4, 5).

Both liveness and protocol failure refer to extensive failures, both in a communication medium and in protocol stations. Liveness denotes the protocol ability to continue after the final step or a reasonable number of intermediate steps with normal operation when an extensive failure of the communication medium occurs. It is difficult to define the extensive failure generally. Therefore, care must only be taken when the liveness of two protocols is compared. The same reasoning is true for protocol failures (i.e. protocol stations failures).

Some robust communication protocol can be well equipped for coping with such failures.

By protocol verification one can mean the investigation of either the degree of the protocol ability to cope with an extensive failure defined, or the set of extensive failures coped with by the investigated protocol.

Errors caused by poor protocol design (errors from 6 to 10).

These errors may be caused by the erroneous transformation of word specification into formal specification, or by a hidden defect in word specification which may be disclosed only after details of the protocol specification by some formal model have been expressed.

The incompleteness of the protocol definition (error 6) concerns either the incompleteness of the transformation of word specification into formal specification, or the incompleteness of word specification with respect to the requirements of the realization of the communication control as a whole. In the first case one is finding out whether anything has been forgotten; in the second case a substantial part of the required analysis concerns the set of errors and failures.

Deadlocks (error 7) are such states which only have an entrance but no exit. Let us recall that the states can concern either one protocol station, or both protocol stations, or the protocol stations and the communication medium used. The designed protocol must be such that either no deadlocks occur in its state diagram, or the entering into deadlock states is impossible (or, at least, highly improbable). These requirements must hold even when various errors and failures occur. The above protocol property is checked by the protocol verification.

Improper loops (error 8) are essentially special forms of deadlocks in the sense that there are several states with no useful exit. After entering the loop the only possible progress is limited to the states of the loop. Checking for existence of this protocol error again entails expressing the structure of the protocol action by some state diagram or by some other formal means in order to make the loops visible.

The tempo-blocking (error 9) denotes the conditional deadlocks and/or improper loops, namely those which depend on the time duration of some operations of the protocol stations. This means that the deadlocks and/or loops occur only for specific values of the corresponding time intervals. Most often various time-out intervals are concerned.

Sometimes the tempo-blocking error denotes the continuing exchange of control information only, without any data exchange.

The uncertainty under the simultaneous inputs (error 10) expresses a kind of deadlock (or loop) which may occur when two contradictory inputs enter simultaneously either the same protocol station or both the protocol stations. When the protocol designed does not cover such a situation, its further action is nondeterministic. It can either continue correctly, or incorrectly, or it can be locked up into the deadlock or into the loop.

As an example of the above situation the following simultaneous occurrence of inputs can be given. Let us assume that the command from the higher layer to terminate data transfer and the protocol word from the other protocol station requiring the start of data transfer occur simultaneously.

Improper time-outs (error 11).

The influence of the time-out intervals on the possibility of protocol error occurrence has already been mentioned in connection with tempo-blocking. The improperly selected values of the time-out intervals can, though, cause other substantial changes of the protocol action. They can even interrupt its normal operation. Therefore they must be carefully analysed; this comes within the scope of the protocol verification.

The sequence number ambiguity (error 12).

When the selected numbering modulus M is not high enough, the sequence numbers may be ambiguous. The approach to the selection of the numbering modulus M has already been described in Chapter 3.4. When the value of the modulus M is only estimated, or when the communication system is complex, it is useful to verify the selected value. Assertion proofs are used as a formal tool for doing this.

Unkept protocol properties (errors 13, 14, 15, 16).

The loss of data blocks, the duplication of data blocks, and the distortion of data blocks are common errors caused mostly by the communication medium used. Recovery from them is provided by the adequate error control methods which are implemented within the scope of the communication protocol (see Chapter 3.4). But the above error control methods are effective only for a certain set of errors and failures. When the set of actual errors and failures is different, the above methods will not be able to cope with all combinations of errors, i.e. the loss and the duplication of data blocks may occur. The role of the verification for this group of protocol errors consists in the investigation of completeness of the set of errors and failures, or in the analysis of the protocol behaviour for the new set of errors and failures.

Similar considerations hold for the occurrence of changed order of the blocks of received data (error 16).

4.3.4 Tools and procedures of verification

The formal models of communication protocol are used as tools for protocol verification. Some of them have been briefly described in Chapter 4.2, but others are used especially for verification purposes. For various formal models of protocol individual verification algorithms are designed. They are mostly assigned to individual groups of protocol errors.

Formal models are used in two basic ways. When verifying the word specification of the protocol, we must first design the adequate formal model and then we can apply the verification algorithms. When verifying the formal specification of the protocol, we either use the appropriate verification algorithms, or we may even design some other formal models which are more suited for the intended verification.

The protocol verifications described in the literature often use many simplifications.

For example, the protocol station failures are neglected, the influence of the time-out intervals is also neglected, the communication medium is considered to be a simple point-to-point line carrying at most one data block at any time, etc. Such limitations reflect the development of the verification methods from the simpler ones (simple configuration of the communication element, many constraining assumptions, only small parts of protocols) to the more complex ones.

The automatic, computer-based, protocol verification may be regarded as the most appropriate one, although it has not been developed adequately so far.

4.3.5 Bibliographical notes

Verification of communication protocols has developed mainly during the last five years, supported by the achievements in theoretical principles and formal models of protocols. The survey of protocol verification approaches and techniques may be found in two publications of Sunshine [267, 270] and in one specialized bibliography [68].

Deadlocks and loops are described in [24, 28, 56, 57, 100, 200] and tempo-blocking in [100]. Loss of protocol synchronization is dealt with in [24, 57, 100, 242, 270]. In [270] the incompleteness of a protocol definition is emphasized.

Sequence number ambiguities are treated in [22, 262]. The analysis of possible occurrence of losses, duplications, distortions and out-of-sequence receptions is given in [22, 24, 92, 262]. Liveness is dealt with, for example, in [24].

The following formal models of protocols have been used for protocol verification: state diagrams [24, 51, 242], interlocutors [14, 56], finite state machines [21, 24, 56], Petri nets [159], UCLA graphs [199], higher-level programming languages (especially Pascal) [22, 262], formal grammars [105], pairs of graphs — duologues [242], phase diagrams [242], etc.

Algorithms for compatible paths investigation are described in [56, 57]. The assertion proof method may be found in [262].

From among the well known protocols the following ones have been (at least partially) verified: HDLC [22, 105], transport protocols [56, 141], PAR protocols [25, 199, 262], ARQ protocol [24, 28, 100], CCITT — X.25 protocol [24], ARPA—TCP protocol [100], ARPA—ICP protocol [199], CCITT — X.21 protocol [242], etc.

Automatic protocol verification is dealt with in [24, 28, 53, 100, 199, 242].

4.4 Protocol Evaluation and Performance Measures

4.4.1 Protocol evaluation

As we discussed in Chapter 4.1, protocol evaluation is a part of communication system design. After being set up based on the requirements imposed, the protocol must be tested to see how it complies with the predetermined characteristics. Even a well arranged protocol, which has been verified, may not be suitable for the communication system in which it is to be implemented. Thus we arrive at the question of whether a protocol can be evaluated at all without its implementation into the given system.

In a sense — though rather limited — it is possible to evaluate and mutually compare communication control protocols in terms of their overhead. Any protocol realization (sequence of commands and responses for one data exchange) consists of data — information parts (i.e. parts carrying the user's data) and control parts. In the same way as the code redundancy is measured by the ratio of the number of non-information data bits to the data word length (in bits), any protocol can be measured by this ratio (ratio of the control part length to the total length of the protocol realization) too. This measure is, of course, dependent on the way of realization: one value is obtained if the successful data message transfer is pursued and another one emerges in the case that transmission opening does not occur. But for the purpose of comparison and optimization of the protocols, the overhead can well serve as a first rough estimate.

However, in this way we do not receive answers to questions such as: "Is the proposed protocol appropriate to the given communication system?", or "How do we assess the properties of the communication based on the knowledge of the control protocol?"

The performance of a communication or computer system is — as mentioned in Part 2 — a complex property depending on a number of factors which are not mutually independent. The performance itself is a vector whose components represent a whole number of measures and criteria and these are influenced by the users' demands being realizable. But this we have also discussed in Part 2.

In the present chapter we are going to concern ourselves with these performance components, since, although mentioned in the preceding chapters, they could not be dealt with in detail. Thus we pass from the evaluation of the protocol to the evaluation of the communication or computer system, in which the protocol does not act alone, but hand in hand with other tools, outlined in Chapter 4.1.

Evaluation in communication systems can be conducted in two ways:

— from the standpoint of the user, by employing criteria that correspond most exactly with the above-mentioned requirements,

— from the point of view of the measurements and measuring methods enabling the values of the criteria sought to be determined during operation.

It would be ideal if the two points of view were identical; in practice, however, this is achieved only rarely. Usually the values measured correspond little with the users' demands, while the performance criteria that meet the users' demands are difficult to determine. In such case, an adequate model by means of which the measurement is modelled on a computer is determined in addition to the evaluating criteria.

4.4.2 Evaluation of the transfer phase

We shall commence with the evaluation of the most important phase — the data transfer phase. This phase comprises the data exchange along with the error control, flow control, and recovery (if needed). Let us now discuss two of the users' demands, which in this phase act in mutual opposition, viz. readiness and accuracy.

Accuracy is evaluated in terms of residual error rate — RER, defined as the ratio of the number of erroneously accepted data characters together with the number of duplicated and undelivered ones to the number of all data characters transmitted (for details see Chapter 3.4). The residual error rate so understood is character-oriented, as the user deals usually with characters or octets (in character-oriented data messages). Occasionally, however, it is more convenient to employ a bit-oriented error rate, because an erroneous character means any erroneously accepted character, no allowance being made for the number of erroneous bits, so that the character--oriented error rate does not describe the actual degree of error protection quite properly.

RER is only slightly dependent on the transfer rate, whereas another criterion characterizing the accuracy, and defined as the ratio of the error-free transfer time to the entire transfer phase duration, fully depends on the transfer rate. Finally, we must not forget a parameter evaluating the most common method of protecion — feedback with retransmission, referred to as the retransmission rate. This is defined as the ratio of the number of repeatedly transferred blocks to the entire number of blocks, and is employed for an assessment of error rate of data links. In addition to the retransmission rate, the mean number of transfers of one and the same block is used.

The readiness will be evaluated in terms of the throughput and delay. Let us treat first the throughput and transfer rate.

The information theory employs the notion of block coding rate — BCR (see Chapter 3.4), which can be defined as for any method of data transfer protection. Since BCR concerns the performance within one block, it cannot catch duplication or non-delivery of blocks within a data message, hence it does not express the use transfer rate or use throughput, which can be measured as the rate of information throughput — RIT (amount of information in bits transferred from the source to the sink in unit time). Inasmuch as information, and hence also its amount, is an indefinite notion (it can express the syntactic, semantic, or pragmatic aspect of information), the notion of transfer rate of information bits — TRIB — has been introduced; this is defined as the ratio of the number of information bits accepted by the addressee during the data exchange phase to the length of this phase, and is expressed in bit/s. Information bits are only such as carry the user's data; they do not comprise parity check bits, start-stop bits, or format and idle bits. Bits accepted by the addressee mean that from the standpoint of the latter the bits have been received correctly and as such are acknowledged, hence they may be erroneous but the error has not been detected.

To those readers wishing to concern themselves with this theme in more detail, synonyms of TRIB may be of interest; particularly useful are throughput, used during measurements of packet switched networks, the block transfer rate, which concerns blocks successfully transferred during the transfer phase, and the throughput factor, which is the reciprocal of the mean number of transfers of one block. As the TRIB is dependent on the transmission rate (it grows with increasing rate), it is sometimes divided by this rate and becomes thus a dimensionless quantity (and is expressed in per cent values after multiplication by a factor of 100); in this case it is referred to as the transmission efficiency.

Neither the TRIB nor the other analogously defined parameters express completely the communication throughput and cannot be used to evaluate the efficiency of the whole communication system, since they are limited to the transfer phase only. The user is interested in the throughput regardless of the communication phase, and this can be defined as the number of data bits (bits exchanged between the processes) accepted in unit time, and expressed in bit/s, i.e. as the data bit transfer rate.

It is much more convenient to express the throughput in bit/s than in block/s, since it is then independent of the block length. Where the latter approach is encountered, the throughput in bit/s can be readily derived knowing the block length and the overhead. Again, the throughput can be related to the total transferred bits in order to obtain the line efficiency, or to apply the ratio of the time required for the data bit transfer to the total transfer time (the throughput efficiency).

In some special cases, other throughput criteria have been introduced in addition. For instance, for the purpose of evaluation of satellite communication with multiple access, the throughput is defined as the ratio of the number of succesfully transferred packets to the number of available time slots and is measured in packets/slot.

Now we can go on to deal with the delay, which in some instances is more significant than the throughput. While the throughput is a measure of the ability of the system to transfer great data volumes in a time required (and is suitable for batch systems), the delay expresses the readiness of the system to message, block, or packet

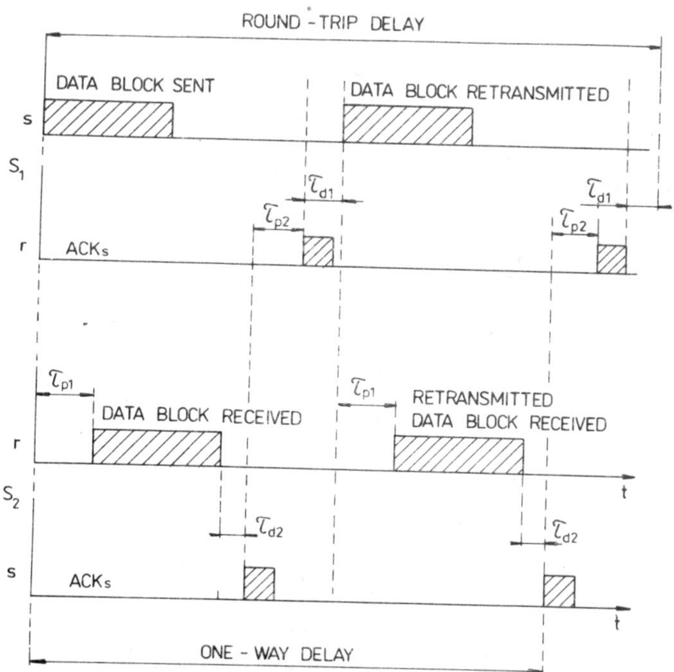

Figure 4.14 One-way delay and round-trip delay in the case of data block retransmission.
(S_1, S_2 = stations, s = sending, r = receiving, τ_{p1}, τ_{p2} = propagation delays, τ_{d1}, τ_{d2} = data block decoding times)

transfer in a time as short as possible, or evaluates the reaction of one station to the action of the other, remote station. Although the two criteria, delay and throughput, are interrelated, one of them cannot be substituted for the other, particularly in relation to the kind of teleprocessing system.

As with throughput, delay is evaluated only within the data transfer or exchange phase which is ultimately associated with the response time in conversation systems, hence delays occurring during the link establishment and transmission opening are disregarded. Delay is defined as the time elapsed between the start of the data block transmission and either its successful acceptance by the addressee (one-way delay) or the acceptance of its acknowledgment (round-trip delay). The difference between the two concepts is shown in Figure 4.14: layout a) demonstrates the length of the one-way delay in the case of block repetition after ascertaining the error, layout b) concerns the round-trip delay under the same conditions.

Again, it is possible to treat in detail the exact determination of the moments of the start and end of the delay; for instance, the first bit of the message and the last bit of the acknowledgment, or the moments of storage of the message in the source and sink buffers in IMP, etc., are considered. This is of importance if we wish to compare the results obtained by different authors using different methods.

The delay as a communication system evaluating measure must not be confused with the data link delay. This is, for instance, the propagation delay on a link between two nodes, the turn-around delay in the case of MDX operation. Naturally, all these — as well as other — delays have a bearing on the overall delay, but they are not the only ones involved; the time of waiting in queues, processing time, etc., also have to be taken into account.

4.4.3 Other performance criteria

Since the throughput (largely) and the delay (always) are related to the transfer phase, other parameters should be available which would concern the remaining phases, during which no data transfer occurs (the link control phase, the transmission opening phase, etc.). There exists a number of such criteria, which, however, are aimed at particular cases and are not universally applicable. This is due to the fact that the delimitation of the phases may be different in the various control layers (or even within one layer).

The simplest way is to evaluate all "nonproductive" phases in terms of their duration, hence of the transfer overhead time — TOT (e.g. in seconds). The channel establishment time and connection establishment time have been introduced especially for the purpose of evaluation of channel switched networks, whereas for packet switched networks the access time, defined as the mean time between the start of the attempt to access and the successful access, suits us much better. The connection establishment time in channel switched public network cannot be influenced, as the link establishment/disconnection procedure has been laid down by international regulations. Moreover it depends on the type of communication system (crossbar systems feature considerably longer link establishment time than semielectronic or electronic systems) and on the method of dialling (the connection is established within 10 s if a sevendigit number is rotary-dialled, while the same pushbutton operation takes 4 s only). The same is true of the access time in public data packet switched networks.

The duration of the non-transfer phases on its own does not allow the effect of these phases on the system performance to be compared, since the ratio of their duration to the transfer phase length or to the volume of the transferred data plays a part too. For this reason, the transfer overhead factor — TOF — has been introduced, defined as the ratio of the overhead delay to the number of information bits accepted within one transfer phase and measured in s/bit. Sometimes the utilization factor — U — is preferred; this is the ratio of the maximum length of the transfer phase to the maximum overhead time.

A number of criteria are available for the characterization of reliability: probability of failure, probability of survival, failure rate, mean time between failures — MTBF, mean time to repair — MTTR, etc. Most commonly used, however, is the availability — defined as the ratio of the time period in which the communication system actually performs the predetermined functions to the base time period. The availability is usually expressed in per cent values. However, it is necessary to specify exactly which functions are involved (in principle, degradation of transfer paths leading to errors that can be corrected is not regarded as failure), and the moments of failure occurrence and repair have to be exactly determined during the measurements.

Since it is not possible to eliminate failures completely, it is convenient to examine also the ability of the communication system to return from the breakdown state to the state of operation. This property is partly involved in the availability (c.f. its dependence on the MTTR); occasionally, however, recoverability is specially defined, viz. as the time within which the system recovers after a failure. This criterion is closely related to protocols, because one of their functions is to control the recovery, but within a complex evaluation of the system this is achieved also by change in structure (topology), rerouting, etc.

Another measure of reliability, with relation to the recovery control and particularly relevant to the evaluation of line protocols, can be found in the literature. This is the degree of control automation and completeness. There exist many protocols that do not comprise all exceptional states, and therefore it is sometimes useful to compare the systems also from this point of view. The protocol performance in some exceptional states is compared, or the systems are evaluated in terms of probability of stopping or of request for a solution (by human intervention or by higher layer protocol).

The last quantitative criterion of performance is the complexity or the cost of the communication system (the two criteria are closely interrelated). Inasmuch as a protocol can be described by the execution algorithm (which is necessary for its implementation), it is possible to determine during the circuit realization the requisite memory capacity and number of basic logical circuits, and to determine during the program realization the number of necessary instructions and memory capacity. The complexity may embrace also the buffer utilization efficiency, defined as the ratio of the mean packet length to the maximum length of the data array in the packet along with the packet storage overhead in IMP.

It is of extreme importance to know the performance criteria of the system, so that they can be evaluated with respect to the user's demands, but not less useful is to know also the susceptibility of the performance criteria to variations in the external conditions, or their stability. This, too, is part of the evaluation of communication systems.

4.4.4 Bibliographical notes

As we have mentioned, it is very difficult to evaluate a protocol *per se*, although such an approach is occasionally encountered [130]. A considerably wider variety of evaluating criteria is available for the assessment of the communication system performance. Several reviews have been published [98, 220, 257], from which the reader can choose the appropriate criteria in accordance with his needs. It is, however, felt that a unified system of evaluating criteria and methods of their measurement is lacking, which makes a mutual comparison of communication systems difficult. The standards so far issued [71, 72] are of national validity, and, moreover, are intended for two-station systems only. The new interim standard [273] which has already been reviewed by ANSI TG X3S35 and is to be approved as an American national standard would form a basis for international standardization.

The throughput has been defined either for a two-station communication model, or for the complete network, e.g. through the N-TRIB (Network TRIB) parameter [214] or by the average number of blocks delivered to the addresses [45, 129]; the question of whether the blocks are accepted correctly or incorrectly being irrelevant in the form as defined in Section 4.4.2 was first suggested in [93] (see also [261], where throughput was measured in messages or packets per second). Some examples of TRIB calculation are given in [93, 220]; in [93] the effects influencing its value are outlined. The throughput or TRIB is employed always when a communication system, particularly a computer-sommunication one, is to be evaluated, although other terms are occasionally used [94, 269, 273]. This is true also of the efficiency, as mentioned in Section 4.4.2 [130, 266, 276].

Residual error rate (RER) has been dealt with in Chapter 3.4; let us only recall that in the standard [72] it is character oriented, whereas in the standard [71] it is bit-oriented.

The delay (one-way as well as round-trip) has been defined, for example, in [266]; another approach has been applied in [128]. In the former paper, this parameter is referred to as the end-to-end block transfer delay, in [214] the message transfer time is defined as the time required for the delivery of a data message from the source to the sink. As to the turn-around delay, this is regarded in [98] as one of the performance criteria. The effects on the magnitude of the delay have been dealt with in [119].

TOT has been proposed as a British standard [71], although in the American standard [72] it is labelled with the same abbreviation, but actually means TOF. Other criteria of this kind (channel or connection establishment time, access time) have been employed in [98, 214, 273]. Examples of TOF calculation can be found in [72, 220]. In [220], moreover, it is suggested that TOF should be measured for each communication phase separately. The utilization factor U is used for evaluation in the standard [71]. The method of measurement of the availability A is given in [71, 72], the values of A of some parts and elements of the packet switched network are reported in [98, 119]. In [98], availability is strictly distinguished from reliability as the ability to maintain the system in operation until the data are sucessfully transferred. This is explained in the case of a system which rejects the data because of failure and thus can possess a low availability but an acceptable reliability.

Recoverability has been mentioned in [45], and in more detail has been treated in [160]. The evaluation of link protocol completeness has been proposed in [220], the complexity is the subject of the papers [219, 266, 269], and the utilization efficiency of the buffer has been used in [129].

The concept of sensitivity has been introduced by Danthine and Eschenauer [58] in connection with the protocol measurement and the effect on changes in the values of some parameters (see also [209]) or values of other performance criteria [128]. In the last case, the stability of the protocol controlling multiaccess is defined as the resistance to changes in the transfer load.

Finally, we must not omit qualitative criteria; of these, at least the resistance to data perturbation and abuse should be mentioned [98].

Appendix A

Basic and Transparent Mode Control Procedures (ISO 1745, 2111, 2628, 2629)

This link protocol was one of the first standardized protocols; its origin is connected with the code for information interchange ISO-7 or CCITT 5. This code is based on 7-unit binary characters and thus comprises 128 combinations, ten of which are reserved for communication control purposes (see Table A.1). The code was approved by the ISO Council in 1967, first as a recommendation, then later as an international standard under the number 646. It appeared in the CCITT White Book in 1968 as a PTT recommendation V.3 under the name IA 5 or CCITT 5, so we shall call it ISO/CCITT code.

Table A.1 Control characters from the ISO/CCITT code

Binary combination	Abbreviation	Meaning
1 0 0 0 0 0 0	SOH	start of heading
0 1 0 0 0 0 0	STX	start of text
1 1 0 0 0 0 0	ETX	end of text
0 0 1 0 0 0 0	EOT	end of transmission
1 0 1 0 0 0 0	ENQ	enquiry
0 1 1 0 0 0 0	ACK	acknowledge
0 0 0 0 1 0 0	DLE	data link escape
1 0 1 0 1 0 0	NAK	negative acknowledge
0 1 1 0 1 0 0	SYN	synchronous idle
1 1 1 0 1 0 0	ETB	end of transmission block

IBM has worked out a link protocol for its RJE terminal product line both with the American version of ISO/CCITT code (USASCII) and with EBCDIC and has called it BSC. In 1968 BSC was adapted as an American standard DLC by ANSI; it was then proposed to ISO which issued its basic mode, again first as a recommendation, in 1971. In 1975 it changed it into an international standard, adding various sections including the transparent mode. For the sake of brevity we shall throughout this appendix use the abbreviation ISO protocol for the complex of IS 1745, 2111, 2628, and 2629. Further description is based on these standards.

The ISO protocol can be applied to HDX point-to-point or multipoint data links for two way data transfer between a control station and one or more tributary stations. Data links may be synchronous or asynchronous; the mode of transmission is arbitrary (serial or parallel).

The ISO protocol performs transmission establishment/termination, error control with fragmentation/reassembly of data messages, flow control, synchronization and phasing, data link capacity sharing, and exceptional states recovery.

Since the control is centralized, only the control station is responsible for establishing and terminating transmission. After the connection over the general switched network is established (if necessary, but this function is not a subject of ISO protocol) the control station may clear the connection by sending EOT to condition all tributary stations to anticipate the transmission establishment. The control station then sends an address (if necessary) followed with ENQ. After receiving ACK from the selected tributary station the transmission is opened; otherwise the control station tries the start again, terminates, or recovers. The transmission may terminate only under the responsibility of the control station which sends EOT (if the link disconnection is not needed) or DLE EOT.

The error control is performed on the basis of a stop-and-wait ARQ method, all-acknowledgment scheme (ACK-NAK) with or without the numbering of data blocks and/or of backward commands. The need for a retransmission is deduced by the invalidity of binary check sums consisting of a checking parity bit (P) in each character which may be optionally accompanied by a block checking character (BCC) at the end of the data block. Although the coding/decoding procedure is the subject of other standards (IS 1155 and 1177), here we recall that P and BCC form a simple iterative code with the detecting capability depending on the length of block. So, the fragmentation of long data messages is necessary.

The flow control avoids only overflow of the receiving buffers and loss of data when a station is unable to receive. The receiving (slave) station may interrupt the sending (master) one with EOT or with the pair DLE⟨. The former command interrupts the transmission immediately while the latter means the sending station should terminate the current transmission at the earliest possible time.

The synchronization (bit and character phasing) is applied when asynchronous data links are used for synchronous transmission. It is achieved and retained by a sequence of SYNs while in the case of asynchronous (start-stop) transmission start and stop units maintain synchronization within each character (details are in IS 1177).

Block phasing is guaranteed even for unequal block lengths by means of separators SOH, STX, ETB, and ETX (STX either separates a header and a data field or serves as the beginning of a data block without any header, ETX terminates a data message and also the last block, while ETB indicates the end of all except the last one, which must not stand alone in a heading and/or data field).

Since the ISO protocol may be implemented to HDX one-way or two-way alternate data transfers over point-to-point and multipoint links, a dynamic channel assignment between pairs of stations is a necessary function which the protocol must provide. The alternating of transfer directions between two active stations is assured on a block basis (each direction is reserved for one block, control or data). The information transfer of multiple communication over multipoint links is assigned for the whole call, beginning with transmission establishment and ending with its termination. Due to unequal block lengths and calls the capacity sharing is unslotted and consists of a polling/selecting procedure under the control of one station. Besides the selection of a single station a multiple station (both group and sequential) is provided with a reply from all stations or one designated station.

The ISO protocol performs a number of recovery procedures for which the control or sending (master) station is responsible. The recovery follows such situations as no or invalid reply to a command and nonrecognition of any control character in blocks. In all cases, after appropriate time-outs the designated station takes action consisting of a retransmission (up to a chosen value of the parameter E) of command, of a transition to another state, or of notifying operator and/or higher level protocol.

Although the ISO protocol is primarily designed for the ISO/CCITT code (other codes may be transmitted provided that they do not contain any of the ten control characters from Table A.1 in a data field) the transparent mode is elaborated enabling a code independent transmission. The code transparency is achieved by inserting a prefix DLE in front of all control characters in data blocks including DLE in a data field (if it occurs). At the receiving site all pairs of characters beginning with DLE (e.g. DLE STX, DLE ETX) are regarded as control characters having the meaning of the second one, except for doubled DLE (DLE DLE) which keeps the original meaning of data character carried by DLE (one DLE is therefore cancelled).

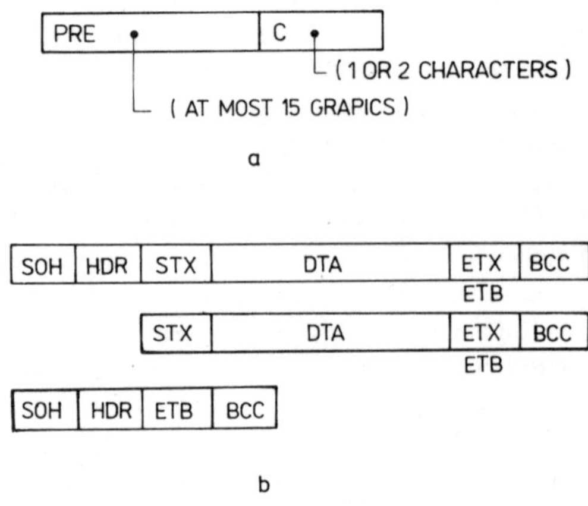

Figure A.1 Types of formats
a) control format
b) data formats

The ISO protocol is defined by a set of 10 control characters (Table A.1), by two types of character-oriented formats (control and data, see Figure A.1), by two types of parameters (the durations of time-outs, the numbers of retransmissions) the values of which depend on the implementation and therefore are not specified in the standards, and by rules for when and how to use control and data blocks and to reply to them. We cannot enumerate all rules here but can add a typical example of protocol realization.

The data and command/reply exchange between two stations (S_1 as a control station, S_2 as a tributary one) is shown in table form (Table A.2). Since both stations are addressed Table A.2 could be considered as a part of the control of a multipoint link.

Table A.2 An example of ISO protocol realization

Station S_1 (control)	Station S_2 (tributary)	Notes
ADR S_2 ENQ		S_1 polls S_2 (transmission opening)
	STX DTA ETB BCC	S_2 replies with the first block of message
ACK		S_1 acknowledges the first block
	STX DTA ETX BCC	S_2 sends the last block of message
NAK		After detecting an error S_1 requests a retransmission
	STX DTA ETX BCC	S_2 repeats the last block
ACK		S_1 acknowledges the last block
	EOT	S_2 terminates its transmission
ADR S_2 ENQ		S_1 invites S_2 to get ready to receive a message
	ACK	S_2 agrees
STX DTA ETX BCC		S_1 sends a one block message
	no or invalid reply	
ENQ		S_1 requests a reply (possibly after a time-out)
	ACK	S_2 acknowledges a message
EOT		S_1 terminates the transmission

The table is divided into three columns: two for station activities, the third one for word explanations. Since stations operate in HDX, each row can represent one station activity. Due to explanatory notes the table needs no comments. For more details, however, we refer to appropriate ISO documents.

Appendix B

Code Independent Error Control System (CCITT V.41)

The recommendation V.41 has been prepared by the SG SpA CCITT (at present SG XVII) and was approved for the first time by the 4th Plenary Assembly (Mar del Plata, 1968). It has been slightly changed during the study period of 1969—1972; this short description of it is based on the Orange Book [34].

The recommendation defines the link protocol to be used for the two-station (point-to-point) configuration where one control station may transmit medium and long data messages transparently over a pair of channels operating in full-duplex: the forward channel for data and commands and the backward one for responses. The link protocol performs primarily the error control joined with the block fragmentation/reassembly function. Two additional communication functions are performed for the automatic operation: synchronization and phasing.

Error control uses the continuous ARQ scheme with numbering of blocks modulo 3 (blocks are labelled by A, B, C, see Table B.1) to avoid losses and/or duplications. Each block is checked at the receiver site (at the tributary station) and acknowledged by a binary 0 maintained on the backward channel until the error is detected, at which time a binary 1 is emitted (an all-acknowledgment scheme). For error detection the pseudocyclic code generated by a polynomial $X^{16}+X^{12}+X^{5}+1$ (over GF(2)) is introduced (for the detection capability of that code see Table 3.4 on page 123) and is applied both to the data field and to the header. The header consists of four bits (see Table B.1 for their meanings). The trailer is formed by 16 bits, the remainder found at the completion of the division of heading plus data bits by the generating polynomial. So, if no error, or an undetected error pattern, occurs the remainder calculated at the receiving site is zero; otherwise it contains at least one 1 signalling the error occurrence. The number of retransmissions E may be limited (typically to 4 or 8).

In order to avoid misunderstanding between the receiving and the sending stations when a block with a detected error is asked for retransmission, the sending station, after monitoring ones in the backward channel within the transmission of the next block, renders it invalid by inverting its last check bit.

The continuity of the ARQ is assured by numbering (although the number of an

Table B.1 The CCITT V.41 commands

Type	Command	Binary combination	Meaning
essential	a	0011	Block A sequence indicator
	b	1001	Block B sequence indicator
	c	1100	Block C sequence indicator
	d	0101	Synchronizing sequence prefix
optional	e	0110	Hold block
	f	1000	End of transmission
	g	0001	Start of message one (5 unit code)
	h	1010	Start of message two (6 unit code)
	j	1011	Start of message three (7 unit code)
	k	0010	Start of message four (8 unit code)
	l	0100	End of message
	m	0111	Data link escape
	n	1101	For service purposes (to be allocated by bilateral agreement)
	p	1110	
	q	1111	
	r	0000	

incorrectly received block is not returned to the sending station) and by the need for the response about a received block to reach the sending station during the transmission of the next block. Thus, the buffers for at least two blocks must be provided at the sending station, and the length of blocks must be kept fixed for ever according to the loop propagation time. Four lengths n are recommended: 260, 500, 980, and 3860 bits, including 4 bits of header and 16 bits of trailer.

The synchronization information is derived from data and the starting procedure is assured by the synchronizing sequence prefix followed by the synchronizing filler of any length, provided it includes at least 28 transitions (from 0 to 1 and vice versa). The phasing necessary to recognize the beginning of blocks is achieved by the continuity of the ARQ scheme with blocks of fixed length and is started by a phasing pattern 0101000010100101. The same response procedure as for error control is used: a binary 0 informs the sending station that a block timing is established at the receiving station. Of course, recovery from synchronization and phasing failures is also included in the recommendation.

The protocol is defined by a set of commands (Table B.1) and by two responses (sequences of all zeros and of all ones), and by two bit-oriented formats with and without a data field (Figure B.1). The protocol parameters are the length of block (n) and the number of permitted retransmissions (E). The syntax (rules for exchanging commands and responses) and the semantics (main situations and states in which the rules are to be applied) are also described. We show them in a simple example.

In Table B.2 the synchronization and phasing establishment and the data message transfer with 7-unit coded characters is pointed out. During the data transfer one block is received in error and it is repeated. As the table form is not the best way to describe the fullduplex operation in both channels, the column headed Notes is included to explain when and why the backward condition (0 or 1) is changed. The rows must be considered as a continuous stream of binary digits (the digit on the left side of each row, except for the first one, for either station is a continuation of the right digit in the previous row).

Besides the communication functions being described above, the protocol permits some exceptional states recovery. The loss of synchronization and phasing has already been mentioned; another problem concerns exceeding the permitted number of retransmissions E. In all such cases the protocol returns to the synchronization and phasing establishment phase.

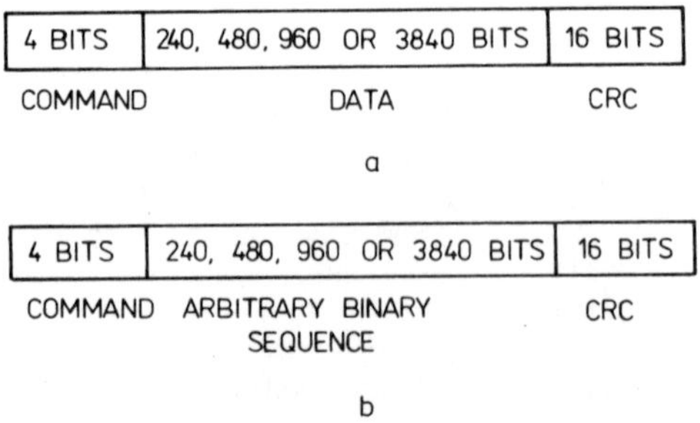

4 BITS	240, 480, 960 OR 3840 BITS	16 BITS
COMMAND	DATA	CRC

a

4 BITS	240, 480, 960 OR 3840 BITS	16 BITS
COMMAND	ARBITRARY BINARY SEQUENCE	CRC

b

Figure B.1 The CCITT V.41 formats
a) data block (commands a—d, g—k, m—r and data)
b) no data block (commands e, f, and l)

Table B.2 An example of CCITT V.41 link protocol rules

Station *S* (sending)	Station *R* (receiving)	Notes
111 1	111 1	idle conditions
0101 synchronizing filler 0101000010100101	111 . . . 100 . . . 0	1→0 is a moment when the phasing has been established at *R*
1010 data CRC	000 . . . 0	the first block of a message with 7 unit coded characters is sent
0011 data CRC	000 . . . 0	the second block (A) is sent and the first block is acknowledged
1001 data CRC	000 . . . 0	the third block (B) is sent but an error is detected, meanwhile the second block is acknowledged
1100 data CRC*	000 . . . 011 . . . 1	when the fourth block (C) is being sent *R* requests a retransmission (the asterisk denotes *S* inverts the last check bit)
1001 data CRC	111 . . . 1	*S* repeats the required block (B)
1100 data CRC	111 . . . 100 . . . 0	*S* repeats the block C and *R* acknowledges the block B
0011 data CRC	000 . . . 0	the last block (A) is sent and the block C is acknowledged
0100 arbitrary binary sequence CRC	000 . . . 0	*S* terminates the message and *R* acknowledges its last block
1000 arbitrary binary	000 . . . 0	*S* ends the transmission

Appendix C

High Level Data Link Control Procedures (ISO 3309, 4335)

The second generation data link control protocols (an example of such a protocol is given in Appendix A) have several disadvantages. When the data messages are short the transmission opening overhead may be significant, the code (alphabet) independency is not obtained effectively enough, and, last but not least, the error control method used is not very good because it does not cover the control part (i.e. commands and responses of data blocks). These imperfections led to the design of new, more advanced, link protocols which are considered to be the third generation data link control protocols.

Again, IBM pioneered work in this area, developing the new SDLC protocol in 1969. The SDLC protocol (or, actually, protocols) served as a background for the standardization activities of the X3S3.4 group of ANSI. These activities resulted in the ADCCP protocol in March, 1971, which is the version of the SDLC standardized in the USA. In the same year, ECMA together with ANSI proposed the draft of the HDLC protocol on ISO. The working group TC97/SC6 worked on this protocol. Finally it was issued in the form of several ISO international standards. First, the formats of the HDLC protocol were standardized in 1976 and then, at the beginning of 1979, the elements of the protocol followed. It certainly is interesting that other firms also have designed their third generation data link control protocols, e.g. the UDLC protocol of UNIVAC and the BDCL protocol of Burroughs. The data link control level of the CCITT X.25 Recommendation (see Appendix D) defines the LAP and LAPB protocols which are versions of the HDLC protocols.

The following, very brief, description of the HDLC protocol is based on two ISO standards, namely IS 3309 and IS 4335 [59]. It should be noted that the standards do not define the HDLC protocol completely (in the sense of the reference specification described in Chapter 2.4), but only define the elements and parts of the protocol. Many actual protocols can be designed from these elements. It would be interesting to deal with many other working documents of ISO which relate to variants and classes of the HDLC, but there is not sufficient space. Therefore readers are referred to the relevant ISO documents.

The HDLC protocol has a bit-oriented format. The data blocks (frames, in the

HDLC terminology) consist of the flag, the address field, the control field, the information field (only in the information frame), the error control field, and again the flag. Figure C.1 shows the frame format and the sizes of the individual fields. The address and control fields may be extended, by multiples of eight bits. The error detection code covers both address and control fields (and, of course, the information field), i.e. everything between the two flags.

The transparency is achieved by two means. First, the flag 01111110 will not occur inside the data block, because of the so-called stuffing (a zero is inserted after each five successive ones and is deleted at the receiving side). Second, the lengths of all fields (with the exception of the information field) are fixed, which provides for the determination of the field beginning and of the data block end by counting bits. However, the stuffing of bits in the information field changes the size of this field which is then not an integral multiple of eight and, therefore, the HDLC protocol is not suitable for the octet (eight bits) parallel transmission.

The HDLC protocol is intended for point-to-point and multipoint data links, centrally controlled. One control (primary) station supervises the operation of one or several controlled (secondary) stations. Any kind of link may be used (i.e. both telephone and radio links, and both switched and leased lines), but it is assumed that they are synchronous (the line synchronization is not a part of the HDLC protocol, although the flags and iserted zero bits could be used for this purpose, because they provide enough transitions for synchronization). Several transmission and either half-duplex or full-duplex operation is assumed.

FLAG	ADDRESS	CONTROL	INFORMATION	FCS	FLAG
01111110	8 BITS	8 BITS	ANY NUMBER OF BITS	16 BITS	8 BITS

Figure C.1 HDLC frame (data block) format

As for communication functions or communication phases, the line establishment/ /release phase is not included in the HDLC. During the transmission opening phase the controlling (primary) station sends SNRM, SARM, or SNRME, SARME commands which initialize the transmission and set the operational mode. Several operational modes are defined in the above documents: two response modes NRM and ARM, two disconnected modes NDM and ADM, and initialization secondary mode IM. Modes can be basic, or extended (i.e. the format with extended control field is used). Of course, the addressing is also carried out during this transmission opening phase.

Flags and fixed lengths of fields provide for the phasing, and also for the transparency. Because all noninformation fields are octets (i.e. eight bits), or multiples of octets, octet phasing may also be performed, even with the HDLC bit-oriented format.

The error control method used comprises the error detection cyclic code, as the one used in the CCITT V.41 protocol (see Appendix B) with a slightly different encoding/decoding procedures, and the continuous ARQ method with retransmis-

Table C.1 Overview of the P/F bit utilization

Modes / P/F bit functions	NRM				ARM			
	TWA		TWS		TWA		TWS	
	P	F	P	F	P	F	P	F
Solicit information	X		X					
Last frame indication	X	X		X				
Solicit supervisory or unnumbered response	X		X		X		X	
Check pointing	X	X	X	X	X	X	X	X

sion. The retransmission can be either selective, when only the incorrectly received (or missed) data block is retransmitted (SREJ command), or nonselective. Windowing is used, both for error control and for flow control. The window size is 7 (or 127 in the extended format). The acknowledgment may be either positive by P/F bits (see Table C.1), negative by the REJ command (or the SREJ command), or combined using sequence numbers. The numbering scheme with the modulus equal to 8 (or 128 with the extended format) is the part of the error control method used. The commands RNR and RR together with the window are used for the "stop and wait" flow control method.

When data are exchanged in both directions, between two or more stations, the HDLC protocol provide for the nontimed link capacity assignment by centrally controlled polling and selection.

Many exceptional conditions are processed by the HDLC protocol, especially the reception of the data block with an error in the control field, and with an abnormal buffer.

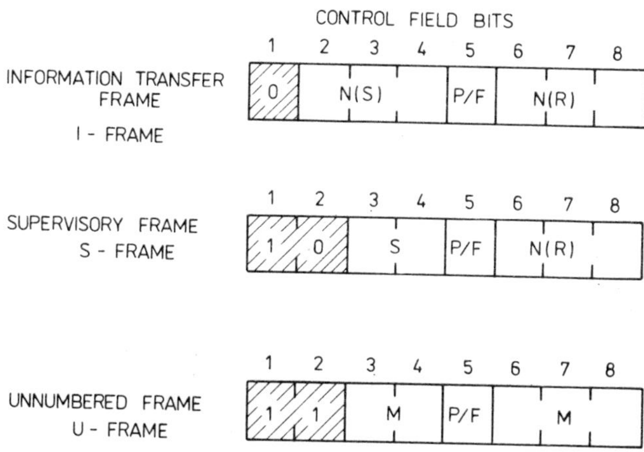

Figure C.2 Control field formats

HDLC commands and responses are transferred in control fields. The control field is divided into several subfields (see Figure C.2) which differ according to the type of frame. N(S) is the sequence number of the data block sent and N(R) is the sequence number of the data block received (other abbreviations are explained in the caption to Figure C.2). The P bit, or the F bit, is the one and same bit which has different names according to the role it plays. An outline of these roles is given in Table C.1.

A list of all commands and responses which have been standardized so far is presented in Table C.2. The binary combination denoting the control field structure is shown in Figure C.2, including the P/F bit and with N(R) in numbered commands.

Table C.2 Commands (P) and responses (F)

Type	Control field bits	Name	Acronym
Numbered xxx = N(R)	1 0 0 0 P/F x x x	Receive Ready	RR
	1 0 0 1 P/F x x x	Reject	REJ
	1 0 1 0 P/F x x x	Receive Not Ready	RNR
	1 0 1 1 P/F x x x	Selective Reject	SREJ
Unnum-bered	1 1 0 0 P 0 0 1	Set Synchronous Response Mode	SNRM
	1 1 0 0 P 1 0 0	Unnumbered Poll	UP
	1 1 1 1 P 0 1 0	SARM Extended	SARME
	1 1 1 1 P 0 1 1	SNRM Extended	SNRME
	1 1 0 0 P/F 0 0 0	Unnumbered Information	UI
	1 1 0 0 P/F 0 1 0	Disconnect/Request Disconnect	DISC/RD
	1 1 1 0 P/F 0 0 0	Set/Request Initialization Mode	SIM/RIM
	1 1 1 1 P/F 0 0 0	Set Asynchronous Response/ /Disconnect Mode	SARM/DM
	1 1 1 1 P/F 1 0 1	Exchange Identification	XID
	1 1 0 0 F 1 1 0	Unnumbered Acknowledge	UA
	1 1 1 0 F 0 0 1	Command Reject	CMDR

As for the HDLC protocol parameters, the following are used: The length of some fields, the numbering modulus, the window size, and the time-out interval concerning the exceptional conditions.

Because it is not possible to deal with the HDLC protocol in more detail here, we only add one example, shown in Table C.3.

Table C.3 Example of HDLC controlled ARM-FDX transmission.
(Notation: I N(S), N(R) P/F or C/R N(R) P/F)

Primary sends	Secondary sends	Comment
SARM, P ↗		Frame lost (not received).
↕ Time-out		(↗ expresses error occurrence)
SARM, P		Retransmitted.
	UA, F	Secondary acknowledges.
↕ Indefinite time		
I0, 0	I0, 0	Contention (both stations start
I1, 0P	I1, 0	to send I-frames simultaneously
↕ Primary time-out	↕ Secondary time-out	Contention solved by different time-outs.
I0, 0		Retransmitted frames.
I1, 0P	I0, 2F	Secondary acknowledges and retransmits.
	I1, 2	
RR2		Primary acknowledges.
↕ Indefinite time		
I2, 2P		Primary continues.
I3, 2	RR3, F	Secondary acknowledges.
I4, 2 ↗		Frame not received.
I5, 2	I2, 4	Secondary continues (with N(R) = 4!).
I6, 2	REJ4	Because out-of-sequence frame I5, 2 was received.
I7, 3	I3, 4	
I4,3	I4, 4	Primary retransmits all frames starting from N(S) = 4.
I5, 4	I5, 5	
etc.	etc.	

Appendix D

CCITT X.25, X.3, X.28, X.29 and X.75 Recommendations

Recommendation X.25, prepared very hastily in 1976, was approved by the Plenary Assembly in 1976 but was revised in 1977 and published together with the new Provisional Recommendations X.3, X.28, and X.29 in 1978. This is the document referenced in this appendix.

Recommendation X.25 defines the DTE/DCE interface characteristics, Recommendation X.3 specifies a Packet Assembly/Disassembly facility (PAD), Recommendation X.28 defines the DTE/DCE interface for a start-stop mode DTE accessing the PAD, and Recommendation X.29 defines the procedures for packet mode DTE to access the PAD.

Moreover, in 1978 Provisional Recommendation X.75 was prepared relating to international interworking between packet switched data networks.

Revisions, amendment, and new Recommendations are expected to be approved and possibly issued in 1980.

Figure D.1 illustrates the positions and subjects of the Recommendations being described here.

We shall now describe briefly each of them, starting with the first and basic one.

Recommendation X.25:

As shown in the title, the Recommendation specifies the interface between DTE and DCE operating in packet mode on public data networks. As a matter of fact, it also concerns the communication of two packet mode DTEs over a public packet switching network (or subnetwork, in the sense of the terminology used in this book). Figure D.2 explains this situation, showing the possible location of an internal network protocol, which is, of course, not defined in the Recommendation because it does not belong to the DTE/DCE interface.

The concepts of so called logical channels and virtual circuits are essential to the X.25. Virtual circuits may be permanent or switched, the latter being denoted as virtual calls.

DTEs and DCEs can be regarded as network elements.

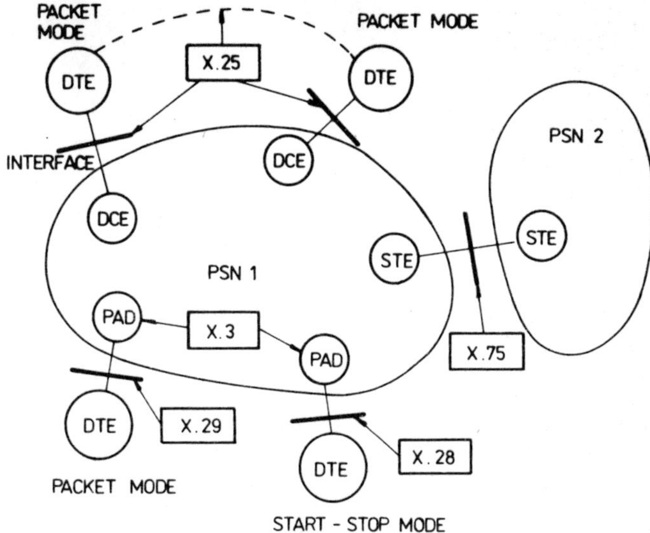

Figure D.1 Overview of the subjects of relevant X-series recommendations. (PSN = packet-switched network, PAD = Packet Assembly/ /Disassembly, STE = Signalling Terminal)

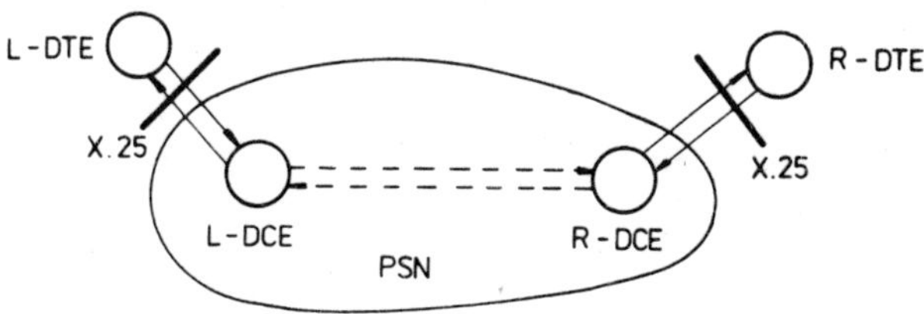

Figure D.2 Communication of two DTEs in the X.25 environment. (L = local, R = remote)

In fact, a three-layer network architecture is defined in the X.25. These layers (X.25: levels) correspond more or less to the lower three layers of the Open Systems Architecture (see Appendix F). We should expect that at least three layer protocols, each for one layer, are defined. And so they are. Figure D.3 depicts the mapping of the architecture into the DTEs and DCEs.

For the lowest layer (X.25: level 1) the DTE/DCE interface characteristics for the physical link between the DTE and the DCE are specified. They can be found in some V-Series or in some other X-Series Recommendations.

Link access procedure (LAP) across the DTE/DCE interface is the protocol being assigned to the second layer (X.25: level 2). In the original X.25 document included in the Orange book a version of ISO 4335 HDLC procedures (see Appendix C) was

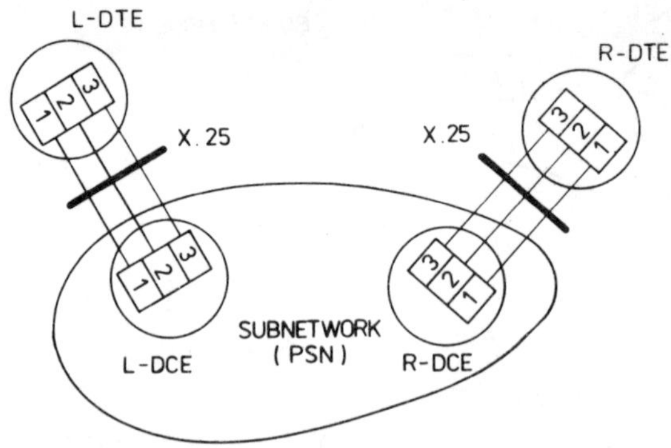

Figure D.3 Mapping of X.25 levels into DTEs and DCEs.
(L = local, R = remote)

adopted. In the amended X.25 document (being described here) the balanced class of HDLC procedures is also included, being denoted as LAPB (B for balanced). Just to illustrate a slight difference between the LAP, LAPB, and ISO 4335 HDLC, Table D.1 is presented in which the commands and responses used in LAPs are shown.

Table D.1 LAP and LAP B commands and responses

Commands	Responses	
RR RNR REJ DISC —	RR RNR REJ — UA	common
SARM —	— CMDR	LAP
SABM —	— FRMR	LAPB

The packet formats and control procedures for the exchange of packets containing control information and user data (data messages or transparent text) between the DTE and the DCE constitute the communication protocol of the third layer, which relates to the Network Layer of the OSA.

Basically three communication phases may be distinguished in the X.25 document, namely the call set up phase, the packet (or data) transfer phase, and the call clearing phase (original terms of the X.25).

Protocol words (in the X.25 identified with packet types) assigned to individual phases or procedures are outlined in Table D.2. Most of them need no explanation.

Interrupt procedure is not intended for mediating interruptions in the DTEs (as, for example, in the INWG 96 protocol), but simply means high priority data transfer (bypassing the flow control bounds). Reset procedure is intended for reinitializing the virtual call or permanent virtual circuit (i.e. for setting all relevant state variables to initial values, e.g. to zero). All data and interrupt packets remaining in the subnetwork are discarded when the reset packet passes over the subnetwork nodes. Restart serves for broader scaled recovery, and causes all virtual calls to be cleared and all permanent virtual circuits to be reset.

Table D.2 X.25 packet types.
(R : denotes remote DTE or DCE)

No.	Packet type		Procedure or phase
	DTE → DCE	DTE ← DCE	
1	CALL REQUEST R: CALL ACCEPTED	R: INCOMMING CALL CALL CONNECTED	Call set up
2	CLEAR REQUEST R: DTE CLEAR CONFIRMATION	R: CLEAR INDICATION DTE CLEAR CONFIRMATION	Call clearing
3	DTE DATA	DCE DATA	Data Transfer
4	DTE INTERRUPT R: DTE INTERRUPT CONFIRM.	R: DCE INTERRUPT DCE INTERRUPT CONFIRM.	Interrupt
5	DTE RR DTE RNR DTE REJ	DCE RR DCE RNR	Flow control
6	RESET REQUEST R: DTE RESET CONFIRMATION	R: RESET INDICATION DCE RESET CONFIRMATION	Reset
7	RESTART REQUEST R: DTE RESTART CONFIRM.	R: RESTART INDICATION DCE RESTART CONFIRM.	Restart

In Table D.2, local DTE-DCE pairs and remote DTE-DCE pairs are differentiated only by means of a capital R. We also could use four columns instead of two, in order to distinguish clearly the two basic communication elements (i.e. one local, and the other remote) both comprising the DTE and the DCE as the protocol stations. Figure D.4 shows a generic scheme related to the procedures numbered 1, 2, 4, 6, and 7 in Table D.2. Acknowledgment (X.25 : confirmation) for control words is single and positive, and is a sort of end-to-end acknowledgment mediated by a tandem of basic communication elements, or communication protocols. The mediating protocol is not specified in the X.25 document.

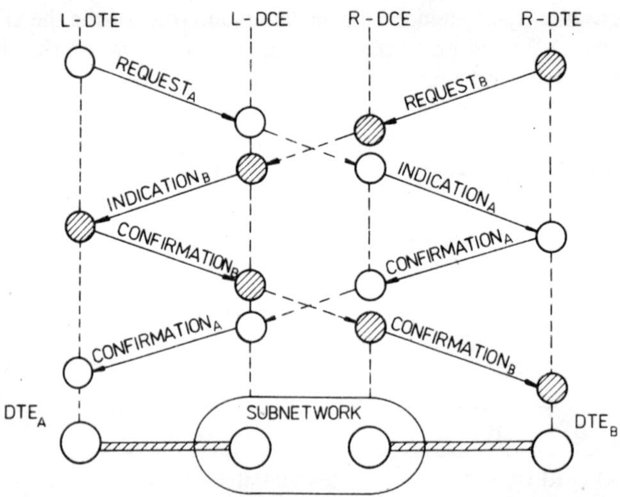

Figure D.4 Handshaking between communicating DTEs

OCTET 1	OCTET 2	OCTET 3
GFI LCG	LC	PTI

Figure D.5 Basic part of the X.25 packet header.
(GFI = General Format Identifier (=0001),
LCG = Logical Channel Group number,
LC = Logical Channel Number,
PTI = Packet Type Identifier)

Fourteen formats of packets (packet headers) are defined in the X.25 document. The lengths of packet headers are different for various packet types. The formats are divided into octets. The first three octets are common for all packet types and are depicted in Figure D.5. In some packet types the PTI field (the control field proper) is subdivided as indicated in Figure D.6.

The P(S) and P(R) sequence numbers belong to the well known numbering scheme used, where P(R) serves as an acknowledgment. A modulus of 8 (or 128 when extended) is used. A window mechanism with $W = 7$ (127) is used, serving for both error and flow control. Only data packets are numbered. Independent numbering for each direction of transmission in a virtual call or a permanent virtual circuit should be provided.

Acknowledgment packets, data packets, and RR, RNR, and REJ packets use the first three octets only. The remaining packet types use one or two octets more in their headers. Status, diagnostic or other additional control information is contained in these additional octets.

8 7 6 5	4 3 2 1	BITS
P(R)	M ¦ P(S) ¦ 0	DATA PACKETS
P(R)	0 0 0 0 1	RR PACKETS
P(R)	0 0 1 0 1	RNR PACKETS
P(R)	0 1 0 0 1	REJ PACKETS

Figure D.6 Subfields of the PTI field for data, RR, RNR and REJ packets.
(P(R) = packet receive sequence number,
P(S) = packet send sequence number,
M = more data indication (multipacket data message))

The format of call request and incoming call packets is not only longer than five octets, but it is also variable or adjustable in length. ALS or ALR subfields (see Figure D.7) of the fourth octet define the length of the subsequent address field. Similarly, the length of the facility field is determined by the contents of the facility length subfield. These two packet types are the only two in which DTE addresses may arrive. The calling DTE tells the subnetwork the called DTE address (ALR subfield nonzero) and the subnetwork (namely, the remote DCE) tells to the DTE called the calling DTE address (ALS subfield nonzero). These two packet types start the virtual call establishment phase, which ends when the virtual circuit is set up. Then all other packet types use the logical channel numbers only, i.e. the virtual circuit established is addressed instead of either called or calling DTEs.

OCTET 1	OCTET 2	OCTET 3	OCTET 4	ALS/ALR OCTETS	OCTET	FL OCTETS
GFI ¦ LCG	LC	PTI	ALS ¦ ALR	A	FL	FCL

Figure D.7 CALL REQUEST and INCOMING CALL packets format.
(GFI, LCG, LG, PTI = see Figure D.5,
ALS = calling DTE address length,
ALR = called DTE address length,
FL = facility length,
FCL = facility (generally, any options to be agreed upon between the communicationg DTEs)
A = address)

As for DTEs addresses, both local or network addresses (or even abbreviations) can be used depending on the agreement in the given subnetwork.

Provisional Recommendation X.75

This is based on Recommendation X.25. As regards the needs of international interworking between national public packet switching networks, the X.75 document defines the interface between gateway/transit switching exchanges (X.75: signalling terminals — STE) residing in different public data networks. This signalling terminal interface (i.e. a sort of STE-STE protocol) is decomposed into three levels, these being very similar to those of Recommendation X.25.

At level 1, physical circuits with bearer rate of 64kb/s or, optimally, 48kb/s are considered.

LAP B protocol is adopted for level 2.

Because of symmetrical stations, a simplified set (with respect to Recommendation X.25) of packet types is used. This is shown in Table D.3. The structure of control words reflects the fact that the STE-STE pair constitutes one basic communication element.

The basic concept of logical channels is, of course, also employed.

Table D.3 X.75 packet types

No.	Packet type (STE — STE)	Procedure or phase
1	CALL REQUEST CALL CONNECTED	Call set up
2	CLEAR REQUEST CLEAR CONFIRMATION	Call clearing
3	DATA	Data transfer
4	INTERRUPT INTERRUPT CONFIRMATION	Interrupt
5	RECEIVE READY (RR) RECEIVE NOT READY (RNR)	Flow control
6	RESET REQUEST RESET CONFIRMATION	Reset
7	RESTART REQUEST RESTART CONFIRMATION	Restart

Provisional Recommendation X.3

In order to facilitate access from simple start-stop mode terminals (DTEs) to public packet switching networks over the public telephone network, leased lines, or circuit-switched public data networks, the packet assembly/disassembly (PAD) facility is defined in the X.3 document.

Essentially, PAD is a sort of converter that should be able to communicate with (and control the communication of) both start-stop mode terminals and other subnetwork nodes (DCEs). The PAD is supposed to reside in some subnetwork nodes.

In the X.3 document basic functions, user selectable functions, and characteristics and possible values of parameters of PAD are specified.

From the basic functions the following examples may be mentioned here: assembly of characters into packets, disassembly of user data fields of packets into characters for individual terminals, handling of virtual call set up, clearing, resetting, and interrupt procedures, formatting and forwarding both packets and characters, handling a break signal from the start-stop mode terminals, etc.

By setting the PAD parameters the most appropriate overall function of PAD can be selected. However, setting procedures are the subjects of Provisional Recommendations X.28 and X.29.

Provisional Recommendation X.28

In this document an interface between a start-stop mode DTE and the PAD is defined.

The procedures supporting the communication between start-stop DTEs and the PAD are: procedures for the establishment of an access path, procedures for character interchange and service initiation (i.e. parameter setting), procedures for exchange of control information, and, finally, procedures for user data exchange.

As a communication medium both public switched telephone network or leased lines with V-series interfaces, and public switched data networks or leased data links with X-series interfaces may be utilized.

PAD and start-stop mode DTE are essentially different stations. Therefore PAD command signals (from DTE to PAD) and PAD service signals (from PAD to DTE) are differentiated. This means that different protocol words are used in different directions.

The tasks of the PAD command signals are: the establishment and clearing of a virtual call, the setting of values of basic PAD parameters (X.28: of a standard profile), the setting of individual PAD parameters' values, and the requesting of status information concerned with the set values of parameters from PAD. The PAD service signals are provided for: transmitting call progress signals to the calling DTE, acknowledging PAD command signals, and informing the DTE about PAD operation.

The two kinds of PAD signals may be regarded as constituting elements of PAD-DTE communication protocol. There is no protocol hierarchy defined in the X.28 document. This means that the protocol concerns the stations (PADs and DTEs) as a whole: no layering is applied.

In the document one can further find detailed definitions of the PAD command and service signals, detailed descriptions of individual communication phases, a list of PAD parameter settings, state diagrams, and sequences of events, etc.

Provisional Recommendation X.29

This defines procedures for the exchange of control information and user data between a packet mode DTE and a PAD (i.e. a sort of packet mode DTE-PAD protocol).

Normally, a start-stop mode DTE can only set the PAD parameters (at least, from outside of the subnetwork). In order to facilitate direct communication between a PAD and a packet mode DTE as a primary means for a packet mode DTE to be allowed to set the PAD parameters, the interface described was defined.

User data fields defined in Recommendation X.25 are used for the exchange of control information and user data. Other X.25 facilities are used as well.

Control words are called PAD messages in X.29 Provisional Recommendation. Again, because the communicating stations are different (PAD certainly differs from various packet mode DTEs), different PAD messages are defined for each of the two transmission directions.

The document contains detailed definitions and descriptions of the PAD messages, including their formats and other information that will not be described here.

Appendix E

INWG 96 and INWG 96.1 End-to-End Protocol

Documents INWG 96 from 1975 and INWG 96.1 from 1977 contain a draft of basic elements of the end-to-end protocol that is intended for communication control of the so called transport stations. These stations belong to the so called transport layer (see also Appendix F — OSA) and are implemented in various network elements as part of network software. Network elements are assumed to be connected to some data network (see Figure E.1).

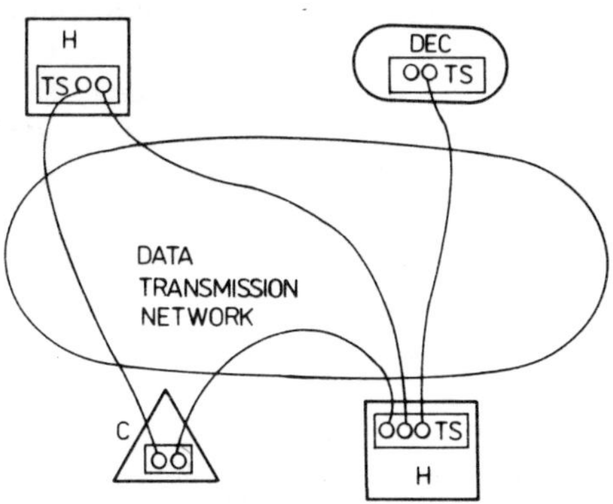

Figure E.1 Configuration for the INWG 96 end-to-end protocol. (H = host computer, DEC = data entry controller, C = concentrator)

The end-to-end protocol described in the documents unifies various designs of data networks, because it specifies the way in which the data network will be used by subscribers. The protocol also supports the uniformity of the design of network software in different computers, minicomputers, and other programmable devices. Such unification is indispensable for achieving a higher level of compatibility in heterogeneous networks.

The primary task of transport stations consists in the realization of protocol stations for the end-to-end protocol. This protocol is also called a transport protocol and it determines a course of transparent communication via data networks. But transport stations perform other tasks as well, e.g. they support interface communication with adjacent layers, or they supply conversions needed for accessing various data networks.

The following data transmission services offered by various data networks are considered in the document:

— datagrams,
— permanent virtual circuits,
— virtual calls (i.e. switched virtual circuits),
— permanent data circuits (leased lines),
— switched data circuits (i.e. circuit-switched).

So both packet switching and circuit switching networks are covered by the documents.

Referring to Open Systems Architecture (see Appendix F), in cases of packet switching networks and circuit switching networks the transport layer is linked to the network layer and to the link layer respectively. From the upper side the transport layer may be either linked to the session layer (in OSA) or it may be linked to function oriented protocols (e.g. file transfer protocol, virtual terminal protocol, RJE protocol) and/or to operating systems.

From the point of view of network architectures (see Chapter 2.3) a data network (or subnetwork) together with transport stations creates a transport subnetwork.

Transport stations are symmetrical. From this it follows that a contention or collision situation may occur when both stations try to establish the connection at the same time. The protocol contains means for dealing with this situation. There are two types of blocks being exchanged between the transport stations: so-called letters and telegrams.

The letters are blocks assigned primarily to the transfer of transparent texts (data messages) of various lengths. The document INWG 96 has limited the letter text field length to approximately 25000 octets (octet = 8 bits). There is no length limitation in the document INWG 96.1.

The telegrams are intended entirely for control purposes.

The documents define two basic modes: the lettergram mode and the liaison mode.

In the lettergram mode the connection establishment and connection termination phases (or functions, in this case) are not utilized. Stations simply send blocks (letters or telegrams) into a subnetwork. No agreement or handshaking is made between the stations preceding the data transfer phase. The sending station may (but does not necessarily) require acknowledgment from the receiving station. The principle of this method is similar to that of the mail service (except that there are no mail boxes in the lettergram mode).

In the liaison mode, firstly the two communicating stations negotiate (during the connection establishment phase, which is called the initialization phase in INWG 96), then data blocks exchange takes place within the scope of one session, and finally both stations terminate the connection during the termination phase. This mode resembles common telephone calls.

As far as communication functions are concerned, in the lettergram mode the only communication function realized is simple error control.

In the liaison mode several communication functions are realized, some of them being optional and selectable by means of codes assigned to the subfield SERVICES (see Figure E.6). The functions are error control (several methods), flow control, and fragmentation/reassembly, packing/unpacking.

In both modes the communication functions of multiplexing/demultiplexing and of addressing are included as well.

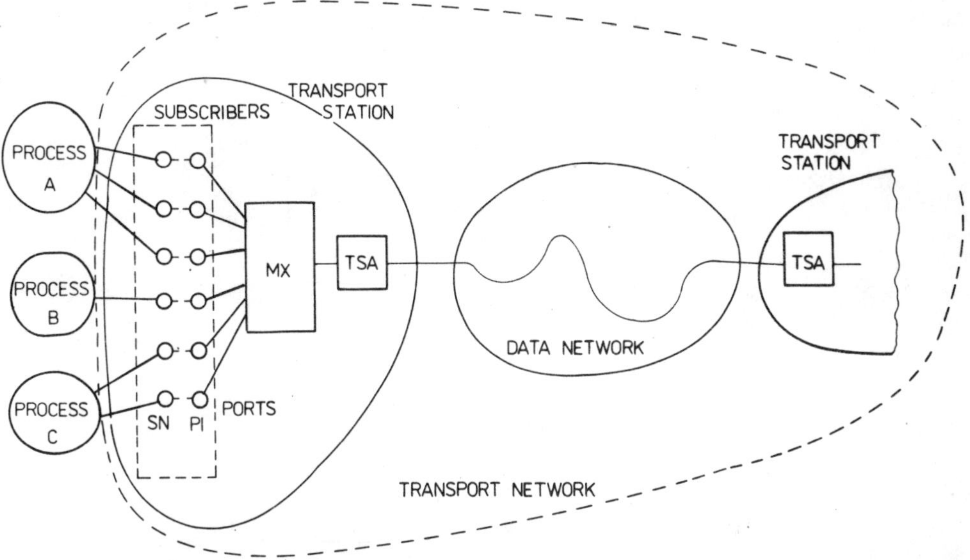

Figure E.2 Multiplexing and address transformation in a transport station. (TSA = transport station address, PI = port identifier, SN = subscriber name)

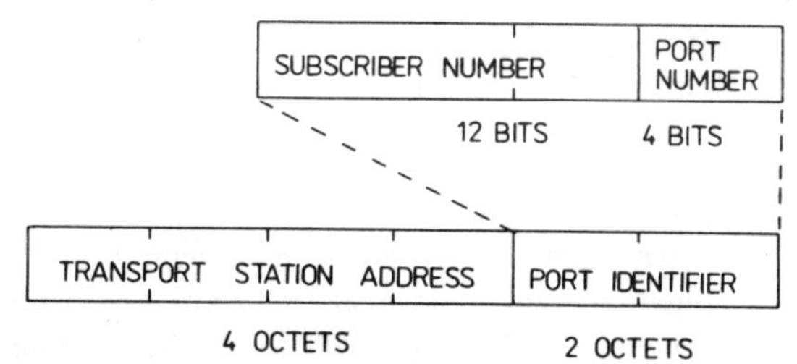

Figure E.3 INWG 96 address format

The transport station, by means of multiplexing, provides for the communication of several processes existing in one network element with several processes in some other network element through one pair of transport stations only (see Figure E.3).

Multiplexing requires a hierarchical structure of the addressing scheme (Figure E.2). Address transformation, which is also realized, is needed because of the introduction of two kinds of subscriber addresses: network addresses (numbers, as in a telephone directory) and original names of communicating processes. Network addresses are related to the so-called ports (see Figure E.2) that are treated elsewhere in the book. Network addresses of ports are called port identifiers, and consist of a port number and a subscriber number (Figure E.3).

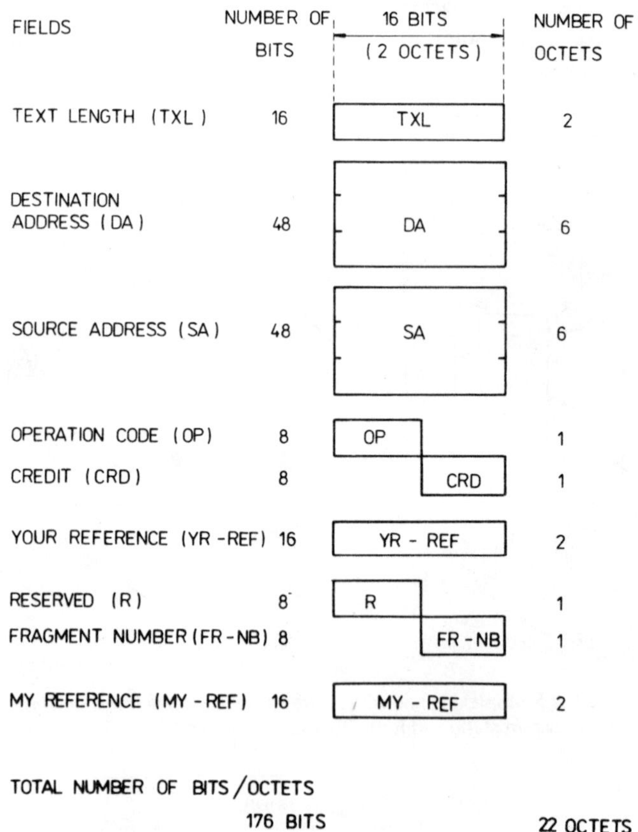

Figure E.4 Format of the INWG 96.1 header

Header format for letters and telegrams is shown in Figure E.4. If letters are long, they are first fragmented and the individual fragments are then sent over the subnetwork. Each fragment is in the block with the header described. Telegrams, having a fixed length of 16 bits, are inserted into the TR subfield (see Figure E.6).

Commands are coded in the OP subfield (see Figure E.5). In the documents three commands for the lettergram mode, two commands for telegrams in the liaison mode, and seven commands for letters in the liaison mode are specified (see Figure E.5). The LI-INIT command serves as a connection establishment request, while the LI-TERM command requires the termination of a connection. The LI-PURGE command can transfer an interrupt to the corresponding station; this command also cancels processing of such letters in a subnetwork that have not been received fully when LI-PURGE is emitted.

Letters and telegrams are numbered independently. The sequence numbers for letters are called YR-REF and MY-REF, whereas those for telegrams are called YR-REF(TG) and MY-REF(TG).

TRANSPORT COMMAND	OP SUBFIELD BITS 0 1 2 3 4 5 6 7	MEANING
LG - LT	R 0 0 1 0 0 0 0	FRAGMETS OF LETTER IN LETTERGRAM MODE
LG - ACK	0 0 0 1 0 0 0 1	POSITIVE ACKNOWLEDGMENT OF LETTER
LG - NACK	0 0 0 1 0 0 1 0	NEGATIVE ACKNOWLEDGMENT OF LETTER
LI - LT	R 0 0 0 0 0 0 0	FRAGMETS OF LETTER IN LIAISON MODE
LI - ACK	R 0 0 0 0 0 0 1	POSITIVE ACKNOWLEDGMENT
LI - NACK	R 0 0 0 0 0 1 0	NEGATIVE ACKNOWLEDGMENT
LI - INIT	0 0 0 0 0 0 1 1	USED TO INITIALIZE LIAISON MODE
LI - TERM	0 0 0 0 0 1 0 0	USED TO TERMINATE LIAISON MODE
LI - PURG	0 0 0 0 0 1 0 1	INTERRUPT AND "PURGING" OF BUFFERS
LI - ERR	0 0 0 0 0 1 1 0	USED TO TELL THE TYPE OF ERROR
LI - TG	R 0 0 0 0 1 1 1	TELEGRAMS
LI - TAK	0 0 0 0 1 0 0 0	POSITIVE ACKNOWLEDGMENT OF TELEGRAM

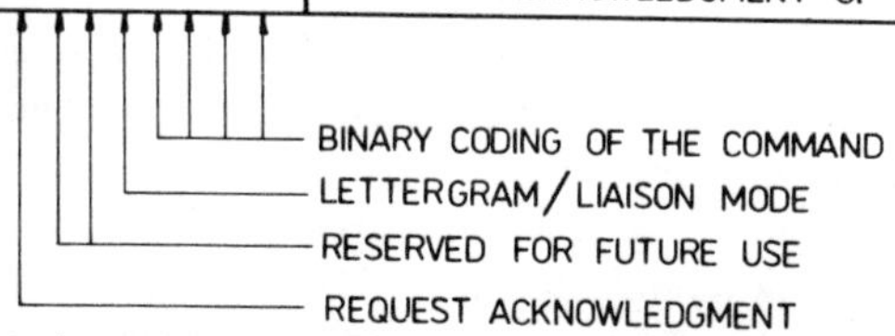

BINARY CODING OF THE COMMAND
LETTERGRAM/LIAISON MODE
RESERVED FOR FUTURE USE
REQUEST ACKNOWLEDGMENT

Figure E.5 Binary coding of transport commands (format of the OP subfield)

During the connection establishment the communicating stations must negotiate which optional communication functions will be used during the session. The optional communication functions are called services in INWG 96 documents. The agreement is achieved by means of the SERVICE subfield which belongs to the LI-INIT command (see Figure E.6). Codes used in the SERVICE subfield are presented in Table E.1.

Table E.1 Coding of the SERVICE subfield — selection of communication functions. (LI — INIT command)

Bit number	The meaning of setting the corresponding bit value to one — optional functions
0	Error control on letters
1	Flow control on letters
2	Multifragment frames
3	Checksum on letters
4 to 7	Reserved for future use

SUBFIELDS OF THE CONTROL FIELD					
OP	CRD	YR-REF	R	FR-NB	MY-REF
LG-LT				FR-NB	MY-REF
LG-ACK		YR-REF			
LG-NACK					
LI-LT	CRD-NB	YR-REF		FR-NB	MY-REF
LI-ACK	CRD-NB	YR-REF			
LI-NACK	CRD-NB	YR-REF			
LI-INIT	CRD-NB			SERVICES	MY-REF
LI-TERM	TERM-CODE	YR-REF			LAST MY-REF
LI-PURG	CRD-NB	YR-REF			LAST MY-REF
LI-ERR	ERR-CODE	YR-REF			LAST MY-REF
LI-TG		TG-TEXT			MY-REF(TG)
LI-TAK		YR-REF(TG)			

Figure E.6 INWG 96.1 control field format (utilization of the control field subfields)

Now two realized communication functions will be described, namely error control and flow control. These are closely related in INWG 96 documents and elsewhere.

Error control in the lettergram mode:

In INWG 96 documents, error control in this mode is specified only in the case of an explicitly requested acknowledgment (bit $R = 1$).

Error control relates to sequence errors only: transmission errors are not considered. No error detecting code is assumed in this mode, and error control is for letters (not for fragments).

The method used is modified ARQ with P-type acknowledgment (LG-ACK), or, if need be, with A-type acknowledgment (LG-ACK and LG-NACK). Numbering modulus 2^{16} is used, together with a time-out (for the whole letter). The modification of ARQ lies in the different decision making related to retransmissions. The retransmissions are not decided by transport stations, i.e. by protocol stations in a layer, but by subscribers in the adjacent higher layer, who must be informed, of course.

Both types of acknowledgment responses (LG-ACK, LG-NACK) contain YR-REF equal to MY-REF of the letter received. They are sent immediately after the last fragment of a letter is received. Fragments are not acknowledged.

Error control in the liaison mode:

This concerns sequence errors only, but optionally (SERVICE bit $3 = 1$) transmission errors may be covered as well. Error control relates to whole letters (not to fragments).

The method used is modified ARQ with group acknowledgment of the P-type (by means of YR-REF which acknowledges a correct reception of letters with numbers

MY-REF equal to or less than YR-REF). The numbering modulus used is 2^{16}, window size is $W = 2^{15} - 1$. Everything above relates to letters (not to fragments). Time-out is used, too. This is started after the last fragment of a letter has been sent. YR-REF (serving as positive acknowledgment) can be inserted in a fragment with LI-LT (when a letter is being sent in the oposite direction), or in a word with LI-ACK.

After the completion of the time-out period the sending station retransmits the unacknowledged letter automatically. The retransmitting may be repeated E times (E is a protocol parameter). When even then the letter is not acknowledged, a decision is shifted to the adjacent higher layer.

Duplicated letters are cancelled, but they must be acknowledged.

Flow control:

This concerns letters and is optional (SERVICE bit 2 = 1). The window mechanism is used to slow down the sending of further blocks. Window size is not fixed, but it is dynamically adjustable by means of CRD-NB. In a way, window size W = CRD-NB. The value of CRD-NB tells the sending station how many letters can be sent to the receiving station (i.e. how many letters can be received).

Because the same mechanism (but with different window size) is utilized for error control, it is clear that with flow control active the common window size will be equal to CRD-NB.

Appendix F

OSA — Open Systems Architecture

The ISO working document entitled "Reference Model for Open Systems Architecture", produced within the frame of ISO/TC 97/SC 96 in November 1978, is very briefly commented on here, though it is the working version only.

This comprehensive document (which is the length of a book) contains not only the detailed specification and description of on actual network architecture (called the Reference Model of Open Systems Architecture), but also contains a uniform explanation of a consistent set of concepts and definitions concerning the basic network architecture elements, and several appendices presenting various surveys, a glossary with definitions, ways of formal description of a network architecture, the interpretation of virtual terminal protocols, of file transfer protocols, etc.

From the point of view of Chapter 2.3 of this book, the OSA is basically the logical network architecture. However, it comprises the mapping of architecture into network elements and into network configuration, and it encompasses a much wider range of network topics. It is based on a more general concept of Open Systems Interconnection — OSI. Roughly, the open system is a system implementing the OSA and, therefore, it is compatible with other systems of this type and also with subnetworks designed in accordance with OSA.

OSA emphasizes services, and in connection with them, also functions (not only communication functions). Layers are characterized by services provided to a higher layer, by services required from a lower layer, and by functions performed within the given layer.

Many novel terms are defined (and explained) in the document, the aim being the elimination of ambiguities in the computer networks and protocols terminology. Some of these terms will be referred to in parentheses (OSA:...).

Before presenting the reference model, consisting of seven layers, some of the principles and concepts will be outlined first.

Figure F.1 shows the graphical representation of the layering used in OSA. Entities are defined in layers. The entities perform functions, provide services (to entities in a higher layer), request and receive services (from entities in a lower layer), and communicate or cooperate (with entities in the same layer). In fact, entities correspond to functional modules, control modules, and protocol stations described in this book. The communication between entities is governed by protocols. There may be several protocols in one layer, and one entity may use several of them. But the term protocol is used in the document both for communication protocols and procedures (see Chapter 2.4). Besides, there is no definition of the communication element (or its equivalent) to be found in the document.

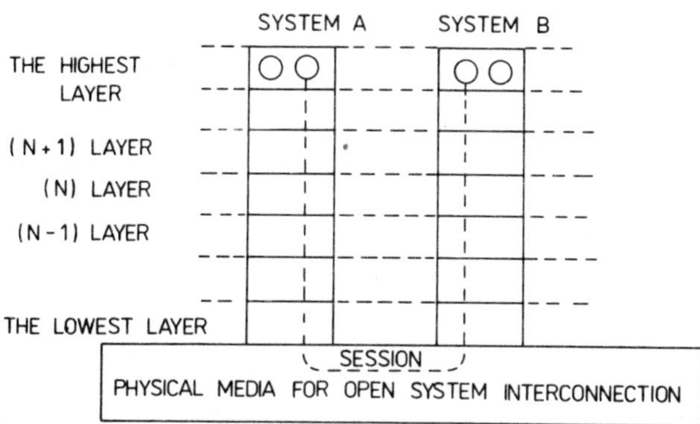

Figure F.1 Principle of layering in OSA

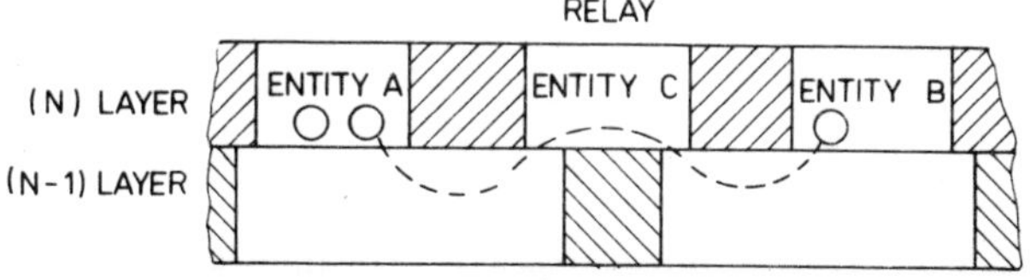

Figure F.2 Relay communication principle

Table F.1 gives a survey of the main services and functions. It can be seen that there is hardly any difference between services and functions as far as their naming is concerned. This is not at all surprising, though, if we take a service to be the result of activities assigned to a communication function.

Services provided by a given layer are rendered not only by this layer but also by a lower layer. Of course, the same holds for the lower layer.

The provision and utilization of services by pairs of entities residing in adjacent layers are determined by an interface which is defined in much the same way as is a protocol: a set of rules and formats (both semantic and syntactic) for the control of data exchange between entities. The interface concept corresponds to the interlayer protocol concept (see Chapter 2.4).

The so called "relay" principle is defined in the document (see Figure F.2) for the communication via intermediate nodes and gateway functions.

Examples of other topics treated and/or defined in the document are: addressing principles, types of data block, establishment and releasing of connections, management functions, etc.

Table F.1 Functions and services picked out from the OSA document

Functions	Services
addressing	network addresses
multiplexing	
establishment	establishment
termination/release	termination/release
option selection	class of service selection
option negotiation	class of service negotiation
layer menegement/administration	session administration
error control	
error detection	
error recovery	error recovery
flow control	flow control
segmenting and blocking	
sequencing	sequencing
routing	routing and switching
transformations/mappings	
data transfer	data transfer
data compression	data compression
encoding/security	encoding
acknowledging	
monitoring	
supervisory functions	
data delimiting/framing	data delimiting
	session control
	restart
	error notification
	recovery

In the document two types of management functions are distinguished: system management functions and layer management functions.

System management functions concern the resources shared by all layers, i.e. complete network elements (OSA: systems). These functions comprise the activation and deactivation of nodes, links, and software modules including the loading, initialization, auxiliary connection establishment and releasing, etc. Apart from these, various monitoring and recovery functions are also included, e.g. measurement control for purposes of diagnostics and/or statistics, and actions to be taken in the case of failures such as restart and reconfiguration.

Layer management functions exert control over the activities of layer entities, i.e. activities taking place inside the layers. Examples of these are: the establishment, maintenance, and releasing of connections to support communication between top layer entities, testing, measuring, and reporting in each layer.

Figure F.3 shows the relation between the two types of management functions and their location in layers of the architecture. System management functions are to be found in the top layer only.

The principle of using lower layer facilities as a communication means is strongly emphasized in the OSA. It can be expressed by means of the communication control element (see Figure 2.11), where communicating entities may be regarded as user stations and a connection is represented by the pair of protocol stations together with a communication medium.

The resulting network architecture, which is called a reference model in the document, consists of seven layers (see Figure F.4).

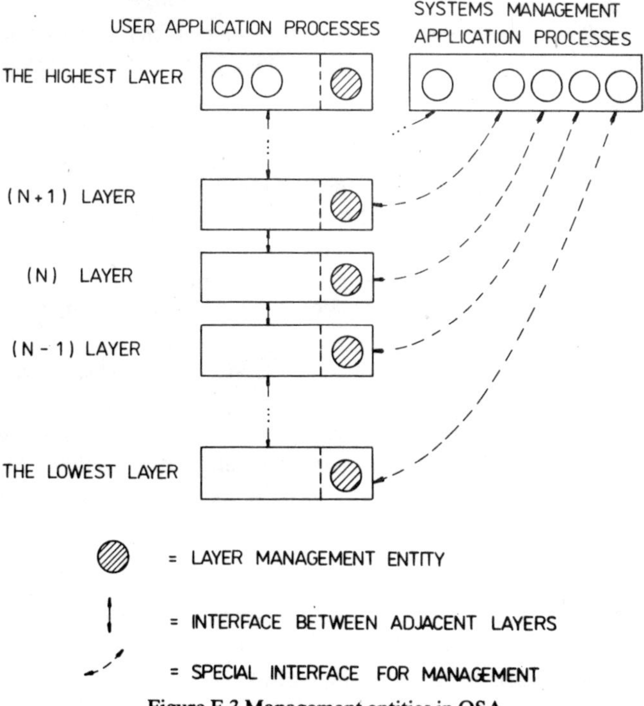

Figure F.3 Management entities in OSA

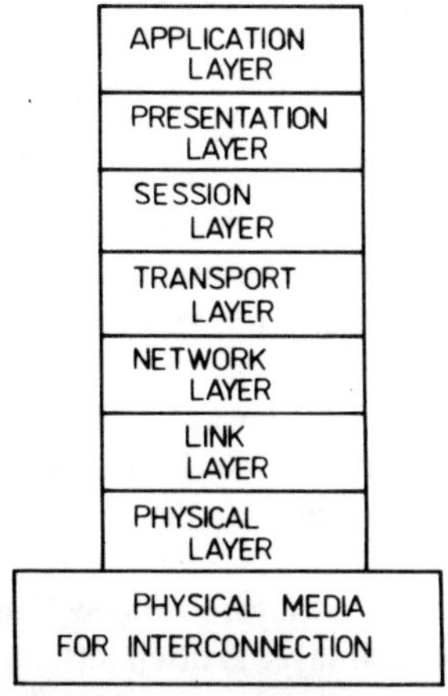

Figure F.4 Reference model of Open Systems Architecture (OSA)

The Physical Layer relates to physical links (OSA: data-circuits) and supplies mechanical, electrical, functional, and procedural characteristics needed for their establishment, maintenance, and releasing.

Some examples of standards relevant to this layer are CCITT V.21, V.24, V.28, V.34, X.21, X.21bis, etc.

The Link Layer comprises the data link control which is characterized, for example, by the standards ISO 1745 (see Appendix A), ISO 3309, and ISO 4335 (see Appendix C — HDLC).

The Network Layer relates in principle to the exchange of packets (OSA: network-services-data-units) via the packet switching network. In comprises the functions which are to be added to the functions of the preceding two levels. Routing and switching are typical functions of this kind.

From among the standards and documents relating to this layer the following can be given as examples: CCITT X.25 (virtual circuits), some documents of ISO/TC97//SC6, projects 17 and 24, and some INWG (IFIP, TC6) documents (datagrams and datagram service).

The Transport Layer concerns the transport service, transport stations, end-to-end protocols, etc. It is intended to provide connections permitting the creation of sessions between entities of the Session Layer. Again, some documents of INWG and those of projects 17 and 24 of ISO/TC97/SC6 can be mentioned as applying to this layer.

The Session Layer is concerned mainly with the control of the sessions, these being connections ensuring communication between application processes. The services provided by the Transport Layer are utilized, of course, for the implementation of the sessions.

The Presentation Layer provides mainly for transformation, conversion, and control services necessitated by differences in data structures and in control procedures in various network elements (terminals, file systems, etc.). The recommendation CCITT X.29 and documents concerning the virtual terminal protocol are examples of documents relevant to this layer.

The Application Layer covers processes (OSA: application-processes) that are the final users of services of all lower layers. The communication between processes is governed by communication protocols (OSA: Application Layer Protocols).

Application processes represent any processes capable of communicating. These may be processes in computers and in all other programmable devices/equipment, manual processes encompassing the cooperation between human operators and input devices, or industrial processes connected with communication of various process control equipment.

OSA is intended to form a general background for the development of a set of compatible standardized protocols and interfaces. Therefore it is natural that there are no communication protocols specified in the document. The main feature of OSA is approach through services.

The link, network, and transport layers can be found in many other types of network architecture. The physical layer is often left out from the network architecture and is considered to be part of the physical media for transmission.

In differentiating between the upper three layers we may be entering an area where standards are as desirable as they are difficult to agree upon.

Appendix G

Selected Abbreviations

A	Availability
A, AD, ADR	Adress, Adress field
ABM	Asynchronous Balanced Mode (HDLC, CCITT X.25)
ABME	Asynchronous Balanced Mode Extended
ACC	Accepted (data, block)
ACK, AK	Acknowledgment (ISO, CCITT)
ADCCP	Advanced Data Communication Control Procedure (ANSI)
ADM	Asynchronous Disconnected Mode (HDLC)
ADP	Automatic Data Processing
AFNOR	Association Française de Normalisation (French Standard Association)
ANSI	American National Standards Institute
ARM	Asynchronous Response Mode (HDLC)
ARPA	Advanced Research Project Agency
ARQ	Automatic Request for Repetition, Automatic-Repeat-Request
ASA	American Standard Association
ASCII	American Standard Code for Information Interchange
ATDM	Asynchronous Time Division Multiplex
b	bit
B	Byte
BC	Binary Checksum
BCC	Block Check Character (ISO), Bit Character Count
BCD	Binary Coded Decimal (code)
BCK	Block
BCR	Block Coding Rate
BCS	Block Check Sequence
BDLC	Burroughs Data Link Control Procedure
BER	Bit Error Rate

BP	Block Parity
BSC	Binary Synchronous Communication (IBM)
BSI	British Standard Institute
BTF	Bulk Transfer Function
BTMA	Busy Tone Multiple Access
C	Control, Control field
CCITT	Commité Consultatif International Télégraphique et Téléphonique (International Consultative Committee on Telegraphy and Telephony)
CH	Character
CMDR	Command Reject (HDLC)
CMEA	Council for Mutual Economic Assistance
CRC	Cyclic Redundancy Checking
CRD	Credit (INWG)
CSMA	Carrier-Sense Multiple Access
DCA	Distributed Communications Architecture (Univac)
DCE	Data Circuit-Termination Equipment
DDCMP	Digital Data Communications Message Protocol (DEC)
DG	Datagram
DIN	Deutsche Industrie-Norm (German Industry Standard)
DIS	Draft International Standard
DISC	Disconnected (HDLC)
DLC	Data Link Control (ANSI)
DLE	Data Link Escape (ISO, CCITT)
DM	Disconnect Mode (HDLC)
DNA	Digital Network Architecture (DEC)
	Deutschen Normenausschuss (German Standard Committee)
DSE	Data Switching Exchange,
	Distributed System Environment (Honeywell)
DT, DTA	Data
DTE	Data Terminal Equipment
EBCDIC	Extended Binary Coded Decimal Interchange Code
ECC	Error Correcting Code
ECMA	European Computer Manufacturers' Association
EDAC	Error Detection Automatic Correction
ED&C	Error Detection and Correction
EIA	Electronic Industries Association
EIN	European Informatics Network
ENQ	Enquiry (ISO, CCITT)
EOH	End of Heading
EOL	End of Letter (INWG)
EOT	End of Transmission (ISO, CCITT)

ERR	Error
ETB	End of Transmission Block (ISO, CCITT)
ETX	End of Text (ISO, CCITT)
F	Flag, Final bit (HDLC)
FCS	Frame Check Sequence (HDLC)
FDM	Frequency Division Multiplex
FDMA	Frequency Division Multiple Access
FDX	Full-Duplex
FEC	Forward Error Control
FLD	Field
FR	Fragment
FRMR	Frame Reject (HDLC, CCITT X.25)
FTSC	Federal Telecommunication Standard Committee
FTP	File Transfer Protocol
GPD	General Purpose Discipline (IBM)
GSMA	Global Scheduling Multiple Access
HDLC	High Level Data Link Control Procedure
HDR	Header, Heading
HDX	Half-Duplex
IA	International Alphabet
ICP	Initial Connection Protocol
IEC	International Electrotechnical Commission
IFIP	International Federation of Information Processing
IIASA	International Institute for Applied Systems Analysis
IM	Initialization Mode (HDLC)
IMP	Interface Message Processor (ARPA)
INFO	Information, Information field
INQ	Inquiry
INWG	International Networks Working Group
IS	International Standard
ISO	International Organization for Standardization
ITA	International Telegraph Alphabet
ITB	Intermediate Transmission Block (BSC)
ITU	International Telecommunication Union (=UIT)
LAP	Link Access Procedure (CCITT)
LAPB	Link Access Procedure — Balanced (CCITT)
LG	Lettergram (INWG)
LI	Liaison (INWG)
LRC	Longitudinal Redundancy Checking
LT	Letter (INWG)

MA	Master Station
MKKTT	CCITT (in Russian)
MOS	ISO (in Russian)
MLP	Multilink Procedure (CCITT X.75)
MRQ	ARQ with Memory
MSAP	Mini-Slotted Alternating Priority
MSG	Message
MTBF	Mean Time Between Failures
MTK	ITA (in Russian)
MTTR	Mean Time to Repair
NAK	Negative Acknowledgment (ISO, CCITT)
NBS	National Bureau of Standards
NCP	Network Control Program
NDM	Normal Disconnected Mode (HDLC)
NPL	National Physical Laboratory
NRC	Network Routing Centre
NRM	Normal Response Mode (HDLC)
NRZI	Nonreturn-to-Zero Inverted (coding)
NSC	Network Switching Centre
NSP	Network Service Protocol (DNA)
NVT	Network Virtual Terminal
NW	Network
OSA	Open Systems Architecture (ISO)
OSI	Open Systems Interconnection (ISO)
P	Parity, Polling bit (HDLC)
PAD	Packet Assembly and Disassembly (CCITT)
P-ALOHA	Pure ALOHA (multiple access)
PAR	Positive Acknowledgment and Retransmission
PB	Parity Block Check
PMS	Processor-Memory-Switch
PRE	Prefix
PS	Packet-Switching
PSN	Packet Switched Network
PSTN	Public Switched Telephone Network (CCITT)
PTI	Packet Type Identifier (CCITT X.25)
PTT	Postal Telegraph and Telephone (office, administration)
R	Recommendation
RCH	Redundancy Check
RCV	Receiver
RD	Request Disconnect (HDLC)
REF	Reference (INWG)
REJ	Reject (HDLC)

RER	Residual Error Rate
RIM	Request Initialization Mode (HDLC)
RIT	Rate of Information Throughput
RJE	Remote Job Entry
RNR	Receive Not Ready (HDLC)
RPT	Repetition
RR	Receive Ready (HDLC)
RSET	Reset (HDLC)
RVI	Reverse Interrupt (BSC)
S, STA	Station
SABM	Set Asynchronous Balanced Mode (HDLC, CCITT X.25)
SABME	Set Asynchronous Balanced Mode Extended (HDLC)
S-ALOHA	Slotted ALOHA (multiple access)
SARM	Set Asynchronous Response Mode (HDLC)
SARME	Set Asynchronous Response Mode Extended (HDLC)
SBT	Six-Bit Transcode (IBM)
SC	Subcommittee (ISO)
SDLC	Synchronous Data Link Control Procedure (IBM)
SG	Study Group (CCITT)
SIM	Set Initialization Mode (HDLC)
SL	Slave Station
SMVT	Scroll Mode Virtual Terminal
SNA	Systems Network Architecture (IBM)
SNRM	Set Normal Response Mode (HDLC)
SNRME	Set Normal Response Mode Extended (HDLC)
SOH	Start of Header (ISO, OCITT)
SREJ	Selection Reject (HDLC)
SRMA	Split-Channel Reservation Multiple Access
SRUC	Split Reservation Upon Collision
STDM	Synchronous Time-Division Multiplex
STDMA	Synchronous Time-Division Multiple Access
STE	Signalling Terminal (CCITT X.75)
STX	Start of Text (ISO, CCITT)
SYN	Synchronization (ISO, CCITT)
TASI	Time Assignment Speech Interpolation
TC	Technical Committee (ISO, ECMA, IFIP)
TCP	Transmission Control Program
TDM	Time-Division Multiplex
TDMA	Time-Division Multiple Access
TG	Telegram (INWG), Tasking Group (ECMA)
TIP	Terminal Interface Processor (ARPA)
TMR	Transmitter
TOF	Transfer Overhead Factor
TOT	Transfer Overhead Time

TRIB	Transfer Rate of Information Bits
TS	Transport Station
TTD	Temporary Text Delay (BSC)
TTXT	Transparent Text
TWA	Two-Way Alternate (HDLC)
TWS	Two-Way Simultaneous (HDLC)
TXT	Text
U	Utilization Factor
UA	Unnumbered Acknowledge (HDLC)
UDLC	Univac Data Link Control Procedure
UI	Unnumbered Information (HDLC)
UIT	Union International des Télécommunications (=ITU)
UP	Unnumbered Poll (HDLC)
USASCII	USA Standard Code for Information Interchange (=ASCII)
USASI	USA Standard Institute
VAN	Value Added Network
VC	Virtual Circuit
VRC	Vertical Redundancy Checking
VT	Virtual Terminal
VTP	Virtual Terminal Protocol
WACK, WAK	Wait Before Acknowledgment (BSC)
WG	Working Group (IFIP)
X	Transparent, e.g. XSTX (BSC)
XID	Exchange Identification (HDLC)

Appendix H

Supplementary Bibliographical Notes

We present here some update to the list of literature references. This supplement reflects mainly the trends of recent development of the subject.

Although the number of papers concerning communication protocols, network architectures, communication functions, etc. is steadily and rapidly growing, the books have only emerged recently. Besides the already mentioned book of Davies, D. W. et al. on computer network protocols [66], the publication edited and written (partially) by Cerf, V. G., and McQuillan, J. M. [H.1] may be recommended to readers.

The number of conferences and workshops dealing with topics of the subject is also growing. We present here, just as examples, the references to the workshop on communication in distributed systems which was held at Berlin in December, 1979 [H.2] and to the two winter schools on properties and functions of computer networks which were held at Karpacz, Poland in March 1979 and 1980 [H.3, H.4].

The special issue of IEEE Transactions on Communications on computer network architectures and protocols [H.5], which is also mentioned in the preface to this book, contains twentythree papers on network architectures, on protocols and functions of a physical level, a link control level, a network level, and higher levels, on network interconnections, and, finally, on formal models and methods of verification and implementation of communication protocols.

With growing number of computer networks and public data networks the problem of compatibility seems to become the most important. This is reflected by the interest paid to the ISO material on Open Systems Architecture [H.6], or Open Systems Interconnection. The further very frequent topics are those of network interconnections and network standards. They are closely related to the OSA concept. Higher layers of network architectures are the final topic of recent interest.

Principles of the OSA are explained by Zimmermann, H. in [H.7]. Various comparisons of the OSA seven-layer model and other architectures and/or networks are treated in the following papers: CCITT—OSA [H.8], SNA—OSA [H.9, H.10], Transdata — OSA [H.10], X.25 — OSA [H.12], etc.

Network interconnection issues may be found, for example, in [H.12, H.13]. One NATO Advanced Study Institute workshop, held in Bonas, France in 1978, was fully devoted to the network interconnection problems [H.14].

The new development of the ISO—HDLC standard and some CCITT X-Series Revised Recommendations will be commented further.

In order to match the link level of X.25 (LAP B) to the HDLC protocol (IS 4335) a tertiary station (termed combined) and an asynchronous balanced mode (ABM) were proposed within the HDLC in addition to the existing primary and secondary stations and the corresponding modes (see Appendix C) in 1977 by the ISO TC/97 SC/6 document No. 1445. This document was reissued after some amendments as No. 1804 in 1979 and appeared in January 1980 as Draft Addendum 2 to the IS 4335 [H.15] for accepting by the ISO Council.

A proposed balanced configuration consists of two combined stations having identical responsibility for exchanging data, commands, and responses and initiating error control functions. Four new unnumbered commands and one response have been introduced: set ABM (SABM) and set ABM extended (SABME) for placing the addressed station in ABM and ABME modes, respectively, reset (RSET) for resetting the receive state variable, and frame reject command and response (FRMR).

During the CCITT Study Period 1977—1980 new recommendations X.3, X.28, X.29, and X.75 were issued and recommendation X.25 was revised (their versions from 1978 [216, 217] are briefly characterized in Appendix D). In 1979 there were several meetings (Paris, Ottawa, Montreal) where documents mentioned above were further revised and amended and finally have been issued as white documents [H.16, H.17, H.18]. We shall sketch main proposals.

Within the scope of X.25 the new service — datagram is proposed as an additional service provided by some networks. Such an amendment necessitated to change the most of original sections in [216] and to add a new one (Procedures for datagram service). Datagram service serves for exchanging short data messages (up to 128 octets in each datagram) without call set-up and clearing. The numbering as well as the window mechanism for flow control are similar to those for virtual circuit service. Also the reset and the restart procedures are introduced in this service. For these functions original packet types DCE and DTE RR and RNR, DTE REJ (optionally), RESET and RESTART REQUEST and INDICATION, DCE and DTE RESTART CONFIRMATION (see Table D.2) are utilized. Besides these types three new ones are defined: DCE and DTE DATAGRAM and DATAGRAM SERVICE SIGNAL.

The format of DCE and DTE DATAGRAM type packet is the same as that of CALL REQUEST and INCOMMING CALL type packets (see Figure D.7) with the exception that no PTI field is involved, and formats may be extended to modulo 128 (similarly as DCE and DTE DATA packet formats). DATAGRAM SERVICE SIGNAL packet format holds the cause field serving for the indication of reasons for service signal (for example, such reasons for the datagram rejected type are local procedure error, invalid facility request, incompatible destination, network congestion, etc.).

Some optional user facilities within the datagram service are provided: datagram non-delivery indication (a datagram is discarded by the network but the user may transmit it later), datagram delivery confirmation, abbreviated addressing, etc.

Other recommendations are proposed to change only slightly. The final draft revision of X.75 [H.18] introduces the multilink procedure (MLP) for data exchange over multiple parallel links (physical circuits) between two STEs. The revisions of X.3, X.28, and X.29 [H.16] define several new PAD parameters with their possible values, new PAD command and service signals, time-outs as well as their provisional values.

All documents are expected to be approved at the 7th CCITT Plenary Assembly in November 1980.

Standardization of protocols of higher layers concerns mainly the virtual terminal protocols [H.19, H.20, H.21, H.22] and file transfer protocols [H.23], but network jobs [H.24] and network processing control [H.25] are treated as well.

The approach to communication control through communication functions, which is typical for this book, may be found in quite a number of papers now.

Of course, there are many papers dealing with individual communication functions. Some of them are referred to as follows: addressing [H.26, H.27], synchronization (of processes) [H.28, H.29], error control methods [H.30, H.31], routing [H.32, H.33, H.34, H.35], flow control [H.36], deadlocks avoidance [H.37].

Some other topics relevant to this book: interprocess communication [H.38], models of protocols and protocol verification [H.39, H.40], a model of the SNA architecture [H.41], communication software implementation [H.42, H.43].

The following list of references contains mostly the literature that has arrived after delivery of the manuscript of this book to the publishing house.

References:

[H.1] McQUILLAN, J. M., and CERF, V. G., Tutorial: A Practical View of Computer Communication Protocols. IEEE Press, New York, 1978.

[H.2] Kommunikation in verteilten Systemen. Schindler, S., and Schröder, C. W. (Eds.), Springer Verlag, Heidelberg, 1979, (338p.).

[H.3] Properties and Functions of Computer Networks. Part 2: Communications (In Polish.) Bazewicz, M. (Ed.), Politechnika Wroclawska, Wroclaw, 1980.

[H.4] Properties and Functions of Computer Networks. Part 3: Information Resources (In Polish.) Bazewicz, M. (Ed.), In preparation.

[H.5] IEEE Trans. on Communications, COM-28, No. 4, April 1980.

[H.6] Reference Model of Open Systems Interconnection. Version 4. ISO/TC 97/SC 16 N 227, June 1979.

[H.7] ZIMMERMANN, H., "OSI Reference Model — The ISO Model of Architecture for Open Systems Interconnection". IEEE Trans., COM-28, No. 4, April 1980, pp. 425—432.

[H.8] Structure for and Use of a Reference Model for Public Data Networks Applications. CCITT, COM VII, Temp. Doc. No. 2 (Revised), Sept. 1979.

[H.9] DEBACKER, P., "Systems Network Architecture in Relationship with the Open Systems Interconnection Reference Model". In: Schindler, S., and Schröder, C. W. (Eds.), Kommunikation in verteilten Systemen. Springer Verlag, Heidelberg, 1979, pp. 226—237.

[H.10] GLAS, G., and LODE, D., "Öffnung homogener geschlossener Herstellernetze im Sinne des ISO-Referenzmodelles, am Beispiel von SNATCH, einem Funktionsverbund zwischen Siemens-TRANSDATA- und IBM—SNA-Rechnernetzen." In: Schindler, S., and Schröder, C. W. (Eds.), Kommunikationen in verteilten Systemen. Springer Verlag, Heidelberg, 1979, pp. 255—266.

[H.11] SCHINDLER, S., et al., "The OSA Project — Design and Formal Specification of an X.25 Based Open Transport Layer and its Protocols." In: Schindler, S., and Schröder, C. W. (Eds.), Kommunikation in verteilten Systemen. Springer Verlag, Heidelberg, 1979, pp. 51—86.

[H.12] POSTEL, J. B., "Internetwork Protocol Approaches." IEEE Trans., COM-28, No. 4, April 1980, pp. 604—611.

[H.13] BOGGS, D. R., et al., "Pup: An Internetwork Architecture." IEEE Trans., COM-28, No. 4, April 1980, pp. 612—624.

[H.14] Interlinking of Computer Networks. Beauchamp, K. G. (Ed.), D. Reidel Publishing Comp., Dordrecht, 1979.

[H.15] Data Communication — High Level Data Link Control Procedures — Elements of Procedures (Tertiary Station). Draft Addendum 2, ISO 4335, Jan. 1980.

[H.16] Revised Recommendation X.3, X.28, and X.29. SG VII, Contribution No. 428, 429, and 430, CCITT, Nov. 1979.

[H.17] Draft Revised Recommendation X.25 Introduction and Packet Level. SG VII, Contribution No. 439, CCITT, Nov. 1979.

[H.18] Final Draft Revision of Recommendation X.75. SG VII, Contribution No. 441, CCITT, Nov. 1979.

[H.19] STRUIF, B., "Spezielle VT-Implemetationsprobleme." In: Schindler, S., and Schröder, C. W. (Eds.), Kommunikation in verteilten Systemen. Springer Verlag, Heidelberg, 1979, pp. 199—207.

[H.20] FUNDNEIDER, O., "Das 'Virtual Device Protocol'." In: Schindler, S., and Schröder, C. W. (Eds.), Kommunikation in verteilten Systemen. Springer Verlag, Heidelberg, 1979, pp. 121—135.

[H.21] DAY, J. D., "Terminal Protocols." IEEE Trans., COM-28, No. 4, April 1980, pp. 585—593.

[H.22] MAGNEE, F., ENDRIZZI, A., and DAY, J. D., "A Survey of Terminal Protocols." Computer Networks, Vol. 3, No. 5, Nov. 1979, pp. 299—314.

[H.23] RAYNER, D., and JONES, A. W., "UK Network Independent File Transfer Protocol." In: Schindler, S., and Schröder, C. W. (Eds.), Kommunikation in verteilten Systemen. Springer Verlag, Heidelberg, 1979, pp. 110—120.

[H.24] KERUTT, H., and SPETH, R., "Job Transfer in Open Systems." In: Schindler, S., and Schröder, C. W. (Eds.), Kommunikation in verteilten Systemen. Springer Verlag, Heidelberg, 1979, pp. 136—160.

[H.25] WATSON, R. W., and FLETCHER, J. G., "An Architecture for Support of Network Operating System Services." Computer Networks, Vol. 4, No. 1, Febr. 1980, pp. 33—49.

[H.26] KUO, F. F., "Message Services in Computer Networks." In: Beauchamp, K. G. (Ed.), Interlinking of Computer Networks. D. Reidel Publishing Comp., Dordrecht, 1979, pp. 387—395.

[H.27] LININGTON, P. P., and HATHWAY, V., "The Addressing Requirements of a Transport-Service." In: Schindler, S., and Schröder, C. W. (Eds.), Kommunikation in verteilten Systemen. Springer Verlag, Heidelberg, 1979, pp. 35—50.

[H.28] BULLIS, K., and FRANTA, W., "Implementation of Eventcounts in a Broadcast Network." Computer Networks, Vol. 4, No. 2, April 1980, pp. 57—69.

[H.29] BÖHME, K., and PETER, G., "Process Communication Structures for Distributed Systems." In: Schindler, S., and Schröder, C. W. (Eds.), Kommunikation in verteilten Systemen. Springer Verlag, Heidelberg, 1979, pp. 296—316.

[H.30] EASTON, M. C., "Batch Throughput Efficiency of ADCCP/HDLC/SDLC Selective Reject Protocols." IEEE Trans., COM-28, No. 2, Febr. 1980, pp. 187—195.

[H.31] AROZULLAH, M., CRIST, S. C., and BURNELL, J. F., "A Microprocessor Based High Speed Space-Borne Packet Switch." IEEE Trans., COM-28, No. 1, Jan. 1980, pp. 7—21.

[H.32] ROSEN, E. C., "The Updating Protocol of ARPANET's New Routing Algorithm." Computer Networks, Vol. 4, No. 1, Febr. 1980, pp. 11—19.

[H.33] KAMOUN, F., and KLEINROCK, L., "Stochastic Performance Evaluation of Hierarchical Routing for Large Networks." Computer Networks, Vol. 3, No. 5, Nov. 1979, pp. 337—353.

[H.34] MERLIN, P. M., and SEGALL, A., "A Failsafe Distributed Routing Protocol." IEEE Trans., COM-27, No. 9, Sept. 1979, pp. 1280—1287.

[H.35] DAVIES, D. W., "Congestion Control in Hierarchical Networks." In: Beauchamp, K. G. (Ed.), Interlinking of Computer Networks. D. Reidel Publishing Comp., Dordrecht, 1979, pp. 397—410.

[H.36] MERLIN, P. M., and SCHWEITZER, P. J., "Deadlock Avoidance in Store-and-Forward Networks — I: Store-and-Forward Deadlock." — II: Other Deadlock Types." IEEE Trans., COM-28, No. 3, March 1980, pp. 345—354, and pp. 355—360.

[H.37] GERLA, M., and KLEINROCK, L., "Flow Control: A Comparative Study." IEEE Trans., COM-28, No. 4, April 1980, pp. 553—574.

[H.38] RAUBOLD, E., "A Model for Inter-process Communication." In: Beauchamp, K. G. (Ed.), Interlinking of Computer Networks. D. Reidel Publishing Comp., Dordrecht, 1979, pp. 185—200.

[H.39] MERLIN, P. M., "Specification and Validation of Protocols." IEEE Trans., COM-27, No. 11, Nov. 1979, pp. 1671—1680.

[H.40] BOCHMANN, G. V., and SUNSHINE, C., "Formal Methods in Communication Protocol Design." IEEE Trans., COM-28, No. 4, April 1980, pp. 624—631.

[H.41] SCHULTZ, G. D., et al., "Executable Description and Validation of SNA." IEEE Trans., COM-28, No. 4, April 1980, pp. 661—677.

[H.42] MAO, T. W., and YEH, R. T., "Communication Port: A Language Concept for Concurrent Programming." IEEE Trans., Vol. SE-6, No. 2, March 1980, pp. 194—204.

[H.43] KEMEN, H., "Zur Programmierung verteilter Systeme." In: Schindler, S., and Schröder, C. W. (Eds.), Kommunikation in verteilten Systemen. Springer Verlag, Heidelberg, 1979, pp. 317—338.

References

[1] ABRAMSON, N., "The ALOHA System — Another Alternative for Computer Communications." Proc. AFIPS FJCC, Vol. 37, 1970, pp. 281—285.

[2] ABRAMSON, N., "The ALOHA System." In: Abramson, N., and Kuo, F. (Eds.), Computer Communication Networks. Prentice-Hall, Englewood Cliffs, 1973, pp. 501—517.

[3] ABRAMSON, N., "The Throughput of Packet Broadcasting Channels." IEEE Trans., COM-25, No. 1, Jan. 1977, pp. 117—128.

[4] AKKOYUNLU, E., BERNSTEIN, A., and SCHANTZ, R., "Interprocess Communication Facilities for Network Operating Systems." Computer, Vol. 7, No. 6, June 1974, pp. 46—55.

[5] ANDRYUSHKOV, Yu. T., and PRANEVICHYUS, G. I., "E-Nets As a Tool for Formal Description of Computer Systems." (In Russian.) Proc. Natl. Conf. Packet Switching Computer Networks. Zinatne, Riga, 1979, pp. 170—175.

[6] A Network Independent Transport Service. Study Group 3, The Post Office, User Forum, Feb. 1980.

[7] ARAZI, S., "Improving the Throughput of an ARQ Stop-And-Wait Scheme for Burst Channels." IEEE Trans., COM-24. No. 6, June 1976, pp. 661—663.

[8] ARPANET Protocol Handbook. Network Information Centre, SRI International, Menlo Park, 1978.

[9] BARBER, D. L. A., "IFIP WG6.1 — International Network Working Group." Proc. Int. Symp. Computer Networks and Teleprocessing, NJSZT, Budapest, Oct. 1977, pp. 255—262.

[10] BARCHANSKI, J. A., "The Approach to Computer Network Protocols Design." (In Polish.) In: Bazewicz, M. (Ed.), Properties and Functions of Computer Networks. Politechnika Wroclawska, Wrocław, 1979, pp. 202—226.

[11] BARCHANSKI, J. A., "Evaluation of Some Acknowledgment Strategies for Packet-Switched Computer Networks." Proc. 4th Int. Conf. Remote Data Transmission, Vol. 1, DT ČSVTS, Karlovy Vary, Sept. 1979, pp. 22—35.

[12] BARTA, J., and POŘÍZEK, R., "Computer Networks." (In Slovak.) Proc. SOFSEM '77, VVS, Bratislava, Nov. 1977, pp. 199—254.

[13] BARLETT, K. A., SCANTLEBURY, R. A., and WILKINSON, P. T., "A Note on Reliable Full-Duplex Transmission over Half-Duplex Links." Comm. ACM, Vol. 12, No. 5, May 1969, pp. 260—261.

[14] BAZEWICZ, M., "Modelling of Computer Networks Protocols." (In Polish.) In: Bazewicz, M. (Ed.), Properties and Functions of Computer Networks. Politechnika Wroclawska, Wrocław, 1979, pp. 166—201.

[15] BAZILEVICH, E. V., and PRAMNEK, G. F., Computer Based Message Switching Systems. (In Russian.) Svyaz, Moscow, 1971.

[16] BELL, D. E., and BUTRIMENKO, A., "An Adaptive Routing Technique for Channel Switching Networks." Proc. IIASA Conf. Computer Communication Networks, Laxenburg, Oct. 1974, pp. 185—188.

[17] BENICE, R. J., and FREY, A. H., "An Analysis of Retransmission Systems." IEEE Trans., COM-12, No. 12, Dec. 1964, pp. 135—145.

[18] BENICE, R. J., and FREY, A. H., "Comparison of Error Control Techniques." IEEE Trans., COM-12, No. 12, Dec. 1964, pp. 146—154.

[19] BINDER, R., "A Dynamic Packet-Switching System for Satellite Broadcast Channels." Int. Conf. Communications Rec., IEEE, New York, 1975, pp. 41/1—41/5.

[20] BINDER, R., et al., "ALOHA Packet Broadcasting — A Retrospect." Proc. AFIPS, Vol. 44, May 1975, pp. 203—215.

[21] BJØRNER, D., "Finite State Automaton — Definition of Data Communication Line Control Procedures." Proc. AFIPS FJCC, Vol. 37, 1970, pp. 477—491.

[22] BOCHMAN, G. V., "Logical Verification and Implementation of Protocols." Proc. 4th Data Comm. Symp., Quebec City, Oct. 1975, pp. 7/15—7/20.

[23] BOCHMAN, G. V., "Standards Issues in Data Communication." Telecommunication Policy, Vol. 1, No. 5, Dec. 1977, pp. 381—388.

[24] BOCHMAN, G. V., "Finite State Description of Communication Protocols." Proc. Comp. Network Protocols Symp., Liège, Feb. 1978, pp. F3/1—F3/11.

[25] BOCHMAN, G. V., and GECSEI, J., "A Unified Method for the Specification and Verification of Protocols." Proc. IFIP Congress 77, North-Holland, Amsterdam, 1977, pp. 229—234.

[26] BODI, Z., et al., "Synchronization Problems in Teleprocessing Systems." (In Russian.) Proc. 3rd Teleprocessing Symp. RYAD, Varna, May 1976, pp. 4.5/1—4.5/17.

[27] BONN, T. H., "Standards for Computer Networks." In: Computer Networks. INFOTECH, Maidenhead, 1971, pp. 463—475.

[28] BRAND, J., and JOYNER, W. H. Jr., "Verification of Protocols Using Symbolic Execution." Proc. Comp. Network Protocols Symp., Liège, Feb. 1978, pp. F2/1—F2/7.

[29] BRANDT, G. J., and CHRETIEN, G. J., "Methods to Control and Operate a Message Switching Network." Proc. Symp. Computer-Communication Networks and Teletraffic, Brooklyn, April 1972. Polytechnic Press, pp. 263—276.

[30] BRAYER, K., "Error Control Techniques Using Binary Symbol Burst Codes." IEEE Trans., COM-16, No. 4, April 1968, pp. 199—214.

[31] BRAYER, K., "A Comparative Study of Adaptive and Nonadaptive Coding on Real Channels." IEEE Trans., IT-16, No. 1, Jan. 1970, p. 109.

[32] BURTON, H. O., and SULLIVAN, D. D., "Errors and Error Control." Proc. IEEE, Vol. 60, No. 11, Nov. 1972, pp. 1293—1301.

[33] CARR, C. S., CROCKER, S. D., and CERF, V. G., "HOST-HOST Communication Protocol in the ARPA Network." Proc. AFIPS SJCC, Vol. 37, 1970, pp. 589—597.

[34] CCITT Orange Book, Vol. VIII.1, Data Transmission over the Telephone Network, Vol. VIII.2, Public Data Networks. ITU, Geneva, 1977.

[35] CERF, V. G., and KAHN, R. E., "A Protocol for Packet Network Interconnection." IEEE Trans., COM-22, No. 5, May 1974, pp. 637—648.

[36] CERF, V. G., and KIRSTEIN, P. T., "Issues in Packet-Network Interconnection." Proc. IEEE, Vol. 66, No. 11, Nov. 1978, pp. 1386—1408.

[37] CERF, V. G., McKENZIE, A., SCANTLEBURY, R., and ZIMMERMANN, H., "Proposal for an Internetwork End-to-End Transport Protocol." Proc. Comp. Network Protocols Symp., Liège, Feb. 1978, pp. H5—H25.

[38] CHANG, S. S. L., "Theory of Information Feedback Systems." IRE Trans., IT-2, No. 3, Sept. 1956, pp. 29—40.

[39] CHERKASOV, Yu. N., BREYEV, V. P., and RYAZANTSEV, O. V., "Principles of Data Exchanges in a State Computing Centres Network." (In Russian.) Proc. Int. Symp. Computer Networks and Teleprocessing, NJSZT, Budapest, Oct. 1977, pp. 631—646.

[40] CHOU, W., and FRANK, H., "Routing Strategies for Computer Network Design." Proc. Symp. Computer-Communication Networks and Teletraffic, Brooklyn, April 1972. Polytechnic Press, pp. 301—309.

[41] CHOU, W., and GERLA, M., "A Unified Flow and Congestion Control Model for Packet Networks." Proc. 3rd ICCC, Toronto, August 1976, pp. 475—482.

[42] CHU, W. W., "A Study of Asynchronous Time Division Multiplexing for Time-Sharing Computer Systems." Proc. AFIPS SJCC, Vol. 35, 1969, pp. 669—678.

[43] CHU, W. W., and SHEN, M. Y., "A Hierarchical Routing and Flow Control Policy (HRFC) for Packet Switched Networks." In: Chandy, K. M., and Reiser, M. (Eds.), Computer Performance. North-Holand, Amsterdam, 1977, pp. 485—498.

[44] Classes of HDLC Procedures. ISO/TC 97/SC 6, No. 1337, Nov. 1976.

[45] COCHI, B., "Evaluation de réseaux à commutation de pacquets." J. de travail modélisation et simulation de réseaux d'ordinateurs. Le Chesnay, IRIA, Feb. 1976, pp. 55—72.

[46] COOPER, C. A., "Synchronization for Telecommunications in a Switched Digital Network." IEEE Trans., COM-27, No. 7, July 1979, pp. 1028—1033.

[47] COTTON, I. W., and FOLTS, H. C., "International Standards for Data Communications: A Status Report." Proc. 5th ACM-IEEE Data Communication Symp., Snowbird, Sept. 1977, pp. 4/26—4/36.

[48] CROCKER, S. D., HEAFNER, J. F., METCALFE, R. M., and POSTEL, J. B., "Function -Oriented Protocols for the ARPA Computer Network." Proc. AFIPS SJCC, Vol. 40, 1972, pp. 274—279.

[49] CROWTHER, W. R., et al., "A System for Broadcast Communication Reservation ALOHA." Proc. 6th Hawaii Int. Syst. Sci. Conf., Honolulu, Jan. 1973, pp. 371—374.

[50] CYPSER, R. J., Communications Architecture for Distributed Systems. Addison-Wesley, Reading, 1978.

[51] DADDA, L., and LeMOLI, G., "An Introduction to Computer Networks." Alta frequenza, Vol. 43, No. 3, March 1974, pp. 143—151.

[52] DALOS, G., "A Modified Carrier Sense Multiple-Access Procedure for Interactive Radio Terminals: Analysis and Computer Simulation." Proc. 6th Colloq. Microwave Communication, Budapest, Sept. 1978, pp. I/3/17.1—I/3/17.4.

[53] DANTHINE, A., "Petri Nets for Protocol Modelling and Verification." Proc. Int. Symp. Computer Networks and Teleprocessing, NJSZT, Budapest, Oct. 1977, pp. 663—685.

[54] DANTHINE, A., and BREMER, J., "Communication Protocols in a Network Context." Proc. ACM SIGCOMM-SIGOPS Interface Workshop Interprocess Communications, Santa Monica, March 1975, pp. 87—92.

[55] DANTHINE, A., and BREMER, J., "An Axiomatic Description of the Transport Protocol of CYCLADES." In: Haupt, D., and Petersen, H. (Eds.), Rechnernetze und Datenverarbeitung. Springer, Berlin, 1976, pp. 259—273.

[56] DANTHINE, A., and BREMER, J., "Modelling and Verification of End-to-End Transport Protocols." Proc. Comp. Network Protocols Symp., Liège, Feb. 1978, pp. F6/1—10.

[57] DANTHINE, A., and BREMER, J., "Specification and Verification of End-to-End Protocols." Proc. 4th ICCC, Kyoto, Sept. 1978, pp. 811—816.

[58] DANTHINE, A., and ESCHENAUER, E., "Influence on the Node Behaviour of the Node-to-Node Protocol." IEEE Trans., COM-24, No. 6, June 1976, pp. 606—614.

[59] Data Communication — High Level Data Link Control Procedures. Frame Structure, ISO 3309, 2nd edition, July 1979; Elements of Procedures (Independent Numbering), ISO 4335, 1st edition, April 1979 + Addendum 1, Dec. 1979.

[60] Data communication Standards. Folts, H. C., and Karp, H. R. (Eds.). McGraw-Hill, New York, 1979.

[61] DAVEY, J. R., "Modems." Proc. IEEE, Vol. 60, No. 11, Nov. 1972, pp. 1284—1292.

[62] DAVIDA, G. I., and REDDY, S. M., "Forward Error Correction with Decision Feedback." Inform. and Control, Vol. 21, No. 2, 1972, pp. 117—133.

[63] DAVIES, D. W., "The Control of Congestion in Packet-Switching Networks." IEEE Trans., COM-20, No. 3, June 1972, pp. 546—550.

[64] DAVIES, D. W., "Flow Control and Congestion Control." Proc. Int. Symp. Computer Networks and Teleprocessing, NJSZT, Budapest, Oct. 1977, pp. 17—36.

[65] DAVIES, D. W., and BARBER, D. L. A., Communication Networks for Computers. J. Wiley, London, 1973.

[66] DAVIES, D. W., BARBER, D. L. A., PRICE, W. L., and SOLOMONIDES, C. M., Computer Networks and Their Protocols. J. Wiley, Chichester, 1979.

[67] DAVIES, D. W., BARTLETT, K. A., SCANTLEBURY, R. A., and WILKINSON, P. T., "A Digital Communications Network for Computers Giving Rapid Response at Remote Terminals." Proc. ACM Symp. Operating Syst. Principles, Gatlinburg, Oct. 1967.

[68] DAY, J. D., "A Bibliography on the Formal Specification and Verification of Computer Network Protocols." Proc. Comp. Network Protocols Symp., Liège, Feb. 1978, pp. H/1—H/3.

[69] DEATON, G. A., "Flow Control in Packet-Switched Networks with Explicit Path Routing." Proc. Int. Symp. Flow Control in Comp. Networks, Versailles, Feb. 1979 (North-Holland, Amsterdam, 1979).

[70] DECNET — Digital's Network Facilities: Technical Summary. DEC, 1975.

[71] Determination of Performance on an Information Path within a Data Communication System. British Standard BS 5203, BSI, 1976.

[72] Determination of the Performance of Data Communication Systems. American Standard X3. 44, ANSI, 1974.

[73] DIJKSTRA, E. W., "Cooperating Sequential Processes." In: Genuys, F. (Ed.), Programming Languages. Academic Press, New York, 1968.

[74] DOLL, D. R., "Multiplexing and Concentration." Proc. IEEE, Vol. 60, No. 11, Nov. 1972, pp. 1313—1321.

[75] DONNAN, R. A., and KERSEY, J. R., "Synchronous Data Link Control: A Perspective." IBM Syst. J., Vol. 13, No. 2, May 1974, pp. 140—162.

[76] DROZHZHINOV, V. I., and MIAMLIN, A. N., "System Model of a Computer Network." (In Russian.) Upravlyayushchiye systemy i mashiny, No. 5, 1976, pp. 3—9.

[77] DROZHZHINOV, V. I., MIAMLIN, A. N., STARKMAN, V. S., and USOV, S. A., "Project of Fundamental Protocols of the Mail Service of a Computer Network with Packet Switching." (In Russian.) Inst. of Applied Mathematics USSR Academy of Sciences, Rpt. No. 44, May 1977.

[78] ELIE, M., "Décomposition et représentation de la fonction de transport de l'information dans un réseau." Proc. Colloq. ACM-IRIA Réseaux d'ordinateurs, Le Chesnay, March 1972, pp. 63—78.

[79] ELIE, M., and ZIMMERMANN, H., "Towards a Systematic Approach to Protocol of a Computer Network — Application to the CYCLADES Network." Proc. AFCET Congress, Rennes, Nov. 1973.

[80] ENGLISH, L., "Transmission Standards." Data Processing, Vol. 14, No. 1, 1972.

[81] FARMER, W. W., and NEWHALL, E. E., "An Experimental Distributed Switching System to Handle Bursty Computer Traffic." Proc. ACM Symp. Problems in the Optimization of Data Communication Systems, Pine Mountains, Oct. 1969, pp. 1—33.

[82] FITZSIMONS, T. F., "ASCII Extension and Expansion and Their Impact on Data Communication." Proc. 2nd ACM-IEEE Symp. Problems in the Optimization of Data Communication Systems, Palo Alto, Oct. 1971, pp. 73—79.

[83] FLETCHER, J. G., and WATSON, R. W., "Mechanisms for Reliable Timer-Based Protocol." Proc. Comp. Network Protocols, Liège, Feb. 1978, pp. C5/1—C5/17.

[84] FOLTS, H. C., "Evolution Toward a Universal Interface for Data Communictions." Proc. 4th ICCC, Kyoto, Sept. 1978, pp. 675—680.

[85] FRANK, H., "Computer Networks." Networks, Vol. 5, No. 1, 1975, pp. 69—73.

[86] FRATTA, L., "Basic Analytical Techniques and Routing Procedures." In: Grimsdale, R. L., and Kuo, F. F. (Eds.), Computer Communication Networks. Noordhoff, Leyden, 1975, pp. 35—62.

[87] FUJIWARA, C., et al., "Evaluation of Error Control Techniques in Both Independent-Error and Dependent-Error Channels." IEEE Trans., COM-26, No. 6, June 1978, pp. 785—794.

[88] GERLA, M., "Deterministic and Adaptive Routing Policies in Packet-Switched Computer Networks." In: Blanc, R. P., and Cotton, I. W. (Eds.), Computer Networking. IEEE, New York, 1976, pp. 111—116.

[89] GLIKBARG, W. S., and GOLDE, H., "Anatomy of Computer Networks." Proc. 7th Hawaii Int. Syst. Sci. Conf.: Computer Nets, Honolulu, 1974, pp. 1—5.

[90] GLUSHKOV, V. M., et al., "Functional Structure and Elements of Computer Networks." (In Russian.) Upravlyayushchiye systemy i mashiny, No. 3, May—June 1975, pp. 1—10.

[91] GLUSHKOV, V. M., KALINICHENKO, L. A., LAZAREV, V. G., and SIFOROV, V. I., Computer Networks. (In Russian.) Svyaz, Moscow, 1977.

[92] GOOD, D. I., "Constructing Verified and Reliable Communications Processing Systems." ACM SIGSOFT Soft. Engng. Notes No. 2, Vol. 5, Oct. 1977, pp. 8—13.

[93] GORN, S., et al., "Performance of Systems Used for Data Transmission — Transfer Rate of Information Bits — An ASA Tutorial." Comm. ACM, Vol. 8, No. 5, 1965, pp. 280—286.

[94] GRANGE, J. L., and MUSSARD, P., "Performance Measurements of Line Control Protocols in the CIGALE Network." Proc. Comp. Network Protocols Symp., Liège, Feb. 1978, pp. G2/1—G2/13.

[95] GRAY, J. P., "Line Control Procedures." Proc. IEEE, Vol. 60, No. 11, Nov. 1972, pp. 1301—1312.

[96] GREEN, P. E., "An Introduction to Network Architecture and Protocols." IBM Syst. J., Vol. 18, No. 2, 1979, pp. 202—222.

[97] GROSSMAN, G. R., et al., "Issues in International Public Data Networking." Computer Networks, Vol. 3, No. 4, Sept. 1979, pp. 259—266.

[98] GRUBB, D. S., and COTTON, I. W., "Criteria for Evaluation of Data Communication Services." Computer Networks, Vol. 1, No. 6, 1977, pp. 325—340.

[99] HAENLE, J. O., and GIESSLER, A., "Simulation of Data Transport Systems of Packet-Switched Networks." In: Schoemaker, S. (Ed.), Computer Networks and Simulation. North-Holland, Amsterdam, 1978, pp. 101—117.

[100] HAJEK, J., "Automatically Verified Data Transfer Protocols." Proc. 4th ICCC, Kyoto, Sept. 1978, pp. 749—756.

[101] HALSEY, J. R., "Public Data Networks: Their Evolution, Interfaces, and Status." IBM Syst. J., Vol. 18, No. 2, 1979, pp. 223—243.

[102] HANSEN, B., Operating System Principles. Prentice-Hall, Englewood Cliffs, 1973.

[103] HANSEN, B., "The Programming Language Concurrent Pascal." IEEE Trans., SE-1, No. 2, June 1975, pp. 199—207.

[104] HARANGOZÓ, J., "Formal Approaches for Designing Protocols." Proc. Int. Symp. Computer Networks and Teleprocessing, NJSZT, Budapest, Oct. 1977, pp. 195—212.

[105] HARANGOZÓ, J., "Protocol Definition with Formal Grammars." Proc. Comp. Network Protocols Symp., Liège, Feb. 1978, pp. F6/1—F7/9.

[106] HARRINGTON, E. A., "Synchronization Techniques for Various Switching Network Topologies." IEEE Trans., COM-26, No. 6, June 1978, pp. 925—932.

[107] HAYES, J. F., "An Adaptive Technique for Local Distribution." IEEE Trans., COM-26, No. 8, Aug. 1978, pp. 1178—1186.

[108] HEARD, K. S., and WINSBORROW, R. P. J., "Functional Requirements and Capabilities of a Portable Network Transport Station." Proc. EUROCOMP, London, May 1978, pp. 215—227.

[109] HERMANN, J., "Flow Control in the ARPA Network." Computer Networks, Vol. 1, No. 1, June 1976, pp. 65—76.

[110] HOPCROFT, J. E., and ULLMANN, J. D., Formal Languages and Their Relation to Automata. Addison-Wesley, Reading, 1969.

[111] HUGHES, P., and MANN, D., "Private Computer Networks." Proc. IIASA Conf. Computer Communication Networks, Laxenburg, Oct. 1974, pp. 149—159.

[112] HUMMEL, H., "Role and Functioning of the CCITT." Computer Networks, Vol. 2, No. 3, July 1977, pp. 123—124.

[113] HUMMEL, A., "State of CCITT Standardization on Public Data Networks." Telecommunication J., Vol. 46, No. 1, Jan. 1979, pp. 33—39.

[114] IIMURA, J., et al., "Studies on Present and Future Public Data Network Service in Japan." Proc. IFIP Int. Conf. Teleinformatics. North-Holland, Amsterdam, 1979, pp. 293—300.

[115] INOSE, H., and SAITO, T., "Theoretical Aspects in the Analysis and Synthesis of Packet Communication Networks." Proc. IEEE, Vol. 66, No. 11, Nov. 1978, pp. 1409—1422.

[116] IRLAND, M. I., "Simulation of CIGALE 1974." Proc. 4th Data Comm. Symp., Quebec City, Oct. 1975, pp. 5/13—5/19.

[117] IRLAND, M. I., "Analysis and Simulation of Congestion in Packet-Switched Networks." Univ. of Waterloo, Comp. Comm. Network Group, Rpt. E-61, april 1977.

[118] JACQUEMART, Y. A., "Network Interprocess Communication in an X25 Environment." Proc. Comp. Network Protocols Symp., Liège, Feb. 1978, pp. C1/1—C1/6.

[119] JOHNSON, T., Packet Switching Services and the Data Communication User. OVUM, London, 1977.

[120] KAHN, R. E., and CROWTHER, W. R., "Flow Control in a Resource-Sharing Computer Network." IEEE Trans., COM-20, No. 3, March 1972, pp. 539—546.

[121] KANAL, L. N., and SASTRY, A. R. K., "Models for Channels with Memory and Their Applications to Error Control." Proc. IEEE, Vol. 66, No. 7, July 1978, pp. 724—744.

[122] KANYEVSKIY, Z. M., et al., Information Transmission with Feedback. (In Russian.) Svyaz, Moscow, 1976.

[123] KATZ, S., and KONHEIM, A. G., "Priority Disciplines in a Loop Systems." J. ACM, Vol. 21, No. 2, April 1974, pp. 340—349.

[124] KELLY, P. T. F., "Public Switches Data Networks, International Plans and Standards." Proc. IEEE, Vol. 66, No. 11, Nov. 1978, pp. 1539—1549.

[125] KERMANI, P., and KLEIROCK, L., "Virtual Cut-Through: A New Computer Communication Switching Technique." Computer Networks, Vol. 3, No. 4, Sept. 1979, pp. 267—286.

[126] KLEINROCK, L., Queueing Systems. Vol. 2, Computer Appications. J. Wiley, New York, 1976.

[127] KLEINROCK, L., "Principles and Lessons in Packet Communications." Proc. IEEE, Vol. 66, No. 11, Nov. 1978, pp. 1320—1329.

[128] KLEINROCK, L., and GERLA, M., "On the Measured Performance of Packet Satellite Access Schemes." Proc. 4th ICCC, Kyoto, Sept. 1978, pp. 535—542.

[129] KLEINROCK, L., and NAYLOR, W. E., "On Measured Behaviour of the ARPA Networks." Proc. AFIPS, Vol. 43, May 1974, pp. 767—780.

[130] KLEINROCK, L., NAYLOR, W. E., and OPDERBECK, H., "A Study of Line Overhead in the ARPANET." Comm. ACM, Vol. 19, No. 1, Jan. 1976, pp. 3—13.

[131] KLEINROCK, L., and SCHOLL, M., "Packet Switching in Radio Channels: New Conflict-Free Multiple Access Schemes for a Small Number of Data Users." Proc. Int. Conf. Comm.: Communication Technology Better Tomorrow, Vol. 2. New York, 1977, pp. 105—111.

[132] KLEINROCK, L., and TOBAGI, F., "Packet Switching in Radio Channels: Part I — Carrier Sense Multiple-Access Modes and Their Throughput-Delay Characteristics." IEEE Trans., COM-23, No. 12, Dec. 1975, pp. 1400—1416.

[133] KNIGHT, J. R., "A Case Study: Airlines Reservation Systems." Proc. IEEE, Vol. 60, No. 11, Nov. 1972, pp. 1423—1431.

[134] KOBAYASHI, H., and KONHEIM, A. C., "Queueing Models for Computer Communications System Analysis." IEEE Trans., COM-25, No. 1, Jan. 1977, pp. 2—29.

[135] KOSOVYCH, O. S., "Fixed Assignment Access Technique." IEEE Trans., COM-26, No. 9, Sept. 1978, pp. 1370—1376.

[136] LABETTOULLE, J., PUJOLLE, G., and MIKOU, N., "A Study of Flows in an X25 Environment." Proc. Int. Symp. Flow Control in Comp. Networks, Versailles, Feb. 1979 (North-Holland, Amsterdam, 1979), pp. 77—87.

[137] LAM, S. S., "Satellite Packet Communications — Multiple Access Protocols and Performance." IEEE Trans., COM-27, No. 10, Oct. 1979, pp. 1456—1466.

[138] LAM, S. S., "Multiple Access Protocols." In: Chou, W. (Ed.), Computer Communication: State of the and Direction for the Future. Prentice-Hall, Englewood Cliffs, to be published.

[139] LAMPORT, L., "Time, Clocks, and the Ordering of Events in a Distributed Systems." Comm. ACM, Vol. 21, No. 7, July 1978, pp. 558—565.

[140] LANN, S. S., and REISER, M., "Congestion Control of Store-and-Forward Networks by Input Buffer Limits — An Analysis." IEEE Trans., COM-27, No. 1, Jan. 1979, pp. 127—134.

[141] LeLANN, G., and LeGOFF, H., "Verification and Evaluation of Communication Protocols." IRISA, Univ. de Rennes, Feb. 1977.

[142] LeMOLI, G., "A Theory of Colloquies." Proc. 1st European Workshop Computer Networks, Arles, April—May 1973, pp. 153—173.

[143] LeMOLI, G., "Colloquies in Computer Networks." In: Grimsdale, R. L., and Kuo, F. (Eds.), Computer Communication Networks. Noordhoff, Leyden, 1975, pp. 195—230.

[144] LeMOLI, G., "On Networking." In: Schoemaker, S. (Ed.), Computer Networks and Simulation. North-Holland, Amsterdam, 1978, pp. 9—37.

[145] List of Approved National and International Standards, Recommendations, Rules and Regulations Related to Communications. IEEE Trans., COM-22, No. 10, Oct. 1974, pp. 1735—1750.

[146] LYNCH, W. G., "Reliable Full-Duplex File Transmission over Half-Duplex Telephone Lines." Comm. ACM, Vol. 11, No. 6, June 1968, pp. 407—410.

[147] MacDONALD, V. C., "Implementation Issues in Teleinformatics Standardization." Proc.

IFIP Int. Conf. Teleinformatics. North-Holland, Amsterdam, 1979, pp. 287—292.

[148] MARK, J. W., "Global Scheduling Approach to Conflict-Free Multiaccess via a Data Bus." IEEE Trans., COM-26, No. 9, Sept. 1978, pp. 1342—1352.

[149] MARTIN, J., Teleprocessing Network Organization. Prentice-Hall, Englewood Cliffs, 1970.

[150] MASUNAGA, Y., "A Probabilistic Automaton Model of the NMR, HDX HDLC Procedure." Computer Networks, Vol. 2, No. 6, Dec. 1978, pp. 442—453.

[151] McFADYEN, J. H., "SNA: An Overview." IBM Syst. J., Vol. 15, No. 1, 1976, pp. 4—23.

[152] McGOVERN, J. P., "DCA — A Distributed Communications Architecture." Proc. 4th ICCC, Kyoto, Sept. 1978, pp. 359—367.

[153] McQUILLAN, J. M., "Routing Algorithms for Computer Networks — A Survey." IEEE Natl. Telecomm. Conf. Rec., Vol. 2, New York, 1977, pp. 281/1—281/6.

[154] McQUILLAN, J. M., "Enhaced Message Capabilities for Computer Networks." Proc. IEEE, Vol. 66, No. 11, Nov. 1978, pp. 1517—1527.

[155] McQUILLAN, J. M., "Interactions Between Routing and Congestion Control in Computer Networks." Proc. Int. Symp. Flow Control in Computer Networks, Versailles, Feb. 1979 (North-Holland, Amsterdam, 1979), pp. 63—75.

[156] McQUILLAN, J. M., FALK, G., and RICHER, I., "A Review of the Development and Performance of the ARPANET Routing Algorithm." IEEE Trans., COM-26, No. 12, Dec. 1978, pp. 1802—1810.

[157] McQUILLAN, J. M., and WALDEN, D. C., "The ARPA Network Design Decisions." Computer Networks. Vol. 1, No. 5, Aug. 1977, pp. 243—289.

[158] MEIER, H. W., et al., "The System Concept of the Computer Network DELTA." Proc. 4th ICCC, Kyoto, Sept. 1978, pp. 703—708.

[159] MERLIN, P. M., "A Methodology for the Design and Implementation of Communication Protocols." IEEE Trans., COM-24, No. 5, May 1976, pp. 614—621.

[160] MERLIN, P. M., and FARBER, D. J., "Recoverability of Communication Protocols. Implications of a Theoretical Study." IEEE Trans., COM-24, No. 9, Sept. 1976, pp. 1036—1043.

[161] MESAROVIC, M. D., MACKO, D., and TAKAHARA, Y., Theory of Hierarchical, Multilevel, Systems. Academic Press, New York, 1970.

[162] MESAROVIC, M. D., and TAKAHARA, Y., General System Theory: Mathematical Foundations. Academic Press, New York, 1975.

[163] METZNER, J. J., "Improvements in Block-Retransmission Schemes." IEEE Trans., COM-27, No. 2, Feb. 1979, pp. 524—532.

[164] MEZZALIRA, L., and SCHREIBER, F. A., "Designing Colloquies." Proc. 1st European Workshop Computer Networks, Arles, April—May 1973, pp. 351—363.

[165] MIZIN, I. A., URINSON, I. S., and KHRAMESHIN, G. K., Information Exchange in Computer Networks. (In Russian.) Svyaz, Moscow, 1972.

[166] MORI, H., and NORIGOE, M., "Binary-Search Polling — Another Technique of Multiple Access Control." Proc. Int. Switching Symp., Vol. 1, Kyoto, Oct. 1976, pp. 143/2/1—143/2/8.

[167] MORRIS, J. M., "On Another Go-Back-N ARQ Technique for High Error Rate Conditions." IEEE Trans., COM-26, No. 1, Jan. 1978, pp. 187—189.

[168] NEUMANN, A. J., et. al., "A Technical Guide to Computer-Communication Interface Standards." NBS Techn. Note 843, New York, Aug. 1974.

[169] NG, S. F., and MARK, J. W., "A Multiaccess Model for Packet Switching with Satellite Having Some Processing Capability." IEEE Trans., COM-25, No. 1, Jan. 1977, pp. 128—135.

[170] NOGUCHI, S., "Study on Computer Network by Public Telephone Lines." (In Japan.) Tohoku Univ. Rpt. No. 53, Sept. 1978.

[171] NOGUCHI, S., and SHIRATORI, N., "Fundamental Characteristics of Loop Computer Networks." Proc. Int. Switching Symp., Vol. 1, Kyoto, Oct. 1976, pp. 133/2/1—133/2/8.

[172] NUSPL, P. P., et al., "Synchronization Methods for TDMA." Proc. IEEE, Vol. 65, No. 3, March 1977, pp. 434—444.

[173] NUTT, G. J., "Evaluation Nets for Computer System Performance Analysis." Proc. AFIPS, Vol. 41, Pt. 1, 1972, pp. 279—286.

[174] OBYEDKOV, J. S., and SHCHERBO, V. K., "Standardization Problems and Tasks in Data Teleprocessing Networks." (In Russian.) Proc. 1st Conf. Teleprocessing Systems. Zinatne, Riga, 1977, pp. 70—74.

[175] OKABE, T., "Evolution of Standards through the ITU (CCITT Recommendations)." Proc. 4th ICCC, Kyoto, Sept. 1978, pp. 229—235.

[176] OLDER, W., "Qualitative Analysis of Congestion-Sensitive Routing." Proc. Int. Symp. Flow Control in Computer Networks, Versailles, Feb. 1979 (North-Holland, Amsterdam, 1979), pp. 131—154.

[177] OPDERBECK, H., and KLEINROCK, L., "The Influence of Control Procedures on the Performance of Packet-Switched Networks." IEEE Natl. Telecomm. Conf. Rec., San Diego, Dec. 1974, pp. 810—817.

[178] PARDO, R., LIU, M. T., and BABIC, G. A., "An N-Process Communication Protocol for Distributed Processing." Proc. Comp. Network Protocols Symp., Liège, Feb. 1978, pp. D7/1—D7/10.

[179] PAWLIKOWSKI, K., "Channel Occupation in a Computer Communication Systems with Access in the Way." Bull. de l'Académie Polon. des Sciences, Série des sciences techniques, XXVII, No. 3, 1979, pp. 33—41.

[180] PENNOTTI, M. C., and SCHWARTZ, M., "Congestion Control in Store and Forward Tandem Links." IEEE Trans., COM-23, No. 12, Dec. 1975, pp. 1434—1443.

[181] PETERSEN, J., "Remarks on the Implementation of the Packet Level Protocols on Public Packet Switching Networks." Proc. Comp. Network Protocols Symp., Liège, Feb. 1978, pp. A2/1—A2/7.

[182] PETERSON, W. W., "Cyclic Codes for Error Detection." Proc. IRE, Vol. 49, No. 1, Jan. 1961, pp. 228—235.

[183] PETERSON, W. W., and WELDON, E. J., Error-Correcting Codes. MIT Press, Cambridge, 1972.

[184] PETRENKO, A. F., "Formal Determination of Time-outs in Network Protocols." (In Russian.) Proc. Natl. Conf. Packet Switching Computer Networks. Zinatne, Riga, 1979, pp. 89—96.

[185] PETRENKO, A. F., "On Modelling of Network Protocols." (In Russian.) Proc. Natl. Conf. Packet Switching Computer Networks. Zinatne, Riga, 1979, pp. 83—89.

[186] PETRENKO, A. F., et al., "Data Link Control Protocol — Version 01". (In Russian.) Inst. Electronics and Computer Science, LatSSR Academy of Sciences, Riga, 1978.

[187] PETRI, C. A., "Kommunikation mit Automaten." Ph.D. dissertation, Univ. of Bonn, 1962.

[188] PHILPOT, G., "Communication Network Control." Proc. Conf. Communication Equipments and Systems, Venue, June 1976, pp. 297—300.

[189] PIERCE, J. G., COHEN, C. H., and KROPFL, W. J., "Network for Block Switching of Data." Proc. IEEE Conv. Rec., New York, March 1971, pp. 222—223.

[190] PLATET, F., "TRANSPAC — a Public Network Packet Data Transmission." Proc. Int. Symp. Computer Networks and Teleprocessing, NJSZT, Budapest, Oct. 1977.

[191] POŘÍZEK, R., "Evaluation of Network Architectures." (In Slovak.) Proc. Computer Networks Conf., Bratislava, June 1978, pp. 211—217.

[192] POŘÍZEK, R., "Protocols in Network Architectures." (In Polish.) In: Bazewicz, M. (Ed.), Properties and Functions of Computer Networks. Politechnika Wroclawska, Wrocław, 1979, pp. 21—47.

[193] POŘÍZEK, R., "Network Architectures." (In Slovak.) Proc. Conf. Integrated Information Systems, VVS, Bratislava, April 1979, pp. 117—124.

[194] POŘÍZEK, R., "Models of Communication Protocols." (In Slovak.) Proc. 4th Int. Conf. Remote Data Transmission, Vol. 2, DT ČSVTS, Karlovy Vary, Sept. 1979, pp. 171—174.

[195] POŘÍZEK, R., "Communication Protocols Structure." (In Slovak.) Proc. Sci. Conf. Technical Univ. of Brno, Brno, Sept. 1979, pp. 41—44.

[196] POŘÍZEK, R., and PUŽMAN, J., "Variables and Constraints in Data Communications System Design." Proc. IIASA Conf. Computer Communication Networks, Laxenburg, Oct. 1974, pp. 167—171.

[197] POŘÍZEK, R., and PUŽMAN, J., Data Transmission Control Procedures and Protocols. (In Slovak.) VVS-ALFA, Bratislava, 1976.

[198] POSTEL, J., "Official Initial Connecting Protocol." NIC No. 7108, ARPANET, June 1971.

[199] POSTEL, J., "A Graph Model Analysis of Computer Communication Protocols." Rpt. No. 7410, Univ. of California, Los Angeles, Jan. 1974.

[200] POSTEL, J., "An Informal Comparison of Three Protocols." Computer Networks, Vol. 3, No. 2, 1979, pp. 67—76.

[201] POSTEL, J., and FARBER, D. J., "Graph Modelling of Computer Communications Protocols." Proc. 5th Conf. Computing Systems, Austin, Oct. 1976, pp. 66—77.

[202] POUZIN, L., "Network Architectures and Components." Proc. 1st European Workshop Computer Networks, Arles, April—May 1973, pp. 227—265.

[203] POUZIN, L., "A Proposal for Interconnecting Packet Switching Networks." Proc. EUROCOMP, Brunel Univ., May 1974, pp. 1023—1036.

[204] POUZIN, L., "An Integrated Approach to Network Protocols." Proc. AFIPS, Vol. 44, May 1975, pp. 701—707.

[205] POUZIN, L., "Network Protocols." In: Grimsdale, R. L., and Kuo, F. F. (Eds.), Computer Communication Networks. Noordhoff, Leyden, 1975, pp. 231—255.

[206] POUZIN, L., "Standards in Data Communications and Computer Networks." Proc. 4th Data Comm. Symp., Quebec City, Oct. 1975, pp. 2/8—2/12.

[207] POUZIN, L., "Flow Control in Data Networks — Methods and Tools." Proc. 3rd ICCC, Toronto, Aug. 1976, pp. 467—474.

[208] POUZIN, L., "Packet Networks — Issues and Choices." Proc. IFIP Congress 77. North-Holland, Amsterdam, 1977, pp. 515—521.

[209] POUZIN, L., and ZIMMERMANN, H., "A Tutorial on Protocols." Proc. IEEE, Vol. 66, No. 11, Nov. 1978, pp. 1346—1370.

[210] PRICE, W. L., "A Study of Bifurcated Routing in a Data Network and the Effect of Isarithmic Control in This Context." NPL Rpt., COM-72, March 1974.

[211] PRICE, W. L., "Simulation Studies of an Isarithmically Controlled Store and Forward Data Communication Network." Proc. IFIP Congress 74. North-Holland, Amsterdam, pp. 151—154.

[212] PRICE, W. L., "Adaptive Routing in Store-and-Forward Networks and the Importance of Load Splitting." Proc. IFIP Congress 77, North-Holland, Amsterdam, 1977, pp. 309—313.

[213] PRICE, W. L., "Simulation of Routing Doctrines, Flow Control and Congestion Avoi-

dance." In: Schoemaker, G. (Ed.), Computer Networks and Simulation. North-Holland, Amsterdam, 1978, pp. 141—153.

[214] Proposed American National Standard. Determination of Performance of Data Communication Control Procedures. ANSI TG 5, Feb. 1977.

[215] Proposed Communication Heading Format Standard, 2nd Draft, ISO/TC 97/SC, No. 6, 1948, Sept. 1979.

[216] Provisional Recommendations X.3, X.25, X.28, and X.29 on Packet-Switched Data Transmission Services. ITU-CCITT, Geneva, 1978 (See also unauthorized documents from April 1979 and Feb. 1980).

[217] Provisional Recommendation X.75 on International Internetworking Between Packet Switched Data Networks. ITU-CCITT Circular No. 94, Geneva, 1978 (See also unauthorized documents from April 1979 and Feb. 1980).

[218] PUŽMAN, J., "Coding for Decision Feedback Transmission Systems." Trans. 6th Prague Conf. Information Theory, Statist. Decision Functions and Random Processes, Prague, Sept. 1971 (Academia, 1973), pp. 721—732.

[219] PUŽMAN, J., "Evaluation of Data Transmission Control Procedures and Protocols." (In Russian.) Proc. 3rd Teleprocessing Symp. RYAD, Varna, May 1976, pp. 1—3.

[220] PUŽMAN, J., "On Data Transmission Systems Performance Criteria." Proc. Czechoslovak Cybernetic Society Conf., Prague, Nov. 1976, pp. 295—306.

[221] PUŽMAN, J., "The Evaluation of Information Transmission Performance." Proc. 4th Int. Symp. Information Theory, Leningrad, June 1976, Pt. II, pp. 147—149.

[222] PUŽMAN, J., Data Transmission (In Czech.) SNTL, Prague, 1977.

[223] PUŽMAN, J., "Automatic Control of Data Networks." (In Czech.) Proc. Sci. Conf. Technical Univ. of Prague, ACTA POLYTECHNIKA, Prague, June 1977, Vol. 2, pp. 51—58.

[224] PUŽMAN, J., "The Telecommunication Network Constraints on Interactive Systems." Proc. Int. Seminar Experiences of Interactive System Use, Szklarska Poręba, Oct. 1977, pp. 189—197.

[225] PUŽMAN, J., "The Design of Data Transmission Systems in the Czechoslovak Conditions." Proc. Int. Symp. Computer Networks and Teleprocessing, NJSZT, Budapest, Oct. 1977, pp. 313—328.

[226] PUŽMAN, J., "The Design of Communication Control in Computer Networks." (In Czech.) Proc. Conf. Integrated Information Systems, VVS, Bratislava, April 1979, pp. 99—107.

[227] PUŽMAN, J., "Communication Functions and Their Implementation in Line Protocols." (In Polish.) In: Bazewicz, M. (Ed.), Properties and Functions of Computer Networks. Politechnika Wroclawska, Wrocław, 1979, pp. 48—85.

[228] PUŽMAN, J., "Data Transmission Standards — A Progress or a Brake?" (In Czech.) Proc. 4th Int. Conf. Remote Data Transmission. Vol. 1, DT ČSVTS, Karlovy Vary, Sept. 1979, pp. 78—82.

[229] PUŽMAN, J., BÄUML, K., and VODIČKA, F., Data Transmission over Telecommunication Network. (In Czech.) NADAS, Prague, 1968.

[230] PUŽMAN, J., and POŘÍZEK, R., "Communication Control in Computer Networks." Proc. 2nd IFAC/IFIP Symp. Software for Computer Control, Prague, June 1979 (Pergamon Press, Oxford, 1980), pp. IP/I/1—IP/I/9.

[231] Reference Model for Open Systems Architecture. Version 3. ISO/TC 97/SC 6, Nov. 1978.

[232] RICHARDSON, T. C., and YU, L. V., "The Effect of Protocol on the Response Time of Loop Structures for Data Communications." Computer Networks, Vol. 3, No. 1, Feb. 1979, pp. 57—66.

[233] ROBERTS, L. G., "Multiple Computer and Intercomputer Communications." Proc. ACM Symp. Operating Syst. Principles, Gatlinburg, Oct. 1967.

[234] ROBERTS, L. G., "Dynamic Allocation of Satellite Capacity Through Packet Reservation." Proc. AFIPS, Vol. 42, 1973, pp. 711—716.

[235] ROBERTS, L. G., "ALOHA Packet System with and without Slots and Captures." Comp. Comm. Rev., Vol. 5, No. 2, April 1975, pp. 28—42.

[236] ROCHER, E. Y., and PICKHOLTZ, R. L., "An Analysis of the Effectiveness of Hybrid Transmission Schemes." IBM J. Res. and Develop., Vol. 14, July 1970, pp. 426—433.

[237] ROSENBLUM, S. R., "Progress in Control Procedure Standardization." Proc. 2nd ACM-IEEE Symp. problems in the Optimization of Data Communication Systems, Palo Alto, Oct. 1971, pp. 153—159.

[238] RUBIN, I., "Message Delays in FDMA and TDMA Communication Channels." IEEE Trans., COM-27, No. 5, May 1979, pp. 769—777.

[239] RUDIN, H., "On Routing and Delta Routing: A Taxonomy and Performance Comparison of Techniques for Packet-Switched Networks." IEEE Trans., COM-24, No. 1, Jan. 1976, pp. 43—59.

[240] RUDIN, H., "Chairman's Remarks: An Introduction to Flow Control." Proc. 3rd ICCC, Toronto, Aug. 1976, pp. 463—466.

[241] RUDIN, H., and MÜLLER, H., "On Routing and Flow Control." Proc. Int. Symp. Flow Control in Comp. Networks, Versailles, Feb. 1979 (North-Holland, Amsterdam, 1979), pp. 241—255.

[242] RUDIN, H., WEST, C. H., and ZAFIROPULO, P., "Automated Protocol Validation: One Chain of Development." Proc. Comp. Network Protocols Symp., Liège, Feb. 1978, pp. F4/1—F4/6.

[243] RUTKOWSKI, D., "Relay Routing Strategy in a Computer Communication System." Proc. Int. Symp. Computer Networks and Teleprocessing, NJSZT, Budapest, Oct. 1977, pp. 297—311.

[244] SANDERS, R. W., and CERF, V. G., "Compatibility or Chaos in Communications." Datamation, Vol. 22, No. 3, March 1976, pp. 50—55.

[245] SASTRY, A. R. K., "Error Control Techniques for Satellite Communications: An Overview." Conf. Rec. IEEE Int. Conf. Communications, June 1974, pp. 22/B/1—22/B/5.

[246] SASTRY, A. R. K., "Improving Automatic Repeat-Request (ARQ) Performance on Satellite Channels under High Error Rate Conditions." IEEE Trans., COM-23, No. 4, April 1975, pp. 436—439.

[247] SATTLER, C., "Kommunikationskomponenten in Rechnersystemen." Proc. 3rd Int. Seminar Kommunikation in komplexen Informationsverarbeitungs Systemen, Potsdam, Feb. 1976, pp. 255—269.

[248] SCHICKER, P., and DUENKI, A., "The Virtual Terminal Definition." Computer Networks, Vol. 2, No. 6, Dec. 1978, pp. 429—441.

[249] SCHICKER, P., and ZIMMERMANN, H., "Proposal for a Scroll Mode Virtual Terminal in European Informatics Network." Comp. Communication Review, Vol. 7, No. 3, July 1977, pp. 23—55.

[250] SCHROEDER, M. R., "Nonsynchronous Time Multiplex System for Speech Transmission." Bell Lab. Memo., No. 11, Jan. 1959.

[251] SCHUTZ, G. C., and CLARK, G. E., "Data Communication Standards." Computer, Vol. 7, No. 2, Feb. 1974, pp. 32—37.

[252] SCHWARTZ, L. S., "Feedback for Error Control and Two-Way Communication." IEEE Trans., CS-11, No. 1, March 1963, pp. 49—56.

[253] SCHWARTZ, M., Computer-Communication Network Design and Analysis. Prentice-Hall, Englewood Cliffs, 1977.

[254] SCHWARTZ, M., and SAAD, S., "Analysis of Congestion Control Techniques in Computer Communication Networks." Proc. Int. Symp. Flow Control in Computer Networks, Versailles, Feb. 1979 (North-Holland, Amsterdam, 1979), pp. 113—130.

[255] SEIDLER, J., Digital Data Communication Systems. (In Polish.) WNT, Warsaw, 1976.

[256] SEIDLER, J., Analysis and Synthesis of Communication Networks for Teleinformatic Systems. (In Polish.) PWN, Warsaw, 1979.

[257] SEITZ, N. B., and McMANAMON, P. M., "Digital Communication Performance Parameters for Proposed Federal Standard 1033. Vol. Standard Parameters." NTIA Rpt., U. S. Dep. of Commerce, Washington, May 1978.

[258] SEXTON, J. H., "End-to-End Protocols, Virtual Calls and the IIASA Network," INWG Doc. No. 46, June 1976.

[259] SHOCH, J. F., "Packet Fragmentation in Inter-Network Protocols." Computer Networks, Vol. 3, No. 1, Jan. 1979, pp. 3—8.

[260] SINDHU, P. S., "Retransmission Error Control with Memory." IEEE Trans., COM-25, No. 5, May 1977, pp. 473—479.

[261] SPROULE, D. E., "Performance Definitions for User Implementation of X.25." Proc. Comp. Network Protocols Symp., Liège, Feb. 1978, pp. E5/1—E5/5.

[262] STENNING, N. V., "A Data Transfer Protocol." Computer Networks, Vol. 1, No. 2, Sept. 1976, pp. 99—110.

[263] Structure for and Use of a Reference Model for Public Data Networks Applications. In: Rpt. 3rd Spec. Rapp. Meeting Layered Models of Public Data Network Services Applications. San Francisco, Sept. 1979.

[264] STUTZMAN, B. W., "Data Communication Control Procedures." ACM Comp. Surveys, Vol. 4, No. 4., Dec. 1972, pp. 197—220.

[265] SUNDSTROM, R. J., "Formal Definition of IBM's System Network Architecture." Proc. Natl. Telecomm. Conf., Los Angeles, Dec. 1977.

[266] SUNSHINE, C. A., "Factors in Interprocess Communication Protocol Efficiency for Computer Networks." Proc. AFIPS, Vol. 45, June 1976, pp. 571—576.

[267] SUNSHINE, C. A., "Survey of Communication Protocol Verification Techniques." Proc. Symp. Computer Networks, NBS, Gaithersburg, Nov. 1976, pp. 24—26.

[268] SUNSHINE, C. A., "Interconnection of Computer Networks." Computer Networks, Vol. 1, No. 3, Jan. 1977, pp. 175—195.

[269] SUNSHINE, C. A., "Efficiency of Interprocess Communication Protocols for Computer Networks," IEEE Trans., COM-25, No. 2, Feb. 1977, pp. 287—293.

[270] SUNSHINE, C. A., "Survey of Protocol Definition and Verification Techniques." Proc. Comp. Network Protocols Symp., Liège, Feb. 1978, pp. F1/1—F1/4.

[271] SUNSHINE, C. A., and DALAL, Y. K., "Connection Management in Transport Protocols." Computer Networks, Vol. 2, No. 6, Dec. 1978, pp. 454—473.

[272] TAKENAKA, I., et al., "Evaluation of Flow Control Schemes for Packet Switched Networks." Proc. 4th ICCC, Kyoto, Sept. 1978, pp. 141—146.

[273] Telecommunications: Digital Communications Performance Parameters. Interim Fed. Standard 1033, General Services Administration, Aug. 1979.

[274] TOBAGI, F. A., and KLEINROCK, L., "Packet Switching in Radio Channels. Pt. 2: The Hidden Terminal Problem in Carrier Sense Multiple-Access and the Busy-Tone Solution." IEEE Trans., COM-23, No. 12, Dec. 1975, pp. 1417—1433.

[275] Transport Service Functions and Services. ISO/TC 97/SC 6, No. 1861, Sept. 1979.

[276] TRAYNHAM, K. S., and STEEN, R. F., "Interpreting SDLC Throughput Efficiency.

Pt. 1: 3 Models." Data Comm., No. 10, Oct. 1977, pp. 43—51.

[277] TSYBAKOV, B. S., KOGAN, Ya. A., and TAFT, V. V., "Computer Networks with Radio and Satellite Channels." (In Russian.) Zarubezhnaya radioelektronika, No. 4, 1978, pp. 39—65.

[278] TSYBAKOV, B. S., and MIKHAYLOV, V. A., "Slotted Multiaccess Packet Broadcasting Feedback Channel." (In Russian.) Problemy peredachi informacyi, Vol. 14, No. 4, 1978, pp. 32—59.

[279] TWYVER, D. A., "Design and Use of the DATAPAC Network." Proc. Int. Symp. Computer Networks and Teleprocessing, NJSZT, Budapest, Oct. 1977, pp. 529—546.

[280] VAUGHAN, V. N., "Standardization in Data Systems with Emphasis on Telecommunications." Proc. 3rd ICCC, Toronto, Aug. 1976, pp. 594—597.

[281] VITANOV, K., "Some Problems of the Synchronization Setting Between Stations with Existing Method of Line Control." (In Russian.) Proc. 3rd Teleprocessing Symp. RYAD, Varna, May 1976, pp. 1.5/1—1.5/10.

[282] WALDEN, D. C., "A System for Interprocess Communication in a Resource-Sharing Computer Network." Comm. ACM, Vol. 15, No. 4, April 1972, pp. 221.

[283] WALDEN, D. C., "Host-to-Host Protocols." In: Network Systems and Software. INFOTECH, Maidenhead, 1975, pp. 287—316.

[284] WEST, L. P., "Loop-Transmission Control Structures." IEEE Trans., COM-20, No. 3, June 1972, pp. 531—539.

[285] WHITE, G. W., "Message Format and Data Communication Link Control Principles." IEEE Trans., COM-20, No. 3, June 1972, pp. 678—684.

[286] WILHELM, C., et al., Datenübertragung. Militärverlag der DDR, Berlin, 1976.

[287] YAKUBAYTIS, E. A., "Architecture of Computer Systems and Networks." (In Russian.) Inst. Electronics and Computer Science, LatSSR Academy of Sciences, Riga, 1978.

[288] YAKUBAYTIS, E. A., "Transport Network." (In Russian.) Inst. Electronics and Computer Science, LatSSR Academy of Sciences, Riga, 1979.

[289] YAKUBAYTIS, E. A., "Multimachine Associations". (In Russian.) Inst. Electronics and Computer Science, LatSSR Academy of Sciences, Riga, 1979.

[290] YAKUBAYTIS, E. A., PETRENKO, A. F., PODVYSOTSKY, Yu. S., and ROTANOV, S. V., "Protocols of the Experimental Packet—Switched Computer Network." (In Russian.) Proc. 4th Int. Conf. Remote Data Transmission, Vol. 1, DT ČSVTS, Karlovy Vary, Sept. 1979, pp. 154—158.

[291] YEMINI, Y., and KLEINROCK, L., "On a General Rule for Access Control, or Silence is Golden." Proc. Int. Symp. Flow Control in Comp. Networks, Versailles, Feb. 1979 (North-Holland, Amsterdam, 1979), pp. 335—347.

[292] ZAFIROPULO, P., and ROTHAUSER, E. H., "Signalling and Frame Structures in Highly Decentralized Loop Systems." Proc. 1st ICCC, Washington, Oct. 1972, pp. 309—315.

[293] ZIMMERMANN, H., "The CYCLADES End to End Protocol." Proc. 4th Data Comm. Symp., Quebec City, Oct. 1975, pp. 7/21—7/26.

[294] ZIMMERMANN, H., "Communication Systems Architecture and End-to-End Protocols." ISO/TC 97/SC 6, No. 1417, 1977.

[295] ZIMMERMANN, H., and ELIE, M., "Transport Protocol — Standard End-to-End Protocol for Heterogeneous Computer Networks." IRIA CYCLADES Rpt. No. SCH 519. 2, May 1975.

Index

(For abbreviations see Appendex G)